SATANIC PURSES

Satanic Purses

Money, Myth, and Misinformation in the War on Terror

R.T. NAYLOR

McGill-Queen's University Press
Montreal & Kingston · London · Ithaca

© McGill-Queen's University Press 2006
ISBN-13: 978-0-7735-3150-5   ISBN-10: 0-7735-3150-5

Legal deposit third quarter 2006
Bibliothèque nationale du Québec

Printed in Canada on acid-free paper.

This book has been published with the help of a grant from the
Canadian Federation for the Humanities and Social Sciences, through
the Aid to Scholarly Publications Programme, using funds provided
by the Social Sciences and Humanities Research Council of Canada.

McGill-Queen's University Press acknowledges the support of the
Canada Council for the Arts for our publishing program. We also
acknowledge the financial support of the Government of Canada
through the Book Publishing Industry Development Program
(BPIDP) for our publishing activities.

Library and Archives Canada Cataloguing in Publication

Naylor, R.T., 1945–
    Satanic purses: money, myth, and misinformation in the war on terror /
R.T. Naylor.

Includes bibliographical references and index.
ISBN-13: 978-0-7735-3150-5   ISBN-10: 0-7735-3150-5

1. Terrorism – Religious aspects – Islam. 2. Terrorism – Finance.
3. Bin Laden, Osama, 1957–. 4. War on Terrorism, 2001–. I. Title.

HV6431.N394 2006   338.4′330365088297   C2006–902626-2

This book was typeset by Interscript in 10.5/13 Baskerville.

Contents

Acknowledgments   vii

Prologue   3

1 The Crucible – Afghanistan, the Anti-Soviet War, and the Roots
   of the al-Qā'idah Myth   12

2 Vengeful Green Giant? – Bin Lāden, "Fundamentalism," and
   the Rise of the Islamintern   29

3 Conspiracies of Evil – Crime, Law, and the Politics
   of Fear   46

4 Usama of Khartoum – "Anti-Christian Jihād," Nerve-Gas Plots,
   and the Transnational of Terror   59

5 Pipe Dreams and Political Hallucinations – Usama, the USA,
   and the Tāliban   75

6 Trials & Tribulations – Prosecutors in Paradise and Usama
   in Wonderland   88

7 Rocket's Red Glare – Snatching Defeat from the Jaws
   of "Victory"   107

8 To the Shores of Muqdisho – Usama in the Land of Qāt, Clan,
   and Cattle   120

9   Terror Dollars and Nonsense – Finding, Freezing, and Seizing
    the Horde's Hoards   137

10 Quartermasters of Terror – Inscrutable Orientals
    and Underground Banks   152

11 Monetary Mujahideen? – Mall versus Mosque in the War
    on Terror   167

12 Original Sin – Palestine and the Rise of Modern
    Political Terrorism   186

13 Pray or Prey? – Fifth Columns, Cooked Books, and Charitable
    Frauds in America   206

14 Neither to Give nor to Receive – Requiem for Islamic Charity
    in the US?   227

15 Chasing Green Herrings – The Netherworld of Terror Meets
    the Underworld of Crime?   239

16 Conflicts of Interest? – On Bloody Diamonds
    and Tarnished Gold   262

17 Striking Out! – Al-Qā'idah Cells in the Global Petrie Dish   277

18 Securing the Home Front – America's Hunt for the
    Enemy Within   314

    Epilogue   335

    Notes   349

    Index   413

Acknowledgments

On one level this book is the product of the usual kinds of research. I had to ferret through libraries, scour electronic sources, work the telephone and tease (sometimes grind) information out of reluctant informants, then separate digestible wheat from disingenuous chaff. But just as important were more general lessons from more than thirty years as an academic economist, historian, and/or criminologist, as a political journalist, as a financial analyst, and even briefly as a UN functionary. During those decades I had the chance to travel widely and observe firsthand many of the places, a lot of the institutions, and some of the events recounted in the text. While I would never claim "expertise" on all the subjects treated, I hope that experience gave me at least some instinct to differentiate simple fact from simple-minded fiction, bitter truth from saccharine pap, and uncomfortable reality from convenient rationalization.

To range so widely is to invite the occasional error. For that I apologize. However this book is written in the belief that it is better, particularly in difficult times, to be sometimes wrong about issues that matter than always impeccably correct about things of little consequence. I hope that the reader will approach the book in a similar spirit.

Obviously in writing such a work I incurred far more debts than I can even acknowledge, let alone begin to repay. Among those to whom I am indebted are: Peter Andreas, Christine Archer, George Archer, Margaret Beare, Hassan Benchekroun, Issa J. Boullata, Juan

Cole, Jacques Courtois, Chris Funt, Melissa Garcia-Lamarca, Roger Haydon, Asif Hasnain, Ihab Hashim, Homa Hoodfar, Sarah Kemal, Azfar Khan, Rafy Kourouian, Mike Levi, Miriam Lowi, Jonathan Nitzan, Sam Noumoff, Dan Omeara, Nikos Passas, Deane Taylor, and Peter Vajda. I also owe, once again, a very special thanks to Jane Hunter for her insights and assistance. Mehmet Karabela gave the text a close reading and corrected numerous problems with my interpretations of Islamic history and Arabic spellings. Claude Lalumière was so persistent in editing the text that he even managed to get me to remove some of my favorite jokes. A number of authors have done pioneering work that helped to guide the present book – in a subject deluged with absurdities the rational voices of Jason Burke, Anthony Shadid, Dilip Hiro, Ahmed Rashid, and John Cooley deserve special mention. Thanks, too, to the Social Sciences and Humanities Research Council of Canada for supporting the research. Not to be forgotten is Phil Cercone, my editor at McGill-Queen's University Press, who again showed a faith in my books that others lacked. Behind any book, too, lies a substantial organization of dedicated – usually unnamed and unsung – people, in this case the professional staff at McGill-Queen's. And there are some who cannot be mentioned – to do so might expose them to danger or at least to harassment.

However there is one further acknowledgement from which I cannot refrain. I dedicate this book to the memory of my maternal grandfather, who, in the face of Ottoman repression and economic crisis, fled to Canada at the end of the nineteenth century from what was then historical Syria. Salameh Aziz left behind bounteous orchards near his home town of Shib'a in what is now southern Lebanon. His hope was to return to them in his old age, or at least to have his offspring enjoy their sight, taste, and fragrance. I tried several times, only to be blocked by war and occupation that devastated, depopulated, and impoverished the area. Indeed, my fondest hope is that this book will contribute a little to the understanding that necessarily precedes justice, which in turn is an essential prerequisite for the return of peace to the Mashreq (the Arab East) in general, and to southern Lebanon in particular, so I can finally carry out his wishes.

SATANIC PURSES

Prologue

On 9 November 1989 the Berlin Wall fell in triumph, and out of a delighted West came paeans of joy about the "end of history." On 11 September 2001 the Twin Towers collapsed in smoke and flame, and out of a shocked West came cries of warning about a "clash of civilizations." History, it seems, had just pulled the wooden stake from its heart and risen from its grave.

Fingers almost immediately pointed at Usama bin Lāden. As a result an abiding and, for the powers that be, eminently useful myth was born, one that continues to misinform, confuse, and distort public understanding and official response to this day.

Supposedly a fabulously wealthy "fundamentalist" from Saudi Arabia, bin Lāden was, so the story went, the architect of early outrages against us targets, most notoriously the 1998 bombing of the us embassies in Kenya and Tanzania. He had also issued a fatwā (a religious edict) that called for the murder of Americans.

Drawing on his experiences fighting the Soviet Union in Afghanistan, bin Lāden had put together al-Qā'idah ("al-Qaeda" in trailer-park slang), a transnational of terror staffed with Islamic fanatics whom he had indoctrinated, trained, and financed. Together they stood ready to launch jihād (supposedly Holy War) against a decadent West and against "moderate" voices in the Arab and Islamic countries.

Using al-Qā'idah, bin Lāden targeted the usa's economic vulnerabilities.[1] He set out to cut off its energy lifeline by overthrowing the (more

or less) friendly governments of key oil-rich states, to push its military
budget beyond the financial cracking point, and to destroy critical infrastructure. The World Trade Center attack brought the international
financial system to a halt, caused the global tourism industry to collapse, and drove the US economy, the motor of world prosperity, into a
recession that forced the government to offset the damage with an
emergency tax cut. The spectre of a repeat performance continues to
haunt the world, which searches frantically to destroy Usama's Rip Van
Winkle cells before they can rub the sleep from their bloodshot eyes.

Bin Lāden's al-Qā'idah was (is?) able to commit such atrocities because of his financial resources. These included $300 million as his
share of a family fortune, and the profits from his own enterprises, not
least a cut from the enormous Afghan heroin trade. Various subsidiaries and affiliates, too, ran (run?) rackets all over the world, ranging
from financial fraud in the United States to smuggling gemstones out
of West Africa, from dealing in counterfeit consumer goods via Paraguay to circulating phony US currency in East Asia, from trafficking in
Christian child-slaves between Uganda and the Sudan (where he also
had a marijuana plantation) to trading qāt (a popular local "narcotic")
from Somalia to Yemen. In effect, Crime and Terror had coalesced to
their mutual benefit.[2]

On top there was (is?) a steady flow of contributions from fellow-
travellers who abound in today's backward Islamic world. The worst
offender is Saudi Arabia, where princes proliferating like pampered
rabbits compete to lavish money extorted from Western motorists on
gold-plated bathtubs or on financing world terror. The proceeds of
this and more tumbled into bin Lāden's overflowing coffers to enable
him to perpetrate terror from Moscow to Madrid, from Istanbul to
Indonesia, and beyond. Even worse, they provided the financial foundations for al-Qā'idah's program to develop nuclear, biological, and
chemical weapons.[3]

The money to stage attacks was (is?) moved around the world using
every possible technique. They include secret bank accounts in shady
offshore havens, long the haunts of the kingpins of organized crime.
They include the hawāla system, an ancient, clandestine form of money
management beloved of wily Orientals ranging from opium traders to
gold smugglers to oil "sheeks." One more recent, especially important
and particularly insidious method was (is?) to work through Islamic
charitable foundations, which have spread everywhere along with
Muslim populations.

Therefore, the US, in defense of itself and the West at large, has deployed against the new enemy two principal weapons. The first, of course, is military. In remarkably short order the awesome might of the United States was mobilized to strike back. It actually started before 9/11 by going after "chemical warfare" facilities in the Sudan. There, in a country recently taken over by a regime of brooding Islamic fanatics, bin Lāden, after being expelled from Saudi Arabia, temporarily set up headquarters. He soon fled again ahead of the long arm of law, as US prosecutors attempted to mobilize the most lethal weapons in the USA's legal arsenal against him. After 9/11, US attention shifted to his "command and control" centres in Afghanistan, where he had joined forced with another gang of misanthropic miscreants to support a proliferating network of terrorist training camps and to flood the world with narcotics. The power of the United States inexorably moved on to Iraq, where bin Lāden and Saddam Hussein were jointly developing weapons of mass destruction. Then it poised over Syria and Iran, countries that sustained al-Qā'idah directly and provided logistical and financial support to other terrorist groups "linked" to it, particularly Hizbullāh in Lebanon and Hamas in Palestine, both notorious for their own suicide operations.

Nor in its efforts to stop the contagion did the US neglect Somalia, another "failed state" where scattered al-Qā'idah cadres might have been trying to regroup after the Allied victory in Afghanistan. Scene of an earlier US effort to combine humanitarian concern with state-building, Somalia had degenerated into a vicious civil war out of which had emerged an important al-Qā'idah affiliate that had provided personnel and money for bin Lāden's earlier attacks. And the US put additional resources into blocking the further spread of al-Qā'idah in South East Asia, especially in Indonesia and in the Muslim-inhabited areas of the Philippines, where the local al-Qā'idah subsidiary was showing ugly signs of evolving an autonomous terror capacity of its own.

While most eyes have focused on military operations, perhaps less appreciated is that, to deny resources to terrorists, the US also deployed another powerful if less spectacular weapon: an internationally coordinated effort to find and freeze the money, to knock out the front organizations and pseudo-charities, and to bring under regulatory scrutiny the underground banking systems. As George Bush II sagely noted when he first cranked up the Pentagon budget beyond its prior Cold War peak: "Money is the lifeblood of terrorist operations."[4]

At first glance, this widely accepted argument about the causes of and appropriate responses to 9/11 has a compelling logic. But on

closer examination it turns out to be liberally laced with myth and misinformation, much of it based on crude racial and religious stereotypes, with a heavy leavening of deliberate disinformation. In fact, when
the conventional tale is broken down into constituent parts, it is hard
to find anything in it that stands up to scrutiny.[5]

The role of bin Lāden in various terrorist outrages has been grossly
exaggerated; al-Qā'idah is largely a law-enforcement fable akin to the
Mafia myth that has long confused public discourse and muddled legislative responses to crime; the notion of an economic war against the
West is a fantasy peddled jointly by bin Lāden and by the legions of instant "national security experts" whom the purported threat of Islamic
Terrorism permitted to crawl out of the woodwork and into TV studios;
most stories about the bin Lāden terror-treasury are fairy tales retailed
by people overendowed with ambition or imagination and underen-
dowed with knowledge or common sense; and the usual portrayal of
things like the "underground banking system" or Islamic charities is
the result largely of ignorance combined with ethnoreligious bigotry.[6]

In fact, the very notion of an aggressive Islamintern out to destroy the
moral and financial foundations of Judaeo-Christian civilization is preposterous. Leave aside the simple fact that terrorist activity, with its resulting death and destruction, has actually been falling for two decades.
Except for the upsurge in deaths caused directly by 9/11, it has continued to fall even as the US government, seconded by the British one, pro-
claims the opposite – mainly to rationalize their own crimes in Iraq.[7] In
any case, great terrorist atrocities growing out of Middle East conflicts began not with 9/11 or even the embassy attacks of 1998 but with the
bombing of the King David Hotel in Jerusalem by Jewish terrorists fifty
years earlier. If the perpetrators of that outrage had been brought to
book and a modicum of justice imposed on the region by international
action, probably few of the subsequent tragedies to bedevil the area, and
by extension the world at large, would have occurred.

Indeed, given the nature and frequency of Western meddling in the
Islamic world, the real mystery is not why someone occasionally strikes
back with bloody effect, but why those events are so rare. Islam, it seems,
really is as pacific a religion as its name (derived from the Arabic word
for "peace") implies. Public outrage over 9/11 might well have extin-
guished any spark of sympathy for violent political Islam across the
Middle East, North Africa, and Central Asia had not the US chosen to
fan the flames.[8] And most attacks that did (and do) occur subsequently,
however appalling, were (are) more the uncoordinated actions of

people with local grudges who finance them on a shoestring than the
product of careful planning by some Daddy Warbucks of Terror from a
cave in Afghanistan.[9] Most perpetrators never went near that place;
those who did got the type of training available at a militia camp in
Michigan; and the few who actually made it into bin Lāden's presence
came out with little more than a pat on the head, then went home to do
what they were planning all along. In short, they comprised at best more
a Rotary Club than an IBM of Terror, and even that is a considerable
stretch. No doubt at various times in various combinations they were
busy hatching conspiracies – after all, conspiracy stripped to its Latin
roots simply means *to breathe together.*

Incidentally, where anyone got the wacky idea that bin Lāden could
issue a fatwā, a privilege restricted to senior scholars of religious law
(whose competitive pronouncements carry nothing like the authority
of a Papal Bull) remains a mystery. Indeed the very notion that bin
Lāden is a "fundamentalist" is debatable. Given the variety of currents
and eddies, streams and swamps, tides and tsunamis in Islamic thought,
the term is largely meaningless.[10] And whoever insists that jihād must
mean Holy War (its most common meaning is effort or struggle for self-
improvement) probably got the idea from *Islam for Dummies.*[11]

If it is true that bin Lāden's military might was always a fiction, that
his "organization" consisted of a scattered handful of political dead-
enders whose explosive power was mainly (although, alas, not entirely)
in their mouths, and that his terror-dollar treasury had the substance of
an Enron quarterly statement, then clearly something went seriously
amiss, not just in the general understanding of what occurred and why
it occurred but in terms of what is to be done about it. Or did it?

Whatever its egregious flaws, the standard story has served to rationalize a dramatic extension of US military power abroad, an expansion
that, by leading to a sharp escalation of international tensions, can, in a
twisted way, act as its own self-justification – albeit this has less to
do with the arcane conspiracy theories currently proliferating in cyber-
space than with simple political opportunism.[12] It has also provided the
rationale for a drastic expansion of police-and-intelligence activities at
home in directions that the citizenry under normal circumstances
would probably find unacceptable. Since the earliest days of the US republic, and repeatedly since World War II, crises, sometimes real, often
exaggerated, on occasion contrived, and usually blamed on evil aliens,
have been similarly used.[13] The Cold War of the 1950s yielded place to
the Crime War of the 1960s, which morphed into the Drug War of the

1970s and 1980s, which gave way to the Terror War today. Each worked to project power abroad while serving to mold opinion, suppress dissent, and justify an expansion of state authority at home. That expansion is aimed not at laudable goals like stabilizing the macro-economy, improving distributive justice, or enhancing environmental protection but at bolstering the position of the national security and/or law enforcement apparatus while advancing the political ambitions of those promoting the change. Each, too, had a financial component that varied from seeking to find and freeze assets of Communist conspirators plotting to subvert the civil order to tracing and trapping money used by Islamic fanatics to perpetrate terrorist atrocities.

What perhaps is most remarkable is how often, once the immediate hubbub has subsided, once a crisis is exposed as misinterpreted or overblown or downright phony, and once the response to it is shown to be counterproductive or opportunistic or immoral, truth quickly disappears down a yawning memory hole. Then, come the next crisis, politicians, press, and public line up to salute the flag and cheer the boys in khaki, or in blue, all over again. Meanwhile "emergency measures" and the institutions created to enforce them during the previous crisis live on to find a new vocation.

Given the dangers of basing major initiatives on self-perpetuating and (often) self-serving myths, this book has three objectives. First, it seeks to demystify the notion of a great anti-Western Islamic resurgence, and the elusive Islamic Terror Dollar along with it. To do so, it places recent events in perspective. Apart from being a tribute to the degree to which in this electronic age instantly produced virtual reality trumps the old-fashioned kind, the al-Qā'idah legend must be one of the most useful political fantasies in history – since it has so little concrete substance, it can be (and has been) transmogrified and transplanted more or less at will to support agendas (many of them ugly) in virtually any and all corners of the world.

Demystification also requires that events be placed in context. Stories about bin Lāden's activities (military or financial) in the Sudan or in Somalia, legends about his similar roles in Afghanistan, or tales about the antics of his alleged subsidiaries and affiliates everywhere from Indonesia or Xinkiang quickly become either hopelessly simplistic or transparently foolish when examined against the facts.

Therefore the second task is to clarify how (and why) a story so contrary to easily verifiable reality was concocted, then turned into the rationalization for actions that have sown death and disorder abroad while trampling on everything from due process to the right to financial privacy at home. The answer lies partly in the fact that, in the messy world of real human beings, as distinct from that of vapid discourse among university-style eggheads, there is no simple, linear relationship between cause and effect. No matter what the initiating action, the precise form that reactions take reflect all manner of exogenous, even extraneous, influences. Prevailing theopolitical beliefs tint the lenses through which events are viewed, while special-interest groups manipulate matters to their own advantage. Without taking some account of how culturally rooted biases and special agendas have twisted and/or colored the choices, it is impossible to assess the ultimate efficacy (or lack thereof) of any given response to an initiating event, even something as seemingly straightforward as tightened financial regulations much less massive recourse to military power.

Therefore the third purpose of this book is to explore the likely consequences of the choices by which the West in general, and the US in particular, has chosen to react. Of the two levels of response – military and financial – to 9/11 or to predecessors like the embassy bombings of 1998, the rush to assert armed might seems the most straightforward. Politicians who scheme re-election by uniting the nation around an external threat; the military with its irresistible impulse to inflate budgets by finding new enemies; the hunger of the United States to increase control of the world's dwindling oil and gas reserves; and the machinations of the pro-Israel lobby – no doubt they all play some role. To their influence must be added efforts of the Armageddon Industry with its supporting network of media outlets, theological colleges, and tax-exempt institutes staffed by theopolitical fanatics who seek redemption through conflagration in the Middle East. All five have interacted with a deeply entrenched anti-Islamic streak in the consciousness of the United States. The image of the Evil Saracen surrounded by undulating harem voluptuaries and dusky grinning psychopaths runs deeply through the course of US history. It was no accident that the new republic's first foreign adventures involved not designs on remaining British territory in what is now Canada or the conquest of much of Mexico (both of which came later) but naval battles with "pirates" (they were actually privateers) of the Barbary Coast. In fact, opponents of political centralization during the debates around the US Constitution itself cited the evil of Islamic despotism as a lesson to be avoided.[14]

Undoubtedly these factors together go a fair way to explain why, after 9/11, the US government seemed ready to bludgeon its way into the

Middle East and Central Asia, to demonize Muslims worldwide, and to upset long-standing political relations from one end of the globe to another. However they do not explain why the first front to open in the War on Terror was not military but financial. This other campaign parallels and complements the military one; it shares many of the ideological assumptions; it is shaped by much the same political influences; yet it also has its own history and mythology, its own secret agendas and its own consequences, which this book also tries to explain.

Briefly put, the current infatuation with finding, freezing, and seizing the illusory Islamic Terror Treasury is a merger of two earlier and quite distinct trends. The first grew out of the experience of economic warfare, particularly during World War II, with its blacklists of individuals and companies suspected of trading with the enemy and with its efforts to find and freeze enemy assets in order to weaken the enemy's capacity to wage sustained war.[15] The second, which took hold during the Drug War of the 1980s, was premised on the similar idea that seizing the so-called proceeds of crime served to pre-empt further crimes by removing the incentive (profit) and the means (criminal capital).

For a time these two ran in parallel directions. Pursuing the first, the US government developed a seemingly knee-jerk tendency to freeze assets of uncooperative ("rogue") states without debate or recourse. Pursuing the second, police forces inside the US (and elsewhere) secured extraordinary powers to grab not just bank accounts and stashes of cash but cars, boats, condos, and Rolex watches without being burdened with the need for proof capable of standing up in court.[16]

The merger began in the 1990s. Inside the US, the Clinton administration started to apply the logic of asset freezes to designated groups rather than to countries. And a new law, the 1996 Comprehensive Anti-Terrorism and Effective Death Penalty Act, targeted not just alleged terrorists but those who provided "material support" – a concept as conveniently elastic as the ever-broadening notion of "money laundering" with which it could work in tandem. The result was to introduce criminalization by association through the back door. At US instigation, the United Nations also began to use asset freezes against insurgent organizations or even leaders of particular states rather than against the countries themselves.

Then came 9/11 and its most dramatic legislative response, the Patriot Act (with its many imitations around the world). While that law is best known for its expansion of the right of government agencies to probe the private affairs of citizens while denying to those same citizens access to the private deliberations of government, its most remarkable features were its extension of financial controls. Its rationalization combined the Cold War myth of a global financier of terrorism (a role formerly ascribed to Moscow) with the Drug War myth of crime lords sitting on top of oodles of boodle. Hence Usama bin Lāden was painted as sort-of a Pablo Escobar of world terrorism, and the Patriot Act was sold to the public as the necessary response. Thus did the police and the national security industry find common cause and a common tool to combat the Green Peril, which, for ease of public digestion, was personified in a villain who might have stepped out of a Batman comic. In fact, he soon will, once cartoonist Frank Miller completes his *Holy Terror, Batman!*, which will pit Batman against ... "Osama bin Laden" himself![17]

The costs of the Terror War have been enormous, on both fronts. Apart from sending the military to eviscerate wedding parties in Afghanistan and to turn Fallujah, Iraq's sparkling city of mosques, into another Mesopotamian archeological site, the Terror War has converted the world's banking infrastructure into a global espionage apparatus. It has led to a set of legal atrocities in which the main evidence against the accused consists of media gossip, claims by "national security experts" with ethnopolitical axes to grind, and fables spun by informants bribed or coerced into testifying. If Drug War hysteria produced affronts to common sense and common decency such as three-strikes-and-you-are-in-for-good laws, Terror War myths lead to mass roundups based on race and religion and long-term incarceration in concentration camps without the benefit of even bogus charges.[18] Such developments call for not just the occasional red flag but a field full of furiously flapping banners. Hopefully this book will not only help to plant some of those warning flags but perhaps contribute a little fresh air to make them flutter more briskly.

1

The Crucible – Afghanistan, the Anti-Soviet War, and the Roots of the al-Qā'idah Myth

In the aftermath of 9/11, all eyes focused on Afghanistan, a country that, Americans suddenly learned, had been turned into the world epicentre of Islamic terrorism by an alliance between Usama bin Lāden's Arab hordes and local fanatics sporting beards and turbans. Yet, only a short time before, Afghanistan had been a marginal, almost unknown place where nearly two decades of civil wars followed by three years of severe drought had left four million people homeless, five million facing famine, and most of the population vulnerable to a series of winters of exceptional severity – all under the radar screens of the "international community."[1]

Suddenly the world was brimming over with humanitarian concern. In November 2001, Laura Bush, the USA's First Lady, launched a "world-wide effort to focus on the brutality against women and children by the al-Qaida terrorist network and the regime it supports in Afghanistan, the Taliban."[2] This dramatic leap of conscience came six years after the Taliban had seized control, massacred the opposition, and imposed its medieval restrictions on women. Thus did a country ignored through years of bloodshed and misery become the telegenic site of another war, this time fought on two fronts.

The US government responded to 9/11 both financially and militarily. Since Afghanistan was already under strict UN economic sanctions, its (known) assets frozen and its (legal) trade strangled, the US set out to close down the covert international channels used by bin Lāden to pay for atrocities like the World Trade Center attacks and to keep his Afghan hosts flush with cash. Then President Bush sent US forces to take out command and control centres, destroy terrorist training camps dotting the countryside, and round up survivors for interrogation about the deeper secrets of 9/11.

The fact that most available evidence suggested a plot hatched directly by the suicide pilots in Hamburg might, in less urgent times, have raised questions about either the effectiveness of US intelligence services, the honesty of its politicians, or the quality of the navigation equipment used by its military en route to their grim mission.

The most celebrated target in the new war was the Tora Bora cave complex. There, straddling the Afghan-Pakistan border, Usama bin Lāden had reputedly constructed a complex of bunkers stretching as deep into the mountains as the World Trade Center had risen into the sky. He had equipped these facilities with electrical generators and ventilators so sophisticated that they were immune to heat-detection equipment, with storehouses for military equipment including a special stash for weapons of mass destruction and garages capable of holding armored vehicles, with kitchens to feed his legions and ultra-modern hospital equipment to tend their wounds, along with offices containing banks of computers to run his rackets and communicate with his terror squads worldwide. This underground high-tech wonderland, impervious to normal weaponry, was protected by modern anti-aircraft devices manned by one thousand hardened al-Qāʾidah fighters.

That the caves, which quickly crumbled under US bombs, were mainly holes eaten into the mountain rock by rainwater and defended only by the assault rifles of a handful of desperate followers whom Usama had abandoned, once the bombing began, in his precipitous flight in the back of a pickup truck, captured brilliantly the glaring disconnect between public perception and concrete reality that would characterize the entire al-Qāʾidah saga in the days, months, and years to come.[3]

Nor, with the world so enraged and engaged, did there seem to be much public expression of concern that the proof offered to date of bin Lāden's direct role in 9/11 (as distinct from a propensity to indulge his ego after the fact) consisted of rumor, hearsay, and innuendo. This would be troublesome enough as the basis for criminal prosecution of a single individual, no matter how seemingly culpable. It was far more so as justification for unleashing the most awesome murder machine in history against one of the most wretched places on Earth, where a handful of people who had seized power at gunpoint harbored

a fugitive from US law. This was particularly true since the US had refused to extend to the wanted man's hosts the diplomatic recognition
required for formal extradition and admitted publicly that its evidence
would not stand up in court. That those hosts, unsavory though they
may have been, had been desperately trying to find a way to quietly
hand over or to otherwise dispose of their unwanted guest also went
conveniently ignored.[4]

What had taken Usama bin Lāden to Afghanistan in the first place
was not some subterranean intent to plot un-American activities, but
the brutal war between the USSR and its local allies on one side and the
US-sponsored, Saudi-financed, Pakistani-supervised mujahideen resistance fighters on the other. Painted as a struggle for national liberation
against an oppressive political system imposed by an invading Soviet
Army, the Afghan-Soviet war was actually a multisided conflict in which
right and wrong usually took backstage to sectarian interests and traditional feuds and in which it was often unclear if the superpowers were
manipulating local clients or vice versa.

That war produced its own set of abiding myths to influence the geopolitical climate for decades after – that the mujahideen (later assisted
by foreign volunteers) emerged to combat Communist repression; that
the Red Army had stormed into Afghanistan en route to the oil fields of
the Persian Gulf; that US military wizardry sent the Soviet forces fleeing;
that such an ignominious result precipitated the collapse of Communism worldwide; and that one unfortunate side-effect was to leave the
billionaire bin Lāden with a fully trained, highly motivated army (trans-
muted with remarkable alacrity from freedom fighters into international terrorists) ready to shift attention from the Soviet Union to the
United States.[5] The persistence of these myths reflects their usefulness
both in rationalizing current agendas and in evading perhaps the most
important question. If the US was really so concerned both by the threat
to Judeo-Christian Civilization posed by terrorist training camps with
great stocks of weapons and run by instructors in irregular warfare who
infused recruits with suicidal Islamic ideology, and by the existence of
worldwide mechanisms for covertly moving the funds that graduating
militants needed to support their future misdeeds, why had it spent so
much time, energy and money creating all of that in the first place?[6]

The answer lies in the Green Belt strategy, a US plan to quarantine the
USSR from the area south of the border with non-Communist Central
Asia and subvert the Soviet Central Asian republics from within by stok-
ing militant and vehemently anti-Communist Islam both in the Soviet

Central Asian republics and in neighbouring areas. Afghanistan, while not the only manifestation, was certainly the most dramatic.

SEEING RED

The very name "Afghanistan" invokes tenacity and treachery, passionate loyalties and endless blood feuds, played out against vistas of stunning natural beauty and grinding material poverty.[7] It is also a country where nothing is simple and little is as it first seems. Geography, ethnography, politics, and religion interact in complex and unpredictable ways that had defied the dreams and ambitions of kings, conquerors, potentates, and proselytizers for centuries before the US and the USSR chose Afghanistan as the site of their most bitter Cold War contest, only to be shocked by the consequences.

Afghanistan is separated roughly north-south by the Hindu Kush mountains. Until 1964, when Soviet engineers tunnelled through, winter ended communication between north and south. The geographic divide corresponds – roughly though not completely – to the ethnic distribution. To the north are Tajiks, Uzbeks, and Turkmens, parts of Turkic ethnic groups forced into the Russian Empire in the late nineteenth century. The region was later reshaped into the Soviet republics of Tajikistan, Uzbekistan, and Turkmenistan. Pushed into a poor, isolated central region by aggressive neighbors, are the Hazaras, Turko-Mongol by origin and, like the Tajiks, Persian by language but, unlike almost all other Afghans, Shi'a Muslim by faith. Probably the country's oldest inhabitants, they are also the group to suffer most from civil strife over the years.[8] South of the mountains are the Baluchi, traditionally nomads whose caravans haul contraband between Afghanistan, Pakistan, and Iran. Most important in the south and east are the Pashtun comprising nearly half of Afghanistan's population and themselves split, partly between tribal confederations (Durrani versus Ghilzai) and partly as a consequence of imperial Britain having drawn the frontier between Afghanistan and India on strategic rather than ethnic criteria.[9] Those divisions had major consequences for the region's political history and for the course of the Soviet-US war (by proxy), the ashes of which supposedly gave birth to Usama bin Lāden's Transnational of Terror.

Thus Afghanistan has always been a medley of ethnic, tribal, and clan alliances of variable degrees of durability united mainly by a flag, a common currency, and, until 1973, a king whose authority rarely extended beyond the three major cities. It was united, too, by the fact that none of the (fifty plus) distinct groups ever pushed seriously the idea of ethnic secession. Not least, the country was united by a shared distrust of its neighbors.[10]

To the north was imperial Russia, followed by the Soviet Union and now modern Russia, seeking first to assert, then to consolidate, now to maintain strategic and economic control over Turkmenistan, Uzbekistan, and Tajikistan and to head off any threat from ethnic nationalism or militant Islam. To the West was/is Iran, attempting to expand its influence in the areas formerly part of the Persian Empire. To the south and east lies Pakistan, successor to the British Raj, which has its own ethnic balancing act to play. Although most of its population is Punjabi, it shares Pashtuns with Afghanistan as a result of an arbitrary decision in 1893 by a senior British civil servant placing the frontier at the easily defended Khyber Pass. When Pakistan emerged weak and vulnerable from the chaos of British India, Afghan rulers resurrected their historic claims. In the 1950s Pakistan, in retaliation, armed and financed rebels who bombed Afghan government installations. It therefore set a precedent for the two countries to wage proxy war on each other, a precedent the US would exploit to the fullest when, a quarter century later, Afghanistan descended into a full-scale civil war.

This superpower strategy at the top of the world was not simply an inevitable consequence of the Cold War division – with the American eagle attempting to rescue subject nations from the claws of the Russian bear. To the extent those claws had dug deeply into Afghanistan, it was for many years with the tacit consent of the US itself.

Afghanistan's most important asset was never its natural resources but its location, first as an east-west caravan route, later as a buffer between great powers – Britain in India versus Russia in Central Asia, then the US versus the Soviet Union. Every Afghan government understood that survival depended on playing off more powerful neighbors. But the old geo-strategic balance ended when the British pulled out. In the early 1950s, Prime Minister Mohammed Daoud Khan asked for US aid to fill the gap. He was refused. The US had written off Afghanistan as a minor part of the Soviet sphere of influence. The country soon had a Soviet-equipped Army, Soviet experts to develop natural resources, and Soviet training for its teachers and bureaucrats. Finally, in 1965, the US took alarm, prodding the king to dismiss Daoud Khan and bring in the US as a counterweight.[11] That led in 1973 to a bloodless coup and the declaration of a republic. With Daoud Khan's new government full of technocrats intent on "modernization," it also began the slide to a multisided bloodbath.

Outside of the capital city of Kabul, Afghanistan seemed trapped in a time warp with women kept largely in bondage to their male relatives or husbands, peasants perpetually in debt to landowners and money-lenders, and education, such as it was, under the control of village mullahs who combined a fuzzy knowledge of the Qur'ān with a side business of selling magical amulets and traditional folk remedies. Time after time attempts at social reforms, such as literacy campaigns or more secure land tenure for peasants, were blocked by a united front of traditional village and religious leaders. After the coup, the republican government was quickly at loggerheads with them again. But by then other political forces had emerged with radically different ideas about Afghanistan's future.

During the 1960s Burhanuddin Rabbani, a professor of religion and leading cleric, had gathered around him a set of acolytes of whom two – Ahmed Shah Mas'ud and Gulbuddin Hekmatyar – would figure particularly large in Afghanistan's future history, the first becoming a post-9/11 US folk hero and the second an Islamic villain targeted by the US, like Usama himself, for assassination. They, too, wanted to modernize Afghanistan, but with Islamic principles taking priority over both secular law and local customs, putting them at odds simultaneously with the republican government and the old religious leaders. Shortly after the coup, the principal Islamist opposition figures fled to Pakistan. There Rabbani, a Tajik, formed Jamiat-i-Islami, which tried to build a broad-based opposition coalition. Hekmatyar, a Pashtun, founded Hizb-i-Islami, a group committed to more radical action, which would itself split into two factions a short time later. These three were joined in exile by other groups led variously by royalists and traditional clerics whose program was simply to restore the status quo ante coup. Thus the core of the mujahideen, already in discordant factions, took shape several years before Communists assumed power in Kabul. The original backer was not the US but Pakistan, which supplied a place of exile, arms, and money. Pakistan was not motivated by the idea of Islam versus Bolshevism but rather by revenge because Daoud Khan again began feeding arms to the Pashtun hill tribes in Pakistan, then stoked another of Pakistan's trouble spots.

Afghanistan and Pakistan (along with Iran) also share Baluchistan. As nomads and traders, the Baluchi have no respect for central authority.

From little ports along the Indian Ocean, they have long smuggled in booze, cigarettes, and contraband gold, while exporting hashish and, later, heroin, with part of the profits invested in weapons. Within a year of British-controlled Baluchistan being allocated to Pakistan, the area was in revolt. The initial uprisings came to little, but, when Pakistan lost East Bengal after the 1971 Indo-Pakistan war, it was determined to stop further territorial losses. Hence it abolished the Baluchi parliament, clamped down on smuggling, and encouraged the in-migration of Punjabis. That set off an even more serious uprising. In fact the first modern "terrorist training camps" in Afghanistan were established by the staunchly secular Daoud Khan to give Baluchi rebels a base to operate against Pakistan.

At much the same time radical Islamic movements emerged in Afghanistan, so did a Communist opposition, divided into factions whose differences paralleled the split among the Islamists. The most militant group, the Khalq, was largely Pashtun and committed, like Hezb-i-Islami, to radical social change – even if it relied on Marx's *Das Capital* rather than Muhammad's Qur'ān for its inspiration. The other, the Parcham, had a broader ethnic base and was more urban-oriented, a secular analogue to the Jamiat-i-Islami – it even had a Tajik leader. Initially the Parcham collaborated with the republican regime; while the Khalqis quietly infiltrated the Army and the bureaucracy. By 1975 the political wind had shifted. At the time the US was committed to blocking participation of Communists in governments outside the Soviet Bloc, a policy that had already led to the overthrow (and murder) of President Salvador Allende in Chile and would soon have similar consequences for Prime Minister Aldo Moro in Italy.[12] With a nod from Washington, financial inducements from Saudi Arabia and help from the secret police of neighboring Iran, the government drove leftists from office and purged pro-Soviet officers from the military, upsetting the fragile internal equilibrium that had preserved Afghanistan as a buffer between the USSR and the West. That in turn led in 1978 to a joint Khalq-Parcham coup in which Daoud Khan and his family were killed. Inside Afghanistan, opposition intensified; outside it, others began to take a more avid interest.[13]

BEAR BAITING

The US government lost no time denouncing the coup as the first stage in a Soviet plot to threaten the West's energy lifeline. It was good propaganda – even if the idea of Moscow lunging through Afghanistan to seize a warm-water port on the Indian Ocean to put the Gulf oil fields under naval threat would have been laughed out of any war college freshman class. In fact the USSR was far from happy with the Afghan coup. The new government was dominated by Khalqis of whose radicalism the USSR disapproved.[14] When they pushed ahead with a program to spread literacy, redistribute land, cancel peasant debts, and emancipate women, the village mullahs, big landlords, rural money-lenders, and tribal chiefs took up arms. The USSR, already dealing with unpredictable allies embroiled in civil wars in Mozambique, Angola, Ethiopia, and Somalia, and concerned with rebuilding relations with the US after the Vietnam War, tried to keep its distance. When the Afghan president asked for Soviet aid against the internal rebellion, he was offered supplies and advisors but no combat troops.[15]

Others were less reticent. Early in 1979, the US decided to back directly an opposition that embraced monarchists and republicans, ethnic nationalists and pan-Islamists, village traditionalists who wanted to roll back the state to defend local customs and political radicals who wanted to take over that state to build a modern Islamic republic. All would be lumped as the "resistance" even though their resistance was often stronger to each other than to the Afghan government or its Soviet backers. Thus, far from US aid to the mujahideen being a response to a Soviet invasion, it preceded Soviet forces in Afghanistan by several months. In fact, it was intended to provoke just that result. If the US had really been concerned about a Soviet march to the Persian Gulf, its later boast about enticing the Red Army into Afghanistan was an odd way to show it.

Even with that claim, the USA gave itself too much credit. Soviet forces really went into Afghanistan to support a coup within a coup. Hafizullah Amin, deputy leader but de facto boss of the Khalq, ignored Soviet advice to slow down the pace of change. Worse, reforms were accompanied by arrests of local notables and implemented by enthusiastic but ignorant outsiders. More of the population was alienated by the brutal suppression of anti-government uprisings. But Amin also opened negotiations with Washington, raising in Moscow the threat that the US might place missile bases in Afghanistan, close to the border. Hence shortly after Amin ousted (and killed) the president and took power himself, he was ousted (and killed) in another coup backed by Soviet units. With Soviet approval, the new Parcham-dominated government invoked the country's Islamic heritage, rolled back social reforms, and offered amnesty to opposition groups. Thus, far from promoting more Communist oppression, Soviet intervention could almost be interpreted as an attempt to curb some of its worst excesses. In the wake of Soviet tanks, the right-wing press in the US took the occasion, much as it would after 9/11, to beat the war drums, calling for restoration of the draft, a new generation of nuclear missiles, unleashing the CIA from its (modest) legal constraints, and covert aid to the Afghan resistance – something that had already begun.[16]

Still, the USSR expected its military involvement to be brief. Initially most troops were reservists from Uzbekistan, Tajikistan, and Turkmenistan who were expected to work as messengers of socialist good will.[17] But blood proved thicker than ideology. When early attempts to placate the US-backed opposition failed, the early forces were replaced by career soldiers of European origin, who, to the delight of the US, remained bogged down in Afghanistan for a decade. In retrospect, US cynicism bears at least as much responsibility as Soviet thuggery for the tragedy of Afghanistan and for the consequences elsewhere.

THE PIPELINE

Another self-congratulatory myth broadcast by the US was that the key to defeating the Red Army was generous US aid to the mujahideen. Actually in the first few years, the US and Saudi Arabia split a modest annual bill of $30–50 million. Only in the middle of Ronald Reagan's first presidential term, when anti-Communism ceased to be matter of *realpolitik* and took on the air of a religious revival, did aid flows jump, Saudi Arabia still matching dollar for dollar. By the time the USSR withdrew from Afghanistan, each government had kicked in $1.5 billion for a guerrilla force supposedly numbering 200–300,000 fighters. The rapid hike in cost reflected partly that the pipeline not merely leaked but gushed and partly an increasing commitment to bleed the USSR. The unofficial outflow would, in the decade to come, make the US military aid program the biggest single source of supply for the world arms black market from which everyone from insurgent groups to embargoed countries to narco-militias would draw. It would also help cement in place the contraband networks dealing drugs, arms, and consumer goods that today dominate trade in and out of Afghanistan.[18]

In the meantime, the first task of those in charge of the US arms pipeline to the Afghan resistance was to find Soviet-style weapons. They were simple to maintain; they permitted use of captured ammunition; and they allowed the guerrillas to claim that their arms were captured from the enemy, therefore allowing the US "deniability." Some came from CIA stockpiles, from China (whose own production followed Soviet lines), from Egypt (which was then replacing its Soviet arsenal with an US one), and from Israel (which replicated Soviet models, then sold them with the claim that the stuff had been captured from the PLO). Yet more were bought from dealers whose own sources were clouded by layers of deception. Communist Poland, desperate for foreign exchange, was rumored to be a major supplier.[19]

At this stage, some arms were stolen before arrival. Among the beneficiaries may have been the CIA itself. By skimming officially sanctioned Afghan aid, it could evade a Congressional ban on assistance to its covert wars in southern Africa and Central America. Some theft, too, may have been the work of brokers and frontmen. In secret arms deals, it is difficult to bargain over price, monitor transactions, and keep formal records. Prices at source might be too high; dealers might substitute inferior goods; and shippers might pad invoices while diverting material to their own customers.[20]

Once arms arrived at the port of Karachi, Pakistan's Inter-Services Intelligence (ISI) took over. Supposedly this was to prevent the Soviet Union from being able to accuse Pakistan of complicity with Washington, suggesting a rather more limited Soviet espionage capacity than most Cold War observers were inclined to credit. A more convincing reason was that it enabled certain Pakistani generals to retire rich. Another advantage of using the ISI as cutout was to make the mujahideen appear more as genuine freedom fighters than as tools of US foreign policy. It was also a way to absolve the US of responsibility for what might follow – any nasty after-effects could be blamed on the "Pakis."

After Karachi, weapons packed in containers marked "food" and "engineering parts" and the like were taken northeast by rail or in special trucks outfitted with frequently changed license plates and driven by soldiers with special passes to prevent police or Customs from interfering, to special dumps of which the largest was Ojhri Camp between the cities of Rawlapindi and Islamabad. There opportunity knocked again, with both hands. Some weapons were apparently diverted by the ISI to equip anti-government guerrillas in the Indian states of Punjab and, later, Kashmir; others were sold on the black market, particularly to places like Iran, then under a US embargo.[21] Evidence of massive diversion vanished in 1988, just prior to the arrival of a US inspection team, when a huge explosion – officially blamed on Afghanistan's secret service – devastated Ojhiri and killed at least one thousand people, perhaps many more.

From the special dumps, the ISI arranged for more trucks, bearing registration plates issued to Afghan refugees loyal to political leaders Pakistan wanted to favor, to haul arms to Peshawar, Afghan exile headquarters and capital of Pakistan's North-West Frontier Province, or to the border city of Quetta in Baluchistan. From there they were turned over to representatives of the seven major resistance movements – there were actually many more, but Pakistan and the US chose to make only these seven, six run by Ghilzai Pashtuns, the beneficiaries.[22] At that point more diversion occurred. Some of the weaponry turned up for sale in the North-West Frontier Province, where there was also an open market in booze, drugs, stolen cars, smuggled electronics, and counterfeit currency.[23]

The final stage, entrusted to contractors with business or family relations with the Afghan exile leadership, required that weapons be hauled, often by mule, into Afghanistan. Once there, arms were supplied to field commanders – there were about two thousand minor chiefs. No doubt some exaggerated quantities used or lost in battle and sold off the difference.

Along with arms came relief aid for three million refugees who fled to Pakistan. Some of the international agencies were respected and independent. Some were probably fronts for US or British intelligence. But what was unique was the presence of a rapidly growing set of Muslim charities, financed mainly from the Gulf states and staffed by volunteers from across the Muslim world, which fed, clothed, and educated a generation of Afghan refugees, as well as indoctrinating them with anti-Communist rhetoric and Islamic virtue. Apart from genuine aid work, funded heavily by donors from the Arab Gulf states, the charities acted as conduits for contributions from both Arab governments and rich individuals to various Afghan factions or to recruiting agencies for foreign volunteers, all with the open encouragement and collaboration of the US and Britain.[24]

Afghanistan is landlocked. Hence its trade, apart from passing overland through Iran or the Soviet Union, went to a large degree via Pakistan under an old agreement for duty-free transit. Remarkably, during the entire war the arrangements continued to function, with legal trade providing cover for the illegal. Japanese electronics, Chinese silks, French glassware and perfumes, British crockery, and much more went

from the port of Karachi nominally to Kabul, with a lot dumped in
Pakistan en route. Back flowed Eastern European manufactured goods,
cheap enough to undercut legitimately imported or locally produced
items in Pakistan.[25] It was simple enough to piggyback mujahideen aid
flows atop normal contraband. Pakistan's smuggling "mafia" developed
a reputation for absolute reliability whether the cargo was us weapons,
French champagne, or Afghan opium: if a cargo paid for by a client was
seized by Customs or police on either side, and a bribe did not suffice
to liberate it, the goods were replaced free of charge. That traffic also
permitted Pashtun clan leaders in the border region to extort protection money from one side or the other, or both competitively.[26] Further
assisting the contraband flow, Kabul, even under its Communist regime, had a freewheeling money market, usually run by Sikhs and
Hindus, which could finance trade and remittances, legal and illegal
alike. Even the cia used the parallel money market, later denounced
as a major tool for terrorist financing, to pay Afghan commanders.[27]

The distribution of aid was subject to dual political control. First, Pakistan delivered assistance to its seven chosen party chiefs according to
how many "followers" they had, a number determined by the isi steering refugees into the camps of the leaders whom it wanted to favor.[28]
After the war the standard tale was that the isi was to blame when anti-
us factions like that led by Gulbuddin Hekmatayar ended up with all
the goodies – as if Pakistan would favor a group without at least tacit approval from Washington. Still, the story served, once again, for the us
government to attempt after the fact to wash its hands of the consequences of having provided so much sophisticated weaponry to political brigands who would soon turn them on each other, and on the us
and its regional allies.

Second, after the seven parties received their allotments, their leaders decided how much would go to actual commanders. That distribution seemed to depend less on military effectiveness than on whether
the party leadership wanted weapons deployed or held back to await a
reckoning of accounts with supposed allies. Shortly after the Communist coup, the Afghan regions of Nouristan and Hazarajat (traditional
home to the Hazara Shi'a) rebelled to become de facto autonomous
– yet they were given not a cent or a bullet of us aid. If any resistance
commander was denied outside assistance, he had to rely on either
what could be taken from government forces or what he could buy
off the black market – in effect he paid for weapons already purchased for him by us taxpayers. Meanwhile some Afghan leaders were

reputed to have a sharp eye for real-estate investments and a taste for Peshawar villas and foreign bank accounts.[29]

A commander denied assistance also had to seek his own sources of funds, such as protection money from smugglers' caravans or payoffs from the Afghan government to refrain from attacking power plants or transmission lines. Ahmed Shah Mas'ud, field commander for the Tajik-dominated Jamiat-i-Islami, collected from the Red Army payments to permit its convoys unimpeded passage along the highway linking Kabul with the Soviet border. This would later lead to charges that he sat out most of the war in his own turf, left in peace by the Communist government as long as he protected its supply routes from attack by other groups, while he hoarded weapons and supplies for the intra-mujahideen struggle to come.[30]

Probably the most lucrative source of independent financing came from the fact that, as a previous generation of hippies could attest, Afghanistan was world-renowned for its recreational drugs. Cannabis growers made payoffs to resistance groups; and hashish traffickers reputedly showed solidarity by stamping bars with anti-Soviet slogans. "Crumble the Kremlin" was a favorite. Police in Britain reputedly intercepted a shipment of half-kilo slabs emblazoned with crossed Kalashnikovs and the exhortation to "Smoke Russia Away."[31]

Opiates were even more important. When queried about their theological appropriateness, the brother of one faction leader retorted: "We must grow and sell opium to fight our holy war against Russian non-believers ... Islamic law forbids the taking of opium, but there is no prohibition against growing it."[32] Or, apparently, against making it into heroin in the autonomous tribal region of Pakistan, in refineries jointly owned by Pakistani merchants and Pashtun leaders.[33]

From the North-West Frontier Province, drugs moved south, carried by the same ISI vehicles (still protected against Customs and police probes) that brought weapons north.[34] Part was taken by smugglers already moving arms (for anti-government guerrilla groups) into India and whiskey (banned under Islamic law) back into Pakistan. Inside India drugs went to Mumbai, where underworld traffickers who smuggled into India everything from gold to pornographic movies arranged the export. Or the dope headed farther south, where supporters of the Tamil separatist guerrillas (the notorious Tamil Tigers) from Sri Lanka moved it out via their European courier system. Other shipments went to Karachi, where a handful of families, each with a senior officer in their ranks, ran the export. Yet other drugs were hauled overland by

Baluchi tribesmen to Iran, then transferred to Kurdish groups to move across Turkey, where the drugs entered a black-market complex of corrupt officials, political insurgents, career gangsters, and intelligence agents, before taking the Balkan route into Western Europe, where they later helped fund the rise of the US-supported Kosovo Liberation Army. All of this was proof not of some grand "organized crime" conspiracy but of the way a lucrative business opportunity competitively calls forth the infrastructure and entrepreneurs to exploit it. All of this, too, was well known to the US, which tolerated (even encouraged) the traffic because it helped to keep Afghan warlords on side and took a toll among Red Army soldiers, while very little Afghan heroin reached the US.

Despite the flood of new weaponry, for some time the mujahideen seemed to make little headway. There were pessimistic forecasts in the CIA that the Soviet Union could continue the war indefinitely, even that it was winning. The popular explanation was that Soviet and Afghan-government command of the air impeded the resistance's mobility and striking power. In fact, air power is of little use in dealing with irregular troops in rough terrain. A more likely reason was that, to most Afghan warlords, the main point of large groups of followers with fancy weapons was to increase bargaining power when it came to negotiating over allegiance. But blaming setbacks on Soviet planes and helicopters was sexier in terms of media sell and more useful in getting extra taxpayer money for US military ventures. Hence, much the way the Lone Ranger carried his trademark ammunition when he rode to battle villains and oppressors, so this war of (selective and unisexual) liberation had its silver bullet, the state-of-the-art Stinger anti-aircraft missile.[35]

Introducing a weapon hitherto available only to US forces violated the principle of deniability; it exposed a recent piece of technowizardry to capture and copy; and it almost guaranteed some missiles to be on the world black market in short order. Most objections, though, came from the CIA. The Pentagon, already infested by Trotskyists-turned-neocons who had switched from calling for permanent revolution to preaching the virtues of perpetual war, was gung ho. There may have been a pressing reason.

Early in 1986 the USSR decided to withdraw from Afghanistan. In preparation, it parachuted in Mohammed Najibullah as president. As former head of the secret police and a Ghilzai Pashtun, he was better placed to interfere with the mujahideen arms pipeline across the traditional Pashtun territories. He reversed more social reforms and

wrapped his government in an Islamic cloak; and he bought the quies-
cence of warlords in big slices of the country by leaving them to their
own devices, provided they did nothing to support the mujahideen.
With the tide threatening to turn in favor of the USSR, the US response
came in two ways.

One was to send emissaries to Iran bearing gifts – namely an offer of
high tech weaponry to aid its long and bloody war with Soviet-supplied
Iraq in exchange for Iran permitting guerrillas from the two million or
more Afghan refugees it sheltered to start operations against the Soviet
and Afghan forces and for Iran to use its influence to get the Shi'a
Hazaras of central Afghanistan to rise against the government and its Soviet backers. But the only result was the notorious Iran-Contra scandal
that paralyzed diplomacy in the last days of the Reagan Administration.[36]

The second effort to step up the war and reverse Soviet-Afghan government gains was to supply Stingers to the Ghilzai-dominated factions
in the east. This, unlike the Iran opening, was proclaimed a great success. But on closer examination, that turns out to be largely puffery.

True, more Soviet aircraft were brought down. But the number seems
to have been inflated by crediting to the Stinger missile every single
"kill," even those due to an old-fashioned anti-aircraft gun or a drunken
pilot. Even these gains were temporary. Pilots soon adopted evasion techniques, while Soviet military engineers quickly learned countermeasures.
By the time the Soviet pullout was complete in 1989, the Stinger was effectively neutralized as a weapon against technically advanced air forces.
Furthermore, the Soviet decision to pull out had been made before the
Stinger arrived. It is even possible that the introduction of modern US
weapons strengthened the hands of opponents of withdrawal and slowed
it down, something the neocons in the Pentagon may have wanted. Since
most missiles arrived very late in the war, their main impact was to build
up stocks for the black market; this forced the US into a belated, expensive, and not very successful buy-back program – particularly so after civil
airline companies were forced to add hours and thousands of miles to
their itineraries to give the region a wide berth.[37] Among the many future legends around Usama bin Lāden was one that, while he was busy in
the Sudan in the early 1990s, he bought a plane to ferry his personal inventory of Stinger missiles from Peshawar to Khartoum.

RED SUNSET?

Along with the Stinger saga came the tale that, because of US aid, the
mujahideen, bolstered by foreign volunteers, turned from a guerrilla

force into a real army capable of defeating the Afghan government in set-piece battles. The theory was that they would seize a chunk of territory on which to proclaim a provisional government and therefore woo away Najibullah's allies. That was the rationale for the 1989 battle for Jalalabad in which Usama bin Lāden reputedly revealed the prowess of his personal army. Allegedly this mujahideen victory finally convinced the Soviets that it was time to turn tail and flee, leading shortly thereafter to the fall of the Communist government in Kabul.[38]

Again the opposite is closer to the truth. By the time of the battle of Jalalabad, the Red Army had almost completed its withdrawal. Peace was perilously close. Of about two thousand local warlords, 160 had already signed with the Afghan government and another 750 were negotiating. The possibility of a deal that would leave Communists as participants in a postwar government alarmed top mujahideen leaders and their US sponsors. Hence they tried try to stage a dramatic military coup. But Jalalabad was an unmitigated catastrophe. Even though the mujahideen were bolstered by Arab and other Islamic volunteers, they were routed. If Usama bin Lāden and his loyalists had really played a major role at Jalalabad, it was likely not something about which they would brag in the future.[39]

After Jalalabad, the Afghan government got enough of a lease on life to survive even its Soviet mentor. In 1989 the Berlin Wall fell, and a series of Communist governments followed soon after; by 1991 the Soviet Communist Party itself had been banned. In those earth-shaking events, the Afghan war was a sideshow. While it did impose on the USSR heavy costs in blood and treasure and even more in international good will, its importance in the collapse of the USSR was far less than purely internal factors such as the breakdown of the archaic planning system, the growing conviction among the political elite that only an opening to the West for trade and technology would revive a stagnant economy, and the rise of ethnic nationalism. Nor was that ethnic nationalism much related to Afghanistan. Even after the Baltic states had seceded from the USSR, the political class of the central Asian republics looked forward to a more equal union of Slavic and Turkic peoples in a reformed USSR. The impetus to break up the union came from Russia, the Ukraine, and Belarus, not from the Islamic regions bordering Afghanistan.

Three years after the Soviet withdrawal, Russian President Boris Yeltsin, in a bid for US favor, cut off supplies and money. Without Russian subsidies, Najibullah was unable to maintain the payments that had purchased peace with ex-mujahideen commanders. The coup de grâce came when the powerful Uzbek warlord and mercenary Abdul

Rashid Dostum, formerly a supporter of the government (provided it left him in peace in his northern fiefdom), decided to break ranks and join the other side. Even that had less to do with ideological opposition to the regime than with Dostum's desire to keep his Pashtun rivals from taking control. This latest mujahideen "victory" led to a vicious civil war from 1992 to 1996, which wrecked Kabul, a city that had gone through the previous fifteen years of strife without serious damage; and it so soured the population on the mujahideen that many seemed ready to welcome the Taliban to liberate them from their liberators.

By that time the costs of the Afghanistan conflict had been enormous. Of a pre-conflict population of twenty-three million, more than one million died, hundreds of thousands were maimed, and nearly six million had fled as refugees to Iran or Pakistan. The already weak infrastructure was largely destroyed. The only crops to prosper were landmines and opium poppies. The costs included the conversion of Pakistan's North-West Frontier Province into the world's premier arms bazaar, while unleashing on Pakistan a scourge of heavily armed religious, political, and ethnic dissident groups who turned parts of the country, the city of Karachi in particular, into another war zone.[40]

However, according to the instant experts who proliferated after 9/11, the main cost to the world was the many thousands of trained foreign volunteers who could turn their talents to other causes once the anti-Soviet war ended. Some did precisely that, although almost always for local causes, not as part of some global jihad.[41] However most of the volunteers were aid workers and teachers, not fighters, who wanted nothing more than to return home to their former lives. Of those who decided to live by their religious principles, most did so through peaceful proselytizing and charitable work. Still, the existence of the Afghan veterans was enough, once the propaganda mills started to churn, to raise the spectre of a rising Islamintern. Credit for its creation is usually given to an important but distinctly secondary figure in the anti-Soviet struggle named Usama bin Lāden, who would have remained largely unknown had he not suddenly become so useful in the greater scheme of world power politics. Having gathered his supposed followers into a grand Terror International, he was an elastic threat that could be expanded at will and bent to fit almost any agenda in almost any part of the world.

2

Vengeful Green Giant? – Bin Lāden, "Fundamentalism," and the Rise of the Islamintern

Usama bin Lāden, so the story goes, emerged from the maelstrom of 1980s Afghanistan, Kalashnikov in one fist, Qur'ān in the other, primed to lead a worldwide jihād against a decadent West while scheming to overthrow or undermine "moderate" governments in the Middle East. He was believed to have three special qualifications for the job. First, his central role in the Afghan struggle gave him organizational skills, knowledge of irregular warfare, and contacts with countless adoring acolytes ready to heed his call to arms. Second, the power of his violent Islamic convictions sufficed to whip his followers into a homicidal-suicidal frenzy. Third, his privileged birth and business acumen provided him with access to seemingly unlimited wealth based initially on extortion from Western motorists, later, once his global infrastructure was in place, from rackets like drug smuggling, currency counterfeiting, and a host of even more exotic pursuits.

That was the story. The reality was a little more mundane. However many palpitations his speeches and videos may induce, bin Lāden, who had been a minor if distinguished figure in Afghanistan, would likely have remained a marginal and undistinguished figure in Islamic discourse and action – if the US had not done so much to elevate his political stature and grossly exaggerate both his resources and his deeds.[1]

PASSING THE HAT

Certainly little in his background suggested that Usama bin Lāden would anoint himself leader of a new Islamintern, or that anyone would follow him very far if he did.[2] Granted bin Lāden was born to wealth and privilege. His father had been an émigré from Yemen whose success was a tale of rags to riches. Starting as a bricklayer, he built a giant construction firm and so distinguished himself by efficient fulfillment of government contracts that the king decided to make Mohammed bin Lāden his Minister of Public Works. Something that would in some places in the West (though perhaps not in the Bush-Cheney White House) be regarded as a gross conflict of interest was, in Saudi Arabia, simply the way things were (are) done.[3]

Muhammed bin Lāden was apparently devout, but not fanatical, except perhaps in his taste for women – which resulted in fifty-eight offspring, most of whom were cosmopolitan and Western-educated. His early death in an airplane accident and the consequent passing of his fortune to his children was supposedly the foundation of Usama's Terror Treasury. In one version of the story, he inherited $80–300 million. Assuming the father made equal provision for his other nineteen sons, nine of them older than Usama, and ignoring anything left to thirty-eight daughters, even the lower figure would have meant distribution at his death of more than the assets of the company while still leaving it with the wherewithal to grow to its present multibillion dollar size. This would be odd behavior for an Arab patriarch traditional enough to have multiple wives but apparently not sufficiently so to respect the custom of passing control of family assets to the oldest son.[4]

In reality Usama's personal share was a (relatively) measly $1 million per year, and even that was cut off by an asset freeze well before the horrendous deeds later imputed to him. Hence another tale claims that bin Lāden's family secretly kept him rolling in dough. This, of course, assumes that the family was willing to risk both the good will of the Saudi regime on whom its wealth depended and its senior members' status of living in luxury in the US by maintaining clandestine financial links with its notorious sibling once he had become an international pariah. Even after the 9/11 Commission cleared the bin Lāden family, the legend persisted – by then there were too many pundits with a professional or political stake in the myth, and too many lawyers slavering over their possible cut from gargantuan lawsuits, to let facts stand between them and a good story.

Although Usama in his youth was reputed to be more religiously inclined and socially conservative than his siblings, that seems to be the result of personal inclination, not of the influence of his father, much less that of his mother, who, a Syrian by birth, was more assertive than Mohammed bin Lāden's other wives. Nor was his interest in politics piqued by religion. Rather it reflected the geostrategic earthquake to hit the region in 1979. That year the Camp David Accords between Egypt and Israel plunged the Arab world into turmoil; the overthrow of the Shah of Iran by a coalition of leftists (soon purged) and Islamists shook US policy to its roots: a bloody takeover of the Grand Mosque in Mecca challenged the moral authority of the House of Saud, with potentially huge implications for the West's oil security; and the opening salvos of the anti-Soviet war in Afghanistan meant that the temperature of the Cold War had taken a sharp turn upward.

Bin Lāden's role during most of that last conflict was simply to travel the Gulf (under the tutelage of Saudi intelligence, which did little without US approval) to raise money from governments, mosques, and businessmen who had known his father. Not until 1984 did he move to Peshawar to get involved in construction (of residences and training complexes). His efforts were of no great military significance.[5] His reputation grew not because of the kind of "charisma" that wins audience approval on *Oprah* but because of self-sacrifice and generosity. Here was a man from a privileged background ready to put life and fortune on the line.[6] In short, bin Lāden was a committed but not evidently bloodthirsty volunteer for a dangerous but widely lauded cause who formed a relatively small cog in an already well-oiled machine that would have functioned quite effectively in his absence.

That machine fed to the mujahideen three types of aid. One was arms – in which bin Lāden played no role except perhaps to construct storage facilities.

The second was money for Islamic volunteers. Here his function was important but hardly indispensable. Not just across the Islamic world but even among émigré communities in the West, fundraisers with at least tacit US approval worked through the same Islamic charities and foundations denounced after 9/11 as conduits for terrorist financing. Among them was the Maktabah al-Khidmaah (MAK – bureau of services). Funded by Saudi Arabia and run by a Palestinian named Abdullah Azzam, it provided medical aid, propagated Islam, and financed publications in Pakistan about the Afghan war.[7] It was a US favorite, with branches in the US, where Azzam made fundraising tours, because

Azzam, who had broken with the mainstream Palestinian struggle over its stress on nationalism rather than Islam, insisted that the task at hand was the creation of an Islamic government in Afghanistan, not pan-Islamic revolution; and he opposed making war against fellow Muslims. When Azzam was killed in a bomb blast in 1989, control of MAK allegedly passed to bin Lāden, who made it, so the story went, the linchpin of his global terror network with a radically revised mission.[8]

The third form of aid was locating and training foreign recruits. Supposedly it was this role that later permitted bin Lāden to swell the ranks of his al-Qā'idah group to its epic 9/11 proportions. Here, too, the truth is more prosaic.

To help the US keep a low profile, the job of finding foreign volunteers and personnel to train them was turned over to "private" actors. Apart from campaigns across the Muslim world, recruitment centres were set up in major Western cities, including in the US, that hosted large Muslim or Arab populations. Much of the work was done through local mosques, some of which also became post-9/11 government targets. US (and British) firms run by Special Forces veterans were subcontracted the job of training future trainers – mainly volunteers with a military background from Islamic countries. Afterwards the trainers instructed other volunteers in use of small arms and how to improvise explosives from ordinary materials. When Egyptian bombers were caught in the US in 1993 mixing ammonia fertilizer with fuel oil, they were using a method taught to Afghan resistance fighters by US intelligence or its proxies.[9] It was also the technique employed a few years later by Timothy McVeigh to blow up the federal building in Oklahoma City; but by then the formula was available at a mouse click on the internet.

After 9/11 enormous attention was focused on those who had been taught such lethal arts rather than on those who did the teaching. Yet much of the recent proliferation of private military contractors (in Bosnia, Sierra Leone, and Iraq, for example) follows precedents set in the Afghan war. Arguably their emergence is a much greater threat to world peace now and for the foreseeable future than the Islamic Brigade they trained. Long after the last of the Afghan volunteers are dead and buried, some of the private military contractors will likely still be in business – that, after all, is the kind of immortality only a stock-market listing can bring.

The volunteers from dozens of Islamic countries were further divided into a multitude of independent groups who adorned their "organizations" with inspiring names. In the post 9/11 confusion, all would be lumped together into "al-Qaeda" along with claims that bin Lāden was personally responsible for training up to seventy thousand Islamic militants.[10] For someone who spent most of the war passing the hat in the Gulf or digging holes near the Afghan-Pakistan border, Usama really did get around.

The total of volunteers over the decade or so of war was nowhere near seventy thousand – it could have been as low as three thousand.[11] Many, probably most, of those were in Pakistan-Afghanistan in the 1980s to do aid work, not to blow up tanks; and few who took part in the military effort went anywhere near a bin Lāden "camp" – of which there was apparently only one in an area dotted with facilities run by Gulbuddin Hekmatyar and Abdul Sayyaf, Saudi Arabia's favorite Pashtun leader.[12] Nor were those who passed through any facility created by bin Lāden automatically and irrevocably in his thrall.

A parallel belief that would prove important in sustaining the al-Qā'idah legend was the post-conflict unity of purpose of the "Afghan Arabs" – who came from places as varied as Yemen, Mauritania, Xinjiang, and Malaysia. In reality different groups had different geographic, strategic, and ideological agendas. Some called for further struggle against oppressive regimes back home; others were tight with their sponsoring governments; yet others dreamed of pan-Islamic revolution. After the war their destinies were equally diverse. Some went home with honor; others hid out in disgrace; yet others looked for martyrdom. A few were even reputed to hire on with intelligence forces as moles or *agents provocateurs* in Islamic opposition movements, while more were harassed and imprisoned by regimes that had encouraged them to sacrifice themselves in Afghanistan, only to be disappointed when they survived.

NO PLACE LIKE HOME?

Ahmed el-Maati, a Canadian citizen, spent more than two years in Syrian and Egyptian torture cells on the basis of phony information provided by Canadian and US intelligence. Born in Kuwait to a Syrian mother and an Egyptian father, he migrated to Canada with his family at age seventeen. After he dropped out of university and did some odd jobs, he followed his older brother to Afghanistan to join a mujahideen unit in 1991 – at that time the Tāliban did not exist and Usama was back in Saudi Arabia. El-Maati's military training consisted of little more than learning to fire an AK-47. Because of a bum knee, his job was to drive ambulances and supply trucks. That gave him the skills to

work, after he returned home, for a trucking firm near Toronto. He
also took flying lessons, on Cessnas not 747s, to perhaps start an air
taxi; but he was afraid of flying and soon quit. One day in August
2001, after a routine delivery across the border, us Customs pulled
him over, grilled him for eight hours, and fingerprinted and photo-
graphed him. They were particularly interested in a map in his vehicle
with several Ottawa buildings, including a virus lab and an Atomic Energy of Canada facility, numbered on it. Later it was revealed that the
map had been issued by the Canadian government to help visitors find
their way around an area full of government buildings. None of the
sites were secret; the Atomic Energy offices and the virus lab had been
closed long before the map was found; and the map was probably left
in the vehicle by a former driver (since el-Maati's usual truck was being
repaired that day) who used it to locate places where deliveries were
due. But to the United States, and to the Canadian Security and Intelligence Service (csis), it was more likely a plan for a terror attack on
key government installations.

According to el-Maati, just hours after 9/11, csis agents came calling. When he asked for a lawyer, they threatened that, if he did not cooperate, they would refuse entry into Canada of his fiancé from Syria.
Later he saw a news flash that us authorities had found a Kuwaiti man
with pictures of Ottawa government buildings. Worried, he arranged
for a lawyer to contact csis; but csis never called back. A couple
months later he was off to Damascus for his wedding. On arrival he was
jumped by a group of hooded men and hauled off to a filthy underground cell where he was beaten regularly for the next several months
until he broke and invented a story about planning to bomb Canadian
installations. Next stop was Egypt where the treatment was repeated. After more than two years, he was freed to return to Canada, his health
broken and his marriage collapsed.[13]

Usama bin Lāden's homecoming in 1989 was radically different. He
was lionized. As local newspapers extolled his exploits, he seems to
have become increasingly aware of the value of publicity to solicit support for Muslim causes. And he used the opportunity to articulate a
growing sense of political alienation.

Still, his first public address after his return consisted not of an attack
on the Saudi royal family or a denunciation of the decadence of us society but of a speech about Palestine. He pointed out that "American companies make millions in the Arab world from which they pay taxes to
their government. The United States uses that money to send $3 billion

to Israel, which it uses to kill Palestinians."[14] And he called for a boycott of US goods on the logic that "when we buy American goods, we are accomplices in the murder of Palestinians." Not only were those the kinds of sentiments with which everyone from war-tax resisters to organizers of consumer boycotts (for example, against California grapes produced by nonunion labor in the 1970s or the products of Apartheid-era South Africa in the 1980s) could understand, but they were widely shared among the Saudi elite, even if few expressed them so openly. It would take much more to make bin Lāden a pariah in Saudi Arabia.[15]

Probably the key event was the buildup to the 1991 Gulf War. Usama had denounced Saddam Hussein as a "whiskey-drinking woman-chasing apostate" and warned the Saudi king about him well before the invasion of Kuwait.[16] Perhaps now believing his own legend, he boasted that he could defend the kingdom with his mujahideen. Instead of taking up Usama's offer of a phantom army, Saudi Arabia added insult to injury by requesting a token force of ex-mujahideen led by Gulbuddin Hekmatyar, only to cut off Hekmatyar's funding when he sided with Saddam Hussein. Then, using as its pretext bogus pictures of Iraqi troops massing near the Saudi border, Saudi Arabia invited in the Americans. Kuwait was soon liberated – returned to the control of a family dynasty that had accorded partial civil rights to about 10 percent of the country's population, then been so upset at the results as to suspend Parliament. But US forces remained in Saudi Arabia, kept there, the suspicion was, to protect the regime against its own people. This supposed US desecration of the Arabian heartland, sacred as the site of Mecca and Medina, was, along with the corruption of its incumbent rulers, a frequent theme in bin Lāden's discourses once he had fled to exile, first to the Sudan and later back to Afghanistan. That increasing alienation from the Saudi regime also brought bin Lāden front and centre into the most contentious debate in Middle Eastern theopolitics – namely how believers were to deal with a state whose Islamic credentials were in doubt.

ISLAM ÜBER ALLES?

A fair number who identify themselves as Muslims regard it as a part-time spiritual obligation to be discharged in a somewhat perfunctory way (as do so many Christians) or as a cultural identification when dealing with outsiders (as do many Jews). But to others, seemingly a growing number, Islam is an integrated guide to all things social, cultural, spiritual, and material. Leaving aside those who, like monks of certain

Christian orders, prefer to retire to mountaintops to contemplate eternity, those committed to Islam as a *way of life* divide roughly into three very broad categories with very different political implications: religious conservatives, street proselytizers, and violent political activists.[17]

The first, the religious conservatives who interpret the Qur'ān literally, tend to resist political or social change unless it receives the formal endorsement of recognized ulemā, legal scholars whose edicts carry weight not because their exponents are appointed by God but simply because they impress their followers with their learning. Nor do conservatives usually show any great impulse to propagate the faith to the outside world (as distinct from correcting error within Islam itself). What gets conveniently forgotten in Western stereotypes is that, except within the Arabian heartland, Islam was spread overwhelmingly by traders and wandering preachers from mystical orders, not by conquest and forced conversion. That is why, to the consternation of the West, it continues to progress in Africa, for example, where Christianity is associated so closely with colonization.

Nor are Islamic conservatives a monolith. There are several schools of Islamic jurisprudence with different interpretations of acceptable deportment. Even the one prevailing in Saudi Arabia permits any behavior not explicitly forbidden in the Qur'ān. It also permits, indeed requires, that holy texts be subjected to ijtihād, the rational criticism and interpretation of recognized Islamic jurists. Furthermore it is commonplace to further subject Islamic law to interpretation in light of 'urf (customary practices of the community). As a result, those who claim to follow Islamic law can have radically different, yet theologically reasonable, interpretations of what it means. As to the notorious sharī'a law itself (routinely caricatured as consisting largely of lopping off hands and stoning adulterers), it actually has four distinct sources: the Qur'ān (the revealed word of Allāh); plus the Sunna (accounts of the life and activities of the Prophet Muhammad, the early community and the khalīfs); plus ijma (the consensus of scholars on a particular point of Islamic law); plus quiyās (the process of reasoning by analogy).[18] In other words, it is far more varied and flexible than what much of the modern Christian Right fobs off as Biblical Law.

A second group, believers in dā'wa (the calling), proselytize widely, using their (often much looser) interpretation of sacred texts to guide by good works and personal example a program of social transformation that may eventually translate into political change. They are frequently at variance with the established ulemā; and, although they are committed to mass activism rather than violent confrontation, they are often treated with suspicion by the political order. As with those in the conservative camp, their interpretations of religious doctrine can vary considerably. But what they have (more or less) in common is "left wing" attitudes towards social welfare and income redistribution combined with "right wing" attitudes towards culture and family.

Third are radical political Islamists who start with the premise (in many places hard to refute) that the state has become a vehicle of a corrupt elite and draw the conclusion (considerably more contentious) that what is needed is a covert cadre committed to a violent takeover. In the hands of such a vanguard, the state becomes the main instrument for social change – the reverse of da'wa belief. Far from yearning for an imaginary time of ultra-conservative Islamic bliss, today's proponents of radical political Islam are well in tune with modern cross-currents of Western political thought and use Islamic rhetoric principally as a tool for mobilization since it gives local legitimacy to grievances and objectives that can be found almost anywhere in the world among adherents of almost any religion.[19]

Although this third group (commonly but not very accurately called jihādist) attracts by far the greatest attention, it is, numerically speaking, by far the least important – a minority within a minority. Its overall significance is further reduced by it being broken up into mutually hostile subsets, which facilitates infiltration and manipulation by the intelligence services.

Furthermore, while the usual definition of a fundamentalist is one who insists on a literal reading of sacred texts, radical political Islamists rationalize their actions more by appeal to recent writers without theological credentials. The accepted view is that there are five "pillars" of Islamic practice: monotheism; daily prayer; fasting during Ramadan; making the Haj (pilgrimage to Mecca), if possible; and zakāt (an obligatory payment whose proceeds are used for charitable purposes). Radical Islamists add a so-called sixth or hidden pillar, the requirement of jihād, with the further notion that it means military action. Such an obligation owes more to Trotsky than to Muhammad.[20] But it recurs in their writings and from there made its way into the pronouncements of people like Usama bin Lāden.

Radical political Islamists are anathema to conservatives who point to warnings in the Qur'ān about the consequences to those of "twisted mind" who "fake Scripture" for their own ends.[21] Nor are radical political Islamists popular with those who follow the da'wa route. Some leaders of the movement to change society by charitable and educational work are themselves former insurgents who rejected armed confrontation; and the state often takes attacks by violent Islamists (which its security services might deliberately provoke) as a pretext to crack down on the nonviolent Islamic opposition as well.

Therefore, even if all committed Muslims base their beliefs (more or less) on the same religious texts, they differ widely in political goals and methods of achieving them. It makes no sense (except perhaps to "national security experts" from the American Enterprise Institute) to lump conservatives (who usually accept the political status quo), proselytizers (who seek to win over society at large as a prelude to peaceful political change), and political radicals (who use Islamic jargon to rationalize plots against the state) into the catch-all category of "fundamentalist." The distinction is critical to understanding developments in Saudi Arabia, the place that supposedly incubated bin Lāden's militant ideology, and in Egypt, the country that supposedly provided him with the organizational resources to turn ideology into political practice.

HOUSE OF SAUD, HOUSE OF SAND?

Sunnī Islam in Saudi Arabia comprises several competing, even conflicting, trends. There is an official ideology that informs almost all of the country's ulemā and that motivates the country's whip-wielding religious police, scourge of female drivers, male drinkers, exposed ankles, and bare heads. Yet, far from calling for radical political action, that ideology is firmly rooted in current society. Often misnamed "Wahhābī" after Muhammad ibn Abd al-Wahhāb, the sect's eighteenth-century founder, the correct term is salafi (follower), since it demands strict adherence to doctrines laid down not by Abd al-Wahhāb but by the Prophet Muhammad, his immediate companions, and the leaders of the two generations that followed. The objective of the salafi movement is to purge Islam of subsequent accretions, including notions like jihād-as-a-sixth-pillar, which bin Lāden learned from his theopolitical mentors.

However, even in Saudi Arabia the salafi sect has competitors. The da'wa line has a following among the urban educated; there is a small but noisy bunch of jihādists; and there are subvariants. Even the official voice has many tongues. For three decades the grand muftī (the leading religious scholar), Abd al-Aziz ibn Baz, gave the House of Saud legitimacy by issuing rulings in their favor, including one to permit us troops in the kingdom. On his death in 1999, the party line fragmented into competing claims whose influence was reduced further by their perceived status as government hirelings – the state provides them with salaries, cars, and houses and periodically purges those who refuse to toe the line.[22] This, of course, gives urban middle-class Saudis a further pretext to shed their religious accoutrements at the door of their homes, then break out the Scotch whiskey, French cosmetics, and US rock music once safely inside. For the very rich, and those of royal blood, the job of indulging their whims is even easier – they simply ban the religious police from the areas where they choose to live.

If, on closer examination, Saudi Arabia's theological uniformity becomes, along with the puritanical piety of many of its people, a convenient myth, the notion of bin Lāden as a "fundamentalist" agitator who ascribes to the "Wahhābī" creed looks even more dubious. The bin Lāden family comes from a region of Yemen, the Hadhramout, which is a stronghold of Sufi sects. Sufis are in some ways the opposite of salafīs. A Sufi searches for a personal experience of God by meditation, repetitive prayathons, hypnotic dancing and whirling, or even sometimes by drugs. Sufis, too, gather at the tombs of their founders in rituals that, to the Islamic literalist, smack of saint worship of an almost Catholic nature. During a nineteenth-century invasion of Yemen, followers of Abd al-Wahhāb desecrated the tombs of the Hadhrami saints.

Certainly bin Lāden is no Sufi saint; but, to critics, his pronouncements are contaminated with traces of Sufi belief.[23] Leaving aside the question of whether suicide bombers are truly motivated by religion, or simply grab onto it for consolation and reinforcement after they have made the decision to die for the cause, suicide attacks, which bin Lāden applauds, have no legitimacy in the Sunnī tradition. (Most respected Shi‘a clerics also denounce them.) Even more interesting, his Syrian mother was from an 'Alawī family. While the divide between Shi‘a and Sunnī was originally based on a dynastic dispute – the Shi‘a believing that the Prophet Muhammad's son-in-law 'Ali was the rightful successor to the Caliphate – over time it evolved into substantial doctrinal differences, which further muddle the usual simplistic stereotypes. But the Shi‘a themselves produced spinoffs. None are more contentious than the 'Alawī, who seem to regard 'Ali with almost the same veneration that Christians accord to Jesus, making them heretical even in the eyes of fellow Shi‘a and apostate in the minds of Sunnī literalists.[24] Yemenite Sufi and Syrian 'Alawi? Usama's theological heritage might well be doubly dubious in the eyes of a genuine Saudi "fundamentalist."

The real problem Saudi Arabia faced on and after bin Lāden's return was (is) political, not religious. It stems from a rapidly growing population that was (is) youthful, well-educated, unemployed, and resentful of the profligacy of the royal family. That family, despite many disputes and differences, knows fully well that if the country slips out of its collective control, all members will lose their power, their wealth, and perhaps their lives. Hence its increasing reliance on the US for defense. Despite a vicious anti-Saudi campaign conducted by US neocons and the pro-Israel lobby, Saudi Arabia remains to all intents and purposes a US colony. But that exacerbates the problem. An increasing disparity in the distribution of wealth coincides with an extremely privileged expat community, particularly from the United States, with the fact that so many of the kingdom's biggest businesses are linked to US transnationals, and with US control of the training of the National Guard whose main job is to guard the regime against the regular Army. After the 1990 Iraqi invasion of Kuwait, it did not escape notice that a Saudi regime that had funnelled so much national wealth into the pockets of UK and US weapons dealers, while skimming off a big chunk in kickbacks, had to call for US soldiers to defend it. This occurred when soft oil prices meant sharply declining national revenues, a large portion of which went to subsidize the US war effort in Iraq.[25]

Thus the real danger posed by someone like Usama bin Lāden, fresh back from his Afghan exploits, was that he might be a lightening rod for social, political, and economic, rather than theological, discontent.[26] For that reason in 1991 he was expelled from Saudi Arabia and took refuge in the Sudan. Three years later, under US pressure, his assets were frozen. Not that it seemed to bother Usama very much. "We also believe that livelihoods are pre-ordained," he scoffed. "So no matter how much pressure America puts on the regime in Riyadh to freeze our assets and to forbid people from contributing to this great cause, we shall still have Allāh to take care of us, livelihood is sent by Allāh, we shall not want …"[27]

While in exile in the Sudan, bin Lāden was visited by emissaries of the regime, including family members, to ask him to mend his ways. In 1995 Saudi Arabia set an important precedent when it designated him architect of a bomb attack on the Riyadh headquarters of the US company that trained and supervised the Saudi National Guard. Another explosion at a US military installation in Khobar followed the next year. Setting a standard of proof that would be common in future accusations, the claim that bin Lāden was behind that attack as well was based on "confessions" of four captured men who said they had been "influenced" by faxes sent by bin Lāden from abroad.[28] However, when the Saudi intelligence services finished their investigation, they put the blame on Shi'a militants from its oil-producing eastern region who were supposedly acting as Iranian agents. The FBI concurred.[29] Afterwards Saudi Arabia again tried to make a deal – it offered to unfreeze his assets and welcome him home provided he agreed to a public reconciliation. Instead he apparently used the proximity of his new abode to reconnect with old cronies from the birthplace of modern political Islam.

PYRAMIDS AND PRAYER BEADS

Egypt prior to World War II was de facto a British colony. In the Canal Zone and the affluent parts of Cairo and Alexandria, British officials disparaged the locals and their superstitions. In response, Hasan al-Bannā, member of a prominent Sufi order, created al-Ikhwān al-Muslimīn (the Muslim Brotherhood). It spread upward to professionals who embraced its nationalism and downward to lower-income groups to whom it promised social justice, then branched out to neighboring countries, Arab and non-Arab alike. (In Afghanistan it inspired both Jamiat al-Islami and Hizb-i-Islami.) Although Islam was the centre of its ideology, the Brotherhood stood in opposition to establishment clerics trained in Cairo's prestigious al-Azhar seminary, whom it saw as servile to the colonial order. And it stressed social activism – each branch had a mosque, a school, a workshop, a sporting club, and other facilities to supply the community with services that the state (and official clergy) failed to provide.[30]

But there was also a revolutionary current. Supporters waged guerrilla warfare against the British, while the Brotherhood shared members with the Free Officers Movement plotting the overthrow of the monarchy. The spark was the 1948 war in Palestine, where the Brotherhood contributed a military unit. Blaming the Arab debacle on the treachery and corruption of Arab governments, the Brotherhood supported the 1953 coup that brought the Army to power; and it applauded when, after assuming leadership, Gamel Abd al-Nasir, one of the few Arab heroes of the 1948 war, nationalized the Suez Canal. But the Brotherhood (perhaps infiltrated by the British intelligence services) soon came to regard the new government as too cozy with the USSR. Some adherents went again into armed opposition. In response to an assassination attempt, al-Nasir's regime cracked down, sending many Brotherhood cadres to exile in the Gulf. Welcomed there as teachers, bankers, and other professionals, they shared their beliefs with a future generation of émigré Egyptian workers who flooded in after the oil boom started in 1973.

With the death of al-Nasir, his successor, Anwar Sadat, began to encourage the Islamists as a foil to nationalists and leftists faithful to the al-Nasir legacy. Although the Brotherhood was still technically banned, the state permitted it to operate social services; and its members again began to infiltrate the professions and civil service in the hopes of a peaceful takeover. However most attention remained focused on the streets, where the organization created unofficial mosques and Islamic charities to minister to the needs of the poor and dispossessed.

This policy of tacit accommodation with the state led to internal dissent. Out of it emerged a much more radical stream stressing not da'wa but violent action, particularly as grievances against the Sadat regime accumulated.[31] First came the infitah (opening) when, on demand from the IMF, the government slashed subsidies to food and fuel, lifted rent controls and limits on land ownership, reduced restrictions on imports, and promoted tourism. This drove up unemployment along with the price of essentials, while the benefits accrued to foreign investors and cronies of the regime. In 1977 the big cities were shaken by food riots in which the urban poor chanted, "Sadat! You are making millions and we are starving!"[32] Sadat followed with what was widely seen as a surrender to Israel at Camp David. Although the Muslim Brotherhood's magazine, Al Dawa, called for peaceful boycotts of all things Israeli, others thought differently.[33] There followed a series of assaults on regime figures and on economic targets. These attacks culminated in the assassination of Sadat in 1981.

The largest radical faction was Gamā'at al-Islāmiyya. Originally a student movement, by the end of the 1970s its followers were de facto running substantial parts of Upper Egypt. Articulating the needs of the disenfranchised and destitute, in the Cairo slums Gamā'at provided cheap welfare services and ran "street mosques" to counter pro-regime theology from al-Azhar. Thus it never abandoned the Brotherhood's street-level focus. However some adherents supplemented that with armed confrontation, later justified as a defensive response to state repression. Because Gamā'at was very much an underground mass movement, there was no real hierarchy of control. Different factions and groups were capable of operating autonomously – although the state took the opportunity of every violent confrontation to concoct an image of a giant, hierarchical conspiracy.

Al Jihad was different. Reflecting the urban, educated and elitist nature of its leadership, it had no street mosques or charities and took no part in mass action. Rather it favored the creation of a disciplined cadre; and it was organized into clandestine cells, each headed by an "emir" and coordinated by committees to handle issues like fundraising, propaganda, and recruitment. Instead of mass confrontations, it favored assassination attempts against regime figures, few of which were successful.

The Islamist opposition fed off a growing economic crisis. During the 1970s and early 1980s the Egyptian economy had been kept afloat by remittances from workers in the Gulf – in effect their earnings paid for the flood of imported consumer goods that crippled indigenous industries. By the mid 1980s, the oil boom petered out; remittances began to dry up; many thousands of Egyptian workers returned to face unemployment at home or competition for scare jobs with all those who, because of a cold peace with Israel and government fears about unrest in the ranks, had been discharged from the Army. During the 1980s, too, militants from both Gamāʿat and Al Jihad had decamped to Afghanistan, with tacit support from the Egyptian government. By the end of the decade, Afghan veterans were returning to face further deterioration of living standards for the masses juxtaposed with ostentatious wealth accumulated by an elite close to the state. And they returned to be treated not as heroes but as subversives. Some turned to the traditional opiate of the masses, except that in their hands religion changed from narcotic to psychostimulant. In the balance of forces they were probably much less important than those who had never left home and whose desperation reached crisis proportions, particularly given all those who were tortured by the security services and emerged from prison humiliated and enraged. But it was easier to blame outside agitators.

In Cairo the Muslim Brotherhood could finance social services through contributions from its large, sometimes prosperous membership; and it earned respect by legal work and public fundraising for causes like Bosnian relief. Gamāʿat, by contrast, was staffed by marginals, and some of its factions raised money by robbing banks and jewellery stores. Both targets seemed to have religious sanction – the banks were based on usury; and most jewellery stores were owned by Coptic Christians. In fact numerous Coptic Christians in Upper Egypt were

soon targets of attempts by militants demanding gizia, supposedly re-
quital money prescribed in the Qur'ān to be paid by non-Muslims in
lieu of military service (although Islamic law does not permit private
individuals to collect it), with some murdered for refusal – although
how much of this was really the work of Gamā'at factions and how
much was simply extortion by criminal gangs was never clear.[34]
Gamā'at in Cairo overstepped the bounds with an effort to create an
autonomous area in one poor neighborhood and to impose zakāt
payments on the inhabitants. Since Pharaonic times the one thing
guaranteed to provoke a stern reaction from Egyptian authorities was
a challenge to their exclusive right to collect tribute from the masses.
The state sent in the Army. Social networks were smashed and "street
mosques" outlawed. There were mass arrests (up to twenty or thirty
thousand alleged members were at one point in prison), dismissals of
thousands of teachers, sieges of villages regarded as sympathetic to
the Islamists, and extrajudicial killings.

Yet for a time Gamā'at seemed to get stronger. Late in the 1990s
radicals targeted tourism because it encouraged alcohol consumption,
gambling and prostitution while edifying ancient temples to pre-Islamic
faiths. In 1997 a group identified somewhat hazily as Gamā'at supporters killed several tourists at the National Museum in Cairo; a few months
later, another group perpetrated a massacre at Luxor, site of the most famous of Egypt's ancient tombs and temples and the most important lure
(except perhaps for the pyramids) for the tourism industry. Of the sixty-
nine dead, fifty-eight were tourists. Hence revenues plunged. There was
never proof Gamā'at was really behind the deeds. Some believed that
the perpetrators had been manipulated by the security services to give
the state a pretext to finish off the group; while the Gamā'at underground leadership insisted that the attacks were the work of Mossad, trying to divert tourist revenues to Israel.[35] Whatever the truth, far from
the 1997 deeds being a sign of a resurgence of Gamā'at, in some ways
they were its epitaph. By then its leadership was largely dead, imprisoned, or hiding out abroad, its networks broken, its remaining grouplets
heavily infiltrated. And Luxor caused the collapse of public support,
leading the remaining leadership to announce from exile a unilateral
truce. Later that year, when seven German tourists were murdered, it
was the work of a deranged former nightclub singer with no connection
to Islamic militants.[36]

Al Jihad had a similar fate. Facing a regime crackdown at home, it had
shifted more attention abroad, particularly to the Balkans, claiming to

defend Bosnian and Kosovar Muslims against Christian Serbs. That shift accelerated after 1993 when, in an attempt on the life of the Egyptian prime minister, it killed a schoolgirl in a bomb attack. The backlash led to a collapse of public support and caused it to split into warring factions. The most militant, Talaeh al-Fatah (Vanguards of the Conquest) was led by a Cairene doctor, Ayman al-Zawahiri, who fled to Afghanistan and was later promoted by the US government to the rank of second-in-command of al-Qā'idah. At Egyptian and US request, Talaeh al-Fatah members arrested in the Balkans were extradited back to Egypt to face the tender ministrations of the secret police, then in 1999 a public trial, which provided essential elements for the creation of the al-Qā'idah legend and perhaps inspired the US to stage its own show trial a couple years later.

The story that emerged from the Cairo trial was that behind the Egyptian atrocities, including the Luxor massacre, stood none other than Usama bin Lāden. (The fact that the confessions were extracted under torture apparently did not affect their credibility.[37]) Out of the trial, too, came the first stories that Usama had tried to buy in Europe chemical and biological weapons. Most importantly it was the first attempt to present al-Qā'idah as a union of talents. Reputedly the paths of Usama bin Lāden and Ayman al-Zawahiri first crossed in the 1980s in Afghanistan where bin Lāden was dishing out dollars and al-Zawahiri was rallying the troops. After the struggle they returned to their respective homes, only to be both chased into exile again. Since the Egyptian security forces had been so effective in closing off Al Jihad's funding, its leadership turned to bin Lāden for help. The result was a step-by-step merger, Al Jihad providing the personnel and bin Lāden the money. Thus was al-Qā'idah born, as a coalition of the willing and the billing. And the birth was celebrated by the announcement of a united front against Crusaders and Zionists, to which a couple of other marginal groups, previously unworthy of serious media attention adhered.[38] (Gamā'at al-Islamiyya was also cited as a charter member, even though its baffled leadership denied any such thing.) Subsequently great quantities of ink would be spilled speculating on whether Ayman al-Zawahiri was vice-president of the new Terror International or whether he was really the CEO with bin Lāden just talking in public and signing checks in private.

One way or the other, the USA had to mobilize to counter the looming threat. It had not only the military might but, thanks to earlier experiences in dealing with something very similar at home, also some legal tools with which to fight.

3

Conspiracies of Evil – Crime, Law, and the Politics of Fear

In a 20 September 2001 address to Congress and to the US people, President George W. Bush declared that "al-Qaeda" was to terrorism what the Mafia was to crime.[1] Thus he captured in a pithy phrase a common belief – that crime and terrorism were both the work of fabulously wealthy, hierarchically structured, transnational entities whose commitment to tear asunder the moral and economic fabric of US society could be countered only by emergency military or legal measures, both of which he took.

This view, heartily endorsed both by media pundits and by the growing army of post-9/11 "national security experts," did not emerge suddenly from the fevered mind of some Republican Party spinmeister. It had been gaining converts for decades before it crystallized in the legislative and military aftermath of 9/11.[2] The anti-Mafia hysteria that had gripped the United States during the late nineteenth and much of the twentieth centuries provided the images, the vocabulary, and even some of the important legal weaponry deployed in the anti-Islamic Terror campaign of the late twentieth and early twenty-first.

The Crime War also set the precedent followed assiduously in the future Terror War of viewing the danger through racially (and/or religiously) tinted lenses. It started the process, even more evident in the later Terror War, of reading evidence and testimony, both in public enquiries and in trials, not for what it actually said but for how it confirmed existing stereotypes. It permitted US politicians and senior bureaucrats long before 9/11 to use an external threat to advance an internal agenda, including their own careers; while the media learned early the vital commercial lesson that, in bringing such a danger to public attention, nothing succeeds like excess.

MOB RULE?

More than a century before today's Green Scare, when even the Red Scare was in its infancy, the United States was alert to a different color-coded threat: the Black Hand. In the US slums teeming with poor European immigrants, including many from southern Italy and Sicily, a number of independent groups worked a racket in which victims (overwhelmingly Italian) received letters demanding payment with, emblazoned upon them, a black hand or something similar.[3] This would have remained a series of isolated incidents, imputable largely to lack of proper police protection for recent immigrants, had not the press romanticized the notion of a single guiding hand, so to speak. As so often in the future with crime (and terrorism), once publicity confirmed the effectiveness of a brand name (al-Qā'idah became a classic example), its use grew – any threat or action carried out under the logo invoked more mystery and spread more fear, increasing profits and aiding recruitment, while the side publicly committed to countering the threat waxed equally fat on the results.

This first manifestation of the emerging "Mafia" menace was consolidated further in the public mind during the late nineteenth and early twentieth centuries when white small-town USA turned against inner cities reputedly populated with dusky, shifty foreigners. Their vices (mainly booze, but also sex, drugs, and rock 'n' roll, or rather its precursors like ragtime and jazz) were depicted by political hopefuls and fundamentalist preachers alike as grave threats to middle-American values. Italian "organized crime" groups were fingered as the main culprits.[4]

In fact, in a remarkable anticipation of the misconceptions that would surround al-Qā'idah, the Mafia, considered as an organization rather than as a mode of behavior, did not exist even in Sicily, its supposed birthplace. Surviving a succession of foreign conquerors and domestic exploiters, living in a stratified, largely rural society in which individual success depended on a powerful patron, Sicilians had no respect for formal law and held in contempt those who collaborated with the authorities. The population relied on extended family for social support and used informal mechanisms for protection and dispute

resolution. Into the breach stepped the Mafioso, not a criminal entre-
preneur so much as a mediator of violence in a society in which justice
usually meant vendetta.[5]

Nor, contrary to another widely held belief, were various "families"
ruled by some sort of governing council. Instead bosses would occasionally meet to iron out disputes over money and territory. There were
no regulations except the periodic pronouncements of the nominal
head of the family; there was no formal division of duties, although everyone knew, based on tradition, more or less what was expected. The
family was a political and military grouping in no way synonymous and
only peripherally coterminous with a business association. The individual Mafioso might go into business – legal or illegal – but there was no
requirement, apart from convenience and trust, to do so with other
members of the family. The family was important mainly when a member needed help in a conflict with an outsider, whether over money or
honor. In short, what prevailed was no different from the informal support relations found almost everywhere in the world prior to the rise of
the modern state, sometimes even after.[6] Yet once the concept was
transplanted to the US, police, prosecutors, and politicians deduced
from networks of client-patron relations based on custom and trust hierarchically ruled crime cartels run by authoritarian Godfathers who
amassed the profits and redistributed some of the proceeds down-
wards.[7] In decades to come they would do much the same in their attempts to comprehend the new menace of Islamic Terror.

Undoubtedly "Mafia members" arrived in the United States during
the late-nineteenth-century ingathering of the tired, the poor, the
wretched, and the homeless who were generally destined to so remain
for at least a generation or two. Once in the US, they formed not one
but many groups, loose and opportunistic, that, as in the Black Hand
era, targeted mainly their own people and that were often at war. They
did not tend to be well represented in criminal opportunities outside
their neighborhoods.

Then came Prohibition, during which the US public was both saturated with bad booze and infused with the notion that it was the collective victim of Italian-led crime syndicates. Harry Anslinger, a senior
functionary in the Prohibition bureau and later head of the Federal
Bureau of Narcotics, still insisted decades later that the presumed epidemic of booze, and of drugs, was the work of "the Grand Council of
the Mafia, with its plan for an international cartel that controlled every
phase of criminal activity"[8] – in much the way that responsibility for

every major act of international terror would later be imputed to Usama's equally ephemeral and adaptable al-Qā'idah. J. Edgar Hoover, long-time boss of the FBI, pioneered the military metaphor that would become so popular in speaking of both the crime and the terror threats in the future, as well as setting a precedent for those who would hype the size of the Islamic hordes when he warned the Senate's Government Operations Committee that the "armed forces of crime" numbered three million.[9] In this, and in many future instances, the authorities also learned that the ordinary citizen better understood a menace if it was personalized. Al Capone, for example, became to booze-related crime something like what bin Lāden was later to religiously inspired terror – in the future "national security experts" would even cite their names in the same breath and laud the legal tools used to tame the first as a means to curb the activities of the second.

The reality was rather different. Gangsters, the most important of which were as likely Eastern European Jews or Irish as southern Italians, accounted for only a small part of the country's booze supply. Most was homemade for personal use or smuggled by individuals across the Mexican or Canadian borders – Henry Ford (initially an ardent Prohibitionist) was much more important than Al Capone in keeping the nation happily besotted. The only significant gang presence was in a few big cities where the consuming elite wanted high-quality imported merchandise.[10] Even the Capone Gang, the quintessential "Mafia" group, was just a set of informal partnerships with shifting personnel. Nonetheless the uproar over the threat it posed permitted the federal government to send in Treasury agents to "clean up" Chicago.

Although the campaign did nothing to dent the booze supply, it was a brilliant success. In 1931 Al Capone was jailed ... for income-tax evasion. The result was to send to the general public, which until then had refused to take the unpopular income tax very seriously, the message that the Internal Revenue Service was on the job.[11] This was not the first time, nor would it be the last, that a federal anti-crime (or, in the future, anti-terror) initiative would have a hidden agenda more important than the nominal one. It was, however, the first time the crime-busters had focused on the money trail to track and crack a big-time gangster, blazing a path followed in the future when anti-money-laundering initiatives became the presumed panacea for curbing first organized crime, then organized terror.

Although Prohibition was repealed two years later, it left as its legacy a federal anti-crime and domestic intelligence-gathering bureaucracy that would, after World War II, in conjunction with ambitious politicians and sensation-seeking journalists, seek fresh justification for its existence. Together they soon found and exploited a dynamite combination of threats – Red Scare and Cold War; Mafia Scare and Crime War – that, in turn, would set the stage for the Green Scare and Terror War to come.

THE CRIME BUSTERS

One of the most important tools in spreading both general fear and an officially approved version of the nature of the threat has long been the public (and highly publicized) enquiry. While there were antecedents, modern use of the technique in the US probably began in 1950, when Democratic presidential hopeful Estes Kefauver, chair of the Senate Judiciary Committee, launched a travelling investigation of organized crime's control of illegal gambling. It was an enormous hit. One commentator compared the public reaction to its "revelations" to the outrage after Pearl Harbor. The creators of both *Superman* comics and *The Lone Ranger* radio series lauded the hearings.[12]

In this, as in future public enquiries, investigators relied for most of their information on war stories from cops, prosecutors, and law-enforcement bureaucrats. The problem was not just their propensity, even more egregious during the Terror War, to invent or exaggerate threats to secure larger budgets and more arbitrary powers, or the tendency of bureaucracies, having created or magnified a threat to justify their initial formation, to keep it or something similar alive to ensure survival in a jungle of competing demands for resources.[13] Also at work was the structure of news reporting. Reporters, who rarely have the means to make informed and independent judgments, are under pressure to produce stories to sell papers or to attract listeners or viewers to ensure more advertising revenues. Thus an apparent crime (or terror) conspiracy may say less about the organization and profit objectives of the perpetrators than about the organization and profit objectives of the media outlet in which the plot is revealed. Many reporters (and their editors), whether working in print, broadcast, or, now, electronic forms, also share the US proclivity to see the world in terms of Good and Evil. Convinced that the USA represents the first, they search for alien conspiracies (responsible for crime, Communism, or terrorism, or maybe several at once) to explain domestic problems.

To be fair, such hearings did on occasion try to tap genuine members of the crime scene. The problem, a recurring one, was that the results often contradicted the presuppositions. Even if witnesses denied any association with or even knowledge of an organized-crime conspiracy, once they admitted knowing people whom the press, fed by the police, had already labelled as Mafia, no matter how they qualified or hedged, that sufficed to prove the existence of a formal organization. Any minor social interaction or communication, let alone a joint financial transaction, however innocuous, constituted further proof.[14] This practice of imposing on testimony an interpretation that suited both prejudices and political agendas featured prominently in both the Drug War and Terror War to follow.

There were many successors to the Kefauver hearings, and an impressive array of political hopefuls to manipulate them to their advantage. But probably no individual had as much long-term impact on the atmosphere in which official crime (and subsequent terror) enquiries would be held, or on the legislative results, as Robert F. Kennedy. While serving as chief counsel of the Senate Judiciary Committee's Permanent Subcommittee on Investigations, Kennedy christened the Mafia Menace a "conspiracy of evil," ringing a bell that resonated up to George Bush II's discovery of an "axis of evil" half a century later. There was, Kennedy said, "a private government of organized crime, a government with an annual income in the billions – run by a commission [that] makes major policy decisions for the organization, settles disputes among the families and allocates territories of criminal operation within the organizations."[15] In the past, the job of policing rackets had been left to the individual states. But to Kennedy, with crime spreading like a plague, structured in a way that would do a Fortune 500 CEO proud, and earning money by the bucket, "Only through a nationwide network can we fight the widespread penetration of criminals in our economy."[16]

As Attorney General, Robert Kennedy got the chance to put his theories to use.[17] He reorganized the federal bureaucracy to make crime control a primary responsibility, giving it tools that would facilitate the transition to terror control a few decades later. He pushed new laws to prohibit things like interstate travel or interstate postal and telephone communication if they aided "racketeering." What made these new laws unusual for the time, but prophetic for the future, was that the acts proscribed were in and of themselves perfectly innocent – dropping a

letter in a mailbox, for example.[18] Criminalizing technical side-issues
gave prosecutors easy-to-prove charges with which to force plea bargains or confessions and paved the way for anti-money-laundering laws
in which minor administrative transgressions like not filling out a form
correctly would be elevated to the status of high crimes. It was no accident that Bush's first Attorney General, John Ashcroft, bragged of mod-
elling his anti-terror tactics on Kennedy's Justice Department, which
would, Ashcroft said approvingly, "arrest a mobster for spitting on the
sidewalk if it would help in the fight against organized crime."[19]

Robert Kennedy planned to cap these innovations with a new omni-
bus anti-crime bill; but the dual tragedies of the Kennedy brothers
aborted the project. A few years later such a law did pass, thanks in
good measure to someone who graduated from privately bashing in
skulls with baseball bats to publicly revealing the inner workings of the
Mafia mind.

THE INSIDER

In 1970, US Congress passed two landmark statutes. One was the Bank
Secrecy Act, a curious name for a law designed to increase federal scrutiny of private financial transactions. It was the opening round of the
fight to attach to money-laundering a degree of opprobrium just short
of that of original sin. The USA's numismatic jihād, first against crime,
later against terrorism, had taken its first tentative step, one that would
culminate in George Bush's Patriot Act three decades later.

The second step was the Racketeer Influenced and Corrupt Organizations (RICO) statute, passed as part of the Organized Crime Control
Act.[20] RICO proposed to reverse the supposed process by which organized-crime figures were, first, taking over legitimate businesses, then
applying criminal methods to extort profit. Its most important innova-
tion was the concept of a criminal "enterprise," which embraced almost
anything that made money, or even some crimes that did not. RICO
took a group of malefactors who might be "associated" in some way,
and converted it into an economic organization, with the important
proviso that the "enterprise" was made up of groups, partnerships, and
even individuals associated de facto rather than de jure. It allowed the
prosecution to take two or more isolated offenses, drawn from a list of
existing crimes, then combine them in a broad conspiracy case so that
the targets could be charged, not only with the underlying crimes, but
with racketeering on top. Subsequently courts would rule that persons

could be guilty of a "pattern of racketeering" without being aware that they were part of such an enterprise, provided they were aware of their commission of the predicate offenses. Others could be guilty even if they did not participate directly in the predicate offenses but provided support, be it financial or logistical or even political. This was an omen for the future when individuals would be charged with membership in a terrorist organization of whose existence they might be unaware.

The penalties included prison sentences of up to twenty years and a fine. But the real financial kicker was the requirement that the "racketeer" forfeit all assets obtained through "racketeering activity." The act also muddied the traditional separation of civil and criminal procedures by allowing civil suits, by the government or by private parties, to strip supposed racketeers of the businesses they controlled and to impose on them treble damages. It was no accident that civil RICO suits, both with and without government backing, would become a popular incentive for "private citizens" (and hungry lawyers) to enlist in the Terror War to come.

RICO was strong stuff. As its advocates freely admitted, it would have been much more difficult (perhaps impossible) to win acceptance but for sensational revelations by Joseph Valachi, a "Genovese Family soldier" heralded as the first "made-member" of the Mafia to turn informant. Valachi's testimony in various trials and before Congress, along with his published memoirs, is credited with putting an end to residual skepticism about the existence of a formal, hierarchical Mafia with mysterious induction rituals, blood oaths, and a rigid code of enforcement.[21] After Valachi, lawmakers could take the view that organized crime was an entity apart from the criminal activities of its members, and legislate accordingly; much the same model would be applied against organized terror in decades to come. Yet police officers who knew Valachi as a street punk scoffed at his claims; he was too young to have witnessed many of the events he recounted; and, since he had spent so long in jail before turning informant, much of his testimony was hearsay. Furthermore, when subjected to a detached reading away from the glare of the cameras, Valachi's testimony (like that of major witnesses in terror trials to come) presented a totally different picture to that widely claimed.[22] For example, Valachi actually refuted the notion that members of the organized crime "family" were simply employees or subordinates of some Godfather who actually ran the rackets and collected the profits. Instead they were autonomous economic actors.

VALACHI: You don't get any salary, Senator.
SENATOR: Well, you get a cut then.
VALACHI: You get nothing, only what you earn for yourself.[23]

Even the family governance role was distinctly limited – members did favors of a military nature for the boss; and he provided them with protection for their rackets.[24] Nor was this super organization particularly good in looking after its own members.

SENATOR: How did you seek the help of your family when you were picked up?
VALACHI: I used to get my own help. What family do you mean?
SENATOR: The family to which you belonged, the Genovese family.
VALACHI: I never bothered them. If I got picked up, I got myself out. I got my own lawyers.
SENATOR: Did they give you any protection in the 35 years [you were a "member"]?
VALACHI: No.[25]

Yet this kind of testimony rationalized the RICO Statute; and the concept of a centralized criminal conspiracy dominating the market for illegal goods and services would in the years to come provide to law enforcement both an analogy to understand and, indirectly, a legal tool to try to cope with organized terror.

There were three unintended but nasty consequences of the new law. First, by invoking the spectre of great conspiracies, the act, or rather the publicity around it, conferred on police forces an increase in informal powers that may have surpassed the law's effects in bolstering formal ones. Faced with a threat that ate away at society's soul, many things seemed justified – force, blackmail, planting (or suppressing) evidence, buying testimony, perjury, and cover-ups – on the grounds that the collateral loss of a few innocents was inevitable in any such "war." In much the same way the menace of organized terror would later produce at best indifference towards, at worst positive enthusiasm for, all of the above along with arbitrary detention, racial profiling, and even torture.

Second, since RICO required establishing the existence of a criminal "enterprise," it encouraged a transformation of the relations between federal law-enforcement agencies and their nominal targets. In simple crimes like theft, extortion, etc. there is usually a victim to register a complaint, assist the investigation, and (if not intimidated) appear as a witness for the prosecution. But when supposed organized-crime-types supplied illegal goods and services to complicit citizens, there was rarely a victim. Proving the existence of the "enterprise" therefore required informants who were paid in cash, reduced sentences, or a license to continue their own rackets. The tales of paid underworld informants are likely second in unreliability only to stories extracted under torture. While in the past police sometimes operated on the basis of such information, they generally preferred not risk having it tested under cross-examination. But with RICO there was increased reliance on such testimony to establish the core element necessary for prosecution.[26] The police effectively went into partnership with selected underworld figures. Similarly in future Terror Wars, spooks made alliances with criminal, insurgent, and "terrorist" groups, provided they directed their activities against and/or traded information about mutually agreed enemies.

Third, the loose nature of the statute facilitated its use in novel ways. It would be deployed for everything from prosecuting insider trading to crippling anti-abortion protests. In that, too, it was a direct spiritual precursor of the Patriot Act, which, while passed nominally to quell Islamic Terror, was subsequently directed against everyone from bank-fraud artists to marijuana smugglers.

Furthermore, over time the RICO statute assumed a more explicitly political role. In 1986 the Philippines government laid a civil RICO complaint charging that the late Ferdinand Marcos, during his tenure as president, ran not a government but a "network ... set up in the fashion of an organized crime syndicate"; it listed Marcos cronies as "lieutenants" who created an "association-in-fact."[27] Although the Marcos case was a civil suit launched by the Philippines government, it was a milestone. A few years later came another RICO case to target a head of state with the US government as plaintiff and the charges criminal, a case whose success would whet the appetites of prosecutors to later turn the RICO weapon against bin Lāden.[28]

THEIR MAN IN PANAMA

In 1903 the US had sponsored a revolution in Colombia's northernmost province, the planned site for a trans-isthmian canal. Over the next few decades, Panama spawned the world's largest flag-of-convenience shipping centre, one of its biggest Free Trade Zones and the most important offshore financial system in the Americas. It also hosted SOUTHCOM, the US military mission charged with keeping an eye on US interests in Latin

America, and the School of the Americas, where the hemisphere's military forces learned how to stamp out un-American activities among their own citizens.[29] Inside Panama that job was left to the National Guard, which, for most of the 1980s, was headed by a long-time CIA asset named Manuel Noriega – until 1990 when he was kidnapped to stand trial in Miami.

Noriega was certainly not innocent, except probably of the charges on which he was found guilty.[30] In his Panama, the press was muzzled, political opponents brutalized and sometimes murdered, and corruption widespread. Nonetheless unlike most of Central America at the time, in Panama there was at least a modicum of social and economic security; and political repression targeted individuals rather than entire communities. Furthermore, contrary to its reputation as a hemispheric hotbed of crime, Panama under Noriega was arguably more cooperative with US law enforcement than it had been under his predecessors. But in 1986 his enemies planted on the front page of the *New York Times* a story alleging his central role in drugs, arms, and dirty money.[31] That was the opening round in a campaign that would culminate not just in a brutal invasion but in a show trial that might have made Joseph Stalin wince.

First, Senator John Kerry, who, in his first major step to hitch his future presidential ambitions to the anti-crime (and, later, anti-terror) bandwagon, held public hearings into the general's misdeeds. The star witnesses were the usual entourage of convicted drug traffickers willing to trade reduced prison time or improved conditions for newsworthy claims about laundering billions in narco-dollars through Panama while paying multi-millions in bribes to General Noriega.[32]

While these stories were circulating (widely, of course), the US government wielded its public stick in the form of a threat of criminal prosecution accompanied by a private carrot of $2 million if Noriega would just disappear. He refused. So the US imposed economic sanctions, much as it later would on Afghanistan to try to make it turn over bin Lāden.[33] When the Panama regime managed to ride out the worst, and when Noriega proved to be better at rigging elections than was Washington, the US decided to invade.[34] It deployed its state-of-the-art equipment and elite troops against a place with a few World War II vintage anti-aircraft guns and several thousand lightly armed militiamen. It was the largest US military deployment in decades – until that record was taken by the invasion of Afghanistan in pursuit of bin Lāden a bit more than a decade later.[35]

Although the plan was probably for Noriega to be killed in the carnage, he managed to survive by taking temporary refuge in the Vatican
Embassy – which then turned him over to the invaders. Attention then
shifted to the legal front. Alas, a search for the smoking gun in the smoking ruins proved less than successful. The Army initially claimed to have
found in Noriega's headquarters fifty pounds of cocaine. However not
even US slum-dwellers were likely to blow their minds on tamale flour.
Nor did any of the huge pile of seized documents revealed anything of
use. Hence the case had to be built exclusively on witnesses. With orders
from the White House to convict at all costs, US Justice Department left
no stone unturned and no turncoat unrewarded.[36]

First the US froze the assets Noriega could have used to hire top defense attorneys (later partially mitigated on court order). Then it got
down to serious business. Most witnesses against Noriega were drug
dealers offered get-out-of-jail-free cards, permission to keep their drug
profits, extra cash, or residency permits. Yet despite being given scripts,
they often contradicted each other; few had actually met Noriega, so
their evidence was largely hearsay; others had personal grudges, usually
because he had been instrumental in their arrests; and some afterwards
threatened to recant if the US failed to live up to its part of the bargains
that had bought their testimony.[37] Their testimony was supplemented
by that of Noriega's political or military rivals, with their own agendas
and grudges, and by that of US officials attempting to protect their own
reputations and positions.[38]

Even had the government not so blatantly stacked the case, nothing
remotely resembling justice could have been done. As with so many
terror trials in the future in which politics similarly took precedence
over any search for truth, the media had already tried, convicted, and
hung the accused, in this case Manuel Noriega, in effigy, saturating
the public (including potential jurors) with tales of his wrongdoings,
his uncertain sexual orientation, and his idiosyncratic religious beliefs. Even so, it became clear that most of the stories about Noriega as
a kingpin of crime were grossly inflated – at worst he was just one more
corrupt cop – and the tales of his hordes of ill-gotten loot were similarly bogus. But he was still sentenced to life imprisonment, most of it
spent in solitary confinement.[39]

Not that truth (nor the fate of the hundreds, perhaps thousands of
civilian victims of the invasion) mattered when it came to important
matters of state. What did count was that in the future it might be possible to again use the courts to attack an important political target, even

if that target was allegedly a wealthy mastermind of terror rather than a greedy kingpin of crime and even if both images were, if not completely false, at least highly embellished versions of the truth.

In the case of bin Lāden, another problem the prosecutors faced was actually retrieving a live body to parade before the courts. The wealthy quartermaster of terror had a habit of hanging out in places a lot less accessible or vulnerable to a quick "police action" than a kingpin of crime.

4

Usama of Khartoum – "Anti-Christian Jihad," Nerve-Gas Plots, and the Transnational of Terror

When Usama bin Lāden fled Saudi Arabia for refuge in the Sudan, at first glance he had chosen an ideal incubator in which the recently born al-Qā'idah could grow into a global menace. The country, it seemed, was a hotbed of Islamic fundamentalism and hence receptive to bin Lāden's message. It provided a setting from which bin Lāden could develop the worldwide business connections through which to subsequently direct his covert flow of terror dollars. Because it was engaged in a holy war against its own Christian minority, it provided a testing ground for the larger jihād Usama had in mind. Indeed these three attributes seemed complementary – the anti-Christian pogroms launched by the Muslim-Arab government of Khartoum provided bin Lāden with the chance to train his legions, deepen his black-market arms contacts, and diversify his sources of funding from the legal to the illegal – it was by running rackets in the Sudan that bin Lāden first began to complement his role as the era's most dangerous terrorist with an equally inglorious career as an international baron of organized crime.

Of course, once again, there is another version of the story, one suggesting that for bin Lāden the Sudan was neither a natural nor, as matters turned out, a very hospitable haven. True, the country had once hosted the Muslim world's first successful religiously inspired revolt against European colonialism. And us neocons never tired of denouncing it as an incubator of Muslim radicalism.[1] However its political elites had more than enough problems at home to be much inspired by calls for a general rising against a Crusader-Zionist alliance.[2] While there was plenty for a civil engineer to do in Africa's largest country, which decades of civil war, drought, and famine had made into perhaps its biggest basket case, the place was vulnerable to Saudi economic blackmail; the intelligence services of Egypt and the US kept it under close surveillance; and, far from being a font of terror-treasure, the country's legal economy, in whose development bin Lāden invested heavily, was a sinkhole for his already depleted financial resources.

BACK TO FUNDAMENTALS?

The Sudan's theological traditions weren't exactly the sort with which a supposed "Wahhābī fundamentalist" would feel particularly comfortable. Since the sixteenth century, religious debate in the Sudan has turned not on mainstream ulemā wrangling over the meaning of Qur'ānic texts but on the teachings of various Sufi orders. In fact the country had no official ulemā or sharī'a law until the Turko-Egyptian conquest in the 1820s, which, in turn, gave way to de facto British rule a few decades later. Opposition to imported religious orthodoxy played as much a role as resentment over foreign rule to spark rebellion. In 1885 Mohammed Ahmed ibn Sayed Abdullah, a Sufi leader who modestly designated himself "al-madhī" (the rightly guided one – a quasi-messianic concept that mainstream Sunnīs regard with suspicion), subjected the British to a humiliating defeat. Although the British returned to slaughter the "fuzzy-wuzzies" with machine guns several years later, they wisely decided to leave the Sudan to its own theological devices, but to turn them to political and economic advantage.

The mahdī himself died before the second British invasion – which killed his son and heir. But when the British resolved to turn the Sudan into one huge cotton plantation, the grandson and his family, among the country's biggest landowners, were their chosen instrument. The grandson also established a political arm, the Umma Party, to collaborate with the British in administering the country. As hereditary leader of the Sufi sect, he sent his acolytes out to preach the faith and inform on their rivals to the colonial intelligence service.[3] However the main barrier to his ambitions was the Marghani family. Leading the second most popular Sufi order, it had opposed the Mahdiist uprising and demanded its own reward. So the British conceded to that family control of urban commerce and encouraged them to create the rival Democratic Union Party. Upon independence in 1956, the Sudan was essentially bequeathed to the care of two dominant but antagonistic family dynasties, rooted respectively in commercial agriculture and urban trade and preaching rival religious doctrines, while the country was administered by a British-trained civil service and Army.

This neat family compact faced a triple challenge. Shortly after independence, a secessionist movement sprang up, led by Christians among mostly animist peoples of the South. In the Northern urban centres, the Communist Party became influential in trade unions and professional groups. And by the 1970s the Muslim Brotherhood began to flex its muscles.[4]

The Brotherhood had a tough sell. Since the Sudan was a country of multiple religions and even Islam, by far the largest, took heterodox forms, the Brotherhood had to water down its message. Furthermore its parentage caused it to be viewed, correctly or not, as an agent of Egyptian influence, prompting it to reorganize under the name National Islamic Front (NIF). Even with that, its urbane, multilingual, foreign-educated leader, Hassan al-Turabi, was widely distrusted.

Four developments combined to allow the NIF to eventually dominate the government. First, the old-line parties, unable to deliver peace or prosperity, were ousted in 1969 by Ja'far Nimeiri, the Army chief of staff. Second, after an abortive coup in the early 1970s, the military government set out, with a nod from Washington, to crush the Communist Party, creating more political space for the NIF. Third, the NIF infiltrated the educational system, giving its views a much greater audience than just numbers of adherents would have warranted. Fourth, it received ample outside financial assistance.

Throughout the 1970s the oil boom attracted a million Sudanese workers to the Gulf states. Already there in exile from Egypt were Muslim Brotherhood cadres. Since the region's financial infrastructure was primitive, the Brothers guided pious members of the Gulf elite into setting up Islamic banking institutions both at home and abroad, including in the Sudan. Although most remittances from the émigré workforce went home via parallel and underground channels, increasingly the Gulf States cooperated in channelling them through the new Islamic banks. That gave Sudanese branches of those banks access to seemingly endless amounts of money compared to more conventional, local competitors. Inside the Sudan their position was consolidated further by a religious exemption from taxes. And they focused lending on small-scale industries and urban commerce, exactly the sectors where the Muslim Brotherhood was recruiting, creating a new commercial class directly competitive with those associated with the old Democratic Union Party. Soon the banks demanded as a condition for loans that applicants provide a letter of reference from a NIF member.[5] The result was that NIF influence rose sharply, something President Nimeiri acknowledged in 1983 when he brought back sharī'a law, not seen in the country since the days of Turko-Egyptian rule. Apart from giving Nimeiri harsh, supposedly Qur'ānic punishments to keep troublemakers in line, one effect of the new laws was to ban outright non-Islamic forms of banking and therefore further entrench NIF-influenced institutions. However, the imposition of sharī'a law was also one of the sparks that reignited rebellion in the South.

THE GREAT DIVIDE

The view, promoted in the US by the Christian Right and the pro-Israel lobby, was/is that conflict in the Sudan derives from race and religion: an aggressive Muslim-Arab North against a victimized Christian-African South. Such a caricature won sympathy for the guerrillas and had the further advantage of suggesting that Arabic-speaking and/or Muslim Sudanese were invaders into black Africa much the way Palestinians supposedly were into Biblical Israel.

In reality the geopolitical split was the work mainly of the British, who not only neglected the South but, to block South-North interaction, established an Apartheid system with special pass laws, much like those they had introduced into South Africa. Furthermore the geographic division in no way corresponded to a simple ethnoreligious one. The Sudan has about three hundred ethnic groups who speak eighty languages. The approximately 50 percent who claim to be "Arab" are actually a hodge-podge of Arab, Nuba, and sub-Saharan African. Another 30 percent are Northern (and western) Sudanese who do not regard themselves as culturally Arab even though they are overwhelmingly Muslim. But even here there is a fair amount of cross-identification. In the Darfur region, for example, scene of the most recent outbreak of "Arab versus African" civil war, everyone is Muslim; and once "African" farmers have accumulated enough cattle to emulate their pastoralist neighbors, they begin to identify themselves as "Arab."

Nor was/is the stereotype of a Christian South accurate. During the colonial era, Christian missionaries, French and English, tried to create a Bible Belt to separate the main population centres of sub-Saharan Africa from the more restive Muslim Northern parts, so that places like Ghana, Cameroon, Nigeria, and Chad now have a religious division somewhat corresponding to the geographic one. However, in the Sudan, Christianization in the non-Muslim South was much less pervasive – Christians today may account for only 5 percent of the country's total population. While access to money from US Christian "fundamentalists" (really a hodge-podge of Biblical literalists, Pentacostals speaking in tongues, and assorted right-wing religious cults) and to guns from Ethiopia and Israel ensured that rebel leadership in the South would be mainly Christian, the great majority involved were/are followers of animist religions. Even then not all Southern ethnic groups backed the secessionist movement – some regarded it as a tool by which the largest local ethnic group, the Dinka, could dominate their "African" neighbors.

Far from being a rebellion against Muslim oppression, the struggle actually began in 1955, a full year before independence, when the country was still a British protectorate, with a pogrom against Northerners.[6] There was a temporary reprieve in 1972, when a peace accord nominally gave the South more autonomy. But the South complained that Northerners continued to dominate decision-making, while Khartoum continued to deny the South its share of development funds. Meanwhile the economic importance of the South increased. First came the discovery of oil. Then came plans to drain the vast marshlands fed by the lower reaches of the Nile from which huge amounts of potential irrigation water evaporated.

Although much of the Sudan is desert, it contains great tracts of potentially fertile land. Traditional farming relied on rainfall to grow food using a well-established pattern of crop rotation along with periodic fallowing. Alongside that, during the British era, there emerged large-scale plantations producing cotton for export, requiring irrigation works and continuous cropping. A few decades after independence, with world cotton markets glutted, came the idea of shifting to mechanized farming of food crops like wheat and sorghum for export to the Gulf. With the backing of big international lenders, Arab states and private Gulf investors, the Sudan was to become the breadbasket of the Arab world. But, as elsewhere in the so-called developing world, the result was to squeeze traditional farmers off their land and reduce them to cheap agricultural labor for absentee landlords. Pastoral lands were dug up, and wood lands razed. Denuded of indigenous vegetation, large tracts were planted to cash crops for a few years, then, once the soil was exhausted, abandoned to desert. Soon masses of environmental refugees who had sold everything – livestock, tools, personal possessions – migrated across the country in search of relief. Thus were planted the seeds for a new civil war.[7]

In 1983, following the mutiny of a Southern garrison ordered to duty in the North, formal rebellion broke out again. Unlike its predecessor, the new movement insisted it was not secessionist but an attempt to win justice for all of the Sudan's rural poor – hence the name Sudan People's Liberation Movement, with its military wing, the Sudan People's Liberation Army. Most of its foot soldiers were young, uneducated, and poor – they were also unpaid, which made looting attractive. In fact many of the operations for which the SPLA was given credit were just cattle raids by tribal malcontents and local bandits against their (also "African" and occasionally "Christian") neighbors. Then the SPLA would arrange to smuggle the loot into Kenya, Ethiopia, or Uganda, the main sources of its weapons. While, to win the hearts and minds of black congressmen, its US supporters broadcast tales that Khartoum had resurrected slavery among "Africans," the SPLA was recruiting forced labor from minority ethnic groups in its zones of control to build infrastructure like roads to improve its links to the outside world, with little or no media comment. In border areas the SPLA also ran a parallel government to collect excise duties on booze, to set prices for basic goods, and to tax gold and cattle smugglers crossing into Kenya or Ethiopia.[8]

The focus of SPLA military action was less Sudan's Army than its economy. The SPLA killed or kidnapped foreign oil workers and sabotaged work on the waterway project. Not one drop of oil was pumped to alleviate the country's acute foreign exchange shortage until as late as 1997; not one drop of water flowed to bolster irrigation and alleviate the ever-worsening famines.[9] Meanwhile, across the South, raids by the SPLA left a trail of mass murder, rape, and pillage in villages inhabited by peoples who failed to cooperate. In future years atrocities would be compounded by splits within the SPLA, which gave rise to an alphabet soup of "liberation" movements with inconsistent and shifting objectives, some of which went no further than the urge to liberate their neighbors' livestock and young women.

The turmoil of civil war came on top of existing social strife. Historically quarrels between pastoralists and farmers over water and land use were brief and fought with spears or muskets; tribal elders could sort out matters (and free any captives) with a few compensation payments; and the two groups ultimately complemented each other by sharing resources and exchanging surpluses. However, with the breaking up of traditional agricultural patterns and the plowing up of pasture lands, nomadic pastoralists intruded more and more on the shrinking resources of farmers, while outside parties – Libya, Kenya, Uganda, Israel, Ethiopia, Eritrea, and Chad at different points and in different combinations – flooded the countryside with modern weapons.

The Northern government, which had an appalling record of its own through both the Army and the local militias it created, made a number of pleas for negotiation, which the SPLA spurned. The declared objective of the SPLA chief, the late John Garang, was to make the South ungovernable and to bring the whole country's economy to its knees prior to marching on Khartoum. In 1985, with the Army in disgrace, Nimeiri was ousted. The successor governments, awkward coalitions of the two old-line parties, quarrelled for a while until finally offering to the South the prospect of federalism. Even sharī'a law was put on the bargaining table. That alienated two groups. One was the middle officer corps, who were convinced that the war could be successfully prosecuted, if only incompetent senior officers were removed. The second was the NIF, which saw in sharī'a law a major step in advancing its agenda. Hence in 1989 the two joined to stage a coup. General Omar Hassan Ahmed al-Bashir took formal control; while Hassan al-Turabi became the éminence grise, his influence extending into the cabinet by NIF control of key ministries, particularly Justice and Finance.[10] The new government crushed independent unions; purged the civil service of leftists and secularists; and launched a crackdown on the black market (except the parts run by NIF supporters) that threatened the government's tax revenues and foreign exchange reserves.[11]

The results were hardly brilliant. The government was soon blacklisted by the IMF and therefore by all major international lending institutions; its support of Saddam Hussein in 1991 led to the Gulf states cutting off official aid; a program of agrarian self-sufficiency failed for lack of ability to finance essential inputs; and, despite repeated ceasefire offers by the government along with a proposal to permit each province with a non-Muslim majority to use English common law instead of sharī'a, the SPLA escalated the fighting. John Garang, still presented in the world press as leading a black civil-rights and self-determination struggle, declared repeatedly that the objective was not Southern independence or even autonomy but the overthrow of the Khartoum regime. Hence he brushed off an offer by former US President Jimmy Carter to mediate. Indeed, while so much of the world denounced the new government as "Muslim fundamentalist," Garang dismissed Khartoum's offer of a referendum on whether or not sharī'a law ought to be abolished with the words: "It is blasphemous to say that God's laws should be judged by human beings." No doubt that played well to his army of right-wing Christian backers in the USA.

Early in 1991, ironically enough the same year that Usama arrived, the government under its (Muslim Brother) Justice Minister introduced a new legal code that eliminated some of the worst features of sharī'a law and exempted the Southern provinces from its application. That kicked some ideological props out from under the SPLA. Later that year came the overthrow of the Communist government in Ethiopia, until then the SPLM's major supporter. These events produced another SPLA split – into three factions that dissipated resources and energy settling accounts with each other. Soon breakaway groups were negotiating with the government. Furthermore, in an effort to curry favor with the US and the IMF, the Khartoum government declared an austerity program, putting it back on the road to financial orthodoxy. But the US had other plans. In 1993 it moved to destroy the Sudanese government's (always tenuous) legitimacy and wreck its (always precarious) finances by formally adding the Sudan to Washington's list of state sponsors of terrorism.

The US decision was a surprise. The US ambassador on the scene insisted that, while elements in Sudan's government had "links" to Islamic groups elsewhere, there was no evidence to implicate the government itself. Indeed, most of the alleged infusion of Islamic militants into the Sudan had been done directly under the auspices of the NIF prior to the 1989 coup when it was attempting to build up its own militia force to counter that of the other parties. Jimmy Carter, still hoping to broker a North-South settlement, asked an American Assistant Secretary of State for the evidence on which the claim of Sudanese state support for terrorism was based, only to be told that there was no proof, just "strong allegations."[12] The CIA later discovered that its sole informant had been a professional fabricator; and it quietly withdrew the reports, although the media continued to parrot earlier accusations.[13]

However, listing the Sudan as a state sponsor of terrorism was a clever stroke. It gave a green light to Chad, Eritrea, and Uganda, three US client states, to replace Ethiopia as a source of arms and supplies to the SPLA. And it signaled John Garang to hang tough with Khartoum. He celebrated by attacking government-held towns, settling scores with rival groups who showed an inclination to negotiate, and looting international emergency aid. The Catholic bishop of one of the most afflicted areas accused the SPLA of stealing 65 percent of relief rations. Indeed, there were some who suggested unkindly that the US government arranged through NGOs to flood the South with refugee aid precisely so the SPLA could divert most of it to the black market to finance purchases of weapons and fuel. Not least, the US designation blocked the Khartoum government's efforts to enlist out-side financial aid at a time when famine was again ravaging much of the country. That, incidentally, made the Sudan desperate for any alternative sources of development funds, including those which a certain homeless self-appointed Islamic holy warrior might be able to provide.[14]

THE NOMAD

Although Sudanese Sufi orders may have been awaiting a divine visita-tion, no one was likely to mistake Usama bin Lāden for the new madhī. He was welcomed only because of the money he (still) controlled and because of the business and construction savvy he could bring to a country ravaged by war and cut off by economic sanctions. Certainly there was no great meeting of minds between bin Lāden and the NIF. The mainstream Muslim Brotherhood was held in low regard by the new generation of Islamic militants. Ayman al-Zawahiri, boss of Egypt's Al Jihad, who is credited with turning bin Lāden from a glorified social worker into a proponent of guerrilla warfare, harshly criticized the ef-fete politics of the Brotherhood back home. How much more distaste would they have for the watered-down doctrines of the NIF?

On the other side, Hassan al-Turabi denounced the retrograde be-liefs of some of his contemporaries. He welcomed to the Sudan to help train the NIF militia not just Sunnī radicals but representatives of Shi'a militancy like Lebanon's Hizbullāh and Iran's Revolutionary Guards, something that would drive a true Sunnī "fundamentalist" into a rage. Not only did he concede (probably because he had no practical op-tion) religious freedom for the Sudan, including the right of people to assume the highest political office regardless of faith, but he attacked harsher interpretations of sharī'a law and the subjugation of women. Any Muslim, he stated in a claim that would lead to him being denounced as an apostate, had the right to change his mind and his re-ligion at will.[15] Indeed, al-Turabi's evident mistrust of imported ideolo-gies applied personally to bin Lāden, whom al-Turabi initially suspected of being a US agent. Over time al-Turabi modified his views – he came to see bin Lāden as just a political simpleton. ("All Osama could say was jihad, jihad, jihad," al-Turabi mockingly told an enquiring journalist.[16]) Bin Lāden was seen as useful only because of the money the government could milk out of him. But bin Lāden's already overhyped attractiveness in that regard diminished considerably in 1994, when his family denounced him and cut off the $1 million a year he had been receiving from his inheritance.

While in the Sudan, bin Lāden's anti-American, anti-Saudi activities remained largely rhetorical. He busied himself building a major highway, raising the level of a hydroelectric dam, restoring Khartoum airport, and reclaiming land at a time when the country was swept by drought and threatened by desertification. He promoted exports of sorghum and sesame and tried to arrange for the bankrupt regime to import oil on credit. For a time he served to attract other Gulf investors who appreciated both the Islamic orientation of the government and the clean management bin Lāden provided to projects in which he was involved. For a man later accused of financing global terrorism through clandestine financial transactions, he seemed remarkably blasé – during his Sudanese exile, he had bank accounts around the world, including in his own name. In fact, the umbrella company subsequently held responsible for much "al-Qaeda" terrorist activity out of the Sudan had the audacity to proclaim its existence with the official title, "Ladin International Trading Company."[17]

All of this activity was, if not unappreciated, unrequited by a government that could not repay in cash and ultimately would not repay in political capital. Once the NIF-run regime had taken bin Lāden for a financial ride, it was happy to curry favor with Washington in much the way it had with France two years before. During bin Lāden's early days in the Sudan, the country had also hosted "Carlos," the infamous jackal-of-all-terrorist-trades. France, where was Carlos accused of murdering two intelligence agents, badly wanted him back for trial. It got its wish. So, too, did Washington, which had no criminal case against bin Lāden and just wanted him out of sight. And how much further out of sight could anyone be than in Afghanistan? Hence Usama departed for another exile, denouncing al-Turabi as a thief and claiming he had lost $100 million in the Sudan. In a sense Usama ended up right back where he started, and broke. He might well have been a spent force politically. Then Fate, Allāh, or perhaps Monica Lewinsky intervened.

With bin Lāden no longer a cause of friction, the Sudan tried to woo the US. It announced unilateral ceasefires with and amnesties for the rebels; and it reiterated its refusal to allow the country to be used as a base for terrorist acts anywhere in the world. The SPLA response was to intensify its campaign; while the US response, in April 1996, was to pressure the UN Security Council to impose diplomatic sanctions – all other UN members were asked to follow the US lead in closing their embassies. This was supposedly in response to Sudanese complicity in an assassination attempt on Egyptian President Husni Mubarak. In reality that job had been planned for a year by a faction of Egypt's homegrown Gamā'at al-Islamiyah; and its principal triggerman, who did hide out in the Sudan, later went public to denounce the NIF for its "distorted and deviated" form of Islam before fleeing elsewhere.

Along with this diplomatic action came a stepped-up campaign by the Christian Right and its pro-Israel lobby allies to denounce the Sudanese government for resurrecting the "slave trade" in war-ravaged areas. The reality was that the government had little control over anything beyond Khartoum. With the Army tied up defending infrastructure from SPLA attack, it had subcontracted "defense" in much of the country to tribal-based militias. Local warlords were happy to use their new firepower to settle old scores, raiding traditional enemies for cattle and captives as well as stealing relief aid shipments. In fact the practice spread beyond the Sudan into Uganda. For if politics makes for strange bedfellows, the besieged Khartoum regime, to relieve pressure from the SPLA and to punish Uganda for supplying the insurgents, made a choice of conjugal partners that was beyond idiosyncratic and well into the realm of the bizarre.

" ... AND THE LORD TAKETH AWAY "

Much as with the Sudan itself, Uganda's problem was geographic with an ethnic overlay whose origins lay in the way British colonialism had exploited, indeed in some ways created, a North-South divide. The country's agricultural wealth (especially cotton and coffee) was largely in Southern areas inhabited by Bantu groups who also dominated the post-independence civil service. The much less numerous Nilotic peoples in the North drew their livelihood mainly from raising cattle and serving in the Army. However, unlike in the Sudan, most Northerners were Christian: Uganda's Muslim population, about 15 percent of the total, was more to the east, the result of the spread of Islam down the

Swahili coast from Oman rather than up the Nile from Egypt. When Milton Obote led Uganda to independence in 1962, he based his rule on support from the Army, made up heavily of Northern Acholi people. Chased from office in 1971 in an Israeli-organized coup, Obote won back power in 1980 – only to be ousted again in 1986 by Yoweri Musevini's National Resistance Army, whose followers were mainly from the South and west. On Obote's defeat, his Acholi soldiers retreated to their Northern home base. Subsequent attacks (and cattle raids) by the National Resistance Army, along with a government blockade, added economic desperation to political frustration and ethnic animosity.

Out of the disappointed Acholi came militant revivalist groups. The first, the Holy Spirit Mobile Force, was led by a self-appointed prophetess who promised to purge her people of sinners and witches and to lead them back to Kampala in victory. Assured by her that rubbing their bodies with shea butter would make bullets bounce off, the men took up arms and headed south. After they were slaughtered, their spiritual leader fled to Kenya. A short time later, her cousin Joseph Kony reassembled the battered remnants and, after a few false starts, rechristened them the Lord's Resistance Army. In an apparent concession to ecumenicalism, Kony personally welcomed new recruits in ceremonies in which he appeared wearing white (Muslim-style) robes, holding a (Catholic) rosary, speaking in (Pentecostal-type) tongues, and invoking traditional (animist) spirits. Thus were the recruits enjoined to self-sacrifice to achieve the twin objectives of conquering Kampala and turning Uganda into a country ruled according to the (Hebraic) Ten Commandments.[18]

Three things made the LRA unusual. First, while most of its supplies were local, this quasi-Christian cult also drew support from the "Islamic fundamentalist" regime in Khartoum. To repay Uganda for backing the SPLA, Khartoum allowed the LRA to set up camps in the Sudan, while the Sudanese military provided arms. Perhaps to acknowledge this support, Joseph Kony introduced into his liturgy some comic-book pseudo-Islamic doctrines. Apart from his white robes, these included the notions that Friday rather than Sunday was the Holy Day and that people who raised white pigs were to be executed. Islam bans consumption, not production, of pigs; and it hardly differentiates them by color. But Kony may have had his own reasons. One captured guerrilla explained the practice with the singularly unIslamic notion that, "Pigs are ghosts." When the Sudan reached a mutual agreement with Uganda that the two would cease to back respective insurgent forces, the LRA was forced to compensate by more raiding and looting, which it extended to the Acholi villages on the Sudanese side of the border as well.

A second unusual characteristic was that the LRA applied scorched-earth tactics even within its own sphere of influence. Its soldiers engaged in systematic rape, to both intimidate the population and weaken social bonds among extended family, village, and ethnic groups who opposed the messianic movement; they cut off lips and ears to deter informants; they hacked off legs to reduce chances of people fleeing; they destroyed rural infrastructure, stole cattle, and plundered relief stores. By attacking roads and post offices and telegraph lines, they sealed the area off from communication with the rest of the country.

A third feature of the campaign, which brought considerable international notoriety, was the kidnapping of children. This became more common as the LRA had increasing difficulty obtaining voluntary recruits. Most abductees were trained as soldiers (boys) or held as sexual slaves (girls) for LRA officers. Some, though, were sold abroad.[19] At that point evil Usama reputedly entered the picture.

According to the Ugandan intelligence service, in a tale beautifully crafted to appeal to the US public no matter which of the government's foreign policy pretexts (the Drug War or the Terror War) it liked best, bin Lāden did double dirty duty. He ran huge marijuana plantations north of Khartoum (in an area whose vegetation was mainly scrub and cactus), and he operated them with child slaves abducted from Uganda. Thus, once the Lord's Resistance Army kidnapped children, some were allegedly traded on the slave market of the Southern Sudanese city of Juba while others were bartered to bin Lāden at the rate of one assault rifle per child. According to more detailed reports, Joseph Kony himself, when not regaling his followers with his white robes and rosary, worked as superintendent on Usama's marijuana farm. This drug-and-slave trade was, of course, supported eagerly by Khartoum, which was the recipient of Usama's "millions" and in return played host to no less than "17 terrorist training camps" whose ultimate objective was to install Islamic fundamentalist governments across East and Central Africa.[20]

Of course, there were a few oddities in that story. Even assuming the NIF (which flogged and imprisoned drug traffickers) and bin Lāden (who denounced drug-addled Western cultures) managed to grow the stuff in an area badly afflicted by drought, it was not clear how they obtained their slave labor force. The city of Juba, where

"Arab" slave traders were reputed to be so active, had for years been surrounded and regularly shelled by the SPLA. Furthermore the bulk of the captives who could be traced were located not in the Muslim areas of the Sudan but in agricultural plantations in the Ivory Coast and Ghana, where the buyers were generally Christian.

However, agitation over the Sudanese government's complicity in the slave trade, with or without bin Lāden's aid, paid enormous political (and even some financial) dividends. For the US government it provided a moral club with which to beat the Islamists. The USA's Secretary of State, Madeleine Albright, during one of her African whistle stops, insisted that Khartoum and its LRA allies "destroy villages. They abduct and enslave children too young to know what death is."[21] This, interestingly enough, was the same Madeleine Albright who, two years later, when confronted with evidence US bombings and economic sanctions had killed half a million children in Iraq, declared that it was a price worth paying. The Khartoum-supports-slavery campaign had the further advantage of giving John Garang's SPLA another technique to raise money.

The role of US Protestant churches in "redeeming" Christian captives from the Moors dates back at least to 1678, when New York City religious congregations raised money to free eleven Americans held in Algiers. Indeed, they did it with such gusto that there was enough money left over to build a new church. Erected at the corner of Broadway and Wall Street, it aptly captured that unique combination of faith, fantasy, and greed that would underpin so much US foreign policy in the future.[22] Three hundred years later leadership in the "redemption" movement was taken by Christian Solidarity International, a Swiss-based organization that did most of its fundraising in the US. There, everyone from millionaire sports celebrities to elementary schoolchildren was encouraged to donate from their respective lunch monies. In the Sudan the funds were used, through SPLA-approved intermediaries, to ransom captives. However some of those intermediaries apparently arranged for locals to have their own children "kidnapped" – intermediaries, parents, and local SPLA officers split the "ransom," while the media flashed around the world news of another successful "redemption." Even when the ransomings were genuine, the policy was counterproductive. It put a hard currency value on kidnap victims formerly taken mainly for reasons of intertribal feuding, and therefore precluded the traditional dispute-settlement apparatus run by the tribal elders from functioning.[23]

NERVE GAS AND HOT AIR

In 1998, in a desperate effort to break out of its isolation, the Sudanese government introduced legislation to permit multiple parties, then followed with a new constitution embedding secularism: this made all civic offices open without distinction on the basis of religion. That same the year the IMF congratulated the Sudan for its "economic reforms" (bad news for the poor) and removed it from the blacklist. However, the US had a different way of rewarding Khartoum for its good behavior. After the US embassies in Nairobi and Dar es-Salaam were bombed (to which the Sudanese government responded by denouncing the acts and offering its help to catch the culprits), the US launched missile strikes, one against alleged bin Lāden "terrorist training camps" in Afghanistan, another to destroy the Al Shifa pharmaceutical plant in Khartoum.

The US seemed to have ample cause, in fact five different causes: the plant was owned by bin Lāden; it was a high-security facility protected by the Army; it had no civilian function; it was making precursors for nerve gas; and it formed a key WMD link between bin Lāden and Saddam Hussein's Iraq.[24] In fact the owner of the factory, a Saudi, had no personal or financial relationship to bin Lāden. The renowned US investigative agency, Kroll Associates, afterwards confirmed that they had never even met. Western technical advisors who had helped operate the plant reported that they had been free to go anywhere on site; there were no secret areas or military restrictions; and they saw nothing suspicious. Reporters arriving at the ruins of a plant supposedly dedicated to chemical weapons found shattered bottles of Ibuprofen and veterinary medicines scattered about. The chemical, EMPTA, which the US claimed to have found in a soil sample smuggled from the site, turned out not to be on the list of restricted precursors after all; and subsequent analysis suggested that the stuff might not be EMPTA but a standard agricultural fungicide with molecular similarities. As to the Iraq connection, five years short of Gulf War II, no one took that very seriously.[25]

Presumably all this information was readily obtainable before the missile attack. But, of course, with the US embassy already closed, conveniently there was no one on site to inform the US officially that the el-Shifa plant was innocent.

Back home critics of the attack belittled the plant as an "aspirin factory" and bemoaned a US government "mistake" that had killed a nightwatchman. In fact the US had destroyed the only producer of affordable medicines and vaccines for things like tuberculosis and malaria in a country ravaged by drought, civil war, and economic sanctions, as well as the sole manufacturer of veterinary medicines for an area that was heavily pastoral. Since the country was financially crippled and still subject to US sanctions, and since the US followed up by freezing the owner's assets for the next five years, there was little chance to import replacements or to rebuild rapidly.[26] That raises the question of whether it was really a misjudgment. In 1995 the US ambassador (then still resident) had threatened Sudan with "the destruction of your economy" if it allowed anti-American activity. Not only was this well before Usama bin Lāden had become an international media star, but there was no reference to him in the warning.[27]

By the time missiles were raining on the Khartoum pharmaceutical factory, that status had certainly changed. Yet by then Usama was hiding out in another geopolitical backwater equally shattered by social strife, where his ideology was also alien, where the rulers were similarly uncertain about their uninvited guest, and where his presence would soon ensure even more lavish attention from the US military.

5

Pipe Dreams and Political Hallucinations – Usama, the USA, and the Tāliban

When the Sudan decided in May 1996 to unburden itself of bin Lāden after unburdening him of most of his money, there was a real question about where he would go. Saudi Arabia did not want him back unless he agreed to publicly kiss and make up; and the United States regarded him as a loudmouth whom it preferred to have out of sight, sound, and, hopefully, mind, particularly after its Justice Department had determined (before the embassy bombings) that there was still insufficient evidence for a criminal indictment.[1] In the meantime how much trouble could he possibly make almost broke in Afghanistan, a shattered backwater riddled with spies, where his former mujahideen cronies were busy murdering each other, in which there was no decent external communications facilities except those monitored by the US and no functioning banking system, and whose economy had been reduced to ruins out of which the only thriving sector consisted of smuggling consumer goods into the country and opiates back out?

Yet somehow within a few years bin Lāden was given credit with transforming such an unappealing context into the epicentre of world terrorism while transforming himself into a mini-nuclear force and world-class drug lord. All this while political and military power was steadily accruing to a new group with which bin Lāden had no ties, which was inclined to view him and his entourage with suspicion and which was working towards a quiet rapprochement with the US.

BACK TO THE WOMB?

When Afghanistan's Communist government fell, so did the last vestige of unity among the clans, sects, and warlords. The most dangerous division was between Burhanuddin Rabbani, the Tajik head of Jamiat-i-Islami and proclaimed president of "liberated" Afghanistan, and Gulbuddin Hekmatyar, the Pashtun head of Hizb-i-Islami and briefly prime minister. Iran and, belatedly, Russia backed Rabbani. But Pakistan favored Hekmatyar. Since he put Sunnī Islam ahead of Pashtun nationalism, he was no threat to Pakistan's control of its border tribes; he would keep a distance from Iran; and, as a Ghilzai, there was little chance he could run a strong central government that might interfere with Pakistan's other interests – to use Afghanistan for strategic depth in the event of another war with India and as a base to supply anti-Indian guerrillas in Kashmir.[2]

But Rabbani, in his bid to maintain power, had two aces up his sleeve. Ahmed Shah Mas'ud was the most effective of the anti-Communist field commanders. And Abdul Rashid Dostum, leader of the northern Uzbek enclave, aligned with Rabbani to block Hekmatyar's ambitions. Although one small Pashtun faction (Abdul Sayyaf's Ittehad-i-Islami) also backed Rabbani, the reality was that, for the first time in three hundred years (but for one brief interlude in the 1920s), the Afghan government was in the hands of an alliance of non-Pashtun minorities. However Dostum soon flipped again, to join Hekmatyar in an assault on Kabul.

The subsequent four years of inter-mujahideen fighting destroyed much of the capital.[3] During that time, the rest of the country fell into the hands of local warlords. In the Shi'a Hazarjat, eight factions bloodily settled accounts until brought into a more or less stable alliance by Iran. In Herat, Ismail Khan, the man whose uprising had signaled the start of armed rebellion against the Soviet-backed government, and who had then fled to Iran, was back ruling the city and surrounding region, collecting customs fees from trade across the Iran-Afghan border. In the city of Qandahar, three different warlords squabbled over the profits from drugs and extortion from truckers. Across much of the country robberies, rapes, and mutilations so alarmed the population that they welcomed, if only temporarily, a new power that promised to tame the warlords and impose a modicum of order.

The rise of the Tāliban, most of whom were Durrani Pashtun who had been largely ignored by Pakistan and the US during the anti-Soviet war, followed a big shift in the geopolitical context. With the collapse of the USSR and the unexpected capture of Kabul by Tajik-dominated factions, Pakistan decided to create a new commercial axis from Quetta in Pakistani Baluchistan through to Qandahar, in the Durrani heartland, and from there extend its influence into central Asia. Hence it was ready to dump Hekmatyar, now despised and discredited. Saudi Arabia, angry at his snub during the Gulf War, also cut him off. Meanwhile the "trucking mafia," which controlled smuggling between Pakistan and Afghanistan, upset over extortion by multiple local warlords, began to finance the upstart Taliban.[4] After the warlords were unseated, Mullah Muhammad Omar, the Taliban leader, accumulated from grateful truckers a war chest of crumpled bank notes, which he dished out as fancy moved him from a old metal box in his Qandahar headquarters. From Qandahar, the Taliban took Herat, its first conquest outside the Pashtun areas, again sending Ismail Khan fleeing to Iran. Then the Taliban turned its eyes on the rest of Afghanistan.

Its success depended on three key resources. One, of course, was weapons Pakistan made abundantly available out of stocks (paid for by the US and Saudi Arabia) it had accumulated during the anti-Soviet war. A second was cash to buy the loyalty of regional chiefs. That required outside sponsors with deep pockets – and the Saudi intelligence department, run by a powerful pro-US prince, was happy to oblige. The third was military expertise.[5]

Although its sudden rise had taken everyone by surprise, the initial expectation was that the Taliban would soon work out a deal with other factions. Instead came a series of betrayals and massacres. During the new civil war the remnants of the Communist Party fractured along more-or-less ethnic lines with Pashtun Khalqis rallying to the Taliban. That proved to be a turning point, for it meant that the Taliban was reinforced by professional Soviet-trained soldiers who were happy to join on, partly through ethnic solidarity and partly because the Taliban could pay. The results showed up quickly in tactics, strategy, and results. Other factions, despite arms and money from Iran and Russia, still dissipated energy and resources in internal disputes. The Taliban gradually fought them off or bought them off.

The Taliban probably had another, somewhat more coy, sponsor without whose approval neither Saudi Arabia nor Pakistan would have acted. If the Iran-Contra scandal had resulted, at least in part, from US intrigues in the 1980s to draw Iran into helping the anti-Soviet campaign in Afghanistan, the victory of the Taliban, which regarded both Persian cultural influences and the Shi'a faith with equal disdain, was at least in part the result of US intrigues to reverse Iranian gains. The US, too, wanted to block a resurgence of Russian influence in the region. Hence, with at least tacit support from Washington, the Tāliban went on not only to take Kabul but to conquer the Hazara heartland and (briefly) seize Dostum's territories. Within a year of Usama's return, his old mujahideen comrades had been subdued or scattered. Only Ahmed Shah Mas'ud and his Tajik forces in the north stood, with Russian and Iranian aid, between the Tāliban and total victory.

Few recent political movements have earned as much bad press as the Tāliban, who imposed on areas they conquered a degree of puritanism that might have made passengers of the *Mayflower* jump ship. While commonly portrayed as the outgrowth of fundamentalist Islam, the Tāliban program was inspired more by ancient Pashtun tribal codes than by a literalist reading of the Qur'ān. That, incidentally, put the movement at loggerheads with radical political Islamists like Gulbuddin Hekmatyar or, for that matter, Usama bin Lāden, who believed in building modern institutions on Islamic principles. Even Iranian clerics who espoused what, prior to the Tāliban, was supposedly the quintessence of Islamic fundamentalism, denounced the Tāliban for giving Islam a bad name.

Nowhere was criticism more fierce than in the Tāliban's treatment of women. Under the Communists, women had worked as lawyers, judges, doctors, and journalists and had played important roles in education, health, and welfare. Under the Tāliban they were driven out of the workplace and into domestic seclusion. Together with the denial of education to girls, these developments seemed to confirm the worst fears about Islam to the US feminist movement. Henceforth the abiding symbol of oppression by Muslim fanatics became Afghan women who could venture out only if clad in the burqah, a head-to-foot tent-like covering. That the burqah is actually an ancient Pashtun custom that is not remotely Islamic was another minor detail that got ignored.

What was true of the burqah was true of many Tāliban edicts on women. Much of Pashtunwali (the Pashtun code of honor) contradicts Islam. In Islamic law divorce is possible for a woman to initiate, even if it is more difficult than for a man. In Pashtunwali divorce is totally prohibited to women. The Qur'ān does prescribe the execution of women (and men) for adultery. But that requires four eyewitnesses, rather difficult to find unless the act is committed in broad daylight in a public park – in which case the fate of those so engaged seems more like assisted suicide than execution. By contrast, in Pashtun practice, women can be executed for adultery on the basis of hearsay. While Islamic law accords women a right equal to men to own property, Pashtunwali forbids it, seeing women as de facto male property to be used as a medium of exchange to cement alliances and end feuds. In fact while Islam calls for the forgiving of unpayable debts, Afghan custom permits families to discharge them by handing over their daughters to the creditor.[6]

Parenthetically it is interesting to ask where all those outspoken US feminists were during the years when a Communist government in Kabul enacted sweeping changes in family law, put women in senior positions, encouraged female education (including compulsory literacy classes in the rural areas), limited the size of dowries, and forbade the exchange of women for cash or kind? The US-backed mujahideen used opposition to exactly those kinds of social reforms to rally the countryside against Communist oppression. While women had been prominent, for example, in the Algerian revolution against the French, or in Iran during the uprising against the US-backed Shah, they were conspicuously absent among Afghan "freedom fighters" battling the Soviet Union. On the other hand four militia commanders appointed to the Afghan Communist Revolutionary Council were women.[7] Indeed those normally strident femocrats were equally silent in 1992 when the US-backed mujahideen celebrated victory over the Communists by letting parents take their girls out of schools (which the Taliban later closed) for fear that educating them would lower their future value as brides and by imposing the veil in Kabul where it was formerly rare or absent.

In any case, the USA's official distaste for Taliban excesses seemed muted for some time. Even after the extension of gender-based repression across the country, the US still played footsies. No doubt the public uproar over President Clinton's difficulties in keeping his zipper done up, and its possible electoral repercussions, helped change the official mind. Even so, the Taliban and Washington continued their minuet – dampened, no doubt, by the Taliban prohibition on music and dancing. To win recognition from the US, the regime was willing to trade three things: a route for pipelines, the stuff of pipe dreams, and Usama himself.

TROUBLE ON OILED WATERS

The collapse of the USSR ushered in a minor revolution in the world petroleum trade. While the reserves of the Caspian region had made

Baku in present-day Azerbaijan the biggest centre of international oil intrigue during the late nineteenth and early twentieth centuries, after the Bolshevik victory outsiders were barred.[8] Once huge fields were discovered in Siberia, the Soviet urge to stake a stronger claim to a sparsely populated area coveted by Asian rivals meant limiting exploitation of Caspian reserves in favor of Siberian. Therefore the end of direct Russian control in 1991 opened up a new international hydrocarbon frontier. Although stock-market shills exaggerated the reserves, they were ample. That combined with a growing danger of depletion elsewhere, including in the US and in the British-controlled North Sea, gave the Caspian special significance – so did the pro-Israel lobby's eagerness to reduce US dependence on Arab sources (unless under direct US military control). If the US could position itself to dominate the Caspian, it would weaken Russia strategically and make its economy more dependent on US financial largesse, which would come only with tight strings attached.[9]

Control of hydrocarbon assets did not necessarily mean physical ownership (which usually remained vested in the state) or the legal right to exploit them (which governments generally contracted to transnational corporations). Caspian oil and gas had to be transported overland to market. All Soviet-era pipelines headed north. The questions were: in which directions and over which pieces of real estate would new ones run, and who would do the running?[10]

Russia could easily extend its existing pipeline system to haul, for example, Caspian oil to a Bulgarian tanker port on the Mediterranean and hence to the world. That would bring transit revenues to the Russian Treasury, position Russian companies to demand a share of exploitation rights, and give Moscow the power to say *nyet* to any distribution plan that did not fit its geostrategic agenda. Washington, not surprisingly, disagreed, even though its own oil companies favored the Russian option. The Russian project also had another weakness – the main route ran through Chechnya, whose rebellion Usama bin Lāden, naturally, was blamed for stoking.

Then there was Iran, with a different and, in terms of commercial geography, even more sensible answer – it could link pipelines to tankers calling at its Persian Gulf ports. But that, too, was a nonstarter in Washington, which was as keen to insulate Central Asia from Iranian "fundamentalism" as to block Russia. However Washington had to find another way for its companies to make good on their huge investments in the region.[11]

The alternative was to run a pipeline 1,750 kilometers westward from Baku across Georgia, then via Turkey to finish at the Mediterranean port of Ceyhan – which also guaranteed supplies to Israel. This bypassed both Russia and Iran and put security in the hands of a faithful (so far) NATO ally – which had its own aspirations for empire, commercial if not political, across the Turkic-speaking areas of Central Asia. However that long and expensive route required driving Russia out of Georgia, where it was backing secessionist movements in Abkhazia and South Ossetia, and it required Turkey to keep a tight lid on Kurdish aspirations to independence along the main pipeline route. The strategic benefits from having Turkey guard US oil infrastructure built to reduce dependence on Arab sources was neatly summarized in 1999, when the intelligence services of Israel, the US, and Turkey cooperated to kidnap Abdullah Öcalan, principal spokesman for the Kurdish separatists, from Nairobi and fly him back to Turkey, where he was sentenced to death.

In vain, sensible voices tried to point out that the real energy problem was not to find an alternative pipeline route but an alternative to hydrocarbons before the world faced climate catastrophe. Nor did it make much sense to assume that the threat of militant Islam (really a catchphrase for any form of political dissent in the region), supposedly one reason to shift the world's energy centre of gravity away from the Persian Gulf, would be any less a problem in Central Asia in the future, particularly given the corrupt and oppressive nature of its post-Soviet, US-backed regimes.[12]

The second major US project pointed in quite a different direction. The gas reserves of Turkmenistan are about the cheapest (in monetary terms) in the world to extract. But again the sole pipeline to external markets ran through Russia, which bought the gas for half the world price, delayed payments, then resold it for hard currency. Later there was a short line to Iran that could not carry gas for US allies because of US trade sanctions but did make the US more committed to finding an alternative. First came Bridas, an Argentinean firm, to which Turkmenistan granted exploitation rights to a new gas field. Bridas proposed to the shaky post-Communist government in Kabul to run from Turkmenistan to Pakistan via Afghanistan an open pipeline that could also pick up northern Afghanistan gas to feed both to urban centres in Afghanistan and to export markets. It was by far the biggest foreign investment project for post-Soviet Afghanistan; and Bridas managed the almost unthinkable – signed deals with all major Afghan faction leaders. Pakistan was delighted at the prospect of both increased energy security and the transit fees it would collect in hard currency. To increase credibility, Bridas had brought in as a possible partner the US company UNOCAL – which pulled a fast one; UNOCAL linked up with a powerful group of Saudi investors to access a different, already proven Turkmen gas field, then opened independent negotiations with the Taliban, which had by then conquered Herat and therefore sat astride the proposed pipeline route.

The UNOCAL project was to be a closed pipeline through Afghanistan, which, by eliminating any need to get northern warlords on side, therefore also eliminated a powerful incentive to strike a viable truce. Like the Bridas project, it would run to Pakistan, where the gas would be liquefied and sent by tanker to the Far East. But it also called for a spur into India. At the receiving end was a massive electricity plant owned mainly by the soon-to-be-notorious Enron Corporation, whose other major investments included the political aspirations of George Bush II. Originally planned to provide 20 percent of India's electricity, the project had so far depended on burning naphtha, which made its electricity cost several times the Indian average. Cheap gas might save it from a bankruptcy, which would augur badly for its overstretched parent. Once Turkmenistan had signed with UNOCAL, the company hired Robert Oakley, former US ambassador to Pakistan (and political overseer of the mujahideen), to negotiate with the Taliban. Since there was no way UNOCAL was going to carry its rival's gas, the huge concession won by Bridas in Turkmenistan was rendered valueless. To add insult to injury, a US court threw out a multibillion-dollar damage suit that Bridas had brought against UNOCAL.[13]

SMACKING THE WEST?

A second thing on the table as the US and the Taliban continued their shy courtship was Afghanistan's burgeoning opium crop. While Afghanistan had always grown abundant cannabis, opium really blossomed during the anti-Soviet struggle. A Red Army counterinsurgency campaign destroyed irrigation works and transportation networks for legal crops and uprooted trees en masse on the pretext that they provided cover for insurgents. Both sides promiscuously sowed the fields with landmines. For devastated farmers, opium, a tough weed that yielded very high returns on small amounts of marginal land, was an obvious alternative. Behind them stood warlords, who taxed the growers. The aspiring opium barons were sometimes mullahs who gave the stuff theological sanction and demanded a 10 percent religious tithe. When challenged, they offered as a rationale the need to raise money to fight communism. But, oddly enough, opium was most prolific in areas controlled by those warlords with greatest access to US-supplied weaponry.

After the overthrow of the Communists, production actually increased in the northern power base of Rabbani and Mas'ud, and in the Ghilzai regions near Pakistan. Returning refugees had to generate income quickly; and, in another triumph of capitalism over communism, former state farms taken over by warlords were turned over to growing poppy.[14]

Far from the opiates business being organized in great transnational "cartels," farmers would plant, harvest, and haul the crop (less the 10 percent tithe) to the local Friday bazaar, where buyers would offer many times the price of alternative crops. Furthermore money lenders (whose activities the former Communist government had tried to curb) would only advance against opium, not against wheat or corn with their much lower returns and shakier prospects. From the local bazaar, the stuff went by truck, taxi, or mule to refineries, sometimes passing through several other intermediaries en route. During the Soviet era, refining into heroin was done in the tribal areas of Pakistan, where the government's writ did not run. But over the 1990s, with precursor chemicals more easily available, increasing amounts took place on site. Since morphine and heroin were only 10 percent by weight and volume of the opium from which they were extracted, refining both raised the returns per unit and facilitated smuggling.[15]

The old routes via Pakistan and India still flourished. So, too, through Iran, where contraband was usually run by Baluchis with family ties across borders. In the past it sufficed to pay off Iranian border guards. But as Teheran began to fear that smuggling would finance an insurgency like the one that had shaken Pakistan in the 1970s, it cracked down. In response drug caravans bristled with anti-aircraft missiles and heavy machine guns.[16] An important new heroin route also opened along the old Silk Road through Central Asia, spreading corruption, political instability, and arms trafficking along with it.

Much of this could have been prevented with a serious international reconstruction effort after the Soviet withdrawal. But the US, which had played such a major role in wrecking the country, decided on a postwar policy of neutrality. Nor were international agencies very forthcoming. In Nangahar Province, adjoining Pakistan, the local warlord, Haji

Abdul Qadir, had promised farmers that the United Nations Drug Control Program would build roads, irrigation canals, schools, and medical clinics if they switched from poppy. When the UN pledges were broken, Qadir threatened to ask farmers to plant even more.[17] Production did accelerate, at least until 1996, when the Taliban offered Qadir a big cash bribe and a promise that Pakistan would not freeze his bank accounts if he quickly decamped.[18]

In the past, poppy growing techniques were appropriate to the local ecology and farmers withheld seed for the next year's planting. Now, with nothing to fear from government authority, buyers lent to farmers so they could buy artificial fertilizer, seeds genetically enhanced to raise drug yields, fuel, and other materials to produce on an industrial scale, expecting to be repaid at harvest. The result was heavy debts to buyers, often large landowners and rural money lenders. Farmers, in turn, would lend to workers foodstuffs or sometimes cash to tide them over the winter. This chain of debt meant that, when anything interfered with marketing, when crops failed because of drought, or when prices dropped precipitously in the face of bounty, small holders unable to pay their debts might lose their land while their workers faced starvation.

After the Taliban, the situation changed radically – in the opposite way to that suggested by recurrent stories about the regime's drug addiction. The Taliban had offered to cut the crop in exchange for foreign aid. Very little was forthcoming – in part because Taliban intransigence forced many aid agencies to leave. With little outside assistance except from Muslim charities, the Taliban refused to risk alienating local chiefs; and without reconstruction aid, the alternative to opium for farmers was not wheat or corn but loss of land and possible exile. A Taliban decision to accommodate opium growing was easier because opium use was (unlike hashish) not part of traditional Pashtun culture.[19]

Even when, in its early years in power, the Taliban accepted opium production, it was in no way an official monopoly. Where possible, pro-Taliban commanders (whose loyalty was often wallet-deep) muscled aside local bosses to collect taxes. Their importance, though, was never very large. Since Afghan farmers rake in about 1 percent of the final sales value of their opiates, even if the Taliban had been able to impose their alleged 20 percent tax (double what religious authorities allow on irrigated land) in every producing region (from some of which they were barred completely), the total take could never exceed $20 million.

Under the circumstances, it had to be much less. Most regime revenues came not from drugs but from levies on and contributions from the "trucking mafia" together with secret subsidies from Saudi Arabia (and the United Arab Emirates) until it cut off the Taliban and froze its assets in 1998.

In 1999, under pressure from Saudi Arabia (which publicly beheaded drug dealers), the Taliban announced a total ban. The UN drug-control office verified that, within two years, output in Taliban-run areas dropped from about four thousand tons to around eighty. With the help of an earlier drought, the Taliban had basically achieved that US ideal of being (non-prescription) drug free. There were still stockpiles. Far from a Taliban plot, stockpiling was the normal response of small farmers whose savings were mainly in kind rather than in cash. And stockpiles eventually go bad or run down.[20] The great bulk of the annual harvest shifted to areas controlled by the remaining opposition.[21] If the Taliban regime were to end and warlord rule returned in its place, it did not take a Nostradamus to predict what would happen – the US victory in the Afghan Drug War would come to resemble rather closely the US victory in the Islamic Terror War.

OVERSTAYING HIS WELCOME?

Apart from pipelines and pipe dreams, also on the agenda between the US and the Taliban was the fate of a certain guest. What had brought Usama back to Afghanistan was hardly its status as a terrorist paradise. He had nowhere else to go. Nor did his decision to relocate have anything to do with the Taliban. He was initially sheltered by one of his former mujahideen allies. His relations with the Taliban were poor from the start and got worse as they warned him to avoid international grandstanding that might bring the wrath of the US down on their heads. Nor were members of Usama's entourage enamored of their new home – they complained of bad food, shifty locals, Taliban obscurantism, and terrible communication with the outside world. Apparently they were also turned off by Usama's increasing egomania, something that would further foul relations with the Taliban. That bin Laden was unable to fulfill his promises about assisting desperately needed reconstruction projects no doubt helped to further sour his hosts.[22] If the "fundamentalist" regime running the drought-stricken war-ravaged politically isolated Sudan had managed to raise considerable political capital by selling "Carlos" (a former stalwart of the same causes in which the regime purported to believe) to France, why could not the "fundamentalist" regime running drought-stricken war-ravaged politically isolated Afghanistan ease the way for outside financial aid by trading to the US someone who had been a comrade-in-arms mainly of their mujahideen enemies? After all, senior members of the Tāliban, like the Sudan's Hassan al-Turabi, openly mocked bin Lāden for his "jihād jihād jihād" refrain.[23]

The turning point was the 1998 embassy bombings and the decision of the US that it did have a criminal case against bin Lāden after all. With a nod from Washington, Saudi Arabia started negotiations with the Tāliban that could have culminated in bin Lāden's extradition. At one point the rumor was that the Tāliban asking price was a modest $400 million.[24] Then it went badly wrong. If Helen of Troy's radiant face wrote a major chapter in ancient world history when it launched a fleet of a thousand ships, Monica Lewinsky's puckered lips deserve at least a footnote in more recent annals for helping to inspire an equally fateful flight of cruise missiles.

Faced with a dramatic triple challenge – from the unfolding scandal over the president's sexcapades, from a resurgent Republican Party in the run-up to the 1998 Congressional elections, and from the terrorists who blew up the Nairobi and Dar es Salaam embassies – the Clinton administration needed an equally dramatic enemy around which to rally the nation. Thus did Usama find himself elevated from the status of a dangerous political dissident to that of an international cult figure. Good (in Red, White, and Blue) was again about to confront Evil (which had obligingly switched colors from Red to Green) on a world scale.

Having created their Islamic monster, the US authorities felt duty bound to strike back. To two bomb attacks on their embassies they responded in 1998 with two missile attacks. The first was against the "chemical weapons" factory in Khartoum. The second was against several "terrorist training camps" in Afghanistan. Two of these camps, which trained guerrillas to fight in Kashmir, were run by Pakistani military intelligence, which was given no notice of the pending attack. While less physically devastating (destroying a few thousand dollars worth of tents and shacks) than the one against Khartoum, this attack had much more profound political aftershocks. In Pakistan, home of most of the dead and the place where most of the injured were treated, outrage was so great that mosques echoed with demands for revenge against Americans, civilian and military alike.[25] It was an omen for the future. The pipeline deal collapsed. Also aborted (temporarily) was the arrangement to hand over bin Lāden, with Taliban negotiators acidly pointing out that the US accused bin Lāden of precisely the crime, the murder of innocents, that the US itself had just committed.[26]

6

Trials & Tribulations – Prosecutors in Paradise and Usama in Wonderland

In November 1998, a federal grand jury in the District Court of the Southern District of New York issued a criminal indictment against Usama bin Lāden alleging a long-term conspiracy to kill US citizens and to attack US facilities overseas. To further such a plot, the indictment claimed that bin Lāden's "al-Qaeda" forged an alliance with other terrorist organizations; purchased land and other facilities to train terrorists; created a command and control structure to manage their actions; constructed a secret financial network including NGOs (AKA Muslim charities) to handle the necessary funds; arranged to run weapons and explosives around the world; made a deal to work with Saddam Hussein's Iraq to manufacture weapons of mass destruction; trained and joined with Somali "tribesmen" to kill US soldiers engaged in UN-sponsored relief work; and even had the audacity to recruit Americans to carry money and messages to the main organization's foreign subsidiaries and affiliates.[1]

It was one of those spectacular, everything-but-the-kitchen-sink-but-even-that-will-be-tossed-in-later rap sheets that US prosecutors use for four purposes: to generate lots of publicity; to avoid the work necessary for genuine evidence-based charges; to try to ensure that not all the charges will be summarily tossed out; and to paint with such a wide brush that defendants will likely run out of resources and be forced to plead guilty to some of the less horrendous accusations. If, as in this case, there was not much chance that the main target would face the music in person, the publicity also gave the US a political tool to beat other regimes into line. By the time an actual criminal process did start, the wild accusations would have so swayed future jurors as to almost guarantee convictions of any minor defendants who did not simply capitulate.

The 1998 conspiracy indictment was neither the first that bin Lāden faced nor the prosecution's preferred choice of legal weapons. In 1996, after the Riyadh and Khobar Towers bombings, a New York grand jury had alleged that bin Lāden had participated in a conspiracy to attack US defense facilities – even though the Saudi Interior Minister, no fan of bin Lāden, publicly cleared him. The trigger was not new evidence but that bin Lāden had issued a "fatwā" calling for the murder of Americans.[2]

Two months later came the embassy bombings. They were preceded by a warning, not from bin Lāden but from someone claiming to speak for Egypt's Al Jihad, that vengeance against the US was pending. Shortly after came another "fatwā," very brief, with none of the rhetorical flourishes of a bin Lāden diatribe, and conveying no real political message other than a call for the general slaughter of Americans, something that bin Lāden's other public declarations explicitly repudiated. Although the embassy attacks led to a new indictment against four alleged top aides to bin Lāden, he was still not included. However, less than a month later, that indictment was superseded by another in which he was charged along with the other four with murder and conspiracy.[3]

In fact, that was a last-minute change. The original idea, resuscitated after 9/11, had been to charge bin Lāden under the RICO Act.[4] Using a law written to attack organized crime could target all members of bin Lāden's "organization" together; it would allow the state to prove bin Lāden and his confederates guilty of offenses merely by demonstrating "membership" in al-Qā'idah, which amounts to criminalization by association; and, at a time when the official view was swinging to the idea that bin Lāden was more a financier than an actual operations manager, it raised the possibility of seizing his presumed terror treasury in much the way that the law had been used to strip "kingpins of crime" of their assets. Most important, talking about RICO indictments helped to consolidate in the public mind an image of al-Qā'idah as a hierarchically controlled, fabulously wealthy, transnational organization that played in terror a role similar to that of the Mafia in crime.

The only thing missing was a live body – RICO had never been applied in absentia. After the missile attacks on Afghanistan, there was little chance of actually parading bin Lāden before judge and jury. That

led to the government shelving the idea of a separate bin Lāden RICO
trial and simply adding him to the others in the embassy bombing conspiracy trial, albeit the prosecutors seem to have taken the precaution
to toss into the new indictment virtually all the clichés and stereotypes
that would have been trotted out in a RICO case.

RICO as an anti-terror tool did not die. After 9/11, a chorus of voices
demanded its resuscitation against bin Lāden. It would permit him to
be found guilty of 9/11 even without direct evidence. All the government had to show was that the attack had occurred while bin Lāden was
a member (he did not even have to be proven leader) of the group.[5]
Although the Bush administration decided to simply kill bin Lāden if
they could catch him, RICO still had its role to play in the War on Terror. Because the law permitted civil and well as criminal actions, "private citizens" launched a series of RICO civil lawsuits to seek billions of
dollars (in one case, a trillion) in restitution from presumed global financiers of Islamic terror, not just from Usama but from a host of Islamic
banks and charitable foundations along with some of the most prominent (and wealthy) individuals in Saudi Arabia.[6]

But all that was in the future. In the meantime the government had a
conspiracy trial to win. And the key to success would be former insiders
willing to reveal the sordid details, both of the dastardly deeds like the
embassy bombings and of the financial resources that made them possible. In the case of Usama bin Lāden, the US got lucky indeed. After
trying to peddle a story to various Middle Eastern countries whose intelligence services wrote him off as a lightweight fabricator, Jamal
al-Fadl wandered into a US embassy somewhere to sell his services.
Thanks to al-Fadl, the embassy-bombings trial would successfully consolidate an image of both al-Qā'idah and the Godfather of Terror who
stood behind it that was chillingly novel yet reassuringly familiar
enough for the public to understand.

THE INFORMANT

Much the way Joseph Valachi's account was taken to confirm an image of
the US Mafia as a corporate body, so most understanding of bin Lāden's
Holy War Inc. as a multidivisional entity that financed itself by global
businesses, legal and illegal, and functioned as the master treasury for attacks across the world, derives from claims by Jamal al-Fadl during the
trial of alleged perpetrators of the 1998 embassy bombings.[7] Valachi had
been too young to witness many events on which he expounded and too

marginal to participate in others. Similarly al-Fadl, a former "al-Qaeda financial executive" who had broken with bin Lāden after being caught taking kickbacks, left bin Lāden's employ before the worst acts ascribed to al-Qā'idah were committed. Nonetheless he performed to order. His testimony bolstered the comic-book version of Islam, the Hollywood caricature of Arab society, and the law-enforcement fantasy about al-Qā'idah. What crusading prosecutor could ask for better than al-Fadl's explanation of jihād?

Q: You mentioned that the money was for jihad. Can you explain to the jury what jihad is.
A: Jihad. It's war for Muslim. It means fighting the enemy.

In fact the most common meaning of jihād is effort or struggle to become a better person. It is often interpreted as a call for believers to work towards social justice, for example by assisting the poor. In Afghanistan the former Communist government announced a jihād against illiteracy, while the post-2001 regime called for a jihād against opium. In Malaysia some clerics say that it refers to hard work. Some Islamic activists see the struggle for democracy as a jihād; while to Sufi sects the only true jihād is against one's own ego. There are times when jihād can legitimately mean "fighting the enemy" in a more conventional sense. But Muslim clerics differentiate between greater jihād, a process of self-improvement, and lesser iihād, which can, under special circumstances, condone *defensive* military action. Even then only the state can declare war and against political not theological enemies, with the further requirement of a fatwā from the most respected religious scholars (like a muftī) – there is no religious sanction or precedent in Islamic history for an individual like bin Lāden to do so.[8]

Al-Fadl also depicted "members" swearing to al-Qā'idah a loyalty oath (bay'a), which no doubt appeared to jurors like a combination of a Mafia induction rite and the US Pledge of Allegiance. ("I make bayat to al-qaeda ..."[9]) The reality of bay'a is very different. The practice dates back to the early years of Islam and had been largely in abeyance until either bin Lāden or the FBI chose to resurrect it. Today most people from the Middle East have only a fuzzy understanding of its meaning or, as with some defendants in the trial, none at all. Strictly speaking it is not a loyalty oath but a *conditional* pledge, and not to an "organization" but to an individual, to follow his guidance as long as it is compatible with Islamic principles. The best-known incidence of its use in Islamic history was when a tribal sheikh pledged loyalty to 'Umar, the second khalīf, while warning the khalīf that failure to follow the shari'a would be met not with theological wrangling but with the pledgee's drawn sword – a position that Khalīf 'Umar publicly endorsed.[10] Under such circumstances Usama bin Lāden might seem less an adored Godfather than the captain of a pirate ship whose armed and dangerous crew watch his every move with suspicion while the first mate plots his chance.

Al-Fadl further pleased his paymasters by confirming a grand merger of terrorist organizations that bore a striking resemblance to tales about a giant coalition of "organized crime" groups peddled a few years before by ex-Cold War "national security experts" who had recycled themselves into crime-control gurus.[11] Nor was al-Fadl's depiction particularly original. In 1996 Yousef Bodansky, the same Israeli "expert" who would later frighten the world with tales of Usama's nuclear-armed, high-tech hideout in the Tora Bora caves, and who was then "research director" for the Republican Party's House of Representatives Task Force on Terrorism and Unconventional Warfare, discovered that the mad mullahs of Teheran had concocted a scheme to bring together the world's most notorious terrorist groups. They included: Hizbullāh (the organization whose military wing was driving the Israeli Army out of south Lebanon); al-Harakat al-Muqāwama al-Islāmiyya (Hamas), Islamic Jihad, and the Popular Front for the Liberation of Palestine (the three Palestinian groups most committed to fighting Israeli occupation); Egypt's Al Jihad (held responsible, probably incorrectly, for assassinating Anwar el-Sadat in revenge for the Camp David accord); and, to please Israel's closest Middle Eastern ally, the PKK (the Kurdistan Workers' Party in rebellion in eastern Turkey). In Bodanksy's remarkable depiction, resolutely anti-Communist Shi'a and Sunnī militants had agreed to bury their differences and cooperate with former-Christians-turned-atheists who ran the unabashedly Marxist Popular Front. Coordinating this "Hezbollah International" was an elite committee of three, one of whom was Usama bin Lāden.[12]

In that spirit, al-Fadl, too, claimed an organizational link between the emerging threat of al-Qā'idah and the old one of Hizbullāh, which, apart from being militantly Shi'a, had never operated as a guerrilla force outside Lebanon; and he spun stories about al-Qā'idah hosting (in Khartoum rather than Teheran) a veritable Shriner's Club Convention of terrorist groups. But al-Fadl did much more. He presented the multi-sided civil war in the Sudan as a struggle of Muslims against Christians in which al-Qā'idah had a lead role in aiding the "Arab" government against its "African" subjects – although the last thing Khartoum would want in its efforts to isolate and delegitimize the SPLA was bin Lāden running around the South chanting "jihād, jihād, jihād." Al-Fadl also reported overhearing one of Usama's top aides modestly claim: "Everything in Somalia, it's our responsibility." Since Usama was not represented by counsel, there was no one to rise to their feet and indignantly demand that hearsay be stricken from the record.

Part of his testimony was intended to portray al-Qā'idah recruits as a truly transnational collection of ruffians. When he introduced them, he attached a tag to indicate place of origin. For example, members of the Libyan Fighting Group who migrated to the Sudan to link arms with bin Lāden supposedly had the phrase "al-Liby" added to their names – Saif al-Liby; Abu Jaffar al-Liby; Abu Anas al-Liby, etc. Everyone who came from Lebanon was known as so-and-so al-Lubnani; everyone from Yemen as al-Yemeni; everyone from Egypt as al-Masri (from the Arabic name of the country; even the US prosecutor had enough sense not to suggest the term al-Egypti). According to al-Fadl (or, in deference to his birthplace, Abu Bakr al-Sudani), the practice even extended to recruits from beyond the Arab world.

Q. Do you know who was in charge of the boat?
A. Yes, Abu Habib al Pakistani and Abu Mohamed al Yemeni.
Q. Does that mean he is from Pakistan?
A. Yes.

It means nothing of the sort. While in Arabic some family names refer to countries (al-Masri, for example) or cities (al-Jaffi, etc.), any tight connection between person and place vanished centuries before. There is no modern tradition of replicating that old practice, which is doubly improbable with a new country like Pakistan. The main objective seems to have been to sell to the jury and to the media the image of a truly international conspiracy. That may have had, a few years later, unfortunate consequences for at least one person.

Khaled al-Masri was a naturalized German citizen born not in Egypt (Masr, in Arabic) but in Kuwait and raised in Lebanon. Facing family problems, he took off to Macedonia for a short holiday. Unfortunately he had attended a mosque in Ulm that was under surveillance – some members had enlisted for Chechnya; and it had been visited by a "suspected al-Qaeda member" (arrested, then released) who had once borrowed a car from al-Masri's wife. And another Khaled al-Masri with "suspected ties to al-Qaeda" was on the US watch list. That was enough for this Khaled al-Masri to be grabbed at the border and hauled to Skopje, where, despite his German passport, he was accused of being an Egyptian Afghan vet. He was told repeatedly that, if he confessed to membership in al-Qā'idah, he would be released. When he refused, he was taken by masked men, blindfolded, injected with drugs, and flown to Afghanistan on a "private" US-registered plane for interrogation by US agents. Finally he was bundled onto another plane and dumped in Albania. When he got back to Ulm, he found his apartment empty, but for a pile of unpaid bills, and his family decamped to Lebanon.[13]

The most celebrated part of al-Fadl's testimony was his depiction of al-Qā'idah's corporate structure. Much the way analyses of organized crime routinely assimilate fraternal-cum-military groupings with economic enterprises, al-Fadl seamlessly merged two distinct phenomena. One was a political structure – a set of committees or councils to handle fundraising, propaganda, recruitment, theological disputation, etc. that could have been lifted directly from an Egyptian intelligence report on Al Jihad. The second was a set of commercial enterprises controlled by a Sudanese holding company owned by bin Lāden. Presumably this was one thing about which al-Fadl could speak with assurance. Yet much of what he said about bin Lāden's businesses actually contradicted both what he claimed about the rest of the "organization" and the portrait of al-Qā'idah his handlers were trying to paint.

Al-Fadl described bank accounts in the Sudan and around the world held in bin Lāden's name – which would suggest either remarkable arrogance or simple innocence. His explanation for bin Lāden's de facto bankruptcy had nothing to do with speculative losses in the forward market for Stinger missiles. For example:

Prosecutor: Did there come a time when the Khartoum Tannery's ownership changed?

AF: Yes.

P: What happened?

AF: We buy it from the government.

P: Who is we?

AF: Al Qaeda group.

P: How much of the Khartoum Tannery did al Qaeda buy?

AF: We [were] owed money ... from the government, from the Sudan government.

P: What did the Sudanese government owe al Qaeda money for?

AF: We build the Thaadi Road.

His laments about low pay don't jibe with the portrayal of bin Lāden running a wealthy transnational lavishing terror-dollars on fanatical volunteers – they seem more consistent with a skinflint boss of a struggling company committed to reducing expenses. Al-Fadl protested his own pay cut by taking secret commissions from customers of the trading divisions, which he diverted to buy land. Yet, when he was caught, leaders of this Terror International did not hang him up by his heels and light a slow fire under his head, or force him on a suicide bombing mission. Rather they told him he was at heart a fine chap and asked him to repay the money. In so doing the "al-Qaeda executives" seemed to have shown more moral fibre than the man who would become the star witness against them. Instead of coughing up, al-Fadl lit out and went knocking on doors to peddle his story. He got lucky after the 1998 bombings, when the United States decided to make bin Lāden the central culprit and needed a Valachi-style "defector" to give their indictment credibility.[14]

Of course, al-Fadl insisted that he was not paid for his testimony – all he got was an arrangement to move him and his family to the US and a "loan" of $20,000 to start a new life. If true, the government got its money's worth. If not, it was a safe story – the prosecution was unlikely to charge him with perjury. Indeed his performance was probably worth more than the hundreds of thousands of dollars he was rumored to have actually received.[15]

The prosecution's case did not rest only on testimony by al-Fadl, although he was the centrefold. Federal agents reported on interrogations of suspects and defendants. Yet even such friendly testimony repeatedly contradicted the stereotype. FBI Agent Stephen Gaudin reported that one of the defendants "explained to me that it's not necessary for you to actually join al Qaeda to actually serve with them." FBI Agent Abigail Perkins's report of her interviews with defendant Khalfan Khamis Mohamed was even more graphic.

Prosecutor: Did you ask him about the term al-Qaeda?
AP: Yes, we did.
P: And what did he say?
AP: He said that al Qaeda was a formula system for what they had carried out, talking about the bombing.
P: And did you ask him whether or not he'd ever heard of a group called al Qaeda?
AP: We did.
P: And what did he say in response?
AP: He claimed that he'd never heard of a group called al Qaeda.

If that was true of the "organization," what about its boss?

P: Generally speaking, what if anything did KK Mohamed say about bin Laden as a leader?
AP: He described him as a sheik, a scholar and a leader.
P: What if anything did KK Mohamed say about his perception of the relationship ... between bin Laden and the group he was part of in Dar es Salaam?
AP: He stated that he knew that people in Usama bin Laden's group were supportive of people in their group, and he said that based on the fact that those two groups have the same beliefs, that he in fact considered himself as well as others in the group in Dar es Salaam to be part of Usama bin Laden's group.
P: Did KK Mohamed indicate to you whether or not he knew the name of bin Laden's group?
AP: He did not.
P: Did he indicate to you whether or not he had ever met Usama bin Laden?
AP: He stated that he did not.
P: Did you talk to KK Mohamed about the views of others in the Dar es Salaam group with respect to bin Laden?
AP: Yes, we did.
P: What did he tell you?
AP: He told us that ... he thought Hussein had actually met Usama bin Laden in Afghanistan, and he said that possibly Hussein's beliefs about Usama bin Laden had made him do what he did with regard to the bombing.
P: Did you ask KK Mohamed if he was aware of any fatwahs issued by Usama bin Laden?
AP: He stated that he was not aware.
P: Can you tell us whether or not KK Mohamed considered himself to be part of a jihad?
AP: Yes, he did.
P: Did he tell you what he perceived bin Laden to be in terms of whether or not he was a leader of that jihad?
AP: He stated, and this was near the end of the interview in terms of talking about Usama bin Laden, he said that Usama bin Laden is our leader in jihad.

To judge bin Lāden guilty on this basis would be tantamount to saying that he was criminally responsible for acts undertaken without his knowledge or participation simply because someone else decided that these acts were of the sort of which Usama would approve. This is RICO-type logic run amok. Worse, in this case, the defendant had never met bin Lāden, never heard him speak in person or even on radio or television, never transacted any business with him, and, as the defense attorney sardonically pointed out, would probably not recognize bin Lāden if he bumped into him on the street. But then the purpose of the indictment was not to actually try bin Lāden in a court of law. Rather it was to create a media extravaganza, sow public fear, and demonstrate that the government was on the job.

The government did have one witness, Ali Mohammed, a former US Army sergeant, to directly implicate bin Lāden. However his testimony posed a rather large problem. It is bad enough in ordinary criminal cases to use informants who have been offered cash, leniency, or a license to continue their own rackets if they rat out the competition. But when, as in terrorism cases, the government has an ulterior (and superior) objective beyond the courtroom, informants are schooled not merely in what to say against the individual(s) on trial, but what tales to tell about unindicted, perhaps unindictable "co-conspirators" and the broader causes they espouse. Therefore if in strictly criminal cases, turned witnesses need to be treated with skepticism, in political ones it is wise to presume them to be liars unless they are proven beyond reasonable doubt to be telling the truth. In the case of Ali Mohammed, the incentives went much beyond money or reduced jail time. The government told him he could either face trial and a high probability of the death penalty, or he could plead guilty in open court with the promise that the prosecution would only ask for life imprisonment – with the chance for parole. Presumably having a gun to the head (metaphorically speaking) or a set of lethal chemicals poised above the arm (literally true) might have affected his willingness in his scripted plea bargain to accuse bin Lāden of responsibility.

FALLOUT

The embassy trials not only served to consolidate the image of al-Qā'idah as a multidivisional transnational of terror but also disseminated the idea of al-Qā'idah as an incipient nuclear power. Credit again goes to Jamal al-Fadl, who described his own duties in acquiring uranium for the group's WMD program. Although this claim would later be ridiculed, it had serious consequences for other bin Lāden associates hauled before the courts.

One was Mamdouh Mahmud Salim, an engineer arrested in Germany shortly after the embassy bombings, extradited to the US, and there accused of being a cofounder of al-Qā'idah, of issuing religious

decrees (!) calling for Muslims to attack Americans, and of participating in bin Lāden's hunt for nuclear weapons. Jamal al-Fadl insisted that
Salim (who somehow acquired the nom de guerre of Abu Jajer al-Iraqi
even though he was Sudanese) sat on the al-Qā'idah religious committee and was at the centre of efforts to buy highly enriched uranium
from a German lab. Although Salim had been behind bars for three
years before 9/11, he was subsequently accused of a role in that event,
too. Allegedly in time free from his duties buying nuclear materials, he
had opened some bank accounts in Germany that supposedly held the
seed money for the suicide pilots.

Salim was certainly no nice guy. While in custody, he stabbed a guard,
leaving him with permanent brain damage. Ultimately this attempted
murder, not participation in the embassy bombing, led to him being
sentenced to thirty-two years. Interestingly, notes taken from his cell,
apparently to be used in a hostage-taking scheme, read in part: "We are
the Muslims who were falsly [sic] accused of bombing the embassy in
Africa."[16] If he were ever tried for that offense, one possible defense
witness was bin Lāden, who in a 1999 interview with Time stated that
Salim had simply been manager of two of bin Lāden's Sudanese enterprises, one a trading company, the other a corporate farm: he had
nothing to do with militant activity.[17]

Nonetheless the usual gaggle of "national security experts" leaped
on the WMD claims. According to another fable peddled by Yousef
Bodansky, three times in the 1980s bin Lāden attempted to buy nukes.
"By 1990 bin Laden had hired hundreds of atomic scientist from the
former Soviet Union" and put them to work in "a highly sophisticated
and well-fortified laboratory in Qandahar, Afghanistan." Leaving aside
the fact that the USSR did not disintegrate until a year later, its weapons industry along with it, the subsequent US invasion of Afghanistan
failed to turn up a trace. Nor did it find anything to substantiate a variant in which Salim (or in some versions, Jamal al-Fadl himself) acted
as go-between for the purchase of "suitcase nukes" for $1.5 million
from a former Sudanese minister who represented South African sell-
ers in a deal financed through al-Qā'idah's secret bank accounts in
Cyprus. These mini-nuclear devices, about which all manner of conspiracy theories had already been woven, had also been hauled off to
Afghanistan.[18] With so much proof of nuclear ambitions, the experts
concluded that the issue was no longer whether bin Lāden had nuclear devices but when he would get around to using them![19]

Accusations from the embassy-bombing trial prompted other countries to take a closer look at who might be hiding out in their jurisdictions. For example, Mohamed Zeki Mahjoub, an Egyptian who in 1995 had fled to Canada to seek refugee status, was accused of being part of the "inner circle" of al-Qā'idah activists. (Others preferred to identify him as a member of Egypt's Al Jihad – but, since the magic merger, apparently the difference ceased to be legally important.) The "link" was that Mahjoub had worked on a bin Lāden-financed Sudanese land-reclamation project. That was enough for csis, which, in 2001, tossed him in a detention centre pending deportation hearings. There the judge reached the startling conclusion that all fifty people working with shovels and bulldozers under Mahjoub's orders were members of al-Qā'idah; and Mahjoub was cleared to be sent back to Egypt. The only hitch came from a 2002 Canadian Supreme Court decision that ruled against deportation to a country where there was a serious risk of torture – unless there was something "exceptional" about the case. There was. According to the Minister of Immigration and Citizenship, the risk to Canada from a married man with one child born in Canada, with no record of violence, and with only the most tangential relationship to bin Lāden, far outweighed the risk to that man of being subjected to the gentle touch of the Egyptian security services on his return home. In the meantime as a security risk he was transferred from an immigration facility to a prison cell where he was held in solitary without bail and denied proper medical attention for hepatitis C and a heart condition, both no doubt aggravated by his hunger strike, while the legal wrangling continued.[20]

JUST DESSERTS?

In May 2001 the embassy trial culminated in guilty verdicts against four "front line al-Qaeda members," including Wadih el-Hage, accused of being bin Lāden's "personal secretary," of being in charge of payroll for al-Qā'idah in Khartoum, and of trying to acquire for bin Lāden a planeload of Stinger missiles for use against us forces in Somalia. Yet there was little in his background or lifestyle to suggest an Islamic terrorist in the making. He had been born in Lebanon a Catholic and converted later in life. He moved to the us, where he studied urban planning, worked in a donut shop, and married a local girl. Although devout, he was not fanatical. Nor was he known to have serious political views – until he volunteered for Afghanistan. Born with a deformed arm, el-Hage was not a fighter but an educator who delivered textbooks and copies of the Qur'ān to refugee centres. While the media would later describe the office that employed him as "shadowy," it was so secretive that it had bank accounts in its own name, a registered address, and publications under its logo.[21]

Nor was there anything secret about el-Hage's later association with bin Lāden, whom he met during the Afghan struggle. In 1992 el-Hage arrived in the Sudan to take up the post of director of international marketing and purchasing for bin Lāden's enterprises. With his US passport he could travel the world freely, which most of bin Lāden's associates could not. That, of course, meant that he could jet about plotting terrorist actions, or he could fly around placing orders and arranging sales. Naturally, prosecutors assumed the first. His work was so hush-hush that he was permitted to collect address books, diaries, and business cards, which, according to a typically calm *Newsweek* account, "later provided investigators with a kind of terrorist road map."[22]

After two years, el-Hage formally left bin Lāden's employ. Although the departure was at his wife's urging, her objections had more to do with life in the Sudan and with bin Lāden's pressure on el-Hage to take a second wife than a protest against the activities of a man whom she later described as "a great boss." Their new home was Nairobi, where he took over as director of a local NGO involved, as was his former Pakistan-based employer, in relief work. But according to prosecutors, it was a ruse – the real purpose of the Nairobi move was to set up the East African al-Qā'idah "cell" that would later organize the embassy bombings. Perhaps. But, if his real job was a well-kept secret, so was the salary he was got from billionaire bin Lāden – el-Hage had to run an auto-leasing franchise, then, when that failed, dabble in gemstone trading to make ends meet.

In 1997, the year after bin Lāden returned to Afghanistan and a full year before the embassy bombings, el-Hage was in Pakistan meeting with Tāliban officials. According to el-Hage, the trip was simply to arrange a supply of gemstones (Afghanistan produces the world's best lapis lazuli, fine emeralds, and respectable rubies) for his far-from-flourishing business. While he was away, the FBI called at his Nairobi home, seized documents, and frightened his wife and children into returning to the US. When el-Hage himself got back to Nairobi, he found that the US government had pressured Kenya to expel him. He followed his family homeward, which some, no doubt, took as proof that he had been reassigned as a "sleeper" agent in the United States. Even back in the US he seemed to lead a normal life, working in a tire store to support his family. Still, the feds kept pressing.

Two weeks after the embassy bombings, el-Hage had a visit at his US home from an FBI agent with the ironic name Robert Miranda, who afterwards testified that el-Hage had been completely forthcoming in response to questions and had agreed without hesitating or requesting counsel to go to Miranda's office to answer more. The chat revealed a number of oddities in attitude for a committed terrorist with the blood of hundreds of innocents on his hands. El-Hage told the agent that, right after the Nairobi bombing, he had phoned a friend at Kenya's Criminal Investigation Department, located close to the US embassy, to make sure he was all right. When asked if bin Lāden were responsible for the attack, el-Hage expressed doubt. He noted that anyone planting such a bomb would know that it would claim many innocent victims, something he did not see his boss as inclined to do. Nor did he deny further contacts with bin Lāden. In fact he had received phone calls asking him, for example, to undertake a purchasing trip, this time to Slovakia, to obtain not nerve gas components but tractor parts.[23]

It is possible that el-Hage was truly the fulcrum for an appalling terrorist outrage; it is also possible that he was just a sap who ran messages and provided accommodation to former associates from Afghanistan and the Sudan without knowing much about what they may have been concocting. Even if he did play a minor role in a real plot, it was blown out of all proportion in his trial to give the FBI, which had been watching him for years, a chance to reply to critics of its supposedly sloppy intelligence work. Whatever the truth, he was charged first with perjury, later with conspiracy in the bombings, and sent to prison for life.[24]

PLEADING GUILTY?

By the time of the embassy trial, Usama bin Lāden had pleaded his own case before the tribunal of world opinion. He told a rather different story than did the prosecutors; and he continued to tell it even after his alleged crimes had been compounded many times by 9/11 and other outrages.

Far from being wild rants calling down the wrath of Allāh upon infidels, through his interviews and videotaped speeches run five main themes that, even if partly motivated by ego or a duplicitous desire to divert attention from his own crimes, merit attention in their own right.

They are: a critique of US foreign policy and, by extension, the US political system; the defensive nature of the Islamic responses to US aggression; boasts about his supposed campaign of economic warfare against the US; comments on his personal role in various acts; and a simple prescription for ending the war between radical political Islam and the United States.

Palestine, his first complaint on his return from Afghanistan in 1989, remained a running sore. ("While American blocks the entry of weapons into Islamic countries, it provided the Israelis with a continuous supply of arms allowing them thus to kill and massacre more Muslims.") But there was much more. In an ABC interview two months before the embassy bombings, he summed up his main grievance: "America has spearheaded the crusade against the Islamic nation, sending thousands of its troops to the land of the two Holy Mosques ... meddling in its affairs and its politics, and supporting the oppressive, corrupt and tyrannical regime that is in control."[25] In later interviews he recognized the main US motive – oil obtained "at a paltry price" by the West: "They rip us of our wealth, of our resources and of our oil."[26] Because of the greed of the USA's local surrogates, oil brought little but uncertainty and unemployment to producing countries, particularly Saudi Arabia. In fact, his denunciation of the spiralling deficits, unpaid debts, and depreciating currency of his former homeland sound less like the protests of an Islamist radical than the diagnoses of an IMF team demanding a severe austerity program.[27]

Despite his distaste for Saddam Hussein, the sanctions against Iraq and their human cost were further sore points. He pointed out that during Gulf War I, UK and US bombing "destroyed the infrastructure and the milk and dairy industry that was vital for infants and children and the civilians and blew up dams which were necessary for the crops people grew to feed their families."

His critique later went beyond what the US government did to a denunciation of the nature of US society. When bin Lāden described the United States as "the worst civilization witnessed by the history of mankind," he may have been slightly overstating the matter. But by citing its banking system based on usury, its traffic in drugs and intoxicants, its gambling "in all its forms" including stock-market wheeling and dealing, and its propensity to commodify women and use them as sexual lures for mass consumerism, he put his finger on a number of things of concern to a serious Muslim, and a lot of Christians. Nor was he blind to the ecological consequences of this "worst civilization." He noted:

"You have destroyed nature with your industrial waste and gases." To add insult to environmental injury, the US refused to sign the Kyoto Accord "so that you can secure the profit of your greedy companies and industries."[28] Unlike his diatribes against consumerism and vice, this seems scarcely the stuff of a "Wahhābī fundamentalist." Granted, the Qur'ān implores the faithful to nurture nature, but Usama would be hard pressed to find within it the basis for a diatribe against greenhouse gases. It is further proof that his critique was essentially political in nature – religious rhetoric was simply the way in which it was expressed to appeal to his principal target audience.

Originally he seemed to have had some faith in the democratic process in the United States. Back in 1998 he had advised its citizens to "find a serious administration that acts in their interest and does not attack people and violate their honor and pilfer their wealth." In retrospect, many sensible people in the US probably wish they had heard and heeded that advice. By 2004 his attitude soured. Denunciations of Jewish conspiracies to warp the US political system probably found little favor except among a handful of Ku Klux Klan types; but when he stated of George Bush II that "the darkness of the black gold blurred his vision and insight, and he gave priority to private interests over the public interests of America," few careful observers of the US political scene would be inclined to disagree. His further comment about "the warlords, the bloodsuckers, who are steering the world policy from behind a curtain" was somewhat more hyperbolic than President Eisenhower's warning at the end of his term about the military-industrial complex, but it is cut from the same cloth.[29] It also has the distinct advantage that no one could say to Usama as they could to Dwight, "Where were you, Mr President, when all this was happening?"

His second major theme was that the Muslim world had a right to protect itself against US aggression.[30] To the rhetorical question, "Why are we fighting and opposing you?" he replied: "Because you attacked us and continue to attack us." He echoed the notion that the actions imputed to him were reactive up to his 2004 presidential election message. "Just as you lay waste to our nation. So shall we lay waste to yours."[31]

The question of the loss of innocent life gave bin Lāden a little pause. In 1998, in denying a role in the embassy bombings, he had insisted that: "Our religion forbids us from killing innocent people such as women and children." He repeated that sentiment in his initial denials after 9/11. But later he shifted ground. "Whoever has destroyed our villages and towns, then we have the right to destroy their villages and towns. Whoever has stolen our wealth, then we have the right to destroy their economy. And whoever has killed our civilians, then we have the right to kill theirs." After all, who were the Americans to complain? "Through history, America has not been known to differentiate between the military and the civilians or between men and women or adults and children. Those who threw atomic bombs and used the weapons of mass destruction against Nagasaki and Hiroshima were the Americans."

Perhaps aware of how shallow (and, arguably, unIslamic) was that justification, he tried to elaborate that, unlike most Muslims whose oppressive regimes the US maintained in place, Americans have political choice. Since Americans use their freedom to vote for and pay taxes to a government that attacks Muslims, they, too, share the responsibility. Apparently that responsibility was not universal – he further suggested that US freedom and democracy is for whites only, although he conspicuously refrained from remarking on the number of non-whites (and Muslims) killed by the embassy bombings or 9/11.

As to the nature of his retaliatory acts, he cited the example of the USSR, supposedly bankrupted by the war in Afghanistan, i.e., by bin Lāden's own efforts. Although a caricature of reality, Usama was turning back against the US a self-congratulatory theme formerly spouted by the Reagan-Bush administrations. In truth, the real threat to US financial integrity came from its trade and budget deficits, which even an army of bin Lādens could do little to worsen – although a subsequent army of US Marines, soldiers, and National Guardsmen in Iraq certainly could. Yet his words seemed to strike a responsive note with those who ought to have known better. According to the director for the Study of Terrorism and Political Violence at St Andrews, Scotland: "Bin Laden has an excellent understanding of economic targeting."[32] Actually bin Lāden had an excellent understanding of the appetite of the Western media for sensationalism and of the propensity of "experts" for self-delusion.

Modestly, bin Lāden cited his own efforts at "bleeding America to the point of bankruptcy" as only one cause of its pending economic downfall. He gave equal billing to the greed of its own corporations, especially those dealing in arms or oil. However, lest anyone take him for an economic determinist, he scoffed at the idea that the Islamic revival was "due to economic factors. This is not so. It is rather a grace from Allah." His proof? "When the holy war called, thousands of young men from the Arab Peninsula and other countries answered the call and they came from wealthy backgrounds. Hundreds of them were killed in Afghanistan and in Bosnia and Chechnya."

As to his personal responsibility, most interesting was how he reacted to the mention of particular individuals who were supposedly members of his "organization." For example, in reply to a query about whether he knew a man captured in Manila, where he was supposedly plotting to kill President Clinton, bin Lāden described him as "among the most courageous Muslim young men. He was a close friend." But: "As to what you say about him working for me, I have nothing to say." Such questions were meaningless. "We are all together in this, we all work for Allah." In other words, what he and his supposed followers had in common was not membership in some organization but a sense of commitment to a common cause, one blessed by God (not bin Lāden). Sometimes he was more explicit. Against the accusation of his responsibility for attacks on US military installations in Saudi Arabia in 1995 and 1996 (for which he had been officially cleared), he said: "We have ... stirred the nation to drive out the enemy. Yes, we have instigated and they have responded." In other words, he took credit for being the inspiration rather than the organizer.

The obvious rejoinder is that Usama was just being cagey to avoid self-incrimination in case he had to defend himself in a US court. But he knew fully well that he was part of the walking dead, that only by a complete fluke would he survive if the United States caught him, in which case he would never see daylight again.

For nearly a decade in his public declarations he took the same line. He voiced approval of various acts, although not necessarily all of their consequences, but stopped short of admitting he had ordered, planned, managed, or financed them. Thus he could insinuate that he had a global reach without risking explicit repudiation from real architects who might be miffed when they had to share credit. That was even his initial reaction after 9/11. "I am not involved in the 11 September attacks in the United States ... I had no knowledge of these attacks ..." In fact he returned to his post-1998 bombing theme: "... nor do I consider the killing of innocent children and other humans as an appreciable act. Islam strictly forbids causing harm to innocent women, children, and other people. Such a practice is forbidden even in a battle." To drive the point home he reiterated that "we are against the American system, not against its people, whereas in the attacks, the common American people have been killed."

Then came the curious December 2001 tape issued just after US troops landed in Afghanistan, which contained his supposed confession to 9/11. It included the claim that only the four pilots were aware that they were on the suicide mission – the other fifteen were just along for the ride, so to speak. The Bush administration lept triumphantly on this "smoking gun." But even Alan Dershowitz, the egregiously self-promoting lawyer who rarely misses an opportunity to tar Muslims with the terrorism brush and, more recently, to justify confessions extracted from them under torture, insisted that, in terms of criminal law, there was nothing incriminatory in the tape – everything was already public knowledge.[33] Even the supposed revelation that only the pilots were in the know was hardly a surprise – it would have been almost impossible for nineteen people to have lived and plotted for so long under the shadow of certain death without at least one of them cracking and running to the authorities. Parenthetically, to publicly gloat that most participants were dupes was hardly the kind of declaration to be expected from someone eager to recruit for the cause.

Last, and certainly not least, of the major themes running through bin Lāden's discourses was his prescription for ending conflict. Despite his harsh view of US society and its corporate-run political system, he made it clear that he was not interested in a struggle to the death: "Every state that doesn't play with our security has automatically guaranteed its own security." Peace was possible, he insisted, if the United States just followed his (rather sensible but not very realistic) advice to "pack your luggage and get out of our lands."[34] In fact the USA was at that moment doing precisely the opposite; and Usama was its primary excuse.

7

Rocket's Red Glare – Snatching Defeat from the Jaws of "Victory"

The US strikes against "chemical weapons facilities" in Khartoum and "terrorist training camps" in Afghanistan that followed the 1998 embassy bombings played well back home, where commentators followed the missile flights with the reverence that used to be accorded a fireworks display on Independence Day. However, for the Tāliban they were not an unmitigated disaster. They gave the regime international sympathy it had formerly lacked and improved relations with China, whose experts were invited to examine the remains of the US state-of-the-art Tomahawks. According to some tall tales, Usama himself brokered a deal.[1] No doubt improved models were soon deployed by the People's Liberation Army while toy replicas might have joined the Chinese consumer goods flooding the US market.

Still the Tāliban tried to placate the US. After bin Lāden ignored a directive to shut up, the regime cut off his telephone, then floated stories that he had fled to Iraq. When the US pushed through the UN Security Council a sanctions resolution whose immediate effect was to drive the Afghan currency down and the price of food up, at a time when several million people had been designated by the UN as facing danger from drought, the Tāliban made a number of overtures. It asked for evidence that bin Lāden had really been the architect of the bombings and other misdeeds; it promised that bin Lāden would leave Afghanistan voluntarily in exchange for the government not revealing his destination; it asserted that, if he were to remain, the regime would bring him to trial before a panel of Islamic judges; and it suggested that the US post international monitors at the borders to keep an eye on him. The president of Pakistan added his own plea for the US to give the Taliban the evidence. All were rejected. The US demanded unconditional surrender.[2]

The US refusal to offer the Taliban a public fig leaf is perhaps partly explained by the Democratic Party's fear of the potential wrath of the US feminist movement if the administration did not hang tough, particularly with a lame-duck president. Furthermore the US was trapped in a myth of its own creation. Each accusation further inflated the bin Laden legend and made rational discourse increasingly difficult. Perhaps to some that result was not entirely unwelcome. The government's stance bore an eerie resemblance to that during the Kosovo crisis a few years back when, in order to set the stage for a military assault, the Clinton State Department deliberately made it impossible for the Serbian regime to back down gracefully.

By the end of 1999 the Taliban was anxious to dump bin Laden without triggering an internal backlash. Its desperation increased the next year, when a group of Yemeni guerrillas attacked the *USS Cole* in Aden harbor, killing seventeen sailors – the US formally warned the Taliban of its intent to attack if bin Laden was found responsible. According to an intermediary, an Afghan-born US businessman, in a face-to-face meeting with US officials in Frankfurt on November 2000, the Taliban was told that bin Laden could be handed over to the EU, killed by the Taliban, or set up as a target for US cruise missiles. The Taliban promised to arrange that last option. Although Al Gore, President Clinton's heir-designate, was beaten in the elections that month, the Bush administration reputedly agreed with the plan. Yet nothing happened. Then came 9/11. The intermediary insisted that the Taliban was in a panic to hand over bin Laden, to shut down his facilities, and to extradite any of his followers who were wanted in their home countries. But the intermediary was told that there was no need for further discussion. Much as would happen two years later when Saddam Hussein offered US weapons inspectors and oil companies open access to Iraq to head off an invasion, the Afghan war train had left the station; the last thing the United States wanted was the arrest and extradition of bin Laden to stop it in its tracks.[3]

PSYCHED OUT?

The date of no return may actually have been 9/9. Two days before the Twin Towers tragedy, a pair of Arabic-speaking men with phony journalism credentials appeared at a press conference hosted by the leaders of the so-called Northern Alliance, the remnants of anti-Tāliban elements who hated each other as much as they did the common enemy. The two began to grill Ahmed Shah Mas'ud about his attitude towards bin Lāden. With that public introduction, they set off bombs hidden in their cameras. When Mas'ud died, fingers immediately pointed at bin Lāden.[4] Perhaps he really did instigate the plot in an effort to buy support from the Tāliban and to head off its plans to turn him over to the US. But, apart from the concerted effort by the perpetrators to ensure that the world got just that impression, a few things made no sense. In the past bin Lāden had called repeatedly for Muslims (notably his former Afghan allies) to cease their own quarrels in order to concentrate on the real enemy beyond. Nor could the attack on Mas'ud do much to advance bin Lāden's anti-US agenda. While US media began to eulogize Mas'ud after he was dead, he had been, if anything, more in the pockets of France, whose press and intellectuals fawned on him; and he had good relations with Iran and Russia, neither of which was in the USA's graces. Plus his independent income from smuggling rackets and control of the best gem-mining territories in the country made him less amenable to being bought. Certainly not least, he was mistrusted by US intelligence. Supposedly in 1992 he had taken $500,000 of CIA money to close the pass through the Hindu Kush to the flow of Russian supplies for the beleaguered government, then done nothing – the CIA decided it had been conned.[5] Not until the end of January 2001 was there even discussion in the US about funding the Northern Alliance.[6]

On the other hand, there were stories that Washington had offered Mas'ud $5 million for bin Lāden's corpse.[7] Whether the rumors were true or merely disinformation spread in the hopes of provoking a clash, they might have provided a motive for bin Lāden. But, if so, that would seem to preclude bin Lāden from having been aware of what was to follow two days later – he could hardly improve his personal security by bumping off Mas'ud, then calling the entire military might of the US down on his head.

The terror war, like all others, was fought on several fronts. One was psychological, both to mobilize public opinion at home and to demoralize and confuse the enemy abroad. Apart from Laura Bush's discovery that Tāliban misogyny had suddenly reached intolerable dimensions, the US PR campaign stressed three interrelated things: the de facto merger of the Tāliban and al-Qā'idah in politics and in crime; the spectre of weapons of mass destruction in the hands of such a fanatical alliance; and the consequent need to cleanse Afghanistan of "terrorist training camps."

Apparently, the dramatic reconciliation between, on the one side, the Tāliban, a gang of know-nothings led by a know-very-little, and, on the other, "Arab" political refugees bitter over their exile in the back-end of nowhere, was so complete that not only were Usama's hoards replenishing the Tāliban treasury but his hordes had become the mainstay of the Tāliban Army. Foreign policy, too, had been effectively taken over by al-Qā'idah.[8]

Nowhere was this alliance for regress so evident than in the joint Tāliban/al-Qā'idah plot to flood an innocent West with soul-destroying substances. With bin Lāden nearly broke after his Sudanese escapades, he and his followers had reputedly turned to crime.[9] In crime there is no bigger money-spinner than drugs. And Afghanistan is to drugs what Saudi Arabia is to oil, particularly with an obliging gang of miscreants in control. The Tāliban regime, so the story went, decided to cut in bin Lāden for a magical 10 percent in exchange for his aid in marketing through his global network Afghanistan's $8 billion per annum opium crop; and it allowed al-Qā'idah to collect drug taxes from the peasantry.

Imagining such an evil pact is consistent with history. In 1917, as the US was about to enter World War I, its government announced that imperial Germany was flooding the United States with narcotics. In World War II, the culprit was Japan. In the 1950s Harry Anslinger, politically astute boss of the Bureau of Narcotics and Dangerous Drugs, blamed the People's Republic of China. In the Reagan era, the Soviet Union, Cuba, and even the PLO were at various points held responsible. So why would it be a surprise when Usama bin Lāden set out to take over the world heroin trade?[10]

Of course, there was the question of whether a Saudi commanding Arab aliens could shake down Afghan opium farmers protected by clan chiefs, some of whose militias boasted tanks and heavy artillery. There were also curiosities in the arithmetic. Even accepting the highly improbable figure that the Tāliban earned annually $20 million from opiates, that would make bin Lāden's share a measly $2 million less expenses, hardly enough to keep his purported al-Qā'idah worldwide army of countless thousands in Qur'āns, let alone Kalashnikovs.

According to the second theme stressed by US propaganda, one purpose of the drug money was to buy so-called weapons of mass destruction, defined as anything usefully murderous that the US has and does not want anyone else to get. In what could have been a dress rehearsal for Iraq two years later, after the White House had saturated the media with tales of hidden horrors, US troops fanned out across Afghanistan looking for secret facilities. Gas-centrifuge plants to enrich uranium seemed elusive. However there were other dangers. Not only, claimed CIA director George Tenet, was "bin Laden ... pursuing a sophisticated biological weapons research program," but he was also "pursuing a radioactive dispersal device, which some call a dirty bomb." To make a "dirty bomb" all that was necessary was a conventional explosive device surrounded by any sort of radioactive material, even hospital waste.[11] That the main threat from a "dirty bomb" was from the conventional blast, and that there was only a minor risk of contamination, which could be fairly readily cleaned up, did not alter the capacity of the "dirty bomb" story to make people quake before their TV sets.[12]

This alarming news came hard on the heels of information that US Special Forces had located rooms full of papers containing technical plans and chemical formulas. Some were half burned; but whether that was unfortunate or convenient was never clear. Then came reports of a lab under construction near Qandahar where al-Qā'idah had tried to develop anthrax and tales of production facilities for things like cyanide, phosgene, and chlorine gas. Nuclear, biological, and chemical weapons all at once indicated a previously unknown level of terrorist audacity. It also indicated a previously unknown level of engineering sophistication in Qandahar, where the Tāliban idea of high tech was a diesel generator to occasionally turn on the lights and an abacus to calculate the national budget.[13] Nonetheless, if anyone needed more proof, US forces found that a fertilizer plant that *could be* converted to chemical weapons production had been located "near a compound that has been used by Osama bin Laden and his organization."[14]

Ultimately all the stories turned out to have the consistency of Manuel Noriega's tamale flour and were quietly dropped. But they had fulfilled their psychological function. Besides, the US government could always plead that, in the interests of its citizens, it had chosen to err on the side of caution.

The third element in the propaganda campaign focused on "terrorist training camps." Afghanistan had always attracted some odd characters. During the 1960s and early 1970s travellers were mainly Western hippies seeking cheap dope, breathtaking scenery, and a break from taking off their clothes in public and spray-painting slogans on bank walls. During the 1980s, travellers were mainly men from Muslim countries outraged at the Communist takeover or driven out of their countries of origin by political persecution. The 1990s combined elements of both. The new Afghan visitor was, like those of the 1960s, most likely displaced and disoriented, but, like those of the 1980s, more prone to get off on gun smoke than pot smoke. There certainly numbered among them those ready to undertake bloody-minded projects that would generate considerable anguish to innocent victims but little concrete political result. However among them were also people with a genuine interest in aiding reconstruction. A lot of them never made it home, at least not without a side trip to a certain US-controlled corner of Cuba.

THE BIG SQUEEZE

As US bombs and missiles rained down on Afghanistan's already devastated and heavily mined countryside, they set off another mass flight of civilian refugees during another harsh winter. That was apparently no accident. While the Bush administration insisted publicly that the purpose of the assault was to liberate the long-suffering Afghans from the tyranny of the Taliban and the infamy of Usama, in a moment of unguarded frankness, one of the joint chiefs announced that the campaign "will continue until the people of the country themselves recognize that this is going to go on until they get the leadership changed."[15]

Still, with hundreds of thousands displaced, the US military wanted to show its humanitarian side.[16] Therefore along with the bombers came two giant military cargo planes, flying high to avoid surface-to-air missiles, perhaps including some of the Stingers the US had so promiscuously handed out a decade or so in the past.[17] These planes dropped on the troubled land thirty-seven thousand packages of food-aid marked with US flags and emblazoned (in English, Spanish, and French) "a gift from the American people." That was an accurate description since the contents were likely unsaleable surpluses donated by US agribusiness corporations in exchange for a tax write-off.

Of course, in time of war there are always a few hitches. The plastic-wrapped meals (beans and lentils in tomato sauce; peanut butter; strawberry jam; a fruit bar; biscuit, shortbread, and fruit pastry; and a utensil kit of salt, pepper, napkin, and a match) were not made to be dropped from high altitudes – as they fell, the air pressure caused them to expand, and the cold made the plastic brittle causing some to split in the air or on impact, assuming they did not just kill people on whom they landed. Some packages that did survive were contaminated – the

US then claimed that the Taliban was poisoning the population, while the Taliban accused the US of so doing. Furthermore food packs sometimes fell in areas littered with unexploded ordnance – there were still ten to fifteen people killed or injured each day from Soviet-era mines laid by both sides; and food packs were colored yellow, as were the cluster bomblets that the US scattered far and wide.[18] Each of the thirty-seven thousand packages would feed one person for one day whereas the real problem, hundreds of thousands on the move, could only be met by regular convoys of large trucks hauling food over the border. Furthermore the cost of airborne delivery, assuming it could ever reach its target, was nearly treble that of a land-based one. On the other hand, the problem with land-based delivery was that the warlords whom Washington was backing might steal the stuff to give exclusively to their own clansmen or to sell on the black market.[19]

Along with the bombs came Operation Anaconda, a twelve-day mountaintop offensive in early 2002 – by far the largest ground action by the US military since Panama. It was also, according to General Tommy Franks, the man who ran Bush's war on international terrorism, an "unqualified and absolute success." Another senior officer concurred that "we destroyed hundreds of al-Qaeda's most experienced fighters and terrorists." When only a few bodies were found, he helpfully suggested that the rest had been literally obliterated.[20]

Of course, it would have been mean to remind the generals that by the time of the US military action, there may have been relatively few foreign fighters left because the US had already recruited so many for other duties. Largely blacked out from the Washington-New York chatterathon was the fact that hundreds of anti-Soviet vets combined with a second generation of Muslim fighters had been relocated from Afghanistan to Bosnia in the early to mid 1990s, not by bin Laden but by the Pentagon, to bolster Bosnian government forces against the Serbs. That war had seemed to be Muslim underdogs fighting Communist Slavs all over again. After the war the recruits were simply disbanded, some no doubt, in the spirit of Bay of Pigs veterans, to take up drug trafficking and freelance terrorism. If the CIA can be blamed for creating in Afghanistan some sort of Muhammad's Monster, the Pentagon deserves the credit for giving it a round-the-world ticket and a multiple-entry visa.[21]

Certainly there were foreign Islamic fighters in Afghanistan, some veterans, some newcomers, at the time of the US invasion. Some were sure to have been among bin Laden's entourage. But that select group would have gone through a series of winnowings. First, his followers were a tiny part of those who had initially volunteered. Most of those would have gone home on their own at the end of the Afghan war. A small number, unable to return to a normal life, continued in his ranks until resettled in Saudi Arabia or Yemen. A group of those remaining ended up in the Sudan, where they worked for bin Lāden for very little, and likely none too happy about it. When he left for Afghanistan, they were told that they could come along but had to pay their own way. No doubt each move whittled down the number of his purported followers even further, as did conditions inside Afghanistan. That left either the most dedicated or the most desperate.

Furthermore, far from all foreigners in Afghanistan being bin Lāden acolytes, apart from Pakistani recruits to the Tāliban, most seem to have been from neighboring Central Asian states run by post-Communist dictatorships.[22] Hence most of the "camps," too, had nothing to do with bin Lāden. They were run by a hodge-podge of local and foreign militant organizations along with some set up and operated by Pakistani military intelligence to train volunteers for guerrilla warfare against India in Kashmir. True, those camps did train militants – they were taught how to handle small arms, improvise explosives, and engage armies in rough terrain. Little in their training would be relevant for terrorist attacks on urban targets in major Western countries where the enemy was security services with fancy espionage techniques on the lookout for dusky complexions and Muslim names.[23] Yet all were the targets of a US program to slaughter from the air and to round up the survivors on the ground.

Information on who to bomb was given to the US either by the Northern Alliance, antagonistic factions with radically different territorial and ethnopolitical agendas united temporarily by hatred of the Tāliban and love of the dollar, or by warlords bribed to once again change sides, who singled out rivals for local dominance, thereby assuring that US bombs killed hundreds, perhaps thousands, of civilians.[24] Their most important military contribution was to chase down supposed al-Qā'idah militants, then turn them over to the US Army and the CIA for further disposition. They were paid for each delivery. Hence those accosted by US allies on the ground who could not speak fluent Pashtun or Dari (the Afghan dialect of Persian) were either murdered or sold.

AFTERGLOW

There were four criteria by which the US invasion of Afghanistan could be assessed. Did it rid the country of the Tāliban? Did it install a legitimate and widely accepted government? Did it get the Afghan drug traffic under control? And did it render the world safe from further outrages allegedly orchestrated by bin Lāden? It failed on all counts.

Tāliban forces pulled out of the major cities in good order, core troops preserved, to fall back on the countryside in the south and east, where they could wage long-term guerrilla warfare secure in the support of the local population and with minimal need for outside logistical and financial aid. That way, too, they could shed the unreliable allies they had purchased and who might (temporarily) find the pickings better on the US side. Such a strategy also negated US air power, leaving the US facing the nasty reality that, as in so many similar conflicts, the only way to deal with guerrillas was to confront them with far larger numbers of regular soldiers.[25] But a major ground offensive was precluded by the logistical and political drain of the subsequent US adventure in Iraq. Meanwhile the Tāliban could quietly infiltrate its supporters into the ranks of the new Afghan government and Army that the US was creating, with the result that, when the US tried to finance local services or buy loyalty by dishing out money, some doubtlessly ended up in enemy hands.[26] With insufficient US military forces to protect them, government officials, police, and even outspoken reform-minded clerics were often killed, either by Tāliban action or in squabbles between rival warlords claiming to be loyal servants of the new regime. The US, of course, had a simple explanation for the persistence of the war – the Tāliban were being reequipped with fancy weapons paid for by Usama bin Lāden.[27]

The "new" regime did not exactly enter Kabul to the cheers of rapturous crowds. In a replay of 1992–96, when taxes had meant extortion and theft, and social services had meant rape and murder, unruly Tajik, Hazara, and Uzbek militiamen shook down visitors, stoled food and other forms of aid, and tried to peddle the latest "intelligence" or supposed al-Qā'idah relics to eager reporters and voyeuristic spooks.[28] Outside the city they slaughtered Tāliban prisoners by firing squad or mass suffocation.[29] Aptly summarizing the security brought by the change of regime was the archeological treasure house at Jam. Once protected by the Tāliban, after the regime fell, the area was flooded with looters working on behalf of dealers from the US, Britain, and Japan. Allegedly, US servicemen acted as intermediaries, buying antiquities from villagers and reselling them to dealers who then marketed them in London or New York as Seljuk or Persian to hide their real origins.[30] It was a dress rehearsal for the cultural pillage that would occur in the wake of the US invasion of Iraq. Simultaneously old warlords ousted by the Taliban returned to their respective fiefdoms, from which they could usually be bought out only by more lucrative positions in the central government. The result was to give power and legitimacy in the new "national" government to people who deserved a privileged place on any list of Afghan war criminals.[31] Even Gulbuddin Hekmatyar, who had been hiding out in Iran, staged a return, albeit first announcing that he had come to help the Taliban in their hour of need – to which the US responded by trying to kill him with a missile fired from a drone aircraft.

Although the US had muscled Rabbani aside to install as president Hamid Karzai, a Pashtun with a blood feud against the Taliban, the Tajik-dominated Jamiat-i-Islami secured the interior, defense, and foreign ministries and, no doubt, used its control over the intelligence services, police, and Army with customary even-handedness. Meanwhile Karzai, who survived repeated assassination attempts only because of tight US security, was either dismissed by fellow Pashtun as a US stooge or ignored by leaders of other ethnic groups even after his ascendancy was legitimized in an election that made those held by the Communist regime seem open and fair.[32] The main result of his election was to ensure that warlords would proclaim loyalty to him to assure a share of the US cash they needed to fight rivals who were equally vocal about their commitment to Karzai's presidency.[33] His isolation forced him to begin making deals with ex-Taliban almost immediately.[34] Originally disguised as an effort to woo "moderate" factors in the movement, by the end of 2005, Karzai had to call for truce and dialogue with no less than Mullah Omar himself – to which Mullah Omar responded by announcing renewed attacks on US targets.[35] By then the security situation in the Pashtun areas had deteriorated so much that Pakistan and India, over vehement US objections, decided to ice the recently revived project to carry Turkomen gas over Afghanistan and instead rely on another line through Iran, with a possible spur to tap the Turkomen fields. If completed it would deliver another blow to US aspirations to be able to dictate the world flow of hydrocarbon resources and would confirm Iran's central role in the emerging Euro-Asian gas distribution system.[36]

As to the opiate plague, even as US bombs began to fall, farmers, sensing Taliban weakness, began again to plant poppy; while traffickers with pockets bulging with cash quickly got back into business. Although before the invasion the British government had produced lists of drug targets to bomb, the US had brushed them aside for fear of alienating the warlords on whom it would rely for the bulk of the land-based operations.[37] Not surprisingly, official US figures showed that production in 2003 stood at a level thirty-six times its total in the last year of Taliban rule. The other major change was that nominally pro-US militia chiefs soon had a reputation for demanding higher bribes from growers and traffickers than had their predecessors.[38] Output continued to climb until by 2005 Afghanistan was producing nearly 90 percent of the world's illegal opiates. Moreover, with the reopening of trade across the Pakistan-Afghan border to an inflow of precursor chemicals, local warlords were able to capture the profits from the manufacture and export of heroin. The highest quality flowed out via Pakistan to Europe – the inferior northward, where the governments of Uzbekistan, Tajikistan, and even China insisted that the cash from Afghan drugs were fuelling local insurgencies.[39]

In response the US launched a double offensive. Hamid Karzai decreed a ban (which he had no means to enforce since his police and Army were already corrupted by drug money) on cultivation, processing, and trafficking, although it did not escape notice that he did so once planting was already over.[40] Simultaneously the US brushed aside the UN, which had some experience in these matters, to launch its own eradication program whose main feature was not building roads and irrigation systems for other crops but sending British and US soldiers to dish out cash from cardboard boxes. The payouts offered never reached the level of returns the farmers could get from opium, and most of the money, not surprisingly, wound up in the hands of local warlords. Nominally in charge of local implementation of the eradication program, they used the money to hire more guns to knock out their competitors, then reported to the US that they had succeeded in cleansing particular areas where, in reality, poppy flourished as before.[41] And in those few places where poppy was eradicated, farmers heavily in debt to traffickers had no choice but to revert to the old Afghan custom of giving their daughters to their creditors – another step towards female emancipation under US tutelage – and/or to send their sons to seek work outside the country.[42] As to the obvious remedy – to allow Afghanistan to grow opiates legally for the prescription drugs market – any such suggestion was met by obdurate rejection by the US administration.[43] The giant pharmaceutical companies who held patents on synthetic substitutes were no doubt pleased that their (tax deductible) expenditures on Washington lobbyists and Congressmen had paid off so well for their shareholders. The only feasible alternative, an

intense microlevel alternative development scheme with ample sources
of credit to break farmers free of the dependence on the cycle of debt
and drugs, while feasible in a few areas where security was reasonable,
was precluded in great swathes of the country where the writ of the
Tāliban insurgents or the remaining warlords held sway.

Nor were the issues of insurgency and drugs distinct. Although during the Tāliban era, its government had successfully suppressed opium,
once in armed opposition, the Tāliban took the opposite tactic. It
joined just about everyone else in fattening off the trade. Afghanistan
remained an economic basket case, its factories destroyed, its agricultural infrastructure in ruins, its population desperate, leaving an economy that was, so the bitter joke went, 95 percent drugs and 5 percent
rugs. While Tāliban attacks focused on military convoys or containers
carrying petroleum and goods for us and other foreign troops, it was
usually safe to send convoys of drugs by road as long as local warlords
were squared away.[44] The Tāliban local commanders could then use
taxes from drug caravans to buy automatic weapons (including, no
doubt, many formerly siphoned from us aid flows to the old mujahideen) off the Pakistan black market.[45]

Inevitably the deterioration spread to Pakistan. Already losing $2 billion
per annum from Customs and sales taxes evaded by the flows of smuggled goods under the Pakistan-Afghan transit trade deal, the country's
infrastructure continued to crumble, rural poverty reached crushing
dimensions, the bureaucracy and Army became hopelessly corrupt, the
textile industry (probably the most important in the country) came under ever more intense competition from China, armed political groups
took control of large urban areas, and the spectre of ongoing instability
in Afghanistan fed Baluchi secessionist sentiments while the Pashtun-
inhabited North-West Frontier Province (where some houses literally
straddle the border and tribes on the Pakistan side call themselves "Afghans") was progressively Talibānized. Each time the us, on the pretext
of another sighting of Usama bin Lāden or Ayman al-Zawahiri, bombed
villages and killed innocents, it managed to recreate the anger that
had arisen after 1998 missile strikes. Mosques rang with cries for vengeance, more recruits flooded recruitment stations, while cash contributions to the anti-us struggle surged. All the while the Pakistan stock
and property markets, buoyed by an influx of speculative funds from
expats, soared to dizzy heights, just waiting for the crash.

But the most important objective of the campaign surely was to rid
the United States and the West of the threat posed by Usama bin Lāden

and his al-Qā'idah. And what better sign of success against things like the terror-dollar hoards that Usama had assembled or earned in Afghanistan could there be than the autumn 2002 incident in which US troops broke into the office of the mayor of Asadabad, a small provincial capital, ransacked it, and made off with $3,000 in cash?[46] The terror-dollar search also inspired an internet fraud letter supposedly from "Dennis Longe" of the US Special Forces claiming that his group had overrun an al-Qā'idah drug lab and found $36 million in cash that was then deposited in a Kabul "security luggage office." Since the US soldiers could not take the money out of Afghanistan by themselves "as it was against military ethnics [sic]," they offered a partnership to anyone willing to wire them a few thousand dollars to cover expenses.[47]

As to the legions of fanatics this kind of money supported, no less a body than the London-based International Institute for Strategic Studies, the leading British neocon think tank, reckoned that over half of the thirty senior leaders and two thousand rank and file of al-Qā'idah had been captured or killed – not a bad record considering the bin Lāden probably had around him about two dozen committed followers. But, the IISS warned, this ought not to lead to any complacency or demands for an early withdrawal of UK and US troops; for it still left about eighteen thousand "potential terrorists" at large ready to attack again. Others agreed. Down but not out, bin Lāden remained "much more than just an iconic figurehead of Islamic militancy ... ." From his hideout, wherever it was, he still "controls an elite terrorist cell devoted to attacking in the United States."

But just where was that hideout? Some contended that it was in the wilds of Afghanistan. Others insisted that it was in the unruly tribal areas of Pakistan, where "he is being protected by a well-financed network of Pakistani tribesmen and foreign militants who operate in the impoverished border region."[48] Yet others had him going to ground in Kashmir, close enough so he could keep an eye on Afghanistan as well. On the other hand, there were those convinced that, to recoup his strength and regroup his forces, he had headed back across the Indian Ocean into East Africa, into a place where, according to US intelligence, he had a host of avid supporters and had already worked bloody mischief against the USA's efforts towards world peace and prosperity.

8

To the Shores of Muqdisho – Usama in the Land of Qāt, Clan, and Cattle

With Afghanistan so well secured, the United States turned to deal with other threats. For a time it seemed that the next target was to be Somalia. The usual prime-time experts on places to which they had never been, with names they could not pronounce, insisted that Usama received much of his terror treasure from sympathetic Somalis, well known for their hoards of clandestine wealth, that his operatives (including those responsible for the 1998 embassy bombings) had taken advantage of Somalia's lawless society, long shoreline, and porous borders to smuggle guns and operatives, and that bin Lāden himself was intent on making the place his next hideout.[1] He could also use Somalia to run lucrative rackets, particularly in drugs and counterfeit money, to bolster his finances.

To stop the money flows, the US Treasury blocked on a virtually worldwide basis the transfer of funds from the Somali Diaspora to families back home – at a time when those remittances, somewhere between $250–500 million annually, were the only thing keeping the country afloat. To prevent the use of Somalia to move weapons and al-Qā'idah cadres in and out of East Africa and the Red Sea area, the US Navy sent a warship to keep an eye on the country's unguarded thousand-plus-kilometre coastline, which is serviced by enough small smuggling vessels to make southern Florida blush with envy. To deal with the possibility that Usama himself was seeking a Somali sanctuary, the military dusted off plans for direct intervention.

Information about bin Lāden's intimate association with Somalia came from the kinds of objective and disinterested sources so often called upon in the Terror War. They included landlocked Ethiopia covetously eyeing a strip of the Somali coast; Somali warlords who, eager to emulate the Afghan Northern Alliance, wanted to use the US military against local rivals; and the Pentagon, which had its own grudge. Among the misdeeds in Somalia they jointly and severally imputed to the dour Saudi were: his central role in the lucrative traffic in qāt, the popular local "narcotic"; his financing and/or training of al-Ittihād al-Islāmiyya (Islamic Unity), a local terrorist movement that had repaid him by helping to bomb the US embassies; and his role in killing eighteen US soldiers who, in 1993, had been simply helping with relief aid in the famine-ravaged country. Proof of this last offense came during the invasion of Afghanistan, when US troops found in an "al-Qaeda stronghold" a GPS system taken from a US soldier killed in Somalia – where he undoubtedly had been using it to locate pockets of starving people in need of an Afghan-style food drop. Hours after the find was announced, the company that had supplied the unit pointed out, uncooperatively, that it had been manufactured four years after US forces had precipitously pulled out of Somalia.[2]

ENTRANCE STRATEGY?

It remains somewhat of a mystery why the US military blundered into Somalia in the first place. Even the most doctrinaire Marxist would have trouble blaming old-fashioned economic imperialism. Nearly 75 percent of the population lived a pastoral existence; manufacturing was almost nonexistent; and agriculture had been savaged by drought and war. Perhaps the fact that bananas were the main export crop triggered in Washington a conditioned reflex. Although indications of offshore deposits had excited some big oil companies, the discoveries came during a world glut. Apart from camels (hardly to US taste even before 9/11) and cattle (of which the US scarcely needed more), about the only local product foreigners found of interest was the gum from some of Somalia's unique trees, which for more than four thousand years had yielded frankincense and myrrh. While a Christian "fundamentalist" might see that as ample reason to sound boots and saddles, at the time of the decision to intervene the US was under the reign of George I, not his Born-Again son. In any case, the trees were in a part of the country that had already seceded by the time US troops arrived in Muqdisho, the capital city.

Looking beyond the economic to the strategic, in the past one attraction had been the port facilities at Berbera, which the USSR had briefly used. But with the end of the Cold War, the old Soviet fleet was rusting out in home ports; and other littoral states welcomed the US Navy.

Perhaps the answer was simply that George I, who had just lost his re-election bid, wanted as his final act in office to show once again the same kind of humanitarian concern as when he had unleashed his Air Force to bomb slum areas of Panama and kill several hundred (perhaps many more) civilians in order to save them from misrule by a CIA agent allegedly turned drug dealer. A Somali intervention seemed costless (to him) and would bequeath to his successor the problem of extrication.

FAMILY VALUES

While Somalia is ethnically and religiously more uniform than almost any other country in Africa, it is deeply divided into clans (six major ones) and subclans (many hundreds). A geographic division partly overlaps the ethnic one. Greater Somalia as a political entity has never existed. Prior to the colonial era the interior was largely nomadic, while the coastal areas were commercial, with Arabic the lingua franca among those who traded ivory, ostrich feather, slaves, and frankincense. During colonization, Somalis came under five jurisdictions – the French ruled Djibouti; the British grabbed the north of present-day Somalia proper, which seceded again in 1993 to form the Republic of Somaliland; the Italians took most of Southern Somalia; another chunk of the South was incorporated by Britain into Kenya; and, after Ethiopia defeated a late-nineteenth-century Italian invasion, the British encouraged it to grab the Somali-inhabited Ogaden before the Italians could incorporate the region.

Although, to cater to domestic opinion, Somali politicians occasionally called for "reunification," on independence the Italian and British pieces were joined into the Republic of Somalia, which officially accepted the general African consensus not to question colonial-era borders, lest that open a Pandora's Box of competing claims. That was the theory. In practice different states covertly backed ethnic insurgencies on each other's turf, hoping that a successful secessionist movement would, once recognized internationally, opt to join their country. Somalia, for instance, stirred up the ethnic Somalis who comprise 60 percent of the population in northeastern Kenya; and it equipped anti-Ethiopia rebels in the Ogaden. That was just business as usual in postcolonial Africa, until Somalia decided to change the rules.

In 1969 the country was taken over by the military dictatorship of Mohammed Sayed Barre, with support from urban elites fed up with traditional clan-based politics. Facing an Ethiopia strongly supported by the US, Barre responded with slogans about "scientific socialism" in which he combined elements of the Qur'ān with random ideas from Marx, Mao, and even Mussolini. He nationalized banks, insurance companies, electrical power stations, petroleum distribution, sugar estates, and refineries, but not the banana plantations, the sole sector to have substantial foreign interests. The expropriated sectors were subsequently made into state agencies run by his kin and cronies. He also opened his ports to Soviet vessels and his Army to Soviet weaponry.[3]

In 1974 the Ethiopian monarchy was overthrown in a pro-Communist coup. For a time the USSR tried to balance its regional allies. But in 1977 Barre, sensing weakness as Ethiopia battled local insurgents, invaded the Ogaden. The Soviet Union dropped its support of Somalia and shipped massive amounts of weapons to its new protegé. Cuba followed with troops and advisors. Despite initial support from Washington, the now ardently capitalist Barre saw his forces chased from the area, then had to deal with half a million fleeing Ogadenis.[4] Somalia had its first, but not its last, modern refugee crisis, followed by its first, but again not its last, emergency infusion of the foreign food aid, which would later play a big role in the collapse of state, society, and economy.[5]

Barre survived the Ogaden debacle for three reasons. First, he still had the backing of Washington, which was happy to flood Somalia with its own weapons to replace the Soviet ones, some of which may have ended up in Afghanistan.[6] Barre's willingness to give oil concessions to four US companies and port facilities to the US Navy further raised his approval rating. Then came development aid, although the main thing developed was the bank accounts of the president's relatives.

Second, Barre manipulated local rivalries, provoking clashes in a country where family loyalties ensured that vendettas could last for decades. He encouraged the Ogaden refugees to encroach on territory of less compliant clans while he maintained the veneer of commitment to the Ogaden by arming refugees (assembled into the Western Somali Liberation Front) with old Soviet weapons. Meanwhile he kept his own entourage happy with phony loans and foreign exchange advances from state banks along with "contracts" to provide nonexistent services to the state and by turning a blind eye to their contraband.

Third, Barre played the refugee crisis to his own ends. He inflated the numbers, then diverted food aid from international donors to maintain alliances or to sell on the black market. Later an investigation by the US General Accounting Office found that perhaps 20 percent of the US portion of the food aid ended up in the mouths of genuine refugees.

Although the formal economy shrank, the country was kept afloat by contraband, both money and goods. Remittances from tens of thousands (perhaps many more) of émigré workers in the Gulf bypassed the formal banking system to come home via underground channels. Livestock merchants underreported exports to bring the proceeds back via the black market. Most frankincense was snuck off to the Gulf, evading license requirements and taxes – the hard currency earned could be salted abroad or brought home without detection. Wages for government service were a pittance, but the jobs were a license to collect bribes and run rackets. In effect the economy switched from formal production and trade to trafficking and smuggling.[7] It was when Barre tried to crack down on one of the most important parts of the off-the-books economy that his problems began to spin out of control.

HARD TIMES, HIGH TIMES

In December 1992, when the Marines first charged ashore at Muqdisho, they were no doubt convinced that they were about to confront armies of doped-up terrorists plotting to flood the world with mind-blowing substances, then invest the proceeds in nerve gas and nuclear missiles. The US military afterwards bragged that its Somalia operation had been planned with the effects of the national drug habit in mind – the troops arrived at 4:00 AM, when local militiamen were presumed to be sleeping off their last high. Back home, the brass fretted about whether open availability of drugs would undermine "combat readiness" the way opiates had in Vietnam two decades back. No doubt all of them, armchair generals and grunts alike, were startled to find that Somalia's notorious dealers were likely mothers selling little packets of largely innocuous leaves in open markets to raise a few shillings to feed their children.[8]

The leaf of the "tree of paradise" had a long and honorable history in religious ritual and traditional pharmacology before the US woke up to the dangers of another killer plague and became the sole major Western country to ban the stuff. Although folklore credits qāt with many medical miracles, including the prevention of cholera, its main effect is as a mild stimulant; chewing fresh leaf releases alkaloids that suppress appetite and maintain alertness.[9] Sometimes used by manual workers in need of extra energy (much as is coca leaf by Andean Indians) and by shepherds trying to remain alert to predators, it was also adopted by soldiers and Sufi saints.

In the West in the nineteenth and twentieth centuries, troops were encouraged to use tobacco – nicotine kept them wired even when hungry and tired. The main alkaloid in qāt, chemically akin to amphetamine, produces similar results. Hence the drug found favor among militiamen. As in war, so in prayer. Followers of Sufi orders decided (to the despair of orthodox ulemā) that, since qāt was not explicitly banned in the Qur'ān, it was halāl, particularly since chewing qāt helped them to stay up all night reciting prayers. In lay society it was used ceremonially at business and political gatherings. With demand bolstered by the repatriated earnings of émigré workers, it also became a mass recreational drug. However, it was associated with sociability not self-indulgence – etiquette frowns on chewing qāt in private.[10]

The tree is indigenous to highlands in Yemen, Ethiopia, and Kenya – and does not grow in Somalia. Usama's ancestral home of Yemen is self-sufficient. There small-scale farmers hire for the harvest extra labor paid with a share of the crop. Since the product is highly perishable, traders usually purchase only a day or so before harvest, then rush it in small lots to urban centres – the spread of paved roads was a boon to its traffic – for retail sale. An impressive (and probably exaggerated) 90 percent of the adult male population and a growing number of women are reputedly regular users, while some industries pay their workers partly in qāt. In the old South Yemen, a nominally Marxist government had tried to ban use except on weekends, when it was permitted only if grown on state land where production could be taxed. On unification with the North, the regulations were dropped. Subsequently the government relied on exhortation and a 30 percent retail tax, which few dealers pay. However use of the drug is opposed by both orthodox clergy and secular modernizers – the first insist that, despite the absence of explicit mention in the Qur'ān, qāt is harām; the second blame the national pastime for low productivity and for keeping the population in an apolitical stupor.[11]

In Ethiopia and Kenya, since growers are mainly non-Muslim, there is no religious sanction. Furthermore, domestic demand is low except among ethnic Somalis in Ethiopia's Ogaden or Kenya's Northeastern Frontier. There are no great international "cartels" running the resulting traffic. From Kenya, the biggest supplier, the qāt, once harvested, must be rushed by local traders to Nairobi's Wilson Airport (which serves domestic and regional traffic), where Somali buyers have small planes waiting even at times when the airport is technically closed. A few bribes suffice for air-traffic controllers to ignore overloading or lack of flight plans. Then the planes land in Somalia at several small airfields and at the major one in the capital. On arrival, qāt is distributed to a horde of dealers waving bundles of cash. Qāt also moves by sea from Mombassa to Somali port towns south of Muqdisho as well as by land through Somali-inhabited areas of Kenya, although overland loads are vulnerable to hijacking. With the spread of a refugee Somali population across Europe, new markets have opened there as well.[12]

The expanding qāt trade triggered old alarm bells. During Britain's long struggle to impose its will on unruly Somali clans, it pointed the finger at Muhammed ibn Abdullah Hassan, the so-called Mad Mullah, a Sufi leader and poet who, the British claimed, financed his long insurrection through the proceeds of qāt – which the British had tried in vain to regulate and tax. His uprising was the first major effort by Somalis to throw off foreign rule. Enormously costly in death and destruction, the rebellion was only crushed in 1920 after the British deployed air power they had developed in World War I. As to the notorious Usama as reincarnation of the Mad Mullah, while tales still abound of him and his followers, in cooperation or competition with so-called organized crime, muscling in on the supposedly lucrative international traffic, if he were really a "Wahhābī fundamentalist," it would be odd for him to peddle a harām substance to hardcore Muslim followers who allegedly abound in Yemen and in Somalia. Furthermore, the notion that an outsider could impose his will on the trade is another drug-driven fantasy.[13]

Not even the Barre government, with its military and police power, could do that. In 1983 the regime banned the trade, arresting hundreds of people, impounding dozens of vehicles, and confiscating (so it claimed) tens of thousands of kilos. Presumably most of what it did grab quickly returned to the black market before the stuff lost its kick. The government rationalized the crackdown by the need to stop drug abuse. More likely the reasons were that the traffic bypassed the national banking system, which the regime manipulated to its advantage; that much of the profit went to opposition groups; and that cronies of the president saw prohibition as a way to unleash the Army and police on their competitors.[14]

HANDWRITING ON THE (BERLIN) WALL?

Despite Barre's success in mobilizing external support and manipulating internal politics, dissent grew. In 1978 disgruntled senior officers from the clan that dominated the northeast fled to Britain to form the nucleus of the Somali Salvation Democratic Front. Financing for its rebellion came not from an international Islamic terror chest but from Diaspora contributions and from "taxes" on smugglers running coffee and qāt from Ethiopia into Northern Somalia. (By the late 1980s Somalia was exporting fifteen thousand tons of coffee a year without the inconvenience of growing any.[15])

Barre managed to bribe away some SSDF leaders. But 1981 saw the emergence of the Somali National Movement, based on the clan that controlled old British Somaliland in the North. That region had special economic strengths. It was the place of origin of most Somalis who worked in the Gulf and sent their earnings home through the parallel money market. And it was home to the frankincense plantations. With the area increasingly restive, Barre launched a campaign of economic warfare. When he ruled that all frankincense exports required a special license, granted only to Southern supporters, tree owners just smuggled more or unloaded gum weighed down with stones and rocks on official buyers. When Barre jailed some of the owners, clansmen in the Gulf invested in fast boats to run arms into Somalia and frankincense back out again. Then Ethiopia, to repay Barre for his support of Ogaden insurgents, allowed the Somali National Movement to set up base camps.

In a sort of dress rehearsal for Washington's anti-terror-dollar policies in the region, Barre tried (in vain) to get Saudi Arabia to cut off the underground flow of money from émigré workers back to the North; and he tried to squeeze the rebels locally by freezing bank accounts and preventing state banks from giving credit to any Northerners suspected of disloyalty. When the uprising spread, he hired white mercenaries to bomb the regional capital; and he tried to attack the Somali National Movement's mini-navy.[16] His only success was a deal with Ethiopia, which closed down the SNM camps in exchange for Barre ceasing to aid the Ogaden rebels. But that proved his undoing. Ogaden refugees denounced the sellout and linked up with dissidents in Barre's own clan to form the Somali Patriotic Movement. Then, in the area around Muqdisho, the most powerful local clan, alarmed at Barre's efforts to squeeze it out of urban trade, created the United Somali

Congress. By the late 1980s the country had descended into a civil war in which four major clan-based insurgent groups were temporarily united against the regime.

The end of the Cold War also meant the end of Barre's usefulness to Washington. With outside support gone, in 1991 he fled to Kenya and later to Nigeria. Left behind was a civilian population ravaged by war, drought, and famine. Hundreds of thousands ended up in urban shantytowns or in refugee camps; many tens of thousands more fled abroad. The remnants of the formal economy shut down, and the banking system collapsed. As in Afghanistan, people, particularly in the growing Diaspora, had to rely on informal bankers (the soon-to-be-notorious hawāla system) for back-and-forth remittances. Then, in another development also seen in Afghanistan, different factions began to print their own money – people caught with another faction's currency could be shot on sight.[17] As the post-9/11 propaganda mills began to churn, Usama would get the blame for both – the hawāla banks were singled out, along with Islamic charities, as the main targets in the financial War on Terror, while the head of the UN Committee monitoring financial sanctions against bin Lāden gravely noted that "We suspect that al Qaeda has exploited the counterfeit currency trade in Somalia."[18] The UN official managed that brilliant insight at a time when the practice of printing and importing fake Somali currency was so widespread that not just warlords but even ambitious local businessmen were cashing in on the trend.[19]

DIVIDE AND MISRULE

Yet another similarity to Afghanistan in the early 1990s was that victory over the common enemy was followed by a civil war that was even more destructive, at least to the capital city. Smaller clans, formerly content to follow the majors, formed their own militia groups; while the old factions squabbled over power and money.[20] The United Somali Congress, which dominated the Muqdisho area, imposed a businessman named Ali Mahdi as "president." That led the Somali National Movement in the northwest to proclaim independence. The Somali Patriotic Movement took up arms against the USC, then split into two antagonistic subfactions. So, too, a short time later did the USC itself after Mohammed Farah Aideed, its military leader and patriarch of one of its two main subclans, had a falling out with Ali Mahdi, a leading figure in the other. For the next five years Aideed insisted that he, not his rival, was the real "president." The conflicts turned Muqdisho (like Kabul) into a free-fire zone. The city was further plagued by gangs staffed by country boys brought in by Barre to fight the clans, then left adrift with his departure. Owing no allegiance to any faction, they supported themselves by looting, trafficking qāt, and extorting from relief agencies – whose presence may have done more harm than good.[21]

While Somalia had hardly been a model of peace and prosperity, historically it had dealt with the vagaries of nature, if not of politics, reasonably well. Farmers stored grain in good years while, when drought threatened, nomads would exchange ailing or aging animals for farmers' surplus grain. This reciprocity, which served to keep traditional farmer-pastoralist hostilities in check, was a mystery to foreign relief workers who poured into the country along with a massive influx of food aid. The effect was, no doubt, to save some, perhaps many thousands, from immediate starvation, but it threatened indigenous agriculture and helped prolong the wars by doing as much to feed militias with weapons as to provide refugees with nutrition.

In Somalia, political power grew both from the barrels of foreign-made guns and out of the bushels of foreign-grown grain. Control of food supplies by any faction meant priority of distribution to their own clansmen; while diversion to the black market allowed the purchase of more soldiers and more weapons, which, in turn, permitted the particular faction to control more of the food supply. Aid agencies, including the Red Cross and the UN, learned to strike deals with militia leaders for access to port and airstrip facilities; they hired from the militias security guards to protect relief stores and to guard convoys on the way to distribution centres; if necessary they paid off freelancers. Although there were still ambushes of trucks leaving the port, theft from storage sites, extortion en route, and rackets run by truck drivers – all of which drove up expenditures for security – the arrangements worked reasonably well. Furthermore by the summer of 1992 the famine had peaked: the drought had alleviated and local production began to improve. The real emergency seemed over. Then the USA came to the rescue.

As its food-aid program long worked, the US government bought farm surplus from a handful of grain companies, paid US shipping companies to move it, then sold it cheaply to governments of "developing" countries for local currency. They paid into local bank accounts from which the US embassy could draw to influence politics or make mischief. Although now gifts have replaced soft-currency sales, the economic impact is much the same. The influx of grain depresses prices of locally grown foodstuffs and drives small farmers off the land; it builds up a taste for (and infrastructure to process) US grains; it encourages a shift to luxury cash crops (usually grown on large, capital-intensive plantations that further dispossess the small-holder population) for export to the West; and it facilitates the rise of intermediaries who get rich distributing US food aid and who act as cheerleaders for pro-US policies. All of this is applauded by well-meaning NGOs who rush about the globe finding more humanitarian crises to reaffirm their importance and to ensure further funding, either direct from Western governments or from tax-deductible contributions by concerned individuals and grateful agribusiness corporations. Some people are certainly saved from starvation in the short run, while the recipient country is left more vulnerable economically and more dependent politically in the long run.[22]

Throughout 1992, Western media were replete with pictures of starving Somali children and tales of massive looting of relief rations – up to 80 percent in some versions, while the Red Cross itself reported losses at a manageable 10 percent.[23] The stories were usually linked to the qāt trade – militias seized food and sold it on the black market to buy qāt, which in turn drove them into a homicidal frenzy while innocent bystanders were left hungry. One person singled out for particular opprobrium was Osman Hassan Ali, a wealthy businessman who (under the title "minister of humanitarian affairs") played the roles of finance minister and national security advisor to Aideed's self-declared presidency. Allegedly Ali had taken over the racket of hiring out armed guards to aid agencies, taxed the fuel they needed for their operations, and cornered the weapons and qāt trades, paying for both with diverted food aid.[24]

Thus Americans cheered when George I declared Operation Restore Hope – none so loudly as four big oil companies whose concessions had been thrown into doubt by the end of the Barre regime. Conoco even put its compound at the disposal of the newly reconstituted US Embassy, a gift the State Department, with its customary sense of good public relations, accepted.[25] Then the Marines arrived to begin a farce that soon turned into a bloody tragedy and that cost in one year $2–4 billion, enough to feed all of Somalia many times over, and more than enough to restore the infrastructure so that the country could again feed itself.[26] Ultimately it was not even clever politics – by the time the troops arrived, the presidential elections were over and George I was bound for retirement to nurse his wounded pride and to plot a comeback (even if by proxy), an urge the Pentagon would soon share.

Once the US forces arrived, priorities changed. Since much of the food aid that came with them was no longer necessary, it ended up making black-market dealers happy and further retarding Somali agricultural recovery. The primary US objective became to restore not hope but "stable government." Therefore, unlike the Red Cross or UN, the US decided to bypass the existing power structure. Yet General Aideed, who increasingly portrayed himself as a nationalist transcending clan and opposing neocolonialism, had repeatedly warned against a US presence without his explicit permission – never solicited or granted.[27] Instead some four hundred members of the US elite Rangers were sent in (on top of troops already present) with the task of "neutralizing" Aideed. As in Afghanistan, there were two main targets: Aideed himself (the "warlord") on whose head they posted a measly $25,000 reward; but also Osman Hassan Ali ("the financier"). Thus, the United States closed Aideed's airport, proclaiming that they were trying to stop the flow of qāt (which would scarcely enhance US popularity) and weapons. They shut down a radio station that broadcast Aideed's message, killing several demonstrators in the process. They fired missiles from helicopters at a gathering of Aideed's clansmen, killing fifty. They kidnapped Osman Hassan Ali. Then they went looking for the Aideed himself.[28]

Aideed had caused so much suffering that his own clan elders along with his chief advisors were often on the verge of repudiating him. But each time the US confronted him directly, clansmen were required by family loyalty to rally. At least in the ensuing melee, there was no confusing who was who. Somalis were woolly haired and dark skinned, while US elite forces were unrelentingly white, perhaps with a touch of boiled-lobster red from the Somali sun. But things did not go completely according to plan. Aideed's militiamen shot down four US helicopters and killed eighteen Rangers – who evened the score by slaughtering about one thousand Somalis, most of them innocent bystanders and some reputedly hostages murdered by US soldiers in reprisal. The success against the US helicopters would later sustain stories (recounted, for example, by the prosecution during the embassy bombings trial) that Usama himself may have provided the missiles from his stockpile of surplus Afghan Stingers.[29]

Aideed's warlord career did come to an abrupt end a few years later. But it had nothing to do with the US military. First, Aideed quarrelled with his "financier," who bolted to the opposition. Then he got into another war with Ali Mahdi over the control of the banana trade.[30] That struggle, along with Aideed's pretensions to the presidency, was ultimately settled with a single bullet. Unlike when the Rangers tried to do the job, there was no "collateral damage" to innocent bystanders.

For the United States, the abrupt departure of its forces from Muqdisho joined the story of their ignominious flight from Beirut ten years earlier, and perhaps even scenes from the US Embassy in Saigon a decade before that, as incidents best forgotten publicly although not forgiven privately. But after 9/11 came the electrifying discovery of the real cause of the USA's humiliation, namely that Usama had created in Somalia a vicious gang of protegés.

BROTHERS IN PRAYER, PARTNERS IN CRIME?

For a while one Somali faction had stood above the fratricide. The very name of the group, al-Ittihād al-Islāmiyya (Islamic Unity), reflected its members' hopes not to wage global holy war but to unite Somalis (including those in the Ogaden) on the basis of one thing they had in common. Inspired more by the salafi of Saudi Arabia than by the Muslim Brothers of Egypt, much less by radical political Islamists of the bin Lāden stripe, originally members of al-Ittihād kept out of politics but earned public trust because they avoided clan feuds and, using contributions from Islamic charities abroad, devoted themselves to relief work. The Somali Salvation Democratic Front, in whose turf they first operated, left them to their own devices. But within a year of Barre's fall, al-Ittihād rose against clan rule in several towns of the northeast. The SSDF counterattacked, sending the group's armed wing into exile in isolated areas near the Ethiopian border. In 1996 the group was accused of attempting to assassinate the Ethiopian Minister of Transportation, himself an ethnic Somali who was regarded as a traitor to the cause of reunification. Ethiopia scattered al-Ittihād and effectively ended its military career, but not its political usefulness. Typed as a violent Islamic terrorist group that had participated in the "ambush" of US Rangers in 1993, shared training facilities with al-Qā'idah, helped with the 1998 embassy bombings, and was a linchpin in the worldwide system bin Lāden used to raise, move, and deploy terror-dollars, al-Ittihād became a propaganda tool in the hands of both the US and Ethiopia. In fact Ethiopia tried to use the tale of al-Ittihād's Islamic legions to rectify its greatest strategic weakness.[31]

Like Southern Somalia, Eritrea had been an Italian colony. After World War II the victors decided that the way to balance Ethiopia's need for an outlet to the sea with Eritrea's demands for independence was to link Eritrea to Ethiopia as an autonomous region. A decade later Ethiopia formally annexed Eritrea. Although much of the population of Eritrea's Christian highlands is closely related ethnically to that of parts of Ethiopia, a big portion of those living in the coastal area is historically, culturally, and commercially closer to the Middle East – Muslim and often Arabic-speaking. Hence annexation led first to the emergence of the Eritrean Liberation Front, which secured support from both Arab and East Bloc countries. Then a splinter group, the Eritrean People's Liberation Front, emerged, with a Christian Marxist leadership. Despite efforts by Gulf-state donors, especially Saudi Arabia, to bolster the ELF in the face of the new challenge, after a brief but bloody civil war, the EPLF triumphed to become de facto the real voice of Eritrean aspirations to independence.

For a time independence looked like a losing proposition. Most Arab states publicly shunned the new movement; and after the 1974 pro-Communist coup in Addis Ababa, Moscow and Eastern Europe swung behind Ethiopia. The EPLF's principal source of external support became the Sudan, which took the opportunity to repay Ethiopia for its aid to the Sudan People's Liberation Army. But there was also an Eritrean Diaspora whose members were regularly shaken down for contributions; while the Eritrean Relief Association scoured the international scene to collect famine relief aid, some of which was undoubtedly diverted to the struggle. As the rebel movement's lock on the interior improved, it began to charge its own transit duties on goods moving between Ethiopia and the Eritrean ports. The EPLF also created underground factories to make everything from weapons to medicines to consumer goods, while covert support continued to come in from Syria and Iraq. Ultimately a tactical alliance between the EPLF and rebels inside Ethiopia proper brought down the Communist government and set the stage for Eritrea's secession.[32]

Cut off from the Red Sea, Ethiopia tried to compensate through ports in Djibouti. But originally they were too small and too poorly equipped to handle the volume of traffic. Hence Ethiopia began to dream of its own outlet to the sea. The most tempting target was Puntland, the northeast corner of Somalia wedged between the warring South and the seceded North. Under a breakaway faction of the Somali Salvation Democratic Front, Puntland had declared autonomy. But to seize a piece of Somalia, Ethiopia needed both a plausible pretext and Washington's permission. According to Ethiopian military intelligence, behind the Puntland secessionists could be found the plots of al-Ittihād, and behind them could be found the guiding hand of Usama bin Lāden. Puntland, it seemed, was destined to be the new Afghanistan and, with its well-known global communications and transportation infrastructure, the staging point for terror attacks worldwide. In the final analysis, probably the only thing that saved Puntland from forcible annexation to Ethiopia was an internal coup in 2002 that led to it renouncing its autonomous status and rejoining Somalia proper. By then, however, al-Ittihād al-Islāmiyya had earned a special place on the US post-9/11 hit list of forbidden organizations whose assets were to be frozen and contributors prosecuted.

It was an odd choice for inclusion on the list. For one thing, al-Ittihād was hardly the only "fundamentalist" movement in Somalia. The Muslim Brotherhood had a local affiliate, al-Harakat al-Islāh (the Reform Movement), not to be confused with al-Islāh al-Islāmiyya (Islamic Reform) or al-Harakat al-Islāmiyya (Islamic Movement), which were also busy in Somalia. In the realm of politics there was also the Hizb al-Islāmi (Islamic Party) of Somalia. On the other hand, Gama'at al-Tabligh al-Islāmi (Community to Deliver the Message of Islam) shunned politics but did campaign to persuade women to don the veil and men to shun qāt. Add to them the Abi al-Sunna wa al-Gama'a (Community of Sunnī Believers, more or less), the Somali Hizbullāh (Party of God), the Tahāluf al-Qabā'il al-Islāmiyah al-Muwāhada (United Alliance of Islamic Tribes), and several more. Some were of considerably greater consequence than al-Ittihād, especially after its military debacle.[33]

For another, apart from the Ogaden question, al-Ittihād had never shown any interest in events outside Somalia. Nor had it ever numbered more than a few hundred militants, as distinct from people who broadly supported its social program. (This paucity of numbers did not prevent the US from claiming that the group had two to four thousand members armed, while some reports in the Western press credited it with up to seventy thousand.) Furthermore, the sudden discovery that al-Ittihād had helped al-Qā'idah with the Nairobi and Dar es-Salaam bombings must have been a surprise to the US prosecutors who had certainly not been shy about casting the accusatory net as widely as they could. There were also claims that al-Ittihād, acting as Usama's local auxiliary, had aided Aideed in his confrontation with US forces in Muqdisho. Yet Aideed was vehemently anti-Islamist. Reputedly, when a business representative of bin Lāden's arrived in Somalia (probably looking to sell sesame and sorghum), that agent had to flee for his life on a qāt plane heading back to Kenya.[34] As to the alleged terrorist training camps jointly operated by the al-Ittihād and al-Qāʾidah (which, in the run-up to Gulf War II, Saddam Hussein, naturally, was helping to finance), they seemed to have vanished into thin desert air.

Ultimately the US claim of "links" between al-Ittihād and al-Qāʾidah was based on three pieces of evidence. One was that, while Usama was reclaiming land and building roads in Northern Sudan, Khartoum was (briefly) giving support to al-Ittihād in its (rather ineffective) quarrel with Ethiopia, which in turn was aiding the (considerably more serious) scorched-earth campaign of John Garang's SPLA. In short, al-Ittihād al-Islāmiyya was guilty not by association (with al-Qāʾidah) but by association with a country formerly associated with the alleged boss of another association, a remarkable new concept in law and diplomacy.

The second foundation stone for the claim that the two groups were in cahoots was that, during the Battle of Muqdisho, the United States intercepted communications in Arabic.[35] Aside from the fact that Usama and his followers are hardly the only native speakers of that tongue, hearing Arabic on the radio would not be exactly unexpected in Somalia: over the years the country had sent hundreds of thousands of guest workers to the Gulf states; its youth (when the schools operate) start to study the Qurʾān in Arabic at age five; the coastal elites often speak Arabic as a second language, a reflection of both their trade ties to the Middle East and the frequency with which they were educated in universities there; a knowledge of the language became even more desirable after Somalia, in a bid for aid money, defied ethnology and joined the Arab League; and, not least, Somalia's soldiers were routinely trained in Iraq, Syria, Libya, or Egypt.

In any case, Somalis hardly needed bin Lāden to show them the arts of war. Nor, after the slaughter of Aideed's clansmen and the kidnapping of Osman Hassan Ali, did they need al-Qāʾidah to teach them to hate the US military. And how a tall, pale (to Somalis) Saudi was supposed to impose his authority on a society inhabited by people who are loyal first to family, then to subgroup, then to clan (in that order), who are traditionally suspicious of strangers, and who refuse to take orders from any outsider or, for that matter, frequently from an insider, was not immediately self-evident.[36]

Still the story was too useful to die. In 2002 Hassan Aideed, son and heir of the late Mohammed Farah Aideed, offered to the US military bases in Somalia and promised to put his forces at US disposal to deal with all of the nasty al-Qāʾidah/al-Ittihād joint activities he claimed to know all about, in parts of the country still outside his own control.

There was also another third factor keeping al-Ittihād al-Islāmiya locked firmly in US sights: namely its supposed role on behalf of al-Qā'idah in moving terror-dollars through phony charities and underground banking systems. Thus did al-Ittihād, or, more specifically, a set of international banking institutions "linked" to it, become the most important target during the opening salvos of the financial War on Terror.

9

Terror Dollars and Nonsense – Finding, Freezing, and Seizing the Horde's Hoards

On 24 September 2001 the Bush administration issued an executive order under the International Emergency Economic Powers Act blocking property of and prohibiting transaction with persons "who commit, threaten to commit, or support terrorism." It was accompanied by a list of eleven organizations and fourteen individuals to which it immediately applied, with many more added in the weeks, months, and years to follow.[1] Shortly after the initial freezes came a new law, the Patriot Act, with a remarkable increase in government powers to find, freeze, and forfeit terror-dollars and to punish those who allegedly raised, moved, and used them.

Of course, an almost immediate freeze on these persons and groups raises a question: how did the authorities find out so much so fast? It was either such good police work as to belie the need for any additional powers, or the government was just waiting for an excuse to move against individuals and organizations targeted well before 9/11, for other reasons. In that second case the move was either crassly opportunistic or an implicit confession of criminal negligence.

The opening of a financial front of the anti-terror war was not restricted to the US. Naturally the British government panted along, tail wagging. And only four days after the US announcement, the UN Security Council adopted Resolution 1373, which required that all member states crack down on terrorist financing. To drive home the importance of "international cooperation," on 10 November 2001 George II stood before the General Assembly to declare: "Terrorist groups like al-Qaida need the support of a financial infrastructure." Therefore "we must pass all necessary laws in our own countries to allow the confiscation of terrorist assets. We must apply those laws to every financial institution in every nation."

Organizations, too, quickly signed on. Interpol joined with the US to create a worldwide terrorist-funding database.[2] The Financial Action Task Force, the US-dominated anti-money-laundering watchdog that had built its reputation on claims that the world was drowning in drug money, saw a way to protect and, if possible, extend its mandate. As one of its officers frankly explained, it was "logical" to see if reporting systems used to combat drug-money-laundering could be "expanded or used for other ends."[3] Although the US administration postured as if something revolutionary was in progress, the directives of autumn 2001 really grew out of a long history during which ever more attention had been focused on the financial side, first of crime, then of terror, then of their supposed satanic union, using ever-more sweeping and intrusive measures – without any real proof that they ever came close to accomplishing their declared objectives.

CUTTING THE SINEWS OF WAR?

After 9/11 two historically distinct trends came together. The first trend, that of modern economic warfare, manifested itself initially during the Napoleonic Wars, when both sides used trade embargoes and asset freezes to further their military and political goals. The US followed suit. It retaliated against Britain and France alike with Thomas Jefferson's Embargo Acts, whose passage through the Senate by an overwhelming majority President Jefferson prophetically secured by exaggerating the danger to US ships and commerce. The Acts gave him the opportunity to deploy the Army (along with threats of prosecution for treason) against the civilian population in an effort both to curb the smuggling that his own legislation had sparked and to intimidate secessionist forces in New England encouraged by the embargoes. Yet both Britain and France shrugged off the effects.[4]

Largely out of fashion in the nineteenth century, with the era's commitment to (selective) free trade, unregulated (or rather self-regulated) financial systems, and a general retreat of the state (except from its military and policing functions), economic warfare came roaring back in World War I. It became much more sophisticated in World War II, with black lists of individuals and companies suspected of trading with the enemy and with efforts to find and freeze enemy assets. Since then sanctions, embargoes, and asset freezes have been prominent tools of statecraft, overt and covert, unilateral or multilateral, on the assumption that financial measures can complement or even replace military ones to achieve political goals.[5]

In the us the most powerful tool of economic warfare derived from the 1917 Trading with the Enemy Act, which put the assets of persons and companies, foreign and domestic, controlled by or involved in trade or financial relations with the enemy, under the supervision of the Treasury, specifically a division later called the Office of Foreign Assets Control (OFAC). In 1977 this law was updated into the International Emergency Economic Powers Act. Although framed in general terms, the IEEPA was originally directed at the East Bloc. But the government was not blind to the problem of "terrorism." Starting in 1979 the Secretary of State began to report annually to Congress a list of countries that "repeatedly" provided support for "acts of international terrorism," to which trade and aid sanctions could be applied. Over time the State Supporters of Terrorism (SST) list has included Cuba, Iran, Iraq, Libya, North Korea, Sudan, Syria, and South Yemen (which got off the list by ceasing to exist). Although compiled by the State Department, this list, too, is supervised by OFAC.

Thus, for a time, the economic war on Communism and the financial war on terrorism were fought with distinct legislative weapons, although both were aimed at countries. But in 1995 the Clinton administration pioneered use of the IEEPA against nongovernmental groups. Although Clinton cited a national emergency: the objective was to defend not the us but the Oslo Accords between Israel and Palestine. Ten Palestinian groups who opposed, plus, to make a show of impartiality, two Jewish terrorist organizations, were placed on a list of Specially Designated Terrorists (SDT) with whom us residents were banned from conducting transactions. Once an organization (or individual) was listed on the basis of never-disclosed criteria, the Treasury gained virtually unlimited powers to shut it down, grab its assets, and seize its records – with very limited rights to appeal. The Clinton-era precedent was precisely what Bush followed in September 2001 before his own anti-terror-dollar law was passed.

Although IEEPA violations could be treated as criminal offenses, that was rare. A criminal procedure gave a defendant additional rights, although not the right to challenge the designation of a group as a proscribed organization. Hence four years after 9/11 not one organization (or officer thereof) added to the index by the Bush administration had been convicted of a terrorism-related criminal offense. Why bother? Seizing the assets and records, and closing the offices, generally sufficed to knock the target out of existence.[6]

Other measures to combat terrorist financing were explicitly criminal in nature – and they, too, predated Bush. The year after the Clinton regime began to turn the IEEPA from an administrative measure against countries into a tool for political vendetta, it secured passage of the Comprehensive Anti-Terrorism and Effective Death Penalty Act. Apart from undermining writs of habeas corpus, permitting the Immigration and Naturalization Service to deport immigrants using secret evidence, and allowing the CIA and military intelligence to conduct domestic espionage (provided they could concoct a link to an external threat), it created a new criminal offense – material assistance to terrorism. True, supporting terrorism was already a crime; but courts had held that someone who assisted an organization with both legal and illegal functions could only be criminally responsible if they intended to aid the illegal. In its words, there was a fundamental difference between someone who actually committed terrorist acts and "persons who merely associated with terrorist organizations." For years the pro-Israel lobby had pushed for a new law (aimed at US-based advocates of Palestinian rights) that would facilitate prosecution of people who funded such groups, even if the individual was unaware of the planned use of the funds.[7] On the first anniversary of the Oklahoma City bombing, it got its wish. The law represented, like RICO before it, another effort at backhanded criminalization by association fully five years before 9/11 and the Patriot Act.

The law also provided for another list: Foreign Terrorist Organizations. Subsequently the State Department's Office of the Coordinator for Counterterrorism scanned the world for targets that met the statutory criteria: foreign; engaged in terrorist activity *or* with the capability and intent to do so; and threatening the security of US nationals or the USA itself, including its national defense, foreign relations, or economic interests. Once an organization was so designated, it became illegal for any US citizen or resident to provide to it "material support or resources." Furthermore if a "financial institution" became aware that it held funds in which an FTO or its agent had "an interest," it had to freeze the funds and report to OFAC, or just pass the money on to OFAC for custody. SST, SDT, FTO – the current alphabet soup of terrorist lists was rapidly taking shape, and there were more to come.

To differentiate his own powerful name-and-declaim measures from those of his limp-wristed predecessor, George II created by executive order a Specially Designated Global Terrorists (SDGT) list, which soon grew to include more than three hundred names and was turned over to OFAC for the usual treatment. Then, to clarify matters, the Specially Designated Nationals and Blocked Persons (SDN) master list combined the SDG, SDGT and the FTO – and then some. The SDN now includes about five thousand individuals, organizations, and countries named under not only the terrorism laws but also the different sanctions programs. Apart from being supervised by OFAC, what the lists have in common is that it is never clear how any person or group got on them, or how they might get off. Decisions are based on secret information from the intelligence agencies. They, in turn, get most of their "intelligence" if not from the morning newspaper (whose stories might well be based on leaks or rumors from the same intelligence agencies) then from undercover informants who realize fully well that their value, and their paychecks, depend on a steady flow of tips, the more unverifiable the better. This gives informants ample opportunity and incentive to embellish, invent, or simply settle a few personal or political scores. Meantime equally objective information keeps pouring into the State Department directly or via accommodating congressmen from all those taxpayer-funded "think tanks" with ethnopolitical axes to grind.

That did not quite end the matter. There is also the recent Terrorist Exclusion List (TEL), maintained by the State Department and operated in consultation with the attorney general to prevent individuals "associated" with "terrorist organizations" from entering the US, or to deport them if they are already there.[8]

While the various economic-warfare measures were being modified to strike at organizations rather than states, something else was progressing along a second, parallel path. Although European precedents existed for seizing assets of those convicted of crimes or treason, such actions were presumed to be punishment, not prevention. The notion that finding, freezing, and forfeiting illegally obtained assets could remove both the motive and the means for further crimes and therefore serve to pre-empt them, was very much US-style in conception, elaboration, and execution. It resulted from the interaction of an accident of legal history with a law-enforcement myth.

Because the US constitutional makeup left criminal justice largely to individual states, most early federal crime-control forays like drug controls or booze prohibition had to be dressed up as fiscal measures. That usually put the Treasury in the frontlines of any ensuing "crime war" – with the resulting Hollywood image, somewhat baffling to the rest of the world, of US cops kicking down doors, flashing badges, and brandishing guns at cowering criminals while proudly announcing their identity as "Treasury agents."

This constitutional quirk was reinforced by the myth that the Italian gangsters during Prohibition had been brought to book when the IRS nailed Al Capone. This was reputedly the first time that law enforcement successfully shifted its focus from the crime per se to the money trail. The result was that income-tax law and, somewhat later, money-laundering regulations supplemented by asset-forfeiture laws became, in the minds of police and prosecutors, initially a useful auxiliary tool for enforcement and subsequently the ultimate means for pre-emption and prevention. That spirit would soon infuse and confuse the Terror War as well.

Two legislative weapons were particularly significant. The 1970 Bank Secrecy Act imposed new financial reporting requirements to facilitate the tracing of ostensibly illicit money. Then the 1986 Money Laundering Control Act broadened those requirements, strengthened penalties, and, for the first time, criminalized the act of money-laundering. Each had within it two quite distinct objectives: help find illegal funds and ease legal requirements for forfeiting them. To achieve the first, the federal government, in the original acts and subsequent amendments, imposed various requirements: that each deposit in or withdrawal from banks of more than $10,000 in cash be accompanied by the filing with Treasury of a Currency Transaction Report (CTR); that Treasury be informed on a Currency and Monetary Instruments Report of each movement of more than $5,000 in cash or monetary instruments in or out of the country; that with any cash purchase of luxury or durable goods costing more than $10,000, the identify of the transactor be similarly reported; and that banks and other financial institutions make Suspicious Activity Reports (SARs). There was a plan to follow with know-your-client (KYC) rules although it was temporarily blocked by a coalition of civil-rights groups and banking lobbyists. More recently, as concerns spread over possible illicit use of non-bank financial institutions, enhanced scrutiny has extended to everything from brokerage firms to check-cashing services, from exchange houses to wire transmitters. Then the fear frontier shifted to private banking and correspondent accounts. It later embraced so-called underground banking systems. Today law enforcement frowns in contemplation of the seemingly endless laundering capacities of emoney and the internet.

Although at first glance these proliferating regulations look like just another example of the irresistible bureaucratic urge to expand paperwork, they actually involve an insidious sequence. The need for a Currency Transaction Report is triggered automatically by a transaction above a certain sum; the bank acts as a passive conduit; and all parties (client, bank, and Treasury) are fully aware of what is happening. A Suspicious Activity Report, by contrast, is the initiative of the bank itself, which reacts to some feature of a client and/or the client's transaction to report that something seemed amiss; and it cannot inform the client of what is afoot without itself being subject to criminal penalty. A KYC rule shifts focus completely from a transaction to the individual behind the transaction, and more. For to "know" a client, logically a bank would have to know a client's clients, and maybe a client's client's clients. With a KYC rule, the bank ceases to be passive as with a CTR, or reactive as with a SAR, and becomes proactive – in effect, a police spy.

Measures to enhance reporting were accompanied by others to facilitate seizure. Riding a wave of Drug War hysteria, police forces got powers to grab all manner of assets, financial and physical, using civil and administrative rather than just criminal procedures. The result was to not just dramatically lower but actually reverse the burden of proof – it was up to people whose assets had been seized to demonstrate that their property was innocent or else it was automatically forfeit.[9] Enthusiasm in the US was greatly enhanced by the fact that seized assets go not to the Treasury but to the police. Despite a litany of legal horrors, with the mass media retailing tales of Colombian narcobarons reclining in gold-plated bathtubs and lighting Havana cigars with $100 dollar bills, the political will to call a halt was sapped. No one wanted to be seen or heard to be "soft on crime."[10] How much more so when the War on Terror permitted the government to effectively merge the economic warfare measures aimed at "terrorist" groups with the financial initiatives aimed at criminal money-laundering and to make both tributary to the newly expanded national-security functions at home and abroad.

PATRIOT GAMES

Although presented as an emergency response and rushed through Congress without scrutiny within weeks of 9/11, the key elements of the Patriot Act had been, like the subsequent invasions of Afghanistan and Iraq, just waiting for an opportune moment.[11] The law was/is so pervasive and invasive that it needed something like the post-9/11 panic to assure its passage. The preamble baldly proclaimed its scope: "An Act to deter and punish terrorist acts in the United States *and around the world*, to enhance law enforcement investigatory tools *and for other purposes*" [emphasis added].

Most subsequent criticism focused on non-financial aspects of the Act, such as those to turn loose US police and intelligence agencies to monitor private conversations and scan electronic communications almost at will. Less noticed but no less serious were the financial provisions concentrated mainly (though not exclusively) in Title III, the International Money Laundering Abatement and Anti-Terrorist Financing Act. Title III cited as its justification the IMF's claim that laundered funds total 2–5 percent of global GDP. Since the ratio of an unknowable to an unknown could yield any result from 0 to 100 percent, the IMF might be right. The Act further insisted that "money laundering … provides the financial fuel that permits transnational criminal enterprise to conduct and expand their operations to the detriment of the safety and security of American citizens." With that rationalization and rather awkward metaphor, the Act basically conceded to police and prosecutors their long-standing wish list, and more. Some of its measures were perhaps justifiable but bore no relationship to a War on Terror; others were sadly predictable; yet others were simply hair-raising. Combined, they attempted to turn the monetary system at home and abroad into a global espionage apparatus and a financial weapon of mass destruction.

There were some miscellaneous measures, incorporated to pander to this or that special interest group, to buy Congressional support or simply to hitch a legislative ride.[12] Those aside, the major thrust of the Act was in four directions. First, it dramatically changed reporting requirements by greatly extending the range of institutions covered, by shifting institutional obligations from passive to reactive-proactive, and by pulling the resulting information into a grand database that government agencies could access with few or no restrictions.[13]

Subsequent to the Act, all financial institutions were required to implement formal anti-money-laundering programs, no matter their need or capacity. In the securities business, for example, about ten thousand broker-dealers were required to file a Suspicious Activity Report on any transaction that "has no business or apparent lawful purpose or is not the sort in which a particular customer would normally be expected to engage." The law put the onus on the broker-dealer to determine if there was "no reasonable explanation for the transaction after examining the available facts, including the background and possible purpose of the transaction." The implication was that, in the future, anyone who bought or sold stocks, bonds, or commodities ran the risk that their broker might be peeking around lampposts to see if they spent their capital gains on popcorn or kiddy porn, on white powder or blasting powder. The result was to add thousands more to the annual list of about 125,000 SARs filed by other institutions without the slightest evidence they had made any difference to US crime rates. As to their potential use to pre-empt terrorism, when Mohammed Atta, operations chief of the 9/11 suicide pilots, arranged for a wire transfer of $69,985 from the UAE to his Florida account, the bank filed a SAR, but no one bothered to look at it.

In addition, the definition of financial institution was broadened to encompass virtually every business with a cash register. Any business accepting cash of more than $2,000 or more had to file a SAR if it thought the client was up to no good on pain of itself facing criminal charges. Leaving aside the question of whether it is really wise to entrust the job of assessing a client's moral character to a pawnbroker or used-car dealer, the reality is that, when and if operators of several hundred thousand small businesses did comply, their lack of training and their instinct for self-preservation would prompt them to mark a transaction "suspicious" any time someone entered their premises looking vaguely "A-rab."[14] Yet legislators so intent on tightening scrutiny of commercial clients and bank depositors had no qualms about easing requirements for gun ownership.

Then there were a series of new rules to enhance identification procedures, bringing in through the back door the kind of KYC rules that an outcry had stopped a few years earlier, only this time as an Act of Congress instead of a Treasury regulation. Simultaneously the thresholds at which some issuers of financial instruments had to make their mandatory reports were lowered, even though for years Treasury officials had complained of the enormous backlog the existing rules generated.

Some information from earlier reporting requirements had been intended strictly for tax enforcement and could be passed to other agencies only if certain privacy safeguards were respected. After the Patriot Act virtually all data from all reports became electronically retrievable by all government agencies, local, state, and federal, including the intelligence arms.[15]

The second general thrust of the Act was to demand changes in how banks and financial institutions did business, particularly but not exclusively with foreign clients. It required that US banks, when ordered by subpoena, produce evidence about foreign-held accounts. It demanded that they deny correspondent banking rights to any financial institution or country whom the US declared to be guilty of aiding terrorist activities. It required them to ensure that the banks for whom they function as correspondents themselves have proper procedures for monitoring their own clients, even if those clients had no business relations with the US. It banned US institutions from doing business with shell banks (name-plate "banks" set up in financial havens), and it ordered them to take "reasonable steps" to ensure that foreign banks for whom they operated correspondent accounts did not have shell banks as the foreign bank customer.[16]

In the same spirit, although banks (and some other financial institutions) had been expected to consult the OFAC lists, the Patriot Act demanded that they regularly consult "lists of known or suspected terrorists or terrorist organizations provided to the financial institution by *any* [emphasis added] government agency." This wording seemed to allow the Department of Energy, for example, to draw up a roster of anti-nuclear protestors, then make it available to banks so they could deny loans and cancel credit cards. Nor was consulting such lists merely an option. If financial institutions do not periodically check their customers against the updated lists, they can face up to $10 million in fines while their officials can land in prison for up to thirty years.

Among the problems raised by such lists is that all Muslims bear certain names specified in the Qur'ān. Although it stipulates a thousand possibilities (about half female), in practice, to show piety or to follow family traditions, parents choose relatively few. At one point Citibank reputedly found four hundred accounts in the name "Mohammed Atta."[17] Moreover, there is no universally agreed system to transliterate Arabic characters into Latin. And there are major variations in spelling conventions between countries where the indigenous language is other than Arabic (such countries accounting for more than 80 percent of the world's Muslim population).

One person who felt the consequences was a Somali living in Ottawa. He attempted to wire via Western Union the prodigious sum of $116 Canadian (about US$90) to a friend in the Netherlands named Mohammed Ali. Western Union checked the OFAC list to find on it Mohammed Ali, a name that occurs among Muslims with about the same frequency as Peter Smith among Anglo-Saxons. Even though the transaction was by a Canadian citizen in Canada to a friend in the

Netherlands and was handled by a Canadian office, that the transmitter was Western Union sufficed for the funds to be frozen.[18]

Third, the Act hiked the penalties for so-called money-laundering offenses and simplified their prosecution, as well as making seizures easier. For instance, existing statutes already permitted the US government to proceed against a person or institution for money-laundering on civil grounds. Anyone caught in the sights of that clause, facing the full power and resources of the US government, which had only to establish proof on a "preponderance of evidence" rather than "beyond reasonable doubt," would likely capitulate quickly and make the best deal they could. The power was broadened and extended to make it easier for the US government to so proceed against a foreign citizen or institution, too, on civil criteria in a US court.[19]

The Act also extended criminal powers. In the past, for example, someone caught taking more than the threshold amount of $5,000 in and out of the country without filing a report might have the money seized. Now it became a crime per se with no need to link the cash to any criminal origin.[20] One of the anti-money-laundering industry's house organs gravely approved with the observation that "Many of the hijackers flashed wads of large bills as they lived inconspicuously."[21] How it is possible to be inconspicuous while flashing wads of large-denomination bank notes was not explained.

One of the most dramatic measures dealt with seizures of suspect funds abroad. Previously the federal government had worked through treaties to request that a country home to a particular foreign bank freeze funds, then perhaps turn them over to the US, usually with the promise that any subsequently forfeited assets would be shared. But the Patriot Act (sec. 319a) stipulated that "if funds are deposited into an account at a foreign bank, and that foreign bank has an interbank account in the United States ... the funds shall be deemed to have been deposited into the interbank account in the United States" and therefore subject to seizure. Just to make sure there was no misunderstanding, the clause further noted that "it shall not be necessary for the government to establish that the funds are directly traceable to the funds that were deposited into the foreign bank." In other words, if, for example, Mohammed Atta and his friends kept their savings in a neighborhood branch of Deutsche Bank in Hamburg, the US Treasury could seize the equivalent amount from any account that Deutsche Bank held in Citibank, New York, without consultation with the German government. Since most of the world's major banks have interbank accounts with US institutions, the clause made the international financial system a free-fire zone for Treasury and Justice officials. Since judges who approve seizures usually seal the records, foreign institutions had little or no information on which to base a protest. As one federal functionary gloated: not only could the government now grab all kinds of goodies but also "you could knock the economy of a country on its head if it were a big enough case."[22]

Fourth, the Act gave even more arbitrary power to the federal government (in addition to its capacity to freeze and seize interbank accounts) to shake down other countries by holding the contents of their banks, and indeed the health of their very financial systems, to ransom. The Secretary of the Treasury could decide that a certain place or institution was a "primary money laundering concern" and take action. At the mildest, this could involve the imposition of special record-keeping requirements on all transactions done by US banks with the target. At the strongest, the US could prohibit access to the US-run international clearing systems to particular institutions or entire countries.

In addition, the president could expropriate sovereign assets of other countries just by issuing a "finding" (sort of a secular fatwā) that their governments support "terrorism." This might mean that, when a country, especially one in the Middle East, refused to allow US law-enforcement agencies to fish through its bank records, the US could freeze assets held by that country or its leaders in US institutions.

Despite the unprecedented range and scope of the measures, the hyper-patriotic ambiance assured criticism that the Act did not go far enough.[23] Immediately on passage, the anti-money-laundering industry – lawyers, professional investigators, security consultants, and firms making "compliance software" – peddled their services with increased vigor, creating more vested interests to fight any future attempts to water down the law.[24]

Perhaps as important, at least in the short run, was the change in ambiance. After the collective drug-induced psychosis had peaked and public interest in the Drug War began to wane, most businesses conducted their responsibilities under anti-money-laundering statutes in a pro forma way. But when the object became to fight Islamic terror, they fell over themselves to appear to be doing their duty. Thus, a number of US citizens or long-standing legal residents of Pakistani background, despite perfect credit histories, suddenly received demands from their credit-card companies to submit bank records and tax returns on pain of having their cards cancelled. When queried, the companies cited "security reasons." Some of the clients did not comply – and the cards were cancelled. Some complied – and the cards were still cancelled. None of those whose cards were cancelled was on any OFAC list.[25]

Even the process of paying down a credit line could lead to similar results. When, early in 2006, a Texas family of impeccable all-American credentials tried to pay off a large outstanding balance on their Master-Card, they found that their check was sent not to the bank but to a bureaucrat in the new Department of Homeland Security, for scrutiny. Since the amount on the check was deemed larger than the norm of credit-card repayments, the funds were frozen.[26]

That change of ambiance had another, potentially enormous, impact on how financial institutions behaved toward clients. Scarcely appreciated at the time or at least not publicly admitted, the new stress on terror-dollars transformed the way in which financial managers and employees looked at their clients' affairs even in the context of previous legislation. With criminal money, their primary responsibilities were to examine what came *into* their institution – was the size or origin or type of the deposit consistent with the business profile or lifestyle of the particular client, or could there be something suspicious about the *origin* of the funds? Now the focus became what went *out* of their institution – in other words, who was going to receive the withdrawal, transfer, or remittance, and why?[27]

Furthermore, with the capacity of spooks and cops to tap into what had become one giant financial database, they did not have to wait for banks to tip them off. When Badr al-Hamzi, a Saudi radiologist, was arrested by the FBI, shackled, and held incommunicado in San Antonio, his offense had been to make large money transfers from the Middle East, then to book five airline tickets through an online service, supposedly the pattern used by the hijackers the day before 9/11. The money transfers were to fund his medical residency at the University of Texas and the tickets were for him and his family to attend a medical conference. He was cleared and released within twenty-four hours.[28] Few were so lucky.

It was not just the anti-money-laundering statutes that were strengthened. For instance, the Patriot Act expanded the definition of what constituted "material aid" to terrorism to include provision of expert advice and assistance, false documents, lodging, training, communication equipment, lethal substances, weapons, explosives, transportation facilities, personnel, etc. As before, there was no requirement that the aid be actually connected to misdeeds – it could be for completely peaceful

purposes. The offense lay in assisting an "organization," even to provide
baby formula to the starving infant son of a slain militant. Nor was there
any need to prove intent. Meanwhile Attorney General John Ashcroft endorsed the idea of the death penalty for "material support."[29] In a similar
spirit, the Patriot Act amended the IEEPA to authorize the Treasury to
freeze assets on the mere assertion that an individual or entity was under
investigation for potentially violating the IEEPA.

Remarkably, too, but little noticed in all the furor, Title VIII Section
813 explicitly declared that acts of terrorism were to be included in the
definition of racketeering activity. Therefore it swept away remaining
legal hesitations over the use of RICO to go after anyone (and their
assets) designated as a terrorist, from bin Lāden on down, whether in
civil or in criminal actions. Not surprisingly, the Patriot Act was followed by a minor deluge of civil suits for enormous sums directed at
the world's "financiers of terrorism."

Once on the books the Patriot Act, much like RICO but far more
quickly, was used to prosecute every offense from drug trafficking to espionage, from white-collar crime to blackmail.[30] Within weeks of passage the provisions intended to help seize terror-dollar equivalents
from interbank accounts were used to grab money from an account
held by a Belize bank in a US institution, not to stop another suicide
hijacker but to compensate presumed US victims of a fraud run by a
Belize lawyer and financial manager.[31]

There was also a series of later measures to complement the chase for
terror-dollars. For example, in the past, financial institutions such as
banks were subject to administrative subpoenas ("national security letters") from the FBI to get them to produce financial records in terrorism or espionage investigations. But a new measure tucked away in the
fiscal 2004 intelligence community authorization bill (to force any who
objected to it to defend why they were trying to impede anti-terrorist intelligence gathering) required the same information from securities
brokers, currency exchanges, car dealers, travel agencies, post offices,
casinos, pawnbrokers, and other institutions doing cash transactions
"with a high degree of usefulness in criminal, tax, and regulatory matters"[32] – as if it were possible to find anything that could not be interpreted to fall into such a category.

Other laws had the appearance of simply administrative devices but
had a deeper purpose – for example, a provision for better imaging
technology for checks to facilitate them being scanned immediately
into central databases. Supposedly to facilitate clearing, it also, not

coincidentally, facilitated greatly spooks and cops knowing just who is paying what, when, where, and to whom.[33] More importantly, the Patriot Act was followed by sweeping changes in the administration of justice. With the creation of the Department of Homeland Security, the Treasury lost its two most important criminal enforcement arms – Customs and the Secret Service (in charge of, among other matters, combating counterfeiting) to the new bureaucracy. It responded by merging its Financial Crimes Enforcement Network (FinCEN) with OFAC to create a new Office of Terrorism and Financial Intelligence in an attempt to restore its lost pride and public profile.[34]

Of course, rules and regulations are meaningless without means of implementation. Hence, bolstered by new legal powers, a multi-agency task force headed by Customs launched Operation Green Quest to "target" terrorist funds in the United States and abroad with about the same degree of accuracy that US and UK bombers achieved at Dresden in 1945.[35]

10

Quartermasters of Terror – Inscrutable Orientals and Underground Banks

By 9/11, law enforcement felt it had a fair grip on the techniques by which criminals created, managed, and moved their loot. The problem had been that legislatures and courts refused to permit the cops to burrow deep enough into the catacombs of clandestine finance, or gave them only picks and shovels instead of dynamite and bulldozers, much less the financial equivalent of a nuclear bunker-buster, to do the job. The Patriot Act was heavy equipment long overdue. But, to handle terror-dollars, more was required.

Criminal money begins life as an outcast, then usually ends up blending with respectable society. Terror money generally does the reverse, making it harder to spot until after the fact. A war on terror-dollars, too, demands action on three levels: to neutralize hoards before they can be deployed; to block the channels through which money flows from source to user; and to close mechanisms by which funds can be replenished. To do all that, the administration needed the help not just of old-fashioned cops with newfangled tools but of national-security experts capable of innovative and independent thinking.

THE HORDE'S HOARDS

One body eager to assist was the Council on Foreign Relations, which, it claims, "takes no institutional position on policy issues and has no affiliation with the U.S. government." Its president, Leslie Gelb, a former

State and Pentagon apparatchik, senior politico-military aide in the
Carter administration, and, later, *New York Times* editorial writer (where
he demanded that Israel stand firm against the Palestinians and called
for the de facto dismemberment of Occupied Iraq) appointed an Independent Task Force on Terrorist Financing. To ensure impartiality,
he appointed as chair, Maurice Greenberg, an outstanding financial
mind who had built his American International Group into the country's
dominant force in insurance. Greenberg showed much the same degree of "independence" from the toing and froing of everyday politics
as did the Council's president and hence could be relied upon to deliver the same kind of objective judgement. After all, Greenberg had
declined Ronald Reagan's offer of deputy directorship of the CIA. Still,
in time off from building up a personal net worth of $3.5 billion, he
contributed generously to public service. He was a heavy donor to the
campaigns of both Georges – George I took Greenberg on his 1992
Asia Trade Mission, after which (surely as a result of sheer merit), AIG
was the first foreign company allowed to sell insurance in China. And
Greenberg funded the Heritage Foundation, which produced objective
studies on things like the need to cut taxes for the USA's rich and to impose "democracy" on the Arab East.

Gelb arranged for the Task Force to be codirected by two men of
appropriate experience: William Wechsler was a former speechwriter
for the chairman of the Joint Chiefs of Staff and former director of
transnational threats for the Clinton National Security Council; Lee
Wolosky was a former National Security Council member with a stint at
the Georgetown University Center for Strategic and International Studies, affectionately known as UCIA.[1] Their report took swipes at the
Saudi government; lauded the Patriot Act but complained that it did
not go far enough; insisted that the main problem in dealing with
terror-dollars was "lack of political will among U.S. allies"; attacked European states for failing to imitate US anti-money-laundering models;
recycled fables about bin Lāden's wealth; and noted sagely that "Al-
Qaeda's financial network is characterized by layers and redundan-
cies."[2] (How they knew that when the financial sleuths in Treasury, the
FBI, and the CIA were all baffled in their hot pursuit of the money trail,
was never explained.) The report, too, insisted that al-Qā'idah received
funding from charities and direct donors from "all corners of the
Muslim world" and then "moves its money through banks in virtually
every corner of the world." However some corners were more important than others. "For years al-Qaeda has been particularly attracted to

operating in underregulated jurisdictions, places with limited bank supervision, no anti-money laundering laws, ineffective law enforcement institutions, and a culture of no-questions-asked bank secrecy." To find such facilities, al-Qā'idah "did not have to look far." Dubai was singled out as a place where "Many prominent Islamic banks operate under loose regulatory oversight." The Task Force noted that al-Qā'idah was not the only problem. "Other Islamic terrorist organizations, Hamas and Hezbollah specifically, often use the very same methods – and even the same institutions – to raise and move their money." Neither, of course, were then in direct conflict with the us, but both were locked in a bitter struggle with Israel.

But would a financial war on terror actually work? Yes, according to William Wechsler, who in subsequent press conferences argued that the best proof was the great success achieved previously. "We have," he noted, "been going after organized crime's financial network since we put Al Capone away."[3]

Although virtually everything in the report turned out to be flat wrong, that did not deter the Council on Foreign Relations from putting much the same team of luminaries to work on a second one a couple years later.[4] Shortly after, the chairman had his own date with financial destiny. Maurice Greenberg's insurance conglomerate had forced, before firing them, some of its us technical staff to train foreign cheap-labor replacements, then bragged about the money it saved; and it had landed a contract from the Connecticut State Treasurer to manage $100 million of state pension money after paying a $500,000 "finder's fee" to a lobbyist, only to have the state treasurer convicted of taking kickbacks. Following his company's admission that "bad accounting" had reduced its book value by $1.77 billion, Greenberg stepped down as CEO – after he had conferred on his wife ownership of $2.2 billion in AIG shares.[5] When this former head of an enquiry into clandestine financing was approached by government investigators in a criminal investigation, he refused to answer any questions.[6]

Nonetheless his Task Force left an important legacy – it had confirmed the accuracy of the Bush administration's judgement with respect to at least one of the major riddles of 9/11. Usama and his ilk, it seems, had mastered an "ancient secret system" that could make money disappear and reappear magically almost anywhere in the world just by chanting the correct code words or flashing the right hand-signals.[7] The hawāla system, the Task Force concurred, "appears custom-made for al-Qaeda."[8] The us Treasury elaborated that hawāla was "a big problem for us" while simultaneously admitting that it had no idea how it operated.[9] After hearing such claims, not only did reporters rush off to haunt the bazaars of the Middle East and Southwest Asia in search of this numismatic version of the Philosopher's Stone, but they soon conjured up from old files stories about a similar phenomenon known among a small circle of law-enforcement initiates as the "Chinese underground banking system." Could it be that al-Qā'idah had adapted to its needs the technology used by the notorious Triads to manage their take from the world heroin market?

THOSE INSCRUTABLE ORIENTALS!

In reality "underground banking systems" are generally benign in origin and operation. For example, the infamous Chinese fei ch'ien (flying money) was invented not to permit money to evade the sight and grasp of the authorities but to facilitate taxation. The imperial government needed a safe means to move tax receipts from the provinces to the capital; while tea merchants coming to the capital faced the insecurity of a long trip back after they had sold their produce. So the merchant deposited money from tea sales with the office each provincial governor kept in the capital and received a certificate. On his return home, the merchant presented the certificate and was paid out of tax money collected locally, thus eliminating the danger and inconvenience for both parties of long-distance movement of silver.[10] Once the Chinese Diaspora – living in a context of mistrust of formal banks, political turmoil, and persecution of Chinese minorities – wedded informal banking institutions with the technique of flying money, the modern "Chinese underground banking system" was born.[11]

Similar phenomena arose elsewhere, from the Middle East (mainly to facilitate trade without violating the Islamic ban on usury) to Colombia (where it evolved to finance imports from the US at a time when Colombia had strict exchange controls). Nor is the mechanism alien to the West's own history. If Muslim terrorists in recent years actually did use the system to attack Western targets, they were just reversing what had occurred during the Crusades when the Knights Templar employed such a mechanism to run funds to Palestine to pay the costs of sacking cities and massacring civilian populations. Far from covert operators, the Templars were the supreme financial power of their day.[12]

The spread of informal methods to move money is often linked to two growing, and related, tendencies: non-European minorities taking root in the West and transactions taking place across borders but within extended families or ethnoreligious groups. Entrepreneurs of a "trade diaspora" typically make no distinction between social and economic life.[13] Their business firms are international, even intercontinental, extensions of kinship structures. Not only might they feel ill at ease with banking institutions in the host country, but sending money to and from their places of origin could be complicated by poor financial infrastructure or exchange controls.

After 9/11, most attention was riveted on the Indo-Pakistani hawāla system and its offshoots across the Indian Ocean in places like Somalia.[14] This system, too, has legitimate origins, even if hawāldars have recently gained notoriety for black-market foreign-exchange dealings and gold smuggling. India, before the modern era, was dotted with informal financial institutions ranging from village money-lenders to rotating-credit associations.[15] The role of hawāla was to bring long-distance financial services to areas not served by banks – which were, even in the big cities, mistrusted as British-colonial institutions.[16] Hawāla was so much part of the normal business scene in British India that its rules were incorporated into formal commercial law.[17] With the spread of an Indian trade diaspora, the system moved with it, handling commercial payments as well as remittances to family members back home.[18] It was further entrenched during World War II, when British intelligence used hawāldars with family members in Axis-controlled areas to run money to pay for espionage operations and to help identify enemy agents, including those agitating for Indian independence.[19]

After the war, India divided into two intensely hostile states, each with the problem of resettling tens of millions of people who had been forced to abandon homes on opposing sides of the ceasefire lines. With no formal relations between the two countries, people turned to the hawāldars to liquidate property and to move assets from Pakistan to India and vice versa. Their importance grew further during the 1963 Indo-Pakistan war, when India, to try to conserve foreign exchange, discourage hoarding, and reduce tax evasion, banned gold imports and severely restricted individual holdings – in a country that historically had the world's greatest hunger for gold. The result was to call up a gold-smuggling infrastructure that soon linked up with, and gave a new urgency to, the hawāla system.

With the post-1973 oil boom, Indian and Pakistan workers flooded into the Gulf states. If they remitted hard-currency earnings to their families through the formal banking system, the money would be converted into rupees (the local currency) at the official rate, and the authorities could trace the flow for tax purposes. On the other hand, Indian and Pakistani gold smugglers bought gold for hard currency but were paid in rupees back home. In the absence of an alternative mechanism, the rupees would be converted to hard currency in India or Pakistan at the black-market rate and physically smuggled out. Into the breach stepped the hawāldars. Earnings by émigré workers in hard currency would be collected in the Arab Gulf states and turned over to the gold exporters. Gold would move across to India or Pakistan. The gold importer would pay through a hawāldar (sometimes they were the same person) the equivalent sum to the family of the émigré worker in rupees at the black-market rate. No monetary instrument had to pass across borders or cross oceans.

Far from being mysterious or illegal, the core mechanism in "underground banking"– the compensating balance – is quite normal, particularly in dealings with countries with exchange controls and/or legally inconvertible currencies. If Business I in Country A owes $X to Business II in Country B, while Business II in country B owes $X to Business III in Country A, to settle the debts without compensating balances, Business I would send via its banker $X to Business II, and Business II would then send via its banker $X to Business III. This requires two international transfers and four distinct withdrawal and deposit transactions. To settle the debts with compensating balances, Business I in Country A settles the debt owed by Business II to Business III in Country A. There are only two banking transactions, from the account of Business I to the account of Business III and no international transfers.

In practice the exchanges are multilateral and the sums do not exactly balance. But the principle remains; the practice is commonplace; and legitimate brokers specialize in making the arrangements. Such transfers are common, for example, in the legal foreign-exchange business. A currency house might accept a deposit of dollars, for example, in New York, then instruct a German affiliate to make the Deutschmark equivalent available in Frankfort, awaiting a reverse flow when other clients make the opposite transaction.

If the system operates informally, much the same occurs. Someone in Country A seeking to move funds abroad contacts the broker and deposits a certain sum. The broker sends a message to their correspondent to credit the equivalent of the deposited sum (less the fee) to a foreign bank account in the name of the person seeking to move the money out of Country A. The offsetting transaction occurs when someone abroad attempts to move money into Country A. Since no two transactions are likely to offset each other, informal bankers run up debt and credit balances with each other and eventually engage in their own clearing operations by check or wire transfers between accounts the informal bankers maintain in regular banks. Not only can informal bankers often do the transmission job better than formal ones, but they can survive and flourish under conditions in which mainstream competitors collapse.[20]

Nor is the system particularly secret. Unless the identity, wealth, and trustworthiness of the two parties handling transactions on behalf of a third are well known and well established, the system could not possibly function. Hawāla contracts are often negotiated in front of witnesses; the customer usually leaves with a receipt of some sort; and records are kept, even if not in the form demanded of mainstream institutions by bureaucrats. If someone really seeks a low profile, they would usually be better off dealing with the private-banking departments of formal financial institutions, which offer the full paraphernalia of shell corporations, offshore trusts, and coded bank accounts in dozens of secrecy havens around the world.

Granted, the "underground banking system" can be used for illegal operations. Gold smuggling and exchange-control evasion fit that category – in India, but not in Dubai, the financial fulcrum for the Indian Ocean-Persian Gulf hawāla system. But obviously so can formal banks. In fact a case could be made that, particularly in Western countries, hawāla operators are probably more leery than orthodox bankers of being caught handling illegal funds – the scandal could threaten the networks of trust that are the sine qua non of the system. Arguably, too, they "know" their clients in a more thorough way than orthodox financial institutions. Anyway, in terms of world totals, it is reasonable to suppose that the amounts of illegal money flowing through informal banks are trivial compared to those handled by the legal system.[21]

Hawāla persists not because of the nefarious designs of Chinese heroin smugglers or of Arab terrorist plotters but because it is efficient and, for lower-income groups, cheap. Contrary to normal banks, who discriminate in favor of big customers, hawāla operators usually charge lower fees to poorer clients whose remittances are proportionately smaller. Since the system fits into a matrix of ethnoreligious ties, it is also well trusted. The fact that hawāla for Muslims is an alternative to usury-based banks is another asset.[22]

Even if hawāla may seem an ethnocentric oddity in countries where orthodox banks are advanced and efficient, it is vital in situations where the formal financial system either is costly and bureaucratic or has broken down completely. In Afghanistan, for example, even when its banking system did operate, most people preferred to use the hawāla dealers who had financial links across the country and on into Peshawar and Dubai. They handled foreign-exchange transactions and international remittances, offered deposit facilities, and even provided microfinancing for small enterprises. Far from unregulated, the system was superintended by the old and respectable Hawalah Dealers' Association. It survived revolution, war, and even US invasion after the formal system ceased to function and the local currency became widely discredited – not only because of the impact of war but also because the Rabbani government, once tossed out by the Tāliban, continued to flood the country with now-illegal notes and because other warlords issued their own currencies, designed to closely imitate the official one.[23]

The US, in posting its October 2001 hit list, claimed proof that bin Lāden used hawāla to move money in and out of Afghanistan, and it froze the assets of (among others) Haji Abdul Manan Agha, whose Al Qadir Traders, a large hawāla house, was based in Quetta, Pakistan.[24] Yet if Usama really used hawāla to move money, it was not because the system was so well adapted to covert operations but because there was simply no other means (in part because the US-sponsored sanctions had finished off the formal banking system), short of a money belt, to do so.[25] Maybe Usama learned about it by watching the CIA in the 1980s, who had similarly used it to move money to mujahideen commanders; while tribal chiefs in the Pashtun border area relied on the hawāla system, which in some cases they run, to finance their worldwide traffic in weapons skimmed from those thoughtfully provided in the 1980s by the US and Saudi governments. Indeed, even the US-installed post-Tāliban regime in Afghanistan started to use hawāla to make remittances to government functionaries in the provinces – it was more secure and more honest. So did the World Bank.[26]

Yet it seemed to take very little to convince the US authorities that hawāla was, as the Task Force warned them, "tailor made" for al-Qā'idah. If no one could pin down a single instance when it was used to move funds for a terrorist attack, that was obviously because it was so secretive. That must have been a surprise to most hawāla operators, who are very well-known in their area of operation, rarely deal with people outside their communities, transact deals before witnesses, and even produce receipts on request. Throughout Pakistan, until recently, newspapers routinely published two exchange rates, the official and the ever-so-secret hawāla one.

Still, the uproar provided a golden opportunity to advance some causes and settle some scores. Formal banks around the world wanted to eliminate competition from informal ones; governments wanted to bring loose cash into regular financial institutions where it could be made available for formal investments.[27] Hence around the world regulations were tightened or in some cases introduced for the first time. In the US, for example, an amendment introduced into financial regulations by the Patriot Act changed the law regarding money transmitters who operated without state licenses. While in the past it had been a crime to "intentionally" conduct such an "illegal" business, the Patriot Act dropped the requirement of proving intent and changed "illegal" to "unlicensed." In effect it became a crime per se to operate without a state license whether or not the person knew it was required. Yet the offense carried the same penalties as it had when the act was done willfully.[28] One person who felt the consequences was Ahmed Abdu, a Sudanese living in Brooklyn. After he had wired money to banks abroad, the authorities seized $310,000 from correspondent accounts held in Citibank, Standard Chartered, and HSBC-USA on behalf of the recipient foreign banks. Ahmed Abdu later pleaded guilty not to plotting to crash a plane into a nuclear power plant but to running an unlicensed money-changing business.[29]

Pakistan, too, in its efforts in the War on Terror, legislated control of hawāla bankers. Of course it was only by happenstance that such a law was expected to increase business for state-owned banks, curb capital flight, and improve tax collection. Bangladesh also cited anti-crime and anti-terror purposes, when the real issue was that nearly half of its foreign-exchange earnings came home through the parallel market. And it tried to draw its hawāldars under the regulatory net just when a new remittance service backed by the formal banks and the government was to go into operation.[30] While both Pakistan and Bangladesh had functioning (if slow and bureaucratic) formal banking system to pick up the slack, the crackdown on hawāla was a near catastrophe for one of the places in the world that could least afford the loss.

QAT-ASTROPHE IN SOMALIA

The notion that Somalia was financing terror by illegal money transfers from the West dates at least back to the 1993 Battle of Muqdisho. Afterwards US Immigration and Naturalization Service (INS) and police harassed Somali exiles, who were presumed to be dope-crazed welfare

bums dripping with US blood. Even in Canada, normally more generous to refugees, the right-wing press leapt on cases of Somali welfare
fraud to denounce the country's "over-generosity." The best-publicized
instance occurred in Toronto in 1993, when police arrested one brother
and two sisters of Mohammed Farah Aideed's reputed military counsel-
lor. Supposedly his six brothers and sisters, two wives, and thirteen children had been instructed to get on the welfare rolls under false names,
then remit money to buy weapons. A little later in Québec, provincial
authorities claimed that over half of 730 Somali welfare dossiers investigated in the previous two years showed "anomalies." The police
charged more than one hundred people – for double drawing on their
welfare, not for terrorism or weapons trafficking.[31]

Then came 9/11. Probably no country in the world was hit harder by
the aftershocks than Somalia, then kept alive by remittances that not only
fed the population but also financed the few oases of functioning private
enterprise in an economic desert.[32] When the US declared its intent to attack "terrorist finance," and the media carried lurid stories of Usama receiving money from Somali charities funded by Somali refugees in the
US, people in the Diaspora feared that if they continued to send money
home, they would be, at best, exposed as illegal immigrants or, at worst,
rounded up as supporters of terrorism. Even if they had wanted to send
more, it had become almost impossible. Somalia had ceased years before
to have a functioning formal banking system. The only way to make international transfers with a reasonable chance of timely arrival had been via
precisely the institutions now firmly in US sights.[33]

Although several hawāla bankers operated in and out of Somalia, the
most important was Al Barakaat. It was founded by Ahmed Nur Ali
Juma'ale, a former banker, in 1989, after the outbreak of civil war. In
addition to a fast, cheap, and reliable money-transmitting network,
from a headquarters in Dubai its owner ran construction, telegraph,
and transportation companies and a cellphone system. Al Barakaat was
no stranger to controversy. In 1999 its Boston branch had attracted attention from its banker, the Bank of Boston, because of cash payments
into its account just below the $10,000 reporting threshold. Since the
Bank of Boston had been previously been embroiled in an epic money-
laundering scandal, it quickly closed the account.[34] Barakaat Boston
was able to open new ones in other banks. However, it found itself on a
watch list not for terrorism but for handling payments from Somalis
suspected of welfare fraud or importing qāt, the latest killer drug to rav-
age US youth.

Then came 9/11 and accusations that Al Barakaat's founder had "befriended" Usama bin Lāden during the Afghan war (a charge that, if fairly applied, might have landed the whole Reagan administration in jail), that bin Lāden had provided capital to the Juma'ale group (which presumably would make bin Lāden a financier of Somali remittances rather than of terrorism), and that the institution was a front for (according to the US Treasury actually "controlled by") al-Ittihād al-Islāmiyya, the Somali affiliate of al-Qā'idah International. Allegedly, when Somalis used it to send money home, the legitimate funds were comingled (a favorite drug-war buzzphrase) with terror-dollars, and some were siphoned off to al-Ittihād and/or al-Qā'idah to buy weapons. The estimate from Treasury was that Al Barakaat remitted to Somalia about $400 million per annum from which it skimmed for its terrorist owners 5 percent – the resulting $20 million was about five times the total profit the company reported from its remittance business.[35] Apparently Al Barakaat sent so much money to al-Qā'idah that, when it put its cellphone network in place in Somalia, it had to borrow the money from the US company that actually set up the technical system. On top of cash came arms – intelligence was so specific that Treasury officers pinpointed one arms shipment arranged by Al Barakaat for al-Qā'idah with the contents recorded as "blankets," a callous attempt to use humanitarian aid to hide instruments of terror and destruction.[36]

Hence, when the Treasury moved to close Al Barakaat's eight US offices, it stripped them to the bare walls, taking the computers, cash, records, etc. – the only thing left behind was the trash, which had, no doubt, been thoroughly searched. In Seattle the raids also hit a minimart that shared facilities with the local Al Barakaat – the feds took care to also remove the food and the cash register.[37] The freeze on Al Barakaat's US assets was declared by Treasury to be "the most conspicuous act" of the financial war on terrorism to date.[38] Its deputy secretary bragged before the House Financial Services Committee that Al Barakaat was the first test case of the new Patriot Act forfeiture provisions. George Bush II, clearly delighted at events, denounced Al Barakaat as a "quartermaster of terror" and "a pariah in the civilized world"; and he reassured Americans that, "By shutting these networks down, we interrupt the murderers' work."[39] Yet when US officials were asked just what proof existed, they insisted that considerations of national security precluded them revealing anything.[40]

The good news did not stop at the US border. Many countries, particularly in Europe and the Gulf, followed the US lead, freezing tens of thousands of Somali accounts. Thus the Al Barakaat operation set the critical precedent in the financial war that, where Washington led, others would meekly follow.

Of course there was a downside. The move was a body blow to the largest functioning business group in Somalia, and it threatened the precarious livelihood of millions. At the time aid workers estimated that about 75 percent of Somalia's families relied on remittance systems of which Al Barakaat was by far the largest.[41] Not to fear. A senior US Treasury official helpfully suggested that Somalis could instead use Western Union. Leaving aside the question of whether the official was lining himself up for a corporate plum after he left public service, someone from an African NGO decided to check out the suggestion by calling a Western Union office. He was asked by the agent if Somalia was really the name of a country. Certainly there was no such entity on the Western Union service list.[42]

Ahmed Nur Juma'ale tried repeatedly, and in vain, to show to US officials the books.[43] The Treasury, it seems, was too busy to look. However it was not too busy to constantly escalate the accusations. Soon, al-Qā'idah, not al-Ittihād, owned Al Barakaat.[44] Furthermore Juma'ale's intimate circle of friends now included Mohammed Farah Aideed, who had preceded bin Lāden as the USA's primary *bête verte.*[45]

For all the talk of extreme secrecy, the Somalia hawāla system was quite open, even in comparison to its counterparts in Southwest Asia. Someone seeking to remit money presented the sum to a broker and got a written receipt with full details of the amount, currency of choice, destination, and recipient, sometimes with the recipient's clan also mentioned. The broker sent a fax or phone message to his representative or branch office in the recipient's town or the closest town if the recipient lived in the countryside. The recipient had to go personally to the representative with proof of identity in the form of a passport or old ID card, along with the sender's name, country of residence, telephone number, clan name, and any code required on top. The recipient signed a receipt and left with the money. In other words, the know-your-client provisions involved were equal to or better than any legislated in the US or Western Europe.[46]

Juma'ale had his own theories about what lay behind the campaign. He insisted that the rumors had been fed to the US government by his competitors, jealous of the fact that he ran the most successful company in a decidedly unsuccessful country and had the confidence of its "president." He further imputed the stories to the

machinations of qāt dealers after he banned use of the drug by his
company's three thousand employees. He may also have been victim
of a clan-based vendetta.[47]

Certainly allegations that Al Barakaat was a vehicle for al-Ittihād al-
Islāmiyya to collect money abroad for terrorist operations made no
sense. For one thing, al-Ittihād's main commitment had always been
to proselytization and welfare – money it raised went overwhelmingly to
schools and hospitals. No doubt al-Ittihād, like every other Somali
group with overseas supporters, received funds via the Al Barakaat system; but the sums were minor compared to the overall flow through
the network. Furthermore in both North America and Europe, people
who collect money for Somalia do so with the cooperation of clan leaders whose legitimacy al-Ittihād publicly questions.[48] Hence when the US
shut down Al Barakaat, it was attacking the financial resources not pri-
marily of its alleged target but of the clans whom the group opposed.
Not least, by cutting the country's financial lifeline, the US risked driving more young men into the militias to try to earn a living by fighting,
looting, and trafficking qāt.

Also closed was the Somali branch of a Saudi charitable organization, Al Haramain Islamic Foundation, which was accused of employing al-Ittihād members and paying them by remittances through Al
Barakaat. If that was such a heinous offense, it is a surprise that the US
did not also declare the UN a financier of terror, since it made remittances to support its own work in Somalia through Al Barakaat.[49]

In the final analysis Al Barakaat and its senior US operative were indeed charged (and convicted) – with running an unlicensed money-
transmitting firm.[50] A couple of "associates" eventually pleaded guilty
not to material support for terrorism but to "structuring." They had
broken down Somali deposits into amounts under $10,000 to avoid fill-
ing out Currency Transactions Reports that might reveal undeclared
sources of income – more likely from working in a sweat shop than
from peddling qāt in Times Square – before sending the funds to Al
Barakaat in Dubai, which transferred them, less 3 percent, to destinees
in Somalia, Ethiopia, Kenya, and the Sudan.

While the sentences were not particularly long, the defendants appealed on the grounds that the court had failed to apply guidelines
calling for sentences to be reduced if defendants were unaware that the
funds they were structuring were of illegal origin or intended to be
used for illegal purposes. But the appellate court rejected the argument. Even though the charges were criminal, in such cases the burden

of proof was reversed. In the words of one judge, the defendants had to prove three things: "not only that their own activity and purposes were legal, but also that those from whom they received the funds engaged in a lawful activity and those to whom they sent the funds used them for a lawful purpose." According to the court's medieval logic, if the funds were illegal in origin or in disposition, the guilt would automatically transfer to the people transmitting them, even if they had been quite unaware. ("Merely transferring proceeds of an unlawful origin does not wash them of their taint.") The judges noted with approval that the government had introduced into the record compelling evidence like media reports about Somalis engaged in food-stamp fraud and sending money home for "unspecified" purposes. That apparently clinched the case for illegal origin. As to disposition of the funds, the judges ruled that once the defendants had pleaded guilty to structuring charges, they automatically agreed to the facts behind the Treasury's decision (which was based on secret deliberations, and, thus, unchallengeable) to freeze the assets, namely that the owner of the Al Barakaat network was directing some of his profits to a terrorist organization. Ergo the funds were intended for illegal purposes. If more evidence was required, the court noted that the defendants' probation officer had said that it was "well-known in the Somali community that [Al Barakaat] was laundering funds ... for Al Qaeda."[51] So what was the fuss all about?

In one of the few instances where a modicum of belated justice followed the Al Barakaat affair, the Somali owner of the mini-market in Seattle, whose store and inventory were trashed during a 2001 federal raid, was given $75,000 in compensation, while another Somali merchant, owner of an adjacent gift shop, was awarded $25,000. But that did little to damper the enthusiasm of US law enforcement. A few years later federal agents raided seventeen money transmitters in Washington area, mom-and-pop operations that lacked resources to meet all licensing requirements of the Patriot Act. The targets included the Eritrean Cultural and Civic Center, an Afghan grocery store, and three little companies suspected of sending money to the Sudan. At least by that time raids had become a little more equal-opportunity in nature – money transmitters serving Guatemala and Peru were also arrested. It seems that the good guys in blue had come to the happy conclusion that laws passed to nail the bad guys in green could be put to other useful purposes.[52]

About two years after wrecking the Somalia remittance apparatus the US finally got around to asking the UN to drop Al Barakaat along with six other Somali businesses and individuals (although not the owner of Al Barakaat) from its list of terrorist supporters. The public explanation was that those involved "have taken active steps to cut all ties with those entities funnelling funds to terrorism."[53] Since there was never any proof that they had such ties to begin with, cutting them apparently did not present much of a challenge.

However, one senior US Treasury official had been honest enough to admit the real reason for the precipitous action – which had held financially hostage an entire country already ravaged by drought, famine, and civil war. In those first days after 9/11, he explained, "We needed to make a splash. We needed to designate now and sort it out later."[54] Or, as another famous US proverb suggested, they had to shoot first and ask questions later.

11

Monetary Mujahideen? – Mall versus Mosque in the War on Terror

Usama bin Lāden, the Independent Task Force observed, worked his monetary magic with the usual tools of clandestine finance – cash couriers, shell companies, coded bank accounts, and the like. He also employed the notorious hawāla system, although, doubtless for reasons of national security, the Task Force was unable to specify a single instance. And allegedly he had yet another trick up the sleeves of his loose-fitting burnoose.

Over the previous two or three decades, Islamic charitable foundations (along with Islamic banks and investment companies) had spread widely. They could, so the story went, raise money in wealthy places like the Gulf or the US, then move it to finance terrorist outrages while pretending to bring succor to teary war widows and doe-eyed orphans. Most money moving through such charities was of anonymous origin. That was grounds for serious suspicion. After all, what decent American would contribute a large sum to a charity unless they got a public accolade and a fat tax write-off? While an attack on hawāla merely closed a terror-dollar channel, an assault on Islamic charities could also stop actual fundraising. It could also insult the core religious beliefs of 1.3 billion Muslims, but that was just more collateral damage.

MALL VERSUS MOSQUE

Although popular bigotry and political opportunism certainly play a role, part of the West's confusion over Islamic charities arises because the Qur'ān supports an economic ideology very different from the canons of savage capitalism so beloved of today's bond brokers and televangelists. Islamic ethic imposes on Muslims as their primary duty the creation of a just society that treats the poor with respect. It favors equity over economic hierarchy, cooperation over unscrupulous competition, and charitable redistribution over selfish accumulation. In effect, the Qur'ān was an early blueprint for the welfare state.[1]

The most fundamental premise of that ethic is that economic activity is inseparable from spiritual. The ultimate purpose of life is the 'ibāda of Allāh. More than simply worship, this implies total submission to God in all aspects of life, including the economic. Where God and the market disagree, the market must give way.

Therefore private-property rights are not absolute. Ultimately all material things are gifts from Allāh over which humans (individually or sometimes collectively) only have trusteeship.[2] This makes it easier for a state authority, acting nominally on Islamic principles, to set limits on what a person can do with economic assets without invoking the protests common in the West against interference with the divine right of property. Islamic thought also makes a distinction between direct gifts from God and things that owe their existence mainly to human intervention. The first are common property. The Qur'ān so specifies water, pasture, and fire (i.e., wood and forest resources). Some clerics add certain types of mines – like petroleum wells.

Since wealth and resources are bequeathed to humanity in trust, people are expected to exploit them for economic gain; but they cannot waste or destroy; and anything they earn is to be used for God's work. That requires donating to the mosque and to the general defense of the umma and relieving the economic hardship of others. Obviously this egalitarianism is far from perfect in practice. Apart from the frequent economic subordination of women (something, of course, totally alien in the Christian world), it is a fair criticism that some Muslim countries condoned slavery until fairly recently. Indeed one Finance Minister of Saudi Arabia in the 1950s had been a slave by birth. Leaving aside the fact that in Islamic countries slavery was more often a form of bonded personal service than a mode of organizing labor for economic profit, and that Islam made a virtue of freeing a slave, if the West is so socially advanced, it is curious that there has never been a black Secretary of the Treasury in the US or, for that matter, a non-white Minister of Finance in any major European country to this day, several generations after slavery was abolished. Whatever the social failings of places where Islam is predominant, the Qur'ān makes clear that the umma is defined by faith alone, with no reference to race or nationality; and Islamic doctrines with their stress on cooperation and equality to achieve falāh (the welfare of humanity) are less compatible with economic servitude (in both historical and modern forms) than the grab-and-run ideology now rampant in "advanced" countries, with the enthusiastic endorsement of modern "fundamentalist" Christianity.

There are several instruments used to turn Islamic economic philosophy into practical action. These include: restrictions on how business enterprises are structured; a ban on fraudulent practices; condemnation of gains from pure speculation; and, to aid circulation of wealth, injunctions against hoarding in the hands of a few.[3] None would likely earn plaudits on the editorial page of the *Wall Street Journal*. A prohibition on trading in produce before crops are ready for harvest would spell ruin to the Chicago commodities exchange; a demand that employers pay decent wages promptly would hardly be appreciated by today's vulture capitalists who count on rolling back wages and looting employee pension funds to finance acquisitions; and provisions for the intergenerational dispersion of wealth could mean the end of the great family trusts in the US that ensure perpetuation of dynastic control without the nuisance of taxes.

All of these instruments are important. But two others are central to implement an Islamic vision of economic society. One provided the impetus for the rapid growth of Islamic banks and investment funds; the other led to a worldwide expansion of Islamic charities.

IN WHOSE INTEREST?

The first of these fundamental instruments of Islamic economics is the ban on ribā – literally an "increase" in the sum needed to repay a loan. Some jurists argue that it only forbids the pre-Islamic practice of doubling an overdue sum, which sometimes led to enslavement of the debtor.[4] Some contend that it bans "excessively high" rates of interest. Some claim that it prohibits outright all interest payments. Even then there are dispensations. In the past some schools of Islamic jurisprudence permitted certain tricks to disguise interest payments that were imported directly, sometimes with their Arabic names, into Europe when evasion of the similar Catholic ban on collecting interest became widespread during the Renaissance.[5]

There were (are) many good reasons to prohibit at least oppressive rates of interest, as low-income groups in the West today can attest. Well before Islam, societies learned that to avoid famine, economic collapse, and social upheaval, they had to ban the unrestricted accumulation of assets by an elite through the progressive indebting of most of the population. Hence secular and/or religious authorities would periodically cancel debts and redistribute agricultural land (previously lost through unrepayable debts) back to landless laborers.[6]

With the advent of Islam, arguments against usury became more sophisticated. Unlike trade, which involves an exchange of value, with usury the flow is one way. Usury thus violates the core principle that Allāh created wealth for the general benefit. Usury also increases economic inequality, potentially robbing the debtor of dignity and of the means of subsistence, to the advantage of a creditor who does nothing socially useful to justify that income. In Islam, the only rationalization for inequality of wealth is that those with more aid those with less. That does *not* mean debts go unpaid. While the well-to-do are expected to make interest-free loans to the not-so-fortunate, those who borrow are expected to repay promptly. However, if someone is unable to repay because of circumstances beyond their control, the creditor is expected to grant more time or, if the debtor's condition is particularly serious, write off the debt. Such a prescription for pious behavior is likely to send shudders up and down the spines of the directors of Citibank or Chase Manhattan as well as to invoke the ire of the IMF.

Today, too, there are exceptions. In Egypt, for example, in a fatwā contested by Islamic courts elsewhere, the grand muftī of al-Azhar authorized payment of fixed interest rates on savings accounts. Some saw that as just another example of al-Azhar acting as a mouthpiece of the state. Others argued that since the depositor willingly turned over the money to the bank, depositor and bank were partners in an investment, not engaged in a usurious transaction.[7] Similarly some ulemā in the Gulf states endorsed the practice by which the area's banks receive interest when they make deposits in international banks while refusing to pay it to depositors back home. However those clerics usually insist that any profits be used for charitable work, one reason why major banks in Islamic countries are big contributors to Islamic charities.

Despite these dispensations, all forms of interest are, at a minimum, contentious. Hence the spread of financial institutions offering interest-free facilities. Their operations are often "supervised" by a shari'a committee on which sit religious scholars of various degrees of credibility, gullibility, or complicity. Some have been notorious scams – in Egypt, for example, during the late 1980s and early 1990s "Islamic investment companies" headed by bearded, Qur'ān-quoting conmen turned into schemes to steal money from expatriate workers. When the system crashed in scandal, costing depositors (except, reputedly, those high in government) enormous sums, the state took the opportunity to "reform" the financial system – it eliminated exchange controls, put informal (Islamic) bankers out of business, and absorbed remittances from the Gulf into the official financial system, where they could be used not to finance mosques or street-level social services but for purposes like paying interest on Egypt's burgeoning international debt.

Most Islamic banks are quite legitimate. Their basic rule is that they receive not interest but part of the profits of businesses in which they place money, then share those profits with depositors. Similarly Islamic investment funds avoid putting money into fixed-interest debt and shun anything that encourages harām activity like speculation, hoarding, gambling, sexploitation, or use of intoxicants. In that sense they are not much different from ethical-investment funds now operating in the West.[8]

The spread of Islamic institutions was well advanced before 9/11, albeit governments took quite different views. Some (Sudan, Pakistan, and Iran) attempted to Islamize their entire financial systems; some (especially in the Gulf) encouraged Islamic institutions alongside Western-style ones; some (like Egypt and Indonesia) took a more laissez-faire attitude; while some (including, remarkably, Saudi Arabia) actively opposed Islamicization of finance.[9] Then came the story that Al Shamal Bank in the Sudan had been set up with $50 million from Usama bin Lāden. The start-up capital was actually $20 million, and it was posted by a group of wealthy Saudis attracted by the Islamic credentials of the Sudanese regime. True, bin Lāden, like many others, had accounts at the bank; but no one has traced a penny to any act of terrorism. Along with tales about Al Shamal came the story that one of Usama's "relatives" sat on the board of Al Faisal Islamic Bank. These allegations were sufficient to paint the entire sector with the "financing of terrorism" brush, undoubtedly to the delight of certain UK and US banks trying to market their own versions of shari'a-compatible investment services to wealthy clients in the Gulf. Across the world major banks slapped freezes on Al Shamal's assets and

scrambled to apologize for any business relationship with it; while a
few Islamic institutions, facing potential depositor runs, tried to protect their business by threatening newspapers with lawsuits.[10]

Islamic investment companies, too, were hit by the aftershocks. One of
Geneva's oldest and most prestigious private banks, Pictet et cie, operated out of Luxembourg three Islamic investment funds for Middle East
clients, one of whom was a Saudi conglomerate called Dallah Al Baraka
Group. Luxembourg's central bank jumped to the conclusion that it was
the same Al Barakaat that George II had labelled "quartermaster of terror." Assets of all three funds were frozen, although a glance at Dallah Al
Baraka's website would have revealed that the operating philosophy of its
founder ("I dream of an area dedicated to financial institutions, clean industries, tourism, open to the world") seemed to have little in common
with rants about jihād from radical political Islamists.[11]

Sometimes the consequences were more serious, as for Al Taqwa ("piety") Trade, Property and Investment Company. It was both an Islamic
investment company with three thousand clients and the centrepiece of
a worldwide business conglomerate in construction, manufacturing, and
commodity trade, with two offshore banks in the Bahamas. Then George
II declared that Al Taqwa acted in tandem with Al Barakaat to raise, invest, hide, move, and disburse money on behalf of al-Qā'idah – supposedly Al Barakaat skimmed fees from its clients while Al Taqwa provided
investment advice and transfer facilities. Once the US put Al Taqwa on
the terror list and forced the Bahamas to close its banks, the UN and the
EC obediently tagged along.[12]

If the founder of Al Barakaat had as his sin his (nonexistent) friend-
ship with and (bogus) acceptance of seed money from bin Lāden, the
offenses of Youssef Nada, founder of Al Taqwa, were much fuzzier. In his
younger days he had been active with Egypt's Muslim Brotherhood,
which rejects the concept of violent jihād and which does not figure on
anyone's terrorist list – except perhaps that of Mossad, which so classi-
fies any gathering of more than two bearded Muslims. Perhaps the problem was that among his thousands of clients and business associates
numbered members of the bin Lāden family. But never Usama himself.
Anyway, if doing business with people named bin Lāden made someone
a national security risk, at least two US presidents with roughly the same
name deserved to have their assets frozen and to be booked a quick passage to Guantánamo.[13] Moreover the notion that Al Taqwa handled
money for Islamic radicals to conduct violent acts seems odd for a company whose investment fund offered to clients equity participation in

businesses that avoided not only usury, hoarding, speculation, booze, and promotion of sexual license but also weapons production.[14]

Ultimately the only part of the accusations that seemed to have substance was that Nada's partner, an Eritrean named Ahmed Idris Nasreddin, helped found the Islamic Cultural Institute of Milan in the early 1990s. It was later dubbed by the US Treasury "the main Al Qaeda station house in Europe."[15] Proof was that the late imam of the institute was a follower of Umar Abd al-Rahman. This almost-blind and diabetic Egyptian cleric, apparently rewarded for his services to the CIA in Afghanistan with a US residency permit, somehow overcame his handicaps sufficiently to help plan and execute the 1993 World Trade Center bombing – for which he now reposes for life in a US prison.[16] That bin Lāden at various points met and cooperated with Umar Abd al-Rahman, that Nasreddin helped found the Milan mosque at which one of the blind sheikh's "followers" was briefly imām (prayer leader), and that Nada was Nasreddin's business partner apparently sufficed to "tie," "associate," "connect," or "link" Youssef Nada to al-Qā'idah.

MONETARY MUJAHIDEEN?

The proscription of ribā, which prompted the spread of Islamic banks, is probably of less importance than the second major instrument to ensure a fair distribution of income and wealth, the requirement of sadaqa – charitable giving. In some ways the ban on ribā is simply a refinement of sadaqa. Usury involves a movement of unearned income from the (by definition poorer) debtor to the (by definition wealthier) creditor; charity implies a movement of financial resources from the well-to-do to the less fortunate. Charity is so central in Islam that the Sunna decrees: "One who works in order to support a widow and destitute is like a mujahid in the path of Allāh."[17] By contrast, it is doubtful if any Christian country would honor a draft dodger with its highest military accolade on the grounds that he had contributed most of his salary to the Salvation Army.

The only charitable requirement specified in the Qur'ān is the payment of zakāt (literally, purification) levied at a 2.5 percent rate on financial assets in general (usually excluding primary residence and professional tools), a higher rate on land, and highest on idle hordes of treasure. In the past it was usual for the state in Islamic countries to collect zakāt. That still occurs in some, but increasingly Islamist activists distrust their governments and demand that the mosque be the fulcrum, or that the movement itself take charge. In some others the money goes to an approved Islamic charity. How zakāt is subsequently redistributed also varies – the state, the mosque, or Islamic charities can all participate, with state and mosque in turn often steering contributions through established charitable foundations as well.

Zakāt is merely the beginning, not the end of charitable transfers. The Qur'ān is replete with exhortations to give beyond the minimum in expectation of non-financial rewards in the afterlife.[18] In fact spontaneous giving of alms (sadaqat al-tatawwu') confers many times the favor from God than would simply giving the mandatory 2.5 percent. Furthermore if the yield from zakāt is insufficient for community needs, the authorities can demand more. Shi'a are also required to pay khums, a 20 percent levy on commercial profit. Then there is waqf: best known as a means whereby the wealthy deed property to a mosque, or use their money to build one, perhaps along with low-rent housing units or merchant's shops whose rental payments go to maintain the mosque, it actually has many more functions. The wealth deeded can be cash as well as physical property and can go to a hostel for travellers, to a hospital, or to a college. In fact one of the early acts of European colonizers was to destroy the waqf system – which financed education in Muslim states – as the first step to dismantle Islamic law as a competitor to European commercial and civil codes.[19]

When governments of Muslim countries came under US pressure to monitor charitable foundations, they ran up against the religious requirement that a charitable donation be anonymous – the gift is intended to win favor in the eyes of Allāh, not of the neighbors or the IRS. Lack of anonymity detracts from the theological merit of the donation.[20] Therefore in Muslim countries it is regarded as impolite, to say the least, to poke into the affairs of a charity. And any government sufficiently amenable to US demands to trace charitable flows is unlikely to be trusted not to use the information to monitor the political behavior of its own citizens.

Moreover few Muslim countries have income taxes. Historically most relied on indirect taxes on commodities; and even that can face opposition from purist clerics who insist that the only levies permitted are religiously sanctioned transfers such as zakāt or khums, payable to and through the mosque.[21] Hence those countries lack the apparatus normal in the West to monitor financial transactions. When governments of Muslim states capitulate to US pressure, they do not just change regulations but create new institutions, then try to win public acceptance for radical, some might even suggest sacrilegious, innovations.[22]

On top comes the problem of sheer scale. Most of the world's 1.3 billion Muslims follow (more or less) the principles of charitable giving (or receiving). Taking just the Arab countries, that still means about 300 million people. Hence it is impossible to map fully the sources, movement, and ultimate disposition of donations. The problem the Muslim world faces today is the US ambition to do so.

LOOKING A GIFT CAMEL IN THE MOUTH?

Not all Muslim countries were created equal, at least with respect to oil deposits. When Gulf-state revenues exploded in the 1970s, Muslim clergy in poorer countries told their followers that the income belonged to the umma regardless of nationality. Hence hereditary rulers of oil states, painfully aware that the Qur'ān questions their political legitimacy, responded by ostentatiously dishing out billions in aid. To this day most money raised by Islamic charities originates in the Gulf. In Saudi Arabia the 1979 Grand Mosque uprising lent a special urgency to the royal family's efforts to buttress legitimacy at home by building up religious credentials abroad. Private citizens show similar generosity. During the Bosnian war a single telethon brought in $120 million in cash, gold, and jewellery. The country now gives away 6 percent of its GNP each year.

After 9/11 some Saudi-based charities were denounced as bin Lāden fronts and put on the US blacklist. Maurice Greenberg of nonpartisan Task Force fame asserted categorically that al-Qā'idah derived "most of its operating funds" (i.e., an undefined proportion of an unknown amount) from Saudi charities. William Wechsler offered his own expert opinion that Saudi Arabia connived in the misuse of charitable funds.[23] (Naturally he repeated that opinion in his capacity as "expert witness" in a trillion-dollar jackpot lawsuit launched by the families of some 9/11 victim against a host of Saudi businessmen and princes, as well as against almost any Islamic institution that had received negative press coverage.) Even those Saudi charities not held directly complicit were depicted as vehicles of state propaganda designed to convert the world's Muslims to "Wahhābī fundamentalism."[24] By remarkable coincidence, about the same time that stories about Saudi financing of worldwide terror were given wide currency, the Pentagon leaked documents proposing to retaliate by freezing Saudi assets in the US (several hundred billion dollars worth) and seizing its oilfields.[25]

To be fair, the terror-dollar war targeted other country's charities, too. In January 2002, the Pakistan-based Afghan Support Committee, which provided food, medicine, and clothing to destitute, fatherless Afghan families, was accused by the US of being a front for financing Usama bin Lāden's Islamic legions. The US even claimed that bin Lāden himself had created the committee, which was subsequently run by his chief fundraiser. So, too, Kuwait's Revival of Islamic Heritage Society, whose Peshawar branch, also committed to aiding Afghan widows and orphans, was accused of padding the lists of qualified recipients to skim the surplus off to al-Qā'idah.[26]

Of course, in all such cases it is legitimate to ask just what new piece of intelligence the US authorities stumbled upon in the wake of 9/11 to allow them to make such a determination. Perhaps in this case the answer lay in the success of the USA's local allies in the Afghan campaign. Picked up in a sweep of what the Pentagon called "the hardest of the hard" Tāliban and al-Qā'idah fighters were twelve Kuwaiti nationals. They were whisked to Guantánamo and held without charge as illegal combatants. Appeals to the US Supreme Court were rejected – the prison camp, said the Supreme Court, was not part of US sovereign territory (a judgement Fidel Castro was probably happy to hear); hence the court had no jurisdiction and, ipso facto, the prisoners had no rights. As it turned out, the dirty dozen were aid workers employed by eight different charities, including the Afghan Support Committee and the Revival of Islamic Heritage Society. They had been trapped in Afghanistan when the United States began bombing, were led across the frontier into Pakistan, and taken captive by local tribes who had received from the US forces leaflets offering a reward for Arab suspects. The chiefs then sold the captives – teachers, engineers, agronomists, even a government auditor – to the US forces who asked no questions, until Guantánamo.[27]

While captured late in 2001, not until early 2005 was the first of these "hardest of the hard" allowed to rejoin his family in Kuwait. Against him the main evidence seems that he had been wearing a Casio watch – which, his captors insisted, terrorists use to time their explosives. Perhaps they do; but presumably Casio watches can also be used by New York yuppies to time their soufflés. It is unknown if the watch was returned, frozen as a terrorist asset, or permitted to proudly grace the wrist of a US soldier as war booty.

As the popularity of asset freezes grew, any pretense that they had anything to do with US security receded. Their main role became to reward allies, however temporary the ally or repugnant its behavior. For example, after the original list of FTOs was given its post-9/11 enhancement, the US administration bought the support of India and fired a warning shot at Pakistan by putting Lashkar-e-Taiba, one of about a dozen insurgent groups fighting India in Kashmir, on the terror index. Naturally it claimed that the group, which had never shown any interest outside Kashmir, was "linked to" al-Qā'idah. Several charities implicated in raising money for Kashmir were frozen. The good sense of that measure was shown after the autumn 2005 earthquake that killed tens of thousands in Kashmir, while the destruction of roads and torrential rains blocked relief efforts. In some areas only Lashkar-e-Taiba was on site to rescue people from the ruins and feed the survivors.[28]

Bush also demanded that its allies freeze the assets of Ummah Tameer-e-Nau, a Pakistani charity run by two former nuclear scientists who had visited bin Lāden in Afghanistan earlier in the year. No one suggested that the organization was skimming money for orphanages off to build intercontinental ballistic missiles. Pakistani investigators who interviewed the two after they had been detained at US request concluded that the two scientists had no knowledge of use to al-Qā'idah in its atomic ambitions. Even the CIA agreed. Yet recipients of the charity's funds were to pay the price of their sidetrip. Pakistan, of course, acquiesced in the US judgment and froze the assets.[29]

That was also the fate of the Al Khidmat Foundation, run by the Pakistani Jamiat-i-Islami, godfather to the Afghan party of the same name whose leadership the US had just installed to run the Afghan Interior and Defense Ministries. It collected money from street fundraising, which, while aggressive, was probably mild compared to the fire-and-brimstone pitches of US televangelists designed to ensure that their collection cups runneth over. Naturally Al Khidmat was also accused of laundering cash from bank robberies and ransom kidnappings. Of course in Pakistan the police routinely blame every criminal incident on opposition or insurgent groups, partly to cover up their own incompetence, complicity, or corruption. But the accusations sufficed to justify the freeze.

Another target was the Al Rashid Trust, among Pakistan's most visible philanthropic organizations. Besides sending relief money to Chechnya and Kosovo, it was the first Pakistani agency to move into Afghanistan after the inter-mujahideen war. There it built twelve mosques and fifteen medical clinics and dug fifty-eight wells in various areas where refugees were trying to resettle. When the Taliban objected to the World Food Programme hiring female inspectors and forced it out of the country, Al Rashid Trust took up part of the slack. At the time it was designated as a financier of terrorism, it had fifty bakeries across Afghanistan providing bread and flour at subsidized prices, plus distributing hundreds of tons of other relief supplies.[30] Unlike with Al Khidmat, there were no accusations that it laundered criminal money – its funds came from donations, sales of books and magazines in the street, and selling the hides of animals sacrificed at the end of Ramadan. Perhaps its real sin was that the servant who served tea to a visiting *Los Angeles Times* reporter carried a shotgun.[31] Yet some might think that was a rather sensible precaution given conditions in Karachi; and it was certainly surprising to find an LA reporter so startled, given that on a routine drive to work along one of his city's freeways, he could probably have spotted enough heavy weaponry to re-equip the Taliban.

BROTHER-IN-CRIME OR BROTHER-IN-LAW

Apart from those in Pakistan, Saudi charities received the most attention. One singled out for special attention was the International Islamic Relief Organization (IIRO), an offshoot of the World Muslim League, a long-established Saudi-backed umbrella organization. The impetus to action came from the fact that from 1994 to 1996 the man in charge of its Philippines office was Mohammed Jamal Khalifah, an Afghan veteran and old university roommate of Usama. Khalifah seems to have been quite an energetic chap. He allegedly participated in bomb plots in Jordan and the US, including not just World Trade Center I in 1993 but even Oklahoma City in 1996. He was reputedly the man who handled the money for the attack on the USS *Cole* in Aden. Some even claimed that he was the real brains behind 9/11, the terrorist attack that has had more masterminds (and paymasters) than any in history. He even figured on the shakedown list in the trillion-dollar tort-lawyer sweepstakes. All that in his time off from supervising thirty-three orphanages in Muslim-inhabited areas of the Philippines, many of whose occupants had lost their fathers to a vicious Army counterinsurgency campaign against Moro separatists. Still, there was no doubt he was guilty of something – why else would he be married to one of Usama's thirty-eight sisters?[32]

Khalifah, the Philippines military claimed, was more than just a fundamentalist fanatic with access to the bin Lāden billions – he was also an in-
veterate playboy and swindler.[33] How it was possible to be a devout
Muslim, yet lead a life of sexual licentiousness and financial dishonesty,
they did not elaborate. Army intelligence claimed that the orphanages
were just cover for Khalifah to skim cash for the Abu Sayyaf Group, a nasty
bunch whose notoriety for lucrative ransom kidnappings would seem to
preclude any such need. Later both the Filipino president and the Secretary of Justice changed the story. In the prelude to a campaign to get new
anti-money-laundering laws through the country's Congress, they insisted
that Khalifah was really moving money *from* the Abu Sayyaf Group to al-
Qā'idah. Al-Qā'idah in turn used the funds, among other things, to finance the Islamic Army of Aden, the group alleged to have bombed the
USS Cole. Justice, it seems, had Khalifah to rights, coming or going.[34]

However at the time of 9/11, Khalifah was quietly running a fish restaurant near Jeddah. He had already been arrested, held in solitary, and
quizzed by the US for four months, then deported to Jordan where, even
though he faced a sentence of death in absentia, he felt he would get
fairer treatment. He was right. The main witness against him, who had
claimed that Khalifah had promised to send money to a group of plotters, renounced his confession during the trial, claiming that it had been
coerced by threats and beatings. Freed by Jordan, Khalifah returned to
Saudi Arabia, where he was again jailed without charge, then, after several months, told he was in the clear. Even in the Philippines, the allegations (which appeared in an Army report after he had left the country)
never led to criminal charges. When queried, the regime claimed that at
the time of Khalifah's residency, the country did not have proper anti-
terrorism laws under which to charge him. Perhaps not. But thousands of
alleged guerrillas of all makes and models had previously been incarcer-
ated. Furthermore the country had no lack of (selectively enforced) laws
dealing with financial fraud that could have been applied. And it was
strange that, after anti-terrorism laws were put on the books, the response of the Philippines authorities was that, if Khalifah dared to return, he would be put under surveillance but not arrested.[35]

BLESSED BY WHOM?

The USA's second major Saudi target was the Muwāfaq (Blessed Relief)
Foundation and its former director, Yasin al-Qadi, whose surname

sounded suspiciously like al-Qā'idah. The case against Muwāfaq and al-Qadi was, if not the first, then probably the most compelling application of the post-9/11 terrorist math, whose most important axiom states that things that happened to fleetingly touch the same thing, even if at completely different times and under completely different circumstances, are equal to and conspiratorially linked with each other.

Although the largest charitable foundations in the kingdom were government-sponsored, the Muwāfaq Foundation was the initiative of a single individual, Khalid ibn Mahfouz, head of one of the most powerful clans in the kingdom. The rise of the bin Mahfouz family had remarkable parallels to that of the bin Lādens – which set the usual tongues wagging in the usual way.[36] The founding patriarch, Salim Ahmed ibn Mahfouz, an illiterate money changer of Yemeni origin, had persuaded King ibn Saud to let him open Saudi Arabia's first bank. Soon the National Commercial Bank was de facto the royal family's personal banker. Since affairs of state and Saud family were (are) quite interchangeable, the bank also handled the regime's most sensitive transactions, including its role in the Iran-Contra affair. After Khalid, the oldest son, took over the bank, he nearly wrecked it, not once but twice. Among his unfortunate moves was the purchase of 30 percent of the shares of the Bank of Credit and Commerce International. Following that debacle, Khalid paid $252 million to settle charges against himself personally and to help indemnify BCCI creditors. Then he hired some Citibank veterans to rehabilitate the bank, and he let his brother run it. But in 1996 Khalid returned; and, by bad luck or ill management, the bank's portfolio of bad loans soared. In 1999 the government took 50 percent of the shares (later picking up another 30 percent), put Khalid temporarily under house arrest, and declared $2 billion missing.[37]

Rumors about what happened to the missing money proliferated. Did it go to finance the embassy attacks in Nairobi and Dar es Salaam? Was some of it used to fund terrorist activities in the Philippines and India? Was it skimmed to finance suicide bombers in Palestine, an accusation also tossed at Khalifah's IIRO? Or could it be, as some suggested, that the money was washed through the Muwāfaq Foundation and sent to al-Qā'idah to be used for atrocities all over the world?

For example, there were claims that its Somalia office was a mobilization centre for Islamic fighters arriving in 1993 to fight Americans, audacious behavior for a foundation whose international headquarters was at the time in Delaware. There were also claims, notably in *Africa*

Confidential, a London-based private newsletter, that Muwāfaq's Sudan office (on whose board sat the son of Khalid ibn Mahfouz) was "linked to" the attempted assassination of Hosni Mubarak on a state visit to Ethiopia in 1995. Ethiopia responded by expelling the staff of the charity. On the other hand Yasin al-Qadi, the man chosen by Khalid ibn Mahfouz to run the charity, responded by launching a protracted lawsuit. Despite enthusiastic intervention on behalf of the newsletter by the usual US "terrorism experts," the case culminated six years later in the editor reading an apology into the court record.[38]

However, before that could happen, the Saudi government, embarrassed by the bad publicity, and apparently threatened by the US with the release of embarrassing information on the private affairs of some of the princes, ordered Muwāfaq to cease operations. The foundation was defunct by 1997. Yet when the Bush administration published its 12 October 2001 terror list, it described: Muawāfaq (AKA Blessed Relief) as "an al-Qaeda front." It further claimed that "Saudi businessmen have been transferring millions of dollars to bin Lāden through Blessed Relief" – impressive activity indeed from a defunct institution.

The evidence to support US claims was not what most people would regard as exactly overwhelming. For one thing, when Ramzi Yousef, central architect of the 1993 attack of the World Trade Center, was arrested two years later, it was found that he had made a phone call to the Islamabad office of a charity called Mercy International, which shared its office with Muwāfaq Pakistan. That was enough for the Pakistani police to arrest the local head of Muwafāq, toss him in jail, and hold him for months without charges. By the time he was released, a plan for Muwāfaq to build hostels for an Islamic University in Islamabad had collapsed.

For another, it seems that Usama bin Lāden, from his Afghan exile, once mentioned to a reporter that Muwāfaq in the Balkans (where it handled Bosnian relief) was one of the charities he thought were worthy of support. No doubt Usama was trying to help US investigators understand the intricacies of his terror-dollar circuitry.[39]

For yet another, there was Yasin al-Qadi himself. Among the elite of Saudi businessmen with major holdings in real estate, consulting, chemical manufacture, and banking in Saudi Arabia, Turkey, Kazakhstan, and Pakistan, in addition to a portfolio of US stocks, he was renowned as a philanthropist who financed everything from famine relief in the Sudan to Muslim schools in Bosnia. But he was also a major investor and director of Global Diamond Resources, a San Diego-based diamond-exploration company. So, too, was one of the multitudinous bin

Lāden brood. By 9/11, rumors were rife about Islamic terrorists trafficking in "conflict diamonds." Furthermore al-Qadi had provided support to Usama during the Afghan war and praised him on his return
home, as did many other prominent Saudis.

After the us froze al-Qadi's assets, it was asked for evidence. But it
could not comply without compromising confidential information
sources and law enforcement methods.[40] Not to fear. Its allies still followed suit. In Albania, al-Qadi's commercial real estate was put on ice.
In Bosnia, where al-Qadi had financed relief work and a Muslim private
school, all his business ventures, including part ownership of a Sarajevo
bank, were brought under state supervision. Meanwhile rumors were
circulated by financial sleuths that al-Qadi's Balkan business ventures
included smuggling rackets.[41] Apparently the tenth richest man in
Saudi Arabia needed to make more money by running stolen cars.

By the time of the Balkan freezes, the fallout from putting al-Qadi on
the terror index had claimed other victims. In December 2002, news
media breathlessly announced that federal agents had conducted a
"raid" (actually a fully consensual search without court order) on Ptech,
a small software company in Boston area, on the grounds that its main
financier was Yasin al-Qadi. In fact, he had put in some start-up funds,
refused further investment, and sold out in 1999. All this was well
known to the FBI for the simple reason that Ptech had voluntarily
started to share information with them right after al-Qadi's name appeared on the terror-sponsor list. However apparently a group of employees left to start a rival operation, then began telling tales about
their former mentor. When the FBI, apparently satisfied there was
nothing amiss, did nothing, the disgruntled ex-employees called Customs, the FBI's long-time rival and eager competitor in the search for
the elusive Islamic terror-dollar, which began a new prime-time investigation of the company.

Shortly after the "raid," Ptech's banker terminated the personal accounts of five Muslim employees without explanation – the accounts of
non-Muslim employees were left intact. Since Ptech had produced software for, among others, the FBI, the Air Force, the Navy, NATO, and the
Department of Energy (where it had helped design computer systems
in a plant that manufactured plutonium cores for nuclear bombs),
there was consternation at the prospect that Ptech software might
contain a back door through which "al-Qaeda" could insinuate itself
for purposes of cyberespionage or virtual sabotage. How could anyone
not be alarmed at the prospect that Ptech used its software to secure

blueprints of nuclear-waste disposal sites, of Smartcards used in defense facilities, and of the USA's food distribution system, making it easy to introduce contaminated products?[42]

Although clients in the past had been more than happy with the company's product, at the first hint of a "terror" link, instead of standing behind their business associate, they turned tail and ran. Despite a clean bill of health from the government, a year after the "raid," a company that had formerly employed sixty-five people had a skeleton staff of ten and was considering dropping its brand name. Still, no one could say that the suspicions were ungrounded. After all, the owner's first name was Oussama.[43]

BEHEADED

Although Muwāfaq was the initiative of a private individual, albeit at the behest of the royal family, the third major target on the US list was an institution established by the government. Al Haramain Islamic Foundation officially raised about $30 million per annum. The US claimed that the sum was much higher – since donors insist on no public record, the US for a change was probably right – for the wrong reasons. The money was used for everything from building schools to providing famine relief. But early in 2002 the US designated the foundation's Somalia and Bosnia branches as facilitators of terrorism, forcing them to close. Among the terrorist activities in Somalia thereby stopped were eight orphanages housing 3,500 children, a campaign against cholera (which in the previous year had afflicted ninety thousand people), a program that dug wells, and clinics offering free health care. As to the terrorists the US claimed that Al Haramain was assisting, shortly after Saudi Arabia ordered the offices closed, a UN investigation reported no evidence such groups were active in Somalia.[44]

Not deterred, the US also insisted that the Kenyan, Tanzanian, Pakistani, and Indonesian branches be closed. The Kenyan government, after an investigation, let its local office reopen; and the US later admitted (without apology) that it had made a mistake in designating the Indonesian one. Buoyed by these victories in the terror-dollar war, the US soon added offices in Albania, Afghanistan, Bangladesh, Ethiopia, and the Netherlands to its ban. And US pressure got Saudi Arabia to oust Abd al-Aziz al-Aqil, the man who had run the foundation for the previous thirteen years – he was personally designated a terrorist financier.[45]

The Saudis had pleaded repeatedly that, while they could meticulously follow government funds (mainly from one princely pocket to another), they had no right to supervise charitable donations. But the US kept up the pressure; and it had a key ally. After a raid in Gaza, Israel claimed it had seized a document that proved that a senior figure of Palestine's Harakat al-Muqāwama al-Islāmiyya (Hamas) at a "fund-raiser" in Riyadh thanked Crown Prince Abdullah for standing firm against US pressures to cut off Saudi support. A copy was given to the White House while another, on Hamas letterhead, was accidentally handed over to the *New York Times* by a "former Israeli official." Of course, the text was in Arabic. But Israeli military intelligence helpfully provided a translation.

However, when the letter was retranslated, it turned out that, rather than being a blueprint of a Saudi-Hamas connection to turn suicide bombers loose on Israeli shopping centres, it was a summary of the impressions of Hamas officials who had attended a Saudi conference on Muslim charities. Nonetheless it did the job of getting Washington to put more pressure on Saudi officials to block private donations to Hamas.[46] It also neatly shifted the semantic battlefield, putting the onus on the accused to prove they had not make any contribution to Hamas instead of on Israel to stop behaving in ways that gave organizations like Hamas so much popular support.

Finally, in 2004, Saudi Arabia crumbled. It banned cash-donation boxes at mosques – in the future all gifts had to made by check. This reversal of a long tradition was guaranteed to expose more people to arbitrary probes by law enforcement and intelligence agencies. Saudi Arabia also insisted that all charitable organizations in the kingdom obtain a license from the Ministry of Social Affairs; get approval from the Saudi Arabian Monetary Agency (the central bank) to open bank accounts; apply for permission from the central bank to transfer funds abroad; consolidate transactions into a single account; and stop engaging in business activities to raise money on their own. (It would be a spectacular blow against fiscal fraud in the United States if the US were to do something similar to its own burgeoning "non-profit" institutions.) Simultaneously Saudi banks were told to cease issuing debit or credit cards on charitable foundation accounts.[47] Not least, Saudi Arabia rolled Al Haramain, along with several other charities, into a new government-run National Commission for Relief and Charity Work Abroad.[48]

The net result was a dramatic drop in charitable donations. While people still contributed the mandatory zākat, the much more important and voluntary sadaqa al-tatuwwuʻ began to dry up.[49] That did nothing to dampen the enthusiasm of either bin Lāden or various "jihadists" who neither received nor needed Saudi charity, but it was potentially a heavy blow to the real US target, one specially selected by the USA's most important ally in the Middle East.

12

Original Sin – Palestine and the Rise of Modern Political Terrorism

Modern political terrorism in and around the Middle East, including bombings of civilian infrastructure designed to maximize the death toll, did not begin with Usama bin Lāden. Nor was he a pioneer either in using funds of illegal origin to commit his reputed crimes or in deploying clandestine methods to hide and move the money. Decades before al-Qā'idah was even a synaptic leap in some US prosecutor's febrile brain, a future Israeli prime minister, Nobel Peace Prize laureate, and honored guest at the White House was lighting the path, along with (metaphorically speaking) the fuse of the bomb that destroyed Jerusalem's King David Hotel, killing ninety-one people, some of them British soldiers, most of them civilian employees.[1] Menachem Begin's Irgun Zve-Leumi (National Military Organization), along with allies and sometime rivals in the Zionist underground, was also adept at robbery, extortion, counterfeiting, and smuggling to raise money and obtain weapons, along with manipulation of religious fronts and phony charities to move it around.[2]

These were achievements of long-term significance. Begin and his colleagues became an inspiration to future Jewish terrorists. And some notorious Arab groups (which, in turn, inspired others in the Muslim world) emerged in direct emulation of their Jewish predecessors, while almost all were reactions, at least indirectly, to the success of people like Begin in achieving their primary objective: to make Palestine – in the words of Theodore Herzl, Israel's off-site founding father – "just as

Jewish as England is English."[3] Yet it was the Palestinian groups who became to the Western world the cultural icons of "terrorism."

Out of that success of Begin and his successors came political upheaval and military confrontation across the Middle East and beyond for generations to come. It was no accident that the first new cause bin Lāden embraced (at least rhetorically) on his return from Afghanistan was Palestine.

THE MUCH-PROMISED LAND

The modern impetus to create a "Jewish homeland" in the Middle East emerged in the early nineteenth century during the contest between France and Britain for commercial control of the Indian Ocean. After Napoleon I (briefly) occupied Egypt, which commanded access to the Red Sea, he called for European Jews to settle in Palestine, through which ran the caravan route from the Persian Gulf to the Mediterranean.[4] The strategic importance of Egypt shot up with the opening of the Suez Canal. If ever the canal fell into hostile hands, British trade with the East would be forced around Africa. Palestine was both essential to the defense of Suez and a possible route for an alternative canal. Hence leaders of the emerging Zionist movement attempted to convince Britain to seize Palestine from the Ottoman empire and to repopulate it with friendly colonists. They had no success – until World War I.[5]

During that war Britain and France promised the Ottoman-ruled Arab areas independence in return for military assistance, while plotting secretly to divide the Turkish territories between themselves.[6] France would take Syria and Lebanon, while Britain would grab Palestine, Yemen, and Iraq and maintain a protectorate over Egypt and the Gulf states. The British also tried to use Palestine to woo central European Jewish leaders away from allegiance to Germany and Austria-Hungary. The self-declared architect of the deal was Chaim Weizmann, a future president of Israel. Trained as a research chemist in Germany, he offered Winston Churchill, then in charge of the Royal Navy, a new process for manufacturing military explosives. His reward, so he claimed, was the Balfour Declaration, in which Britain offered a "national home" for Jews in Arab Palestine.[7]

Weizmann's self-congratulations notwithstanding, much more was at work. The British political elite was replete with Christian Zionists who saw the ingathering of Jews to Palestine as fulfillment of Biblical prophecy. Churchill himself was convinced that Bolshevism was largely the

handiwork of a "sinister confederacy" of "international Jews."[8] Hence
his notion of Zionism as an antidote. No doubt his anti-Arab racism
made the idea more attractive. He had experienced the youthful thrill
of watching British machine guns massacre the "dervish" Army in the
Sudan in 1898. Later, as a mature statesman, he had authorized the
first-ever use against a civilian population of poison gas, delivered by air
against "recalcitrant Arabs" protesting British takeover of oil-rich Iraq.[9]
Furthermore anything that would demoralize Muslim peoples in the
Middle East would rebound to Britain's favor in India, where demands
for independence, which the British blamed mainly on Muslim agitation, were growing more insistent. Churchill's philo-Zionism was likely
fed further by his opposition to concessions in Ireland – Protestants in
Ulster appeared to him like Zionists in Palestine, pioneers of progress
in a backward land of primitive religious belief. All this swung him, and
others in the imperial establishment, to favor political Zionism. Its leaders reciprocated by backing Churchill's dreams of a political comeback
after his disastrous performance in World War I seemed to have con-
fined him to political limbo.

During Ottoman times Jewish immigration to Palestine grew slowly
but remained largely urban. Takeover of agricultural property was
blocked by Ottoman law, which forbad absentee ownership. The Jewish
National Fund, financial arm of the Zionist movement, got around this
to some degree by having resident Middle Eastern Jews act as fronts.
But real progress came when the near-bankrupt Ottoman Sultan, in
exchange for loans, introduced a new land-registry system that permitted wealthy absentees to gain title. Once the British took over, they accelerated the process. Although Palestine's olive oil and oranges had
already won international acclaim, most agriculture was the work of
self-sufficient peasant farmers. The British hoped to replace them with
wealthy landholders who would be cooperative with the colonial power.
But, when purchase of Arab-owned land was followed by eviction of Palestinian peasants, the result was increasingly violent clashes between indigenous farmers and European Jewish settlers. Race and religion
certainly played an exacerbating role; but the problem was ultimately
derivative from economic insecurity and land expropriation.[10]

Before World War II, the British crushed a Palestinian rebellion, deporting and executing its leadership and disarming the Arab population. Soon after, Britain started training and equipping Jewish soldiers.
But something else was afoot. Before the war, radical political Zionism
had been inspired and nurtured by Benito Mussolini in fascist Italy and

supported by a right-wing government of Poland, happy to cooperate in a project to rid Poland of its Jews. The alliance was aptly symbolized by the career of Menachem Begin, a former officer in the Polish Army. When his group began military activities against the British in Palestine, it was initially with Italian training and Polish weapons.[11] However during the Spanish Civil War, Mussolini, fearing a defeat of fascist forces and anxious for German military aid, cozied up to Hitler, whom he had previously brushed off as a crude upstart. As a result, Irgun leaders patched up their quarrels with Britain. But soon after the war, the Irgun was on the offensive again, for example, with a 1946 plot to murder the British Foreign Secretary and, of course, with the notorious bombing of the King David Hotel.[12]

After the bombing, excited reporters claimed that the Irgun had some four to five thousand armed members. Actually there were relatively few, and their operations were quite cheap. Still, stories about grand conspiracies helped to raise the Irgun's profile and increase its support. They were also useful to British military intelligence, which, by inflating the threat, could secure more resources and prepare an alibi for its own ineffectiveness. The lessons for the post-9/11 world are too obvious to require elaboration.

Still, outside sympathizers were more than eager to help. They raised money, recruited members, and arranged logistics in twenty-three countries, of which the US was the most important.[13] There fundraisers for militant Zionist groups worked on religious congregations, businesses, and households using a mix of persuasion, guilt, and intimidation. People preferred to contribute cash than to fight; and the myth of thousands of guerrillas made the choice easier. In the Bronx even Christians who refused to contribute might find swastikas painted on their doors.[14] Money, too, was kicked in by sympathetic Jewish gangsters.[15] There was even a scheme to sell fake bonds to US Jews and divert the money to the Irgun.[16] Meanwhile inside Palestine, the Irgun benefited from hold-ups of banks, post offices, and a payroll train, plus extortion from Jewish businesses in Palestine, while also stealing weapons and explosives from British Army bases.[17] It had competition.

In 1937 the Lohamei Herut Israel (AKA the Stern Gang) split from the Irgun. The leader, Avraham Stern, wanted to create in Palestine the kind of totalitarian movement he had admired in Europe. He and his followers blamed the Zionist mainstream for alienating Mussolini and tried to convince the Nazis to create a Jewish state militarily aligned with Germany on the French colony of Madagascar. Equally unsuccessfully they proposed to arm and train Jews in the Warsaw ghetto, then move them to Palestine to fight the British.[18]

In 1942 the British killed Stern, opening a succession contest. One night the group's operations chief, Yitzhak Shamir, whom the British had briefly imprisoned on terrorism charges, went for a stroll with his chief rival and came back alone – his rival was later found with a bullet in his head.[19] Like the Irgun, the Stern Gang raised money from robberies – of banks, government offices, the paymaster handling relief funds for Jewish refugees, and possibly from a more prophetic source. Before the Nazis overran Belgium, world centre of the diamond trade, the British had subsidized the movement of Jewish diamond-cutters to Palestine. In perhaps the first manifestation of the "conflict diamond," the Stern Gang, or its imitators, seemed to find their stones and cash a prize too rich to resist.[20] It also received contributions from the same countries that aided the Irgun. Furthermore it developed close relations with the USSR and, a little later, Communist Czechoslovakia, a bountiful source of men and weapons.[21]

Although the Irgun and the Stern Gang earned the most notoriety, mainstream movements used much the same methods. Across Europe and the Americas, in French-ruled North Africa and white-dominated South Africa, the Haganah, the principal political and paramilitary organization, mobilized millions of dollars and tons of arms.[22] Inside Palestine the British permitted the Haganah to impose a tax on Jewish settlements to finance its militia. There, too, Haganah militants raised money by shaking down businesses, by playing the currency black market, and by counterfeiting – a British raid on a safe house turned up equipment for forging British government bearer bonds along with £50,000 worth ready for circulation.[23]

However, most external funding for the Haganah came from the US, from both ends of the social ladder. Mob casino bosses staged Jewish National Fund events in California and Las Vegas.[24] In 1945, anticipating the end of the wartime truce with Britain, David Ben Gurion met in the US with the vice-president of the United Jewish Appeal, the most important Jewish tax-exempt charitable foundation. Together they convened a meeting of nineteen prominent Jews to form a US arm of the Haganah. The UJA would continue to finance legal activities in Palestine; while the new group would take care of covert ones. Prophetically, in light of accusations later levelled at Muslim charities, they organized public fundraising events using as fronts institutions involved in refugee welfare relief. As the money came in, accountants working for respectable enterprises owned by group members channelled it to Swiss banks, thence to Palestine. In addition, members guaranteed for the Jewish Agency a loan secured against the future flow of donations, with the money used for arms purchases.[25]

Not until after 1948, with the conquest of Palestine almost complete, was the tax-exempt status of either the Jewish Agency or the UJA challenged – and temporarily suspended. But, with intervention from the US administration, the suspensions were quickly lifted, and no criminal charges followed. Indeed, despite occasional private efforts, to this day that status has never been successfully contested – the courts dismiss protests on the grounds that individuals do not have standing to challenge administrative rulings by the IRS.[26]

Initially the weapons used to conquer Palestine were mainly from British sources, diverted from local stockpiles or purchased on the black market from corrupt or complicit British quartermasters in North Africa. Later some British officers rerouted shipments of weapons away from the British-led Arab Legion in Jordan to the Haganah.[27] At the end of World War II, Haganah gunrunners, with the help of sympathetic insiders, raided US Army depots in Europe and scoured the US for war-surplus material. Arms, ships, machinery to create arms factories inside Palestine, and even squadrons of fighter aircraft were available at scrap value. US mobster Meyer Lansky, already a financial contributor, arranged through underworld contacts in waterfront unions to facilitate the movement of weapons for Jewish paramilitaries.[28] In addition, the new Communist government of Czechoslovakia provided both weapons and reconditioned fighter planes that were moved, sometimes painted with US insignia, through the US-occupied zone in Germany to Palestine. It was a mutually beneficial alliance. The Czechs allegedly took payment in hard currency, gold, and military technology stolen from the USA, which Warsaw Pact countries could study and copy. The aircraft arrived in time to be decisive against the Arab side.[29]

Not that it was ever much of a contest. While the world has been saturated for decades with the David-and-Muhammed myth, the reality was the reverse. There was a three to one majority in favor of Zionist forces for most of the war; thanks to aircraft from the US and Czechoslovakia, they quickly took control of the skies; and on the ground they greatly outgunned the other side. Their forces were heavily staffed by former British and US soldiers who, at the end of World War II, simply moved to the Haganah, sometimes with their weapons. The Arab armies, by contrast, just beginning to emerge from a colonial tutelage that had kept them weak to ensure they would not be a serious source of opposition, were plagued by poor morale and antiquated equipment, often trained only for the parade ground and commanded by officers whose main military talent lay in embezzling from Army stores.[30]

CREATING A LAND WITHOUT PEOPLE

Before the armies from neighboring Arab states entered Palestine, the Jewish armed forces had already launched an ethnic cleansing campaign that would deliver to the new state of Israel 80 percent of historical Palestine, even though the UN partition plan allocated to Israel about 50 percent. Far from an unfortunate side-effect of war, the ethnic cleansing was based on a plan worked out by the Jewish Agency's Transfer Committee, which, using its tax-exempt financing from the US, had already done an inventory of the contents of nearly five hundred Arab villages.[31] Then came a series of massacres, the results of which were broadcast, along with false reports of epidemics, to terrorize the rest of the Palestinian population into flight. The dirtiest operations were conducted by the Stern Gang and Irgun. Their most notorious act was in the village of Deir Yassin, where 250 villagers of all ages and sexes were lined up against walls and shot; the town was then looted. Deir Yassin was hardly alone. But the fuss made it appear aberrant instead of a single instance in a systematic campaign. Then, after the Palestinian population had fled, the government of Israel blamed "rogue elements" while undercutting the political standing of two groups whose (far-right) ideology ran counter to the official (pseudo-Marxist) one. The Irgun and the Stern Gang were banned – but their fighters were simply absorbed into the regular armed forces and their leaders encouraged to make respectable careers in politics and government service. Once Israel was created, Stern Gang boss Yitzak Shamir went undercover for a while as European head of Mossad, the Israeli intelligence service, orchestrating, among other deeds, a letter-bomb campaign to kill Arab scientists whose skills might be useful for military projects in their own countries. He later entered mainstream politics, capping his career, much as had his old rival, Menachem Begin, as a prime minister of the country he had so large a role in creating.[32]

Duly emptied of indigenous inhabitants, some 380 towns and villages were demolished or handed over to Jewish colonists, who then gave them Hebrew names, with the financial support of tax-deductible contributions to the Jewish National Fund. After securing the countryside, Zionist forces in turn conquered and emptied the major urban centres.[33]

One of the earliest laws of the new state of Israel proclaimed that all who fled (750,000 people) forfeited their property – houses, farm-lands, and personal possessions, along with shops, stores, and factories. The objectives were not just to seize property but to ensure that if the UN applied pressure for a return of refugees, there would be nothing to which to come home. To lose property under this law, the population did not have to pass the frontiers of what became Israel. Those who simply sought refuge in a neighboring village were stripped of every-thing they left behind. In areas where the population was slow to leave, Israeli soldiers evicted people from their homes or blocked farmers from cultivating their lands, making the property forfeit under the law. The Custodian of Abandoned Property wrote frankly about the "vast amount of property spread over hundreds of towns and villages." He sent officers to every house, shop, warehouse, plant, quarry, field, orchard, and bank to do an inventory, to tend large herds of animals, and to pick crops on 800,000 acres of land that legend subsequently claimed to have been desert.

In theory all of the property was to be turned over to the state. In practice Israeli soldiers broke into homes and took jewellery, cash, and oriental carpets while Jewish newcomers, fresh from concentration camps, looted abandoned Arab houses, apartments, and commercial establishments.[34] Israel's onsite founding father, David Ben Gurion, ex-pressed his disgust. The loss of those assets, he felt, would interfere with the new country's ability to use seized Arab property to attract more Jewish immigrants to farm the lands, tend the orchards, and staff the factories and shops whose previous owners had been driven into refu-gee camps in neighbouring countries.[35]

Others, whose consciences were not as selective, were also upset. Among them was Count Folke Bernadotte, the UN mediator in Pales-tine. He had saved the lives of thousands of Jews during World War II, and he insisted that the first priority in a peace settlement be repatria-tion of those Palestinians who had fled. In 1948, he was murdered by the Stern Gang.[36] World pressure to restore to the Palestinians their land and property largely died with him.

Nor did it revive after 1967 when Israel completed its conquest of Pales-tine by seizing the West Bank and Gaza, and then began to apply in slower motion much the same ethnic-cleansing techniques. Land and water were seized under various pretexts to be used for Jewish settlements; political leaders were assassinated; arbitrary imprisonment, deportation, and tor-ture became routine; houses were razed along with their olive trees; and the remaining population was reduced to virtual slave-labor status.[37]

Meanwhile into Israel and the Occupied Territories poured annually billions in US military and economic aid, along hundreds of millions more through charitable and religious foundations who spent the money to finance further colonization. The trick was simple. Any charitable institution so designated by the government of Israel was automatically given the same status by the US one, a privilege granted the institutions of no other foreign country. Anything raised abroad, mainly in the US, by the Israeli government or its official charities went into the official budget to be spent nominally on things like education and welfare within internationally recognized borders, thus permitting the Israeli government to divert more of its other funds to colonization and settlement in illegally occupied areas. Yet, although today the doctrine of fungibility, the idea that it is illegal to allocate money for legitimate purposes if it is intended to free up other funds for illegitimate ones, is applied to ban such practices by groups supporting Palestinian initiatives, curiously, no one in the US government seems to have applied the same notion to stanch the vastly greater flows from the US to Israel, and then on to Occupied Palestine.[38] And each time even mildly critical voices were raised from outside the ranks of officialdom, a massive propaganda machine swung into action to deny and defame until those voices were silenced. Thus, facing world indifference, it was up to the Palestinians themselves to ensure justice. Alas, there were few among them politically capable of the task, and many whose behavior would make that goal much more difficult to accomplish.

REBEL WITH TOO MANY CAUSES?

If any name was slated to top the charts in the annals of "Arab terrorism," at least until Usama bin Lāden came along, it is that of Sabri al-Bannā, better known as Abu Nidal. He will be remembered as the man who organized massacres at the El Al check-in counters in the Vienna and Rome airports in 1985 and the bombing of an Istanbul synagogue the next year, conducted murders and kidnap operations against pro-US figures in the Gulf States, assassinated numerous officials of the Palestine Liberation Organization who were attempting a dialogue for peace with Israeli doves, and ran guns to keep going one of the bloodiest wars of the last fifty years.[39] However much horror the escapades of Abu Nidal may justifiably invoke, it is impossible to call him a rebel without a cause.

Sabri al-Bannā was born to a comfortable middle-class family in Palestine. His father was a successful citrus grower whose orange crop went each year from Jaffa to Liverpool. The family was well off enough to have a second home on the Syrian coast. Perhaps the only thing he shared with bin Lāden is that his mother was an 'Alawī from the Alexandretta area, which France casually ceded to Turkey. In a dress rehearsal for its treatment of the Greek population in Northern Cyprus forty years later, Turkey began suppressing Arabic, driving Syrian nationalists underground, and flooding the area with Anatolian peasants. Then came 1948.

After the city of Jaffa was captured by the Haganah, its soldiers rounded up and expelled the Palestinians; looters from Tel Aviv went to work; and the seized homes and lands were resettled with Jewish refugees from Europe. The al-Bannā home and orange groves were among the chosen. The family itself escaped to a refugee camp in Gaza and later made its way to Nablus in the West Bank, then under Jordanian control. There, no doubt, the family heard tales about Jewish farmers making the deserts bloom with orchards of the very Jaffa oranges that Palestinian farmers had cultivated for generations.

Thus, with the loss of his mother's home to Turkey and his father's to Israel, in effect young Sabri had already been doubly disinherited, and it was going to happen a third time – during the 1967 war. By then he was already determined to fight to regain his homeland. Three things distinguished his future career as a Palestinian militant: one was the sharp mind he applied to business enterprise, political organization, and terrorist attacks; the second was his admiration for the Irgun and the Stern Gang whose methods he consciously set out to imitate (on the theory that, if their tactics had sufficed to conquer Palestine, the same in other hands might win it back); the third was his curious choice of targets.[40]

Although Abu Nidal had already established his own group, he soon dissolved it to become a member of Fatah, created by Yasir Arafat and a small group of other Palestinian exiles in Kuwait in the late 1950s, with financial support from Diaspora students, professionals, and businessmen. Fatah was marginal at the start; it conducted a few desultory raids into Occupied Palestine, whose main result was to give Israel a pretext for massive reprisals. Meantime the supposed official voice, the Palestine Liberation Organization, was created, financed, and controlled by the Arab League so that the Arab states could placate their populations, outraged over the abysmal performance of their armies in the battle to save Palestine, with the illusion of action. When in June 1967 the frontline Arab armies were smashed and the rest of Palestine occupied by Israel, the old PLO fell apart. A new organization of the same name emerged, dominated by Fatah, which began to put together the infrastructure of a government in exile, with Amman in Jordan as the de facto capital.

In those early years Abu Nidal had a role of some significance, mainly because of his business acumen. He opened in Jordan a trading company that also served to front for political meetings and handle payments to guerrillas and their families (the same kind of role of which bin Lāden's Sudanese enterprises would later be accused). He was soon dispatched as Fatah's official representative in Khartoum and later Baghdad. Yet he was critical of Fatah rhetoric and practice. To him, the young Palestinian fighters recruited from refugee camps who strutted about waving Kalashnikovs were mainly noise and hot air. When it became likely that the king of Jordan would order his forces to crush the Palestinian guerrillas lest their rather inconsequential attacks across the river provide a pretext for quite consequential Israeli retaliation, Fatah sent Abu Nidal to Baghdad to obtain reassurance from Iraq that its forces, stationed in Jordan to help defend the country against further Israeli expansionism, would protect the Palestinians. His mission was a failure. The Palestinian infrastructure and much of its fighting force was wiped out, and the remnants fell back on Lebanon, where they were soon repeating the same mistakes, but without Abu Nidal, who had gone permanently into opposition to the Palestinian mainstream. He was not alone.

There had always been challenges to the pretense of Yasir Arafat's Fatah to speak for the Palestinian Diaspora. Much as the Haganah had faced opposition from the Stern Gang and Irgun, so a number of Palestinian factions opposed one or both of Arafat's main strategic initiatives to build the accoutrements of a state in exile and to strive for the independence of the parts of Palestine seized by Israel in 1967, effectively conceding 80 percent of Palestine and confining its former population to permanent exile.

For a long time the most important opposition was headed not by Abu Nidal but by Wadi Haddad and George Habash (a Marxist from a Christian family), who together established the Popular Front for the Liberation of Palestine. While Arafat built his long career on accommodation with the most conservative forces in Palestinian society, Habash was fond of remarking that it was impossible for Palestinians to liberate Palestine before they liberated themselves. While Arafat sought to create a popular movement whose political content was little more than

Palestinian nationalism, Haddad stressed solidarity with radical leftist movements everywhere. In that spirit he teamed up with an odd assortment of romantic sociopaths, including another individual whose notoriety would in its time exceed that of Abu Nidal and come close to matching that achieved by Usama bin Lāden today.

OF MYTHS AND MEN

According to legend, Illich Ramirez Sanchez ("Carlos") was born in Caracas to a family of millionaire Marxists. At age fourteen he was the head of the Venezuelan Communist youth and sufficiently enthusiastic to be recruited by the KGB before his fifteenth birthday. It sent "Carlos" first to Cuba for guerrilla training, then to Moscow's Patrice Lumumba University (sort of an al-Azhar for atheists) for ideological indoctrination. Afterwards, armed and financed by Moscow, he constructed a terrorist multinational whose collective list of reputed feats included: attacks on Lod Airport in Israel (really done by the Japanese Red Army) and on the Israeli team at the Munich Olympics in 1972 (the work of Black September); a (nonexistent) contract job for the "Communist" government of Nicaragua to assassinate former dictator Anastasio Somoza; and a plot to the overthrow of the Shah of Iran (really the consequence of a mass uprising) and direct the takeover of the US Embassy in Teheran in 1979 (a strictly indigenous job). Although this last event led to the defeat of Jimmy Carter at the hands of Ronald Reagan, his Republican challenger, Carlos was subsequently "linked to" an attempt to bump off the new president. His public CV even included a global rampage on behalf of Saddam Hussein at the end of the 1980s to divert attention from Iraq's planned invasion of Kuwait, at a time when Carlos was living in Libya, whose leader personally called for the withdrawal of Iraqi forces. During all this time rumors flowed that Carlos was seeking or, much worse, had already obtained a small nuclear device.[41]

The truth was rather more prosaic.[42] Far from Carlos being born to great wealth, his father was a lawyer of comfortable but not extravagant means who passed his political consciousness to his sons. Against a background of unrelenting corruption, poverty, and repression, Venezuela had given birth to a strong Communist opposition in which Carlos, a nerdy individual who was often the butt of his classmates' jokes, played no role. He never went near Cuba, not even to frolic on the beaches. He did attend Patrice Lumumba University – contrary to Western propaganda, it was a serious educational institution in which

Carlos excelled, not in his studies of engineering, but in his investigations of vodka and girls. Indeed, like most of the romantics who played revolutionary games in Europe at that time, he despised the conservatism of Soviet Communism. Attracted to the Palestinian cause, he linked up with the Popular Front, whose belief in armed struggle across the globe as the only way to liberate the homeland was consistent with Carlos's own dreams of worldwide revolution led by a violent (but definitely non-Islamic) vanguard. Carlos managed to shoot, but not to kill, a major financial contributor to Israel and toss a bomb at a branch of an Israeli bank, as well as to blow apart a popular hangout in Paris, killing many innocents. But his early operations for the PFLP were so incompetently executed, they nearly caused the collapse of its European infrastructure. In 1975, after killing two French intelligence agents on rue Toullier in Paris, he managed a narrow escape and was nearly himself executed by an outraged Wadi Haddad. The French services, to cover up their embarrassment and to strike a propaganda blow, spread the story that Carlos was working for Moscow. Soon the notion of the Soviet Union as world financier of terror took off; and in short order all manner of previous terrorist acts whose authorship was fuzzy were being laid at the joint doorstep of Carlos and Moscow. Haddad decided that, if Carlos could curb his revolutionary zeal for food, booze, and prostitutes, he had his uses after all. Hence Carlos was designated the point man for what became his most notorious coup, a plot to kidnap the oil ministers of the OPEC countries.[43]

However, the plan ran afoul of efforts by the presidents of Austria, Algeria, and Libya. All the ministers survived; and when Carlos attempted to pocket $10 million in ransom money paid by Saudi Arabia, he again came perilously close to ending his career in front of a PFLP firing squad.[44] Still, the OPEC heist secured his reputation. Soon he was allegedly plotting everything from an attack on a French nuclear power plant (possibly true) to a surprise appearance at the 1976 Olympics in Montreal (certainly false). He likely had a hand in a series of outrages in France in the late 1970s and early 1980s; but by then his motives may have had less to do with Palestine than with more personal matters, such as the imprisonment of his then wife. He also developed a new appetite, digesting books and articles about his alleged exploits. Of the small nuclear device he had supposedly acquired, there was no trace.

Although Carlos did have links with the East German intelligence services and briefly had a safe house in Hungary, every effort he made to enter the Soviet Union was rebuffed; and the KGB soon pressured its

European allies to roll up the welcome mat.[45] By the end of the 1980s, he was on the run. Iraq was weary of him; Syria spurned him; Libya's Mu'ammar Qadhafi insisted that Carlos stand trial for the death of a Libyan in the OPEC caper. Like Usama, he wound up in the Sudan. Supposedly he entered on a fake Yemeni diplomatic passport without the knowledge of the local authorities. But once there he was not exactly security conscious – roaring around in his fancy car and hanging out in the hot spots, few and far between in National Islamic Front-run Khartoum. At first his hosts were pleased. But then reality intruded. NIF boss Hassan al-Turabi later commented: "We welcomed him as a combatant … for noble causes. Now he's a hoodlum, his behavior is shameful."[46]

The Sudan was a bad choice of exile. France offered to the Sudan political support in its efforts to escape pariah status and provided arms and training plus the use of a strip of neighboring Central African Republic (run de facto by an ex-French spook) as a backdoor to attack anti-government guerrillas in the South. Sudan may have reciprocated with promises of oil concessions; it certainly delivered on Carlos.[47]

Probably the most eloquent summary of his career was provided by Carlos himself at his trial.[48] He insisted that most of what was known about him was myth, the joint product of spook disinformation, reportorial overimagination, and public hysteria. But it served important purposes. "The myth brought in hundreds of millions of dollars to the Palestinians. Everyone benefited from it. I don't give a damn about the Carlos myth, it's not me who created it."[49] Perhaps not; but the PFLP, the Mossad, and the French intelligence services, among others, used that myth to their own ends, as did Carlos himself. Perhaps Usama was watching and taking notes.

REVOLUTIONARIES AND RACKETEERS

While the Popular Front was indulging in bloody revolutionary fantasies across Europe and sometimes in the Middle East, something much more serious was taking shape in Lebanon. That country became to the Palestinian Diaspora what Pakistan's North West Frontier Province would shortly be for Afghan exiles. From there the Arafat-controlled PLO supported worldwide information and diplomatic services, an Army and social security apparatus for the refugee population, communications facilities, and industrial investments to train a generation of skilled workers and entrepreneurs. From Lebanon, too, PLO activities spread around the world: it was soon supporting model farms in seven countries in Africa, an airport duty-free shop in Tanzania, and agribusiness and textile factories in Eastern Europe. The result of all the PLO economic activities was to make the organization an integral part of the Lebanese economy and to help convert the Palestinian presence from a band of dispirited refugees into a veritable PLO Inc.[50]

Funding for the PLO was separate from that of the political factions that (sometimes) sheltered under its umbrella. Partly it came from the Palestine Liberation Tax of 5–7 percent collected on the salaries of the expatriate Palestinians working in the oil-producing countries and paid to the PLO by the oil-rich Gulf states. This was supplemented by occasional direct contributions from the leaders of Arab states and by gifts (which were rarely tax-deductible) from the Palestinian Diaspora elsewhere in the world. But these sources left the PLO at the financial mercy of the various Arab countries whose leaders had their own agendas. At one point the PLO complained that money raised nominally for Palestine ended up financing the Afghan mujahideen. As a result, more importance was attached to independent revenue – from businesses in Lebanon and abroad, and from a portfolio of bonds, stocks, and money-market instruments all over the world. The main financial manager was the Arab Bank of Amman. This institution had been formed in Palestine back in 1930 to try to provide funds for Palestinians to buy up land from absentee owners in competition with the Jewish National Fund. When its owners fled with their bank to Jordan in 1948, the branches in Palestine were all closed. The bank was subsequently singled out by pro-Israel groups as a financier of global terrorism long before institutions like the Bank of Credit and Commerce International earned such distinction and continued long after BCCI had vanished. Arab Bank even featured in post-9/11 lawsuits as an institution supposedly managing money on behalf of al-Qāʾidah.[51]

Out of this search for financial independence came predictable tales of a giant PLO slush fund from criminal activity – drugs, extortion, skyjacking, etc. Some "national security experts" who later grabbed the spotlight to make erudite pronouncements about Usama bin Lāden's megabillions first earned public fame pronouncing on the "black budget" from which Arafat supposedly financed worldwide terror campaigns. Indeed, the claim that the PLO revenues came equally from three sources – patron states, criminal activity, and its own network of business companies and investment fronts – bore a similarity to the alleged al-Qāʾidah business structure revealed to the world about two decades later.[52]

There was a downside to Arafat's control of money. Smaller Palestinian groups had to find their own sources. The Popular Front, while raising money from sympathizers, engaged in kidnapping, skyjacking, and extorting funds from rulers of the Gulf states in exchange for a commitment not to operate on their soil.[53] So did one of its splinter groups, the Democratic Front for the Liberation of Palestine, formed by Nayif Hawatmeh, another Christian Marxist of even more radical bent. Ahmed Jibril, whose main political view was that armed struggle be coordinated with Arab states, departed to found the Popular Front for the Liberation of Palestine – General Command with money from Syria, which also supported al-Saiqah, formed by Palestinians in Syrian refugee camps. The Iraqi Ba'th party created the Arab Liberation Front; and another defector from Fatah, Abu'l Abbas, set up his Palestine Liberation Front with support from Gulf state businessmen and politicians as well as periodically from Iraqi intelligence. But none could match the financial resources of Fatah. And control over the Fatah treasury in turn gave Arafat the leverage to assert almost a monopoly on decisions about how the PLO budget was allocated.

As the PLO entrenched itself in Lebanon, the country descended into a vicious, multisided civil war with Israel, various Arab states, and different Palestinian factions stoking with arms and money conflicts between that country's multitude of political and religious factions. Meanwhile Israel, concerned less about Palestinian guerrillas crossing the tightly sealed border than the impact of growing PLO power and influence on the Palestinian population under occupation, intensified its shelling and bombing of Southern Lebanon.[54] In 1978 it launched a full-scale invasion, sending nearly half of the population of the area fleeing, either abroad or into the "belt of misery," the mixed Palestinian-Lebanese Muslim refugee camps and slums that ringed Beirut.[55] Then in 1982 it rolled over the border again with one third of its Army. Before the carnage was over, some fifty thousand Lebanese and Palestinians were dead, maimed, or wounded, 85–90 percent of them civilians; some 600,000–700,000 people were displaced; and direct physical damage was three times that of the preceding seven years of civil war. In the aftermath the Lebanese government faced a reconstruction bill it estimated at a minimum of $8 billion, excluding damage to Palestinian-owned institutions, homes, and businesses, while others put the total as high as $27 billion.[56] The enormous destruction would soon be forgotten by the mainstream media until in 2004, when Usama bin Lāden reminded the world by contrasting the attention paid to the Twin Towers to the silence over the wholesale destruction in Beirut, which he claimed, not very convincingly, inspired his own actions.[57]

THE ENEMY OF MY ENEMY?

In the subsequent mop-up operation, Israel seemed to have an unlikely ally. Unlike the leaders of other groups to challenge the dominance of Yasir Arafat's Fatah in the councils of the PLO, Abu Nidal had rarely lacked for material support; and, like Arafat, he kept control in good measure by being master of his mint. After he had created his own organization, the Fatah Revolutionary Council, he received from Iraq all of the mainstream Fatah's Iraqi-based assets – weapons, cash, training facilities, and especially the diplomatic passports that were important for moving arms and personnel around Europe.[58] Still, while the president of Iraq looked on Abu Nidal with favor, his ambitious vice-president, Saddam Hussein, was less impressed and, after he took over the presidency in 1979, moved to expel Abu Nidal. To try to curry favor and buy time, Abu Nidal ran errands. During the early part of Iran-Iraq war, he set up arms deals for Iraq with Poland and Bulgaria and helped train members of the exiled Islamist opposition to the secular Syrian regime, then at loggerheads with Iraq.[59] But he also staged an assassination attempt on the Israeli ambassador to Britain, which provided the pretext for Israel's long-planned invasion of Lebanon – even though the ambassador himself publicly denounced Prime Minister Begin's efforts to use his close brush with death to justify the subsequent atrocities. Finally in 1983, in a bid to placate the US, Saddam Hussein showed the door to Abu Nidal, who, anticipating Usama bin Lāden's complaints about the Sudan a decade later, complained bitterly that Iraq owed him $50 million. Abu Nidal landed in Syria, where, in return for asylum, for several years he helped the government identify and liquidate leaders of the Islamist opposition – the same ones he had helped Saddam train.[60] While Syria prevented him from establishing his own bases in the country, he set up in Lebanon to directly challenge al-Fatah. From there he conducted assassinations against prominent PLO officials around the world.

There was always something strange about his targets and his timing. For example, the attacks on El Al offices in Rome and Vienna took place in the two countries of Europe where sympathy for Palestine was greatest. The attempted assassination of the Israeli ambassador to Britain (the actual triggerman was a survivor of the Deir Yassin massacre) occurred when the PLO was trying desperately to keep the situation quiet in Southern Lebanon.[61] While there was the occasional Jewish target, most of his victims were Palestinian doves attempting, usually with Arafat's blessing, to dialogue with the Israeli peace camp. The most prominent of his victims was Abu Jihad, the Palestinian leader who was most closely in touch with operations during the first intifāda (popular uprising) in the Occupied Territories and whose death was perhaps the single greatest blow struck against the rebellion. Furthermore while everyone knew where his infrastructure in Lebanon was located, Israel, never hesitant to bomb anywhere in that country, left the Abu Nidal camp alone.[62]

Inevitably there were suspicions that his group was infiltrated and manipulated by Israel. On the other hand, the Palestinian movement, hardly the most mature or sensible of the world's national liberation groups, has never lacked for hotheads and cutthroats ready to slaughter one another in the name of their supposed struggle while their enemy looks on in bemused contempt. Abu Nidal was conspicuous in that regard only by his success. Nonetheless it is true that many of the things Abu Nidal did had the remarkable effect of advancing the interests of Israeli hardliners, notably during governments headed by Menachem Begin and by Yitzak Shamir, whose methods Abu Nidal had as a youthful revolutionary so admired and as a mature terrorist sought hard to emulate.[63]

His longevity in the terror business was often imputed to money. There were the usual stories of great fortunes, up to $400 million, from smart investments of the Iraqi endowment and from extortion and gunrunning. How this was possible, when, by his account, Iraq had stripped him of all his assets then expelled him, was not clear. In another eerie similarity to the Usama bin Lāden legend of later years, this story was retailed at the same time as claims that his "followers" engaged in petty scams in Europe and even in the US to raise money. Indeed in 1993 US authorities announced that they had broken an Abu Nidal "cell" in the Midwest. Allegedly a group of Palestinian émigrés managing corner convenience stores in poor areas had been told by the "chief of Abu Nidal's American operations" to raise money in the US by "fraud, theft and extortion" and to obtain by fraudulent means US passports to facilitate the travel of others. Supposedly their activities included high-return capers like stealing a truckload of light bulbs for sale through their stores and running a "massive" nationwide food-coupon fraud ring. Inevitably one of the Palestinians was supposedly

selling cocaine, with part of the money sent out of the country on behalf of the "organization" to finance its operations. Several were sentenced the next year – on federal racketeering charges.[64]

Stories of the Abu Nidal megamillions were accompanied by claims
that the money was stashed in foreign banks in the names of his wife,
son, daughter, and close confederates, all well known to the major intelligence services. He was even supposed to have an account in the
Bank of Credit and Commerce International. It seems that Abu Nidal,
the astute financier, had a sense of financial security as advanced as
that shown by Usama bin Lāden in the Sudan.

In reality his longevity was due to his capacity to find new sponsors.
When he ran afoul of Syria, he ended up in Libya, where he allegedly
help the regime destabilize the Sudan by supporting the SPLA. When
Yasir Arafat, with that instinct for political self-immolation that was long
his trademark, declared support for Saddam Hussein following the invasion of Kuwait, the Gulf States not only cut off the PLO but, report-
edly out of sheer rancor, begun funnelling money to Abu Nidal as well
as to Arafat's Islamist opposition.[65] After Abu Nidal exhausted his welcome in Libya (whose government closed his camps and expelled his
key operatives), he wound up for a time in Egypt, where he tried to sell
his knowledge of Libya, Yemen, and the Sudan and offer his services
against Al Jihad and Gamā'at al-Islāmiyya in return for asylum and freedom to operate. Then, dying from cancer, he headed back for Iraq.[66]

His last exile was grist to the Washington propaganda mill. In 2002,
the Iraqis claimed that he had entered the country using a phony Yemeni passport (whose holders did not require visas), that they tracked
him down following a tip-off from a friendly Arab country, that he was
suffering from leukemia, and that he had shot himself when they came
to arrest him. The Bush administration had a different story. Abu
Nidal, it said, was suffering only from mild skin cancer. He had agreed
in exchange for treatment (in those glorious Baghdad hospitals denied
under the US and UK sanctions X-ray or radiotherapy equipment or
even chlorine to sterilize water) to help Saddam train al-Qā'idah fighters stationed in Iraq (as if Iraq needed an outsider to train paramilitary
forces). When he refused to carry out his side of the bargain (as if a
man with his past would hesitate in such an assignment), he was killed.[67]
Actually, the most likely scenario was that he had entered the country
under the aegis of an Iraqi intelligence service in exchange for information and was bumped off in a desperate last-ditch attempt to placate
the US in the buildup to the 2003 invasion.

In one respect he could die in peace. Following the Lebanon war, then the crushing of the first intifāda in Palestine, the PLO had been reduced, by the death of its most effective leaders, the drying up of financial resources, and the loss of any base near the occupied areas, to a shadow of its former self. Under extreme duress, it agreed to US-brokered "peace accords," which left it acting as Israel's arm in suppressing popular outrage in the West Bank and Gaza.

By then the discrediting of Arafat and secular nationalism by Israeli and US obstinacy meant that the political initiative had shifted to those who espoused radical political Islam. Their ideological appeal was powerfully reinforced by a social and economic one. With Israel seizing most of the arable land and subjecting the urban population to progressive immiseration and humiliation, with the West Bank facing 50 percent unemployment and Gaza closer to 80 percent, and with an absence of governmental social services (Israel refused to grant them, and the PLO had no money) about the only thing keeping the population from mass starvation was UN handouts and a network of charities linked to the emerging Islamist opposition. When after 9/11 the US insisted on targeting the Islamic charities that bin Lāden allegedly used to finance terror, it was already an old story. Both Israel and the US had started well before to do precisely that to Palestinian institutions. The difference was that now the fight intensified and became worldwide.

13

Pray or Prey? – Fifth Columns, Cooked Books, and Charitable Frauds in the USA

When the US government expanded its original terror list to embrace individuals and institutions who provided "material support," it demonstrated its commitment to the First Amendment right to freedom of (selective) religion by freezing the assets of the country's three major Muslim charities: the United Holy Land Foundation for Relief and Development, the Global Relief Foundation, the Benevolence International Foundation. Declaring such a freeze under the International Emergency Economic Powers Act also criminalized any support offered to the foundations by US citizens, even if such assistance, financial or otherwise, had been intended and used for legitimate purposes. Apparently the government was so busy chasing Islamic terror-dollars that it did not have time to move against Hindu zealots collecting money in the US to support anti-Muslim pogroms in India or Zionist groups raising funds to build more West Bank settlements and to remove any pesky Palestinians (along with their houses).[1] But at least the administration showed its sensitivity to Muslim sentiment by closing the institutions during Ramadan. When asked for evidence of wrongdoing, the FBI and the Treasury again cited "national security."[2]

There was a difference between how the three organizations were treated. With respect to Global Relief and Benevolence Foundation, the federal agents made dark hints about "possible links to al-Qaeda" and claimed that the information they had seized from the charities would be "a linchpin in their efforts to shut down al-Qaeda's money pipeline."[3] That seems a fair description of the logic and effectiveness of the war on terror-dollars – to close off a flow through a pipeline requires turning the correct valve while removing a linchpin simply lets a wheel fall off its axel.

However, with the United Holy Land Foundation, the biggest and oldest of the three, there was no real effort to "link" it with al-Qā'idah. The institution had been banned back in 1997 by Israel, which had kept pushing the US to follow suit. In 2001, it finally got its way. In a press conference with Israeli Prime Minister Ariel Sharon at his side, President Bush clarified that the intent of both closing United Holy Land and, unlike the other two Muslim charities, declaring it a designated foreign terrorist organization was to stop the flow of funds not to al-Qā'idah but to Hamas. Attorney General Ashcroft, in announcing a raid on the charity's offices, had similarly declared: "With this action we go beyond the al Qaeda network to target groups whose violent actions are designed to destroy the Middle East peace process." But if Hamas was really such an obstacle to peace, why did Israel devote so much time, energy, and money to create it?

REAPING THE WHIRLWIND?

In the 1970s Israel faced a Palestinian nationalist movement committed to a secular state and ready to make a huge territorial compromise – the PLO would write off losses from 1948 (consigning surviving refugees and their descendants to permanent exile) in exchange for recognition of a sovereign Palestine in the remaining 20 percent, the areas grabbed by Israel in 1967. Since Israel had no intention of surrendering good land or water, its strategy became to undermine PLO influence in Occupied Palestine by attacking it abroad and by creating an Islamic alternative at home. To that purpose, it permitted Ahmed Yassin, spiritual leader of what later became Hamas, to come home to Gaza from his studies in Cairo, then gave him a license to set up al-Mujamma al-Islāmī (Islamic Centre), a charitable foundation responsible for social, religious, and welfare institutions including schools, clinics, and mosques. It was funded partly by zakāt, partly by secret subsidies from the Israeli military governor's office. For nearly two decades, while Israel impeded the inflow of funds to PLO-supported institutions and imprisoned, expelled, or assassinated PLO leaders, it facilitated the influx of money for Islamic charitable work, for creating an Islamic University in Gaza, and for building mosques. The logic seemed impeccable. The PLO was preoccupied with finding a territorial base to rebuild national institutions. Islamists, by contrast, subordinated Palestinian nationalism to concern for the umma as a whole and were mistrustful about, even bitterly antagonistic to, secular and leftist trends within the Palestinian movement.[4]

True, the relationship between Israel and the Islamists was not always cordial. Yassin's collaborationist policy led a breakaway group, Islamic Jihad, to take up arms. That put pressure on Yassin to distance himself, at least rhetorically, from Israel. In 1984, after the alleged discovery of an arms cache, he was sentenced to twelve years in prison. Israel, hardly namby-pamby in defending itself against armed threats, released him the next year. For the next two decades he was alternately jailed and freed, expelled and allowed home, until finally in 2004, frail and in a wheelchair, he was assassinated by Israeli helicopter gunships. Things, it seemed, had not gone entirely according to plan.

When the first intifada broke out in 1988, the Islamists, like the PLO, were caught by surprise and scrambled to catch up with the general population. It was in response to the popular uprising that Yassin organized Hamas. In the struggle for the soul of Palestine for some time the PLO seemed to have the upper hand. But in the run-up to the 1991 Gulf War, following Arafat's astounding blunder in articulating support for Saddam Hussein, the Gulf states pulled their funding from the PLO and began, with Israel's tacit cooperation, to pump more into Hamas. Most contributions from individuals and from governments came via banks that were routinely monitored by Israeli intelligence. Once inside Palestine, the funds were distributed to various charities and religious institutions and to the social assistance networks linked to them.[5] On the other side, the PLO was bankrupt – it had never recovered from Israel's destruction of its Lebanon infrastructure; money for its institutions had largely dried up; and there were strikes by its functionaries over arrears of pay. Financial pressures were one factor forcing the PLO to accept the Oslo Accords, in which it would get not 20 percent of Palestine but about half of that while permanently ceding most arable land and water in the West Bank to Israel and allowing its own governmental functions to be subordinate to and directed by Israeli security forces.

There were powerful rejectionist forces on both sides. The Israeli right, religious and secular, was outraged at the betrayal of the Zionist ideal, while Ahmed Yassin, now seeking to be both religious guide and voice of Palestinian nationhood, rejected the agreement as a surrender. His influence was steadily growing. By the end of the 1990s, the budget of Hamas may have been greater than that of the Palestinian Authority, while reputedly one Palestinian in three received financial aid from the spreading network of Hamas-run social services. There was also military action against the occupation; but it started much later than the charitable work. In all the justified horror over suicide bombings, what gets conveniently forgotten is why and how they began, and the degree to which violence in Palestine by Islamic "fundamentalists" was simply the mirror image of that of Jewish "fundamentalists."

FAITH, HOPE, AND TAX-EXEMPT CHARITY

Zionism was originally the work of secularized Western European Jews. The Orthodox rabbinate of Eastern Europe denounced the project as heretical – to them the ingathering of Jews to Israel was a theological, not a political, concept and was only to occur after the return of the Messiah.[6] When Israel was carved out of (most of) Palestine at the end of World War II, its leaders, although forced to concede points to the religious establishment, still paid more lip service to Marx than to Moses. Hence relations with the more orthodox sects remained tenuous, even hostile. Some who lived in Palestine-Israel simply kept their distance from politics and the state. Others made compromises in return for state funding.

The turning point came with the 1967 war. Afterwards religious nationalism, which combined messianism with territorial expansionism, assumed a stronger position on Israel's political scene. In the US, too, there had been sharp clashes between political Zionists and orthodox sects. But some secular Jews took the 1967 war as a sign from a God in which they previously had rather limited belief, while some religious traditionalists began to accept that the earthly manifestation of Israel could provide both the inspiration and the location for a massive return to the faith.[7]

That shift was neatly captured in the 1970s by the emergence of Gush Emunim (Bloc of the Faithful). Its spiritual mentor, Rabbi Avraham Kook, announced that the recreation of the state of Israel and the arrival of the Messiah were separate events and that it would require human intervention (through annexation, expulsion, and colonization) to turn the first into the second. So encouraged, Gush, with weapons from sympathizers in the Army and money from the government (especially after the 1977 victory of Menachem Begin's right-wing coalition), set out to convince the Messiah that it was time to haul his butt out of bed and get busy. After all, the religious militants claimed to be simply trying to repeat the accomplishments of Joshua, who had subjugated, then destroyed, the Canaanites.[8]

Israeli society still had plenty of dissenters who opposed territorial expansion. They were remarkably more vocal than many Jews of otherwise liberal bent in North America who so often responded to Israeli atrocities by accusing the bearer of such tidings of anti-Semitism. However, growing numbers publicly articulated support for the annexation of all Palestinian land and the permanent expulsion of not just Palestinians in the West Bank and Gaza but also those who had survived 1948 inside Israel.

Along with Gush, the "legal" arm of expansionism, emerged Jewish underground groups conducting assassinations and seizing land at gunpoint while hatching plots to destroy the Haram al-Sharif. This mosque, better known as the Dome of the Rock, is on the site in Jerusalem from which the Prophet Muhammad is said to have ascended to heaven and that once housed the Temple of Solomon. It was (after Mecca and Medina) the third most holy site in Islam. From 1948 to the present, it was the target of many attempts to blow it up, some of them joint ventures of US Born Again Christians and Israeli religious radicals, both seeking to promote the "clash of civilizations" leading to Armageddon and the return of the Messiah. The most notorious effort in the 1980s was the work of the tax-exempt Temple Mount Foundation, headed by the former intelligence director of the Stern Gang. Money for divine demolition came from a US Christian "fundamentalist" who made his fortune swindling investors in oil-and-gas leases, then later tried to use Biblical directions to drill for oil in Israel – on the grounds that it would anoint the Jews and bring them back to Jesus.[9] In the 1990s there were several successor organizations, including the one led by US casino mogul Irving Moskowitz, who financed an "architectural" tunnel alongside the Temple Mount, which led to rioting in which seventy people, Jews and Muslims alike, were killed. Moskowitz was also a generous funder of Jewish settlers in Hebron, notorious for their attacks against the Palestinian majority in that city, and he spent millions on another religious settler campaign to displace Palestinians from Jerusalem. In fact when in 2005 the government of Israel, over strong protests from the religious right, decided to withdraw from Gaza, Moskowitz turned up to promise settlers the funds to resist.[10]

Although these various groups might have no formal organizational link to the Gush or to each other, they were united by a (more or less) shared ideology – the need for the mass return of Jews to Eretz Yisrael, the extension of Jewish rule over all of the Promised Land, the supremacy of Old Testament over secular law, the reconstruction of the Temple of Solomon, and, finally, the arrival of the Messiah. They were united, too, in easy access to funds from tax-exempt religious, charitable, and educational foundations in the US. And they were united in promoting the in-migration of Jews from abroad, including the US.

One of the most articulate newcomers was the late Rabbi Meir Kahane. He was important not so much for numbers of direct followers (they were few) but for the clarity and force with which he publicly articulated positions that many others secretly or not so secretly believed and yet others covertly or sometimes overtly implemented. Kahane got his start in Zionist politics by smuggling guns to the Irgun in prepartition Palestine. But his real notoriety began in the 1960s, when, allegedly with FBI support, he armed and trained Jewish youth in New York to fight Black Power militants and anti-war Vietnam protestors. Out of this emerged his Jewish Defense League.[11]

Kahane knew the importance of money and how to circumvent IRS rules designed to prevent charitable institutions from raising money for terrorist activity. He once suggested to his followers that the JDL itself organize a shul (temple) because "a Shul is never bothered by the IRS and can be held in a store front in Brooklyn ... It's a great investment because then tax deductible contributions can be made with no trouble and the store can be used for meetings." The result was a flow of tax-deductible donations to Kahane's religious and charitable organizations, one of which, the Institute for the Jewish Idea, proclaimed in its flyers such religious and charitable notions as Israel "must create nuclear, chemical and biological weapons for mass deterrent [*sic*]" and "a Jewish state can never make the Arab equal."[12]

In 1971 Kahane was convicted of conspiracy to manufacture firebombs and tossed into prison. On his remarkably early release, he headed for Israel to recreate the JDL in his new abode, initially under the name Kach (Hebrew for *Thus*). Appropriately, its Jerusalem headquarters featured pictures of earlier Jewish terrorists, including leaders of the Irgun and the Stern Gang.[13]

Once in Israel, and seated in the Knesset, Kahane proved both an embarrassment and a backhanded asset. Kahane was a firm believer that the end was nigh, and with it a new beginning. "A horrible world war is coming," he prophesied. "Tens of millions will die. It will be the Apocalypse," he seemed to gloat. "God will punish us for forsaking

him. But we must have faith. The Messiah will come. There will be a res-
urrection of the dead." He insisted that Messianic redemption would
have already occurred if the Israeli government had had the courage to
annex the occupied areas, destroy the Haram al-Sharīf, and rebuild the
Temple of Solomon. That also meant the need to expel the Arabs.
Hence Kahane would make them an offer they could not refuse – accept some money and a one-way ticket, or be physically tossed out with
neither. It was simply a matter of right. "Because there is a Jewish people, we have the right to come to this country, and to take it from the
Arabs." This, he insisted, was not racist. "The biggest racist is the Jew
who doesn't see that to be a Jew is something special." And he said, remarkably prophetically, "There is a wall separating Jews and non-Jews."

What made him unacceptable to the Israeli elite was not that his
views were so extreme – he was hardly alone in holding them.[14] The
problem was that he spoke in English to an international audience –
normally such sentiments were articulated only in Hebrew for local
consumption. And he mocked Israel's political elite for its hypocrisy.[15]
By publicly attacking Kahane and his followers and eventually kicking
Kahane and his party out of the Knesset, the Israeli government could
disassociate itself from a "rogue" extremist group robbing and killing
Palestinians while continuing policies that led to much the same results
on the government's own timetable.

Kahane was no hypocrite. He was more than happy to put his muscle
and his money where his mouth was. With backing from wealthy us
Jews, he and his followers created their own settlement in the West
Bank, while applauding (but claiming not to participate in) Temple
Mount plots. When he said, "I want peace with the Arabs but on my
terms," he was expressing sentiments shared by generations of Israeli
leaders. Still, he went a little further in specifying just what his terms
were. To prepare the ground for the return of the Messiah, Israel had
to expand and grab parts of Egypt, Lebanon, Syria, Jordan, and Iraq.[16]
If this seemed a prescription for perpetual war, that did not faze the
rabbi in the slightest. There would be no peace anyway, he insisted, until the Messiah arrives.[17]

He got a chance to discuss that timetable with the Messiah in person
in 1990 after he was assassinated. His son and heir created a new organization, Kahane Chai (Kahane lives) to carry the work. It was an unfortunate choice of names; for the son himself was killed by Palestinians in
a drive-by shooting at a West Bank settlement a few years later – with
the result that the New Kach movement sprang up to immortalize both.

Nor was Kahane's influence long absent from the Knesset. Three years after he was ejected, a man whom some had seen as a rival and others regarded as a successor, took a seat. Rehavam Ze'evi was a former Israeli military intelligence operative who had earned a reputation for fighting Arab terrorism by throwing suspects out of helicopters over the Mediterranean. After his military career, Ze'evi ran guns to South America in conjunction with three individuals later indicted for drug smuggling. Back home he founded his own political party (Moledet), whose ideology was neatly summed up when, during the early stages of the first intifada, it sponsored the Committee for the Mass Expulsion of Arabs (whom Ze'evi and his followers referred to as "lice").[18] Ze'evi matched Kahane in honesty, telling critics that, "If transfer is not ethical, then everything we have done in this country for the past hundred years is wrong." But because he was native-born and not prone to grandstand before the foreign media, Ze'evi remained in the Knesset and secured a series of cabinet positions. His final post was as Minister of Tourism under Ariel Sharon before members of the Popular Front for the Liberation of Palestine killed him in 2001.

Kahane's lingering influence was also evident in the US. Indeed he managed posthumously and in a backhanded way to precipitate the first serious US crackdown on "terrorist fundraising." It began in 1994, when Baruch Goldstein, a US JDL member who had followed his mentor to Occupied Palestine, walked into a mosque in Hebron with an Israeli Army-issue assault rifle and slaughtered twenty-nine Palestinians at prayer. Killed by outraged survivors, Goldstein was feted by the Israeli religious right as a martyr and national hero. However, the Israeli government declared Kach and Kahane Chai illegal organizations.[19] A publicly enraged President Clinton declared that he would cut off funds to settler-terrorists. And US law enforcement announced that in the future it would prosecute under the RICO statute all individuals and institutions who provided financial aid not just to the Kahanist groups (who were never seriously targeted) but to Hamas or to any of the many charities it ran (for which prosecutors showed considerably more enthusiasm).

It was a brilliant coup. The US government seized on public concern over the mass murder of Palestinians in their place of worship by a Jewish-American zealot equipped with Israeli Army weaponry provided free by the US to divert a law supposedly designed to knock out the kingpins of so-called organized crime to dry up funding for an organization that, whatever else it did, spent most of its money on social support to victims of Jewish terrorism. Furthermore, by hitting Hamas in the pocketbook, the US hoped to tilt the political balance in favor of Yasir Arafat's PLO, which was cooperating in the Oslo Accords. It might well be that this 1994 extension of RICO to purposes its framers could not possibly have expected, not the subsequent misuse of the IEEPA by Clinton or Bush's Patriot Act a few years later, was the real start of the current anti-Arab witch-hunt in the US even if the main target was not burnoose-clad witches but the alleged means by which they bought their broomsticks.

Needless to add, none of approximately one thousand Jewish and Israeli-oriented fundraising bodies in the US was inconvenienced – with one minor exception. In triumph, the Clinton administration announced that it had frozen accounts belonging to Kach – it thus took out of the hands of serial killers and mad bombers the sum of $203. Subsequently Kach and Kahane Chai changed the name of their bank accounts to Kfar Tapuach Fund and announced that they would return checks to their donors who could reissue them in the name of the new organization. Later potential new donors could avoid that inconvenience by simply checking on the organization's websites as to which accounts held in the name of which organizations to send the money.[20] Apparently the FBI and the IRS were either having trouble with their internet connections or were too busy probing the affairs Lebanese grocery-store owners to investigate further.

PIPELINES AND PIPEBOMBS

After the Hebron massacre, the "military arm" of Hamas (the Sheikh Ez al-Din al-Qassam Brigade) began action. It needed very little money, although the myth of great sums of outside support provided Israeli border guards with a pretext to shake down people trying to enter Occupied Palestine with cash or gold. Some weapons were smuggled from supporters in Jordan or Egypt; some were stolen or bought locally from Israeli soldiers, or made, as were bombs, from ordinary house-hold and industrial material. Like the claims about cash smuggling, the supposed flood of sophisticated weapons coursing over the border gave the occupation authorities an excuse to subject the population and its economy to ever tighter controls.[21] While in later years there would be the predictable allegations that suicide bombers were Afghan veterans (and, by inference, instruments of the omnipresent Usama), they, too, were homemade. Furthermore, the Sheikh Ez al-Din al-Qassam Brigade operated not as a coordinated military (as had the PLO's armed wing in years past) but as a set of autonomous "cells." All those features meant that anything done to curb money flows to Hamas would hurt the charitable arms, not the military. But holding the civilian population hostage and, even better, making their lives so miserable they would give up and leave were always the main objects of the exercise.[22]

Much as with the al-Qā'idah myth, claims about the amount of money and the number of fanatics seeking martyrdom escalated almost without limit. By the mid 1990s, accounts (designed to reach Western ears) spoke of three thousand Hamas activists in Jerusalem "waiting for orders to carry out or support acts of terror inside the capital." Apart from question of whose capital Jerusalem really was, the story gave cover to a mini-ethnic cleansing campaign to rid the city of more of its Arab population. Nor was this limited to Jerusalem. "There are also some 20,000 Hamas and other Islamic fundamentalists in Judea and Samaria," the refrain went. "They and their suicide squads are on standby."[23] That served as the pretext for Israel to demolish more homes, uproot more olive trees, and deport more people in the name of ensuring Israel's "right to exist."

While Israel sought to crush the Hamas infrastructure by military means, the US cooperated on the financial front. In 1995 came the Clinton administration's abuse of the IEEPA to freeze the assets of not just Hamas but of Islamic Jihad, the Popular Front for the Liberation of Palestine, and, just for good measure, Lebanon's Hizbullāh. US officials admitted they "do not expect to find many such accounts." Rather the point was "to block donations from US organizations to those groups."[24] Hence the Clinton regime, in another precedent for the latter Bushies, followed with a crackdown on the charities supposedly raising money. The primary target was the Dallas-based Holy Land Foundation for Relief and Development; but also in law-enforcement sights were the Islamic Committee for Palestine (Tampa), the Islamic Association for Palestine (Dallas), the Islamic Centre of America (Detroit), and the United Association for Studies and Research (Virginia), which supposedly functioned as the US think tank for Hamas. At one point the FBI reputedly found that the US office of the International Islamic Relief Organization ran $1.2 million to Hamas, with some of the money originating from the Saudi Embassy in Washington.[25] Why Saudi Arabia would move money to Hamas via its Washington embassy, whose bank accounts are under scrutiny, instead of through bank-secrecy havens in neighboring Gulf states was not readily apparent.

By going after charitable donations, money was not really the issue. As a new community full of refugees, almost all money raised inside North America by US Muslims went to support destitute newcomers or build mosques. The fuss over the money trail served more as a smoke-screen for a search-and-destroy effort aimed at those trying to explain to the broader public why so many people in the Middle East rejected the Oslo Accords.

Probably the pinnacle of the Clinton-era campaign came in 1998 when Attorney General Janet Reno gave the nod to a joint undercover operation of the FBI and Israel's Shin Beit (national police) to test the Shin Beit theory that "most" of the money raised by US Muslim charities for Palestine went to "terrorism." An American who had converted to Islam and had set up the Al Sadaqa Foundation to send relief aid to Gaza gave the FBI permission to bug his office and car. In the past he had shipped things like eyeglasses and sewing machines. Presumably these were hard to criticize unless Palestinian suicide bombers were seriously myopic (in the physiological rather than political sense) and sewing machines could be converted to fire needles at Israeli tanks. But this time, with the cops watching, he sent a few thousand dollars to Ismail Abu Shanab, a "leading Hamas figure," to see if it would be "diverted to terrorism." Abu Shanab redistributed the money to orphanages and health-care facilities. As the informant later commented, "I assume they [the recipient institutions] used it for charitable purposes ... These people were hungry; they were nearly out of food." Not that his opinion helped Abu Shanab, who was later killed by the Israelis in retaliation for such terrorist acts.

There was an even more secretive aspect to the project. According to that informant, another FBI agent offered money directly to Hamas and to Palestinian figures "for terrorist attacks." In other words, rather than just tracing the money flow, the point was to actually instigate actions that could later be used to denounce the institution handling the money.[26] This anticipated the Bush II era, when the Pentagon declared a policy to infiltrate and manipulate groups into action, then, once they showed themselves, obliterate them. Much like police sting operations, to which they bore an obvious family resemblance, any resulting terrorist acts raise the obvious question as to who was the most guilty, though there was never any question as to who was going to face the music.

Parallel to government measures against Hamas fundraising were "private" ones working on a remarkably similar timetable and backed by the same "experts." This campaign began in 1992, when Israel rounded up and expelled four hundred Palestinians, who, sitting in exile in Lebanon, looking back at their homeland, became a major public-relations disaster. With world opinion running sharply against Israel's actions, and, more to the point, increasing disquiet even in the us, came the first claims that Hamas was conducting terrorist fundraising in the us through Muslim charities, that its supporters, especially in the Chicago area, were peddling drugs and running insurance scams, and that the city housed a special command-and-control centre (a grocery store, no less) from which to attack Jewish institutions in the us and abroad and to torture and murder Jewish community leaders. The proof turned out to be a video featuring footage of fiery Arabic-language speeches, crudely spliced, mistranslated, and taken out of context.[27] Shortly after began the long and painful saga of Mohammed Abdul Hamid Khalil Salah, a us citizen and a Chicago resident, arrested in Palestine in 1993 and, he claimed, tortured by the Israelis, and forced to sign a confession in Hebrew (which he did not understand) that he had couriered money from the us to Hamas, allegedly to buy weapons.[28] In fact the money was raised in England by a respected cleric, Abu Obada, to help the families of the four hundred exiles. It was wired to Salah's bank; he took it out in cash, carried it to Jerusalem, where his wife deposited it in the account of a local money-changer and then began to distribute it to the most desperate. Obada confirmed that he later sent several hundred thousand more, but, by the time it arrived, Salah had been arrested. After serving five years in prison he returned to the us and took up volunteer work in the Quranic Literacy Institute, set up by a respected Chicago-area surgeon and real-estate developer to translate and disseminate religious tracts to the increasing Arab Diaspora in the area. The next year the place was raided by the FBI, who, claiming it was a front for Hamas, froze the assets of both Salah and the institute, using as unchallenged evidence the confession Salah had long before repudiated.[29] In 1998 the FBI also charged Salah and two other individuals with financing terrorism, basically the same charges for which he had already served time in Israel. Salah was effectively placed in a kind of internal exile – since he was charged with giving material support to terrorism, in strict theory anyone engaging in any transaction with him, even the sale of a loaf of bread, could also be so charged.[30] Worse, since his assets were frozen, he could not pay the costs of his defense. His lawyer had to request from the government permission to solicit contributions, which was granted provided the FBI could see photocopies of the checks – which it used to confront at least one donor and no doubt scare off many others. Soon Salah was also facing a private lawsuit.

In 2000, the parents of a Jewish teenager killed in Occupied Palestine several years before sued Mohammed Salah and three Muslim charities (the Holy Land Foundation for Relief and Development, the Islamic Association for Palestine, and the Quranic Literacy Institute) for "wrongful death" of the youth. The suit was filed under a 1990 statute (never before used) that allowed victims of terrorist acts abroad to demand compensation in US courts.[31] What made the law attractive was: first, as with RICO suits, people and institutions could be found de facto guilty of horrendous crimes, leaving their reputations in tatters, using only a civil standard of proof; second, the law provided for both compensation for the plaintiff and punitive damages against the defendant; third, victory meant that the judge, also as in RICO cases, could treble the damages. Only in the United States would a law that allows private prosecution of criminal charges under civil criteria and permits oppressive fines to parade as damages, thus payable to the plaintiff rather than the state, be confused with the notion of justice.

The central thrust of the suit, taking up a theme articulated publicly by William Wechsler, future co-director of the "non-partisan" Task Force, was that there was no difference between the military and charitable activities of Hamas, that its political leadership directly controlled the military action. Since there were obviously no formal membership lists in resistance groups, every time a bomb exploded or a shot was fired at Israeli soldiers or settlers, it could be blamed on Hamas as a whole, including the network of social services it ran to relieve the misery of a population in their fourth decade of military occupation and economic oppression. The suit also argued that Hamas had a global presence, with one third of its money raised in the US. More to the point, "leaders" in its European and US "control centres" raised money, laundered it through institutions like charities, then moved it to Palestine, where its primary function was to purchase weapons. The focus on Mohammed Salah (working for free translating passages from the Qur'ān for an obscure literary society) was because he supposedly admitted to his Israeli interrogators that he was the US leader of Hamas! As to the co-defendant Holy Land Foundation, although it put on a charitable front, its real function was supposedly to provide financial support to recognized terrorist groups.

Of course, no one expected the plaintiffs to prove a one-for-one relationship between funds put in the foundation's hands in the US and

their actual use in the purchase of weapons. That was because, to hide
the trail, the perpetrators ran the money through a series of complex
transactions – it changed hands many times; was comingled with funds
from the apparently legitimate charitable and business dealings of
front organizations; was deposited in Swiss banks; and was then put at
the disposal of Hamas. The Arab terrorist group could subsequently
draw from the pool of laundered money at will to finance training,
purchase weapons, and provide lodging, false identification, communications equipment, lethal substances, explosives, personnel, transportation, and other material support for terrorist operations – in effect
the entire laundry list specified as banned activity in US anti-material
support legislation. Furthermore, the plaintiffs claimed, expenditures
from this pool of funds paid for the vehicle, machine guns, and ammunition used to kill their son, for the training of the Hamas hitmen responsible, and for the support of the families of Hamas members killed
while undertaking assassinations or suicide bombings. Under the circumstances, surely they were entitled to compensation for the extreme
physical pain the boy suffered before his death, for the cost of his funeral, and for the loss of his economic value since his earning power
was terminated at age seventeen. They also asked for damages for their
own mental anguish and the loss of their son's company. The demand
was modest – only $100 million in direct compensation, plus another
$100 million in punitive damages, plus costs and attorneys' fees, then
for the whole sum to be trebled.

For some time lawyers wrangled over the applicability of the statute.
Then 9/11 delivered a mini-miracle. Mohammed Salah was already the
target of criminal charges for material support of terrorism; and now
one of the co-defendant institutions, the Holy Land Foundation, was
officially designated as a *bête verte*. Even better, the Quranic Literacy
Institute had apparently received some backing from a certain Saudi
financier. Apart from giving Mohammed Salah (who worked as a volunteer since any salary could have been immediately frozen by the government) $27,000, Yasin al-Qadi had lent $800,000 to the Institute.[32]
Everyone, including the jurors, knew that their government had determined al-Qadi to be one of the people responsible for 9/11.

Late in 2004 the judge decreed that Hamas was guilty of the killing.
Although neither Hamas nor any other Palestinian group had claimed
credit, and although, apart from the dubious confession, no one had
proven an operational link to Mohammed Salah or the Holy Land
Foundation, the judge, perhaps eyeing prospects of a higher court

appointment if he proved sufficiently zealous in the War on Terror, found the defendants liable. That judgment was made, it seems, on the impeccable logic that, if a charity gave some money to someone, and that someone gave some money to someone else, and that someone else bought a weapon that *might* have been the one used in a shooting, the original donor was culpable even if the funds had actually been officially earmarked to pay for funerals of victims of Israeli helicopter gun ships and missiles. The only issue left was how much the jury would demand that the defendants pay. To keep things fair, the judge gave the defendants less than three weeks to mount a defense against a potential $600 million claim. During that time they would have to go through three thousand documents in three languages and find expert witnesses to rebut the testimony offered by witnesses for the plaintiffs (such as Matthew Levitt, a former FBI "terrorism analyst" reincarnated as senior fellow of the Israel lobby's Washington Institute for Near East Policy) who had regaled the jurors with tales of Hamas atrocities and Islamic duplicity. Two of the institutions did not bother to mount a defense; and the lawyer for the third sat through the proceedings more or less in silence. Under the circumstances, it was probably better to save energy for the appeal.

The jurors spent a few days to calculate that the youth's life was worth to his family $52 million, which the judge trebled to $156 million plus court fees and costs. Of course, money was not the real objective. How could it be when the institutions operated on a shoestring using volunteer help and had already had their assets frozen by the government (which therefore had a prior lien)? Rather the motive was to help the government in its war on terror-dollars by going after the "domestic enablers of terrorism."[33] There has to date been no use of the statute by a Palestinian family to try to obtain from a US court damages resulting from the murder of their children by Israeli settlers whose funding comes through tax-exempt Jewish religious and charitable foundations in the United States. Of course, they are victims not of terrorism but of crowd control.[34]

TURNING THE VALVE

By the time of the civil judgment, the Holy Land Foundation was effectively defunct. Certainly it had supported Palestinian charities – that was its raison d'être. No doubt some were affiliated with Hamas – after all, the organization had built, initially with Israeli assistance, the

biggest network of social services in Palestine. But the foundation repeatedly denied that it had anything to do with suicide bombers. Nonetheless, in the year 2000, the State Department asked the US Agency
for International Development to strip the foundation's registration,
eliminating its right to obtain relief supplies cheaply. Then, after 9/11,
on the pretext that it was the premier North American fundraiser for
Hamas, the offices of the charity were closed, its property and documents seized, and its accounts frozen.[35] In effect, complaints aired in
the $600 million civil suit were just recycled into an IEEPA regulatory
action and a subsequent criminal case.

As always, the decision to close the institution was made in secret; the
government only had to show its purported evidence in camera to a fed-
erally appointed judge. The charity did try to challenge the freeze. But
the judge decreed that there was "ample evidence in a massive administrative record" that officers of the charity had met with Hamas leaders
and provided funds for Hamas-controlled charities as well as financial
support to families of Hamas martyrs. No doubt that last accusation was
true – given what a large percentage of the Palestinian population Hamas was helping to support, it would be strange if some family members
of a suicide bomber did not number among the recipients. The judge
opined further that the government evidence was so overwhelming,
there was no point for the charity to even bother to enter a defense –
against evidence it was not allowed to see anyway. The nature of that evidence can be deduced from the phrase "administrative record." In this
and similar cases, the courts base their conclusions not on proof in the
sense of information introduced in open court and therefore subject to
challenge but on secret conclusory affidavits from bureaucrats. When the
Holy Land Foundation tried the Supreme Court, the highest judicial
body in the land refused to hear an appeal.[36]

However, this was only the start of a multi-stage process. Two weeks
after the charity was closed, it, plus Ghassan Elashi, its Palestinian cofounder and chairman, along with his four brothers, all respected
members of the Dallas Muslim community, were charged with material
support to Hamas under the 1996 statute, with conspiracy to violate the
IEEPA, money-laundering, and filing false tax returns.[37] Everyone had
gotten a piece of the investigatory action – including the FBI, IRS, the
new Bureau of Immigration and Customs Enforcement (BICE), the
State Department, the Secret Service, the US Army CID, the Texas Department of Public Safety, and the police departments of Dallas, Plano,
Garland, and Richardson, Texas. The case permitted John Ashcroft to

sternly declare: "Terrorist money men should know this. We are hunting down the murderers you support, and we will hunt you down." Presumably he made that pronouncement in a nationally televised press conference to ensure an impartial jury.[38] Yet, when it came to trial, the material support charges had vanished and the brothers were left with the accusation that they had made false declarations to ship computer parts to Libya and Syria. In the past most export-law violations were handled as regulatory offenses; but when cases involved Arab or Muslim countries, us prosecutors seemed to prefer to make them criminal. They were easy to prosecute; they rarely required informants; and they could usually be proven simply with business documents seized in raids.

Of course, there was additional "evidence" against the Elashi family and their foundation: for instance, the fact that the wife of Mousa Abu Marzouq, deputy leader of the Hamas politburo, was second cousin to the brothers. Apparently, too, the Marzouqs were once detained at Kennedy Airport on their way out with documents that mentioned a $250,000 investment in the brothers' company. To John Ashcroft this was "seed money." Probably it was – seed money for a computer services company. Equally incriminating was the fact that Mousa Abu Marzouq apparently had contributed to the Holy Land Foundation – which some might interpret to mean that Marzouq was supporting the charity rather than the charity supporting Hamas.[39]

Then came phase III. In a separate case in Florida, brought on the third anniversary of 9/11 and in the countdown to a potentially tight presidential election, Adham Amin Hassoun and Mohammed Hesham Youssef, both already facing other criminal charges, were indicted for supporting Hamas. From 1994 to 2001 Hassoun allegedly wrote checks totalling $53,000 to co-conspirators and groups including the Holy Land Foundation and another Muslim-American charity, the Global Relief Foundation, to support "jihād" against the West. Apart from timing of the charges (when one of the accused was already in prison in Egypt), it was odd the two were accused of writing checks *before* the charities were placed on the us terror list. So, just for good measure, they were also accused of trying to help José Padilla, the supposed "dirty bomber" (a designation probably more descriptive of his physical appearance after years of detention than of his intent) get to Afghanistan for "training." And, so the further claim went, they had tried to raise money for terrorists in Afghanistan, Kosovo, Chechnya, and Somalia.[40] At least in Afghanistan and Kosovo, the CIA and Pentagon

the also raised money for terrorist operations, even though they preferred to call their protegés freedom fighters.

Finally, just to keep things tidy, early in 2005, Abd al-Jaber Hamdan,
chief fundraiser for the Holy Land Foundation for Southern California, where he had had been living with his wife and six children for
twenty-two years years, and who had been locked up at the same time as
the Elashi brothers, was ordered deported. His offense was not terrorism. Rather he had been arrested, charged, and convicted of violating
the terms of a student visa issued twenty-five years before.[41]

The second of the major charities closed by Executive Order (although not at the time designated a terrorist organization) was the Global Relief Foundation. It had been the second largest Muslim charity in
the US in terms of assets, the largest in terms of international spread
and activity; and its main though not exclusive humanitarian efforts
had been in war zones. Not only were its assets frozen, but its director,
Rabih Haddad, was arrested. Only years later did it surface that the CIA
had decided that the charity was plotting to attack the US with nuclear
weapons.[42]

The charity appealed the freeze. It pointed out that, among other
things, the IEEPA only allowed the president to regulate property in
which foreigners had an interest (Global was a US-based entity) and
that the law had a clause exempting humanitarian relief from freezes.
This was true – before the Patriot Act. Subsequently the president had
sweeping powers to override such qualifiers if he decided that the exemption would jeopardize his ability to deal with a national emergency.
As to Global's further complaint that such Patriot Act amendments to
the IEEPA constituted legislation designed to apply retroactively, the
court ruled that they were really of a regulatory rather than a criminal
or penal nature; hence the ban on ex post facto legislation did not
apply. Furthermore, rejecting the charity's claim that it was being
subjected to a sentence without trial, the court insisted that the action
of OFAC – wrecking the charity by publicly launching an investigation
of its possible role in support of terrorism without giving it a chance to
defend itself – did not constitute "punishment."[43]

In retrospect the appeal was a waste of energy. After all, a plea from
the charity's lawyer that, unless the freeze was lifted, impoverished
Muslims overseas would face malnutrition or starvation during the
winter was hardly going to cut much ice, so to speak, in a country whose
former Secretary of State could declare that the death of half a million
Iraqi children under the age of five as a consequence of US sanctions

was "a price worth paying." Failure of the appeal was the end of Global Relief, "ruined," as its lawyer put it, "on the basis of secret evidence and without a trial."[44]

As to Haddad, initially accused by the government of funnelling money to al-Qā'idah, after eighteen months in jail he was finally subjected to a secret prosecution – for overstaying his visa. Ultimately Haddad was deported to his native Lebanon, forbidden ever to return, while his wife and young children (against whom there were no accusations, let alone charges) were banned from entering the US for ten years.[45] In this and many similar cases the government would claim that they deported individuals because it was the quickest way of getting them out of the country and therefore protecting the citizenry from anything they might scheme. The alternative explanation is that, by deporting Haddad, the government was de facto admitting that it did not have the evidence to support terrorism accusations and was anxious to be rid of evidence of another blunder. Short of just offing Haddad or burying him alive in some place like Guantánamo, a permanent ban was probably the most effective way to head off potentially embarrassing questions.[46]

The third of the major targets, Benevolence International, which distributed food and clothing and operated hospitals, dental clinics, and orphanages in places as varied as Bosnia, Tajikistan, Afghanistan, Pakistan, Daghestan, and Muslim areas of China, was also bankrupted by an IEEPA freeze – and by the usual lurid accusations from the Justice Department that it was created by a bin Lāden "associate" and that it funded al-Qā'idah's ambitions to chemical and nuclear weapons.[47] It launched the usual appeals – against the freeze and against the seizure of its operating documents. Then, on 29 April 2002, its lawyers filed a motion opposing the use of secret evidence. By the remotest coincidence that same day the government filed a criminal charge against the foundation and its chief executive officer, Enaam Arnaout, for making false statements under oath: "BIF has never provided aid and support to people or organizations known to have engaged in violence, terrorist activities, or military operations of any kind." In effect, by protesting his own innocence, the director became liable for another criminal charge. In an unusual move, the district court agreed with a defense motion to dismiss the indictment. The government reacted by bringing against Arnaout fresh charges of racketeering and conspiracy – for which he potentially faced ninety years in prison. Not surprisingly he crumbled and entered a plea of guilty in exchange for the government dismissing all the highly publicized claims about material support to terrorism, which would have placed him in the highest possible category for sentencing purposes.[48]

The racketeering and conspiracy charges supposedly grew out of a NATO raid on the charity's Balkan offices, a raid that was necessary, so the government claimed, because BIF was "involved in planning attacks against targets in the U.S.A. and Europe." The raid and the subsequent court cases threw a chill into the operations of all the Islamic charities providing essential relief and crucial economic support to the Bosnian and Kosovar economies in a time of crisis. Allegedly this raid turned up all kinds of new information about Arnaouts "ties" to bin Lāden. There were claims that he had: attended organizational meetings of al-Qā'idah in Afghanistan; worked in the late 1980s and early 1990s buying and distributing weapons on behalf of al-Qā'idah; allowed a military advisor to bin Lāden to serve as an officer of BIF in Chechnya; and sought to destroy evidence (documents and photos) linking him to bin Lāden. All this on top of laundering charity money to finance terrorism. In Congressional testimony, Michael Chertoff, then head of the Justice Departments Criminal Division and soon-to-be Secretary of Homeland Security, put the amount of money diverted to Chechen rebels in the hundreds of thousands. Meanwhile his boss, Bible John Ashcroft, in his customary verdict on cases before they were tried, offered the sage thought that: "It is sinister to prey on good hearts to fund the works of evil."

In the final analysis, criminal charges against the organization itself were dropped. Lest this be misinterpreted as Christian charity on the part of the Attorney General, the Justice Department explained: "The benefit of continuing to prosecute Benevolence International was outweighed by the cost of prosecution."[49] In other words, in a practice based closely on Drug War tactics, they had already seized the assets, bankrupted the institution, and destroyed its reputation, so why take the risk it might clear its name in a criminal court? Arnaout himself pleaded guilty to diverting a small portion of the charity's funds, not to bin Lāden, but to Muslim fighters in Bosnia and Chechnya, and not for chemical weapons, but for boots and blankets.

Thus, in exchange for the US government agreeing to drop all references to support for terrorism, the boss of the foundation pleaded guilty to a rather banal white-collar offense involving fiddled accounts, something that, if fairly applied, would have brought much of the US nonprofit sector before the courts. Furthermore, while the heads of some prominent all-American charities were busy living high-on-the-hog at public expense, Aranout gained no personal benefit. Nonetheless, since the trial occurred at a time when us corporate barons were being regularly exposed for gross fabrications of their account books that had enabled them to plunder billions with virtual impunity, the court felt it was important to send a message. Hence it sentenced Aranout to more than eleven years in prison – on top of the sixteen months he had already spent in solitary confinement. While these three victims of the war on Muslim charitable foundations in the United States – the Holy Land Foundation, Global Relief and Benevolence International – attracted most of the headlines, there were to be several other casualties, including, in the final analysis, Islamic charity itself.

14

Neither to Give nor to Receive –
Requiem for Islamic Charity in the US?

The US had good reason to keep a sharp eye out for charitable fraud after 9/11. Along with a burst of philanthropy by people horrified at the events came vultures seeking to turn the tragedy to their own profit. New York State saw the almost immediate formation of about 250 new charities listed with the State Attorney General, plus a host of others who did not bother. They would hit the phone lines to solicit donations by cash, check, or credit card. Undoubtedly most were bona fide, but some would disappear with the money; others used a small portion on genuine relief work, while diverting most to "administrative costs"; and yet others worked the opposite side of the charity ledger.

The State of New York had initiated emergency procedures so that, if a family member of someone killed in the attack signed an affidavit, the State almost immediately produced a death certificate to permit the applicant to receive from government departments and private charities special monetary compensation, for example, to pay for counselling services or to fly family members across the country for funeral services. Since it took some weeks to arrive at an exact casualty list, fake certificates were an easy way to bilk the charities.[1] However, in the aftermath of 9/11 the USA's main focus in the matter of charitable fraud involved a quite different gang of conspirators than a bunch of New York con artists.

Arab and Muslim communities, among the most recent and insecure parts of the USA's rather lumpy melting pot, had their beliefs trashed and their civil rights trampled underfoot when the cops came to kick down their doors and the INS engaged in mass roundups. The authorities had the help of good citizens who flooded police stations with reports of suspicious behavior and formed spontaneous posses to go looking for "rags" (including a few Sikhs in turbans) on whom to demonstrate that the US frontier spirit was still alive and kicking, literally. Meanwhile prominent public figures asked why Arab-Americans were not simply volunteering to be interrogated, tagged, and profiled.[2] Although that kind of hysteria soon died down, much longer lasting was the impact on community institutions. The politicojudicial lynching of the three Muslim charities at the start of the terror-dollar frenzy set the tone – there was much more to come.[3]

SURGICAL STRIKE

One of the more appalling instances occurred in 2003 when eighty-five federal agents stormed the house of an oncologist in Manlius, a suburb of Syracuse, New York. Rafil Dhafir had come to the US from Iraq more than thirty years before. Devout, he spent much of his time and money on charitable activity, both on and off the job. As the only oncologist in town, he treated people of limited means at reduced rates, sometimes for free. In 1993, upset by the impact of economic sanctions and constant UK and US bombing on the Iraqi population, he founded Help the Needy, a charity that (according to prosecutors) raised nearly $5 million from local zakāt contributions, deposited it in US banks, then wired it to Jordan to finance emergency shipments of food and medicine.[4]

For four years seven different federal agencies investigated Help the Needy, gathering bank, tax, medical, and business records and scrutinizing letters, emails, and videotapes. Prosecutors afterwards claimed that Dhafir tried to hide his activities from the government. Yet fundraising events were well enough advertised that federal undercover sleuths were able to attend. Nonetheless, since he had no federal license to send food and medicine to Iraq, he was arrested and charged with conspiracy to violate the IEEPA, with conspiracy to launder money, and with twelve counts of actual laundering. He was later accused as well of tax fraud, using false social security numbers, billing Medicare for chemotherapy sessions at his clinic at times he was not there, diverting donations to acquire real estate (to build a mosque), and donating money to other charities later put on the freeze list. John Ashcroft, in an unusually restrained mood, was content merely to say that: "Those who covertly seek to channel money into Iraq under the guise of charitable work will be caught and prosecuted."[5] But New York Governor George Pataki launched a tirade against "terrorists living here in New York State" and denounced Dhafir's activities, which had yet to be aired in court, as a "money laundering case to help terrorist organizations."[6]

Other US-based organizations outraged at the slow-motion mass-murder campaign the US had undertaken against the civilian population of Iraq (prior to its 2003 decision, on humanitarian grounds, to fasttrack the slaughter) were also shipping food and medicine. The worst any of them had faced was a fine. Why was Rafil Dhafir singled out? Part of the answer, no doubt, lay in general Islamophobia. But the raid with all its media hoopla took place just before the invasion of Iraq, when US law-enforcement agencies had been mobilized (in Operation Imminent Horizon) to target "Iraqi agents" in the US.[7] In fact that campaign had already netted another group of Iraqi refugees in Seattle who had sent $12 million in cash and other supplies to Iraq.[8] Yet Dhafir, who had fled Saddam's regime three decades before and who was a committed salafi, hardly sympathetic to Ba'thist secularism, did not seem the likely head of an Iraqi "sleeper cell." But perhaps, the feds reasoned, as a doctor he had access to particularly strong soporifics.

Also arrested was Ayman Jarwan, executive director of Help the Needy. Since he had degrees in nuclear and radiological engineering, the government, pointing to press reports about plots to explode a "dirty bomb" in the US, asked the court to deny him bail. "This man," the prosecutor insisted, "knows how to use and has access to this material." Although the judge did grant bail to Jarwan, Dhafir had no such luck. He was four times denied. At the last hearing prosecutors cited the fact that he was supposed to have purchased a stash of gold to prepare the ground for a quick dash over the St Lawrence River into Canada. He had never completed the order. Still, intent was the thing; the judge agreed Dhafir was a flight risk and again denied bail.

After thirty-one months in detention without bail and a seventeen-week trial, he was sentenced to twenty-two years on fifty-nine counts of fraud, tax evasion, Medicare and Medicaid fraud, visa fraud, lying to federal agents, violating US sanctions against Iraq, and money-laundering. Yet all of the money he had sent went not in cash but first by check to a local bank, then by cashiers' check to Jordan, where it was used to buy emergency supplies. Not only was it completely open, but Dhafir kept a careful ledger, which the government seized and used as evidence. This is strange behavior for a dedicated money-launderer. Furthermore Dhafir repeatedly insisted that recipient groups issue him proper receipts for tax purposes. (Those in Jordan did so; those in Iraq were afraid of the wrath of Saddam's intelligence services and did not.) After the conviction prosecutors tried to get the judge to further hike his prison time on the notion that he was a national security risk – in effect attempting to win at the sentencing a material-support-to-terror charge they had not submitted to trial.

Another suspicious institution was the SAAR Foundation, which got its name from Suleiman Abd al-Aziz al-Rajhi, a Saudi financier close to the ruling family. It (like the Muwāfaq Foundation) presented the administration with the problem of how to close an institution that had already ceased to exist. Allegedly an "affiliate" of the Saudi-funded World Muslim League, SAAR had been a network of more than one hundred Muslim charities, think tanks, and companies linked by overlapping directorates before it was liquidated in December 2000. After 9/11, the Department of Justice claimed to have tracked its activities retroactively in eighteen countries; and in March 2002 various former offices were raided and old records seized in search of the inevitable "al-Qaeda connection." Since al-Rajhi also had an indirect interest in a Gainesville, Georgia, poultry farm, the result was to let Customs agents rather than foxes loose in the hen houses.[9]

On the surface SAAR was an odd choice of foundation to harass. The World Muslim League program had nothing to do with radical political Islam of the jihādist variety. It was not even close to the salafi creed of the Saudi regime. Rather it followed the da'wa trend of the Muslim Brotherhood. Saudi exiled dissidents reported that for decades SAAR leaders used Saudi cash to promote a more urban and progressive agenda. That may be why the Saudi regime cut off its funding in the mid-1990s, leading after a few years to it winding up.

According to the Justice Department, the raids occurred because the government could find no "reasonable" explanation for an interconnected network of affiliates with multiple internal transactions except the desire to fool law enforcement. That, if fairly applied, would shut down just about every corporation in the USA larger than a 7–11 franchise. Perhaps a better explanation was that Customs, which led the raid, was celebrating its shift from Treasury to the new Department of Homeland Security. That transformed Customs agents from despised tax collectors to people charged with the vital task of protecting the USA against foreign threats.[10]

In some ways the raids were a follow-up to events in Tampa six years before when police probed not a threat to US national security but "anti-Israel activists" led by the presumed world financial kingpin of Palestine's Islamic Jihad group. Afterwards SAAR officials claimed that they met repeatedly with FBI officials and were given a clean bill of health. But SAAR remained in the sights of certain "experts" who fed rumors to the Justice Department.[11]

A year after the new raids came accusations that the SAAR Foundation had run no less than the largest terrorism-financing ring the world. The proof was not a money trail from SAAR to mad Muslim bombers but that some affiliates had used the same banks with which bin Lāden dealt. These turned out to be not Al Shamal Bank in the Sudan but Bank al Taqwa and Akida Bank Private in the Bahamas, tiny institutions run by Youssef Nada and Ahmed Idris Nasreddin, the Al-Barakaat and Al Taqwa entrepreneurs who had been honored by the Bush administration in October 2001. Yet SAAR had no formal transaction with these banks that were, like it, defunct anyway. Rather some executives of its interlocking affiliates had arranged loans in their private capacity. Still, there was other strong proof of wrongdoing. While for years SAAR had duly reported to the US government an annual budget of $1.5 million, its final report covering the year 1998 acknowledged receiving $1.8 billion! There were two possible explanations. One was a typo. The other was a huge influx of secret funds (only discovered by reviewing a public IRS document) to commit terrorist atrocities.

In other words, a foundation already defunct before the acts that initiated the investigation was suspect because at some point in the past some people who had something to do with some of its affiliates borrowed some money for some purposes not related to the foundation's work from banks owned by someone else who was formerly a member of a non-terrorist organization that no one even in their dizziest moments had managed to "link" to 9/11. Still, it was impossible to be too careful. As terrorism expert Rita Katz gravely explained: "A rich Saudi who wants to fund radical ideas or terrorists like Hamas and al-Qaeda knows he can't send the money directly, so he filters it through companies and charities, often in the US and Europe."[12] That also seemed to be the philosophy underlying law-enforcement action against the US branch of Saudi Arabia's International Islamic Relief Organization.

THE ODD COUPLE

It was a story of two friends who fell out, in which Customs managed to "tie," "associate," "connect," or "link" (TACL?) a remarkable number of the USA's *bêtes vertes*. It began in 1985, when an Egyptian named Suleiman Biheiri, in the US on a tourist visa, met a Saudi named Suleiman ibn Ali al-Ali. They went their separate ways. Biheiri remained in the US to set up a company called Beit al-Maal Inc. (BMI) to offer mainly to Middle Easterners shari'a-compatible investments in the US real-estate and leasing markets. Al-Ali returned to Saudi Arabia as a full-time fundraiser for the International Islamic Relief Organization, where he so impressed the ruling family that he was sent back to the US to create a US affiliate with the slightly abbreviated name International Relief Organization. (Already it had something to hide!) Its responsibilities included raising money for Bosnian war relief. IRO also created as an affiliate, Sana-Bell Inc., an Islamic investment company whose name was an anglicization of Sanabil al-Khair (Seeds of Charity), the endowment fund run by IIRO back in Saudi Arabia. The new Sana-Bell was to create a similar endowment fund in the US through which donations could be channelled into investments conforming to shari'a law. That logically called for the money to be entrusted to an Islamic investment company – hence Sana-Bell placed $3.7 million with Biheiri's BMI.[13]

But the two friends quarrelled; and Sana-Bell sued BMI in US court for recovery. In his affidavit, Biheiri claimed, among other things, that al-Ali had withdrawn for his own purposes one million dollars of Sana-Bell's money. He had also apparently put millions of IRO money into a Chicago-based chemical company run by a director of another Islamic charity, Mercy International. That raised serious suspicions since the Nairobi office of Mercy International was the place where Wadih el-Hage, imprisoned for life for ostensibly setting up Usama's East Africa cell, stored his records.[14] In 1997, both the chemical company and IRO were raided by the FBI, which claimed to be searching for evidence of terrorism support and diversion of dangerous chemicals – despite the guarded language, everyone knew what that meant. The US director of Mercy International, though not the charity itself, was eventually charged, convicted, and sentenced – for commercial fraud, not for plotting to wipe out the population of Illinois with sarin gas.

But for the swarthy complexions and curious religious rituals of the principals, two ex-friends suing each other might have seemed not much more than business as usual in the USA. Then came 9/11 and the dredging up of old stories with new twists. Customs, along with the FBI and the IRS, came calling. This time the target was Suleiman Biheiri, the aggrieved party in the earlier civil case. According to a court declaration of the senior Customs agent-in-charge, the feds decided that the individuals on *both* sides of the earlier dispute were involved in material support for terrorism, money-laundering, and IEEPA violations, with tax evasion thrown in for good measure. According to the government, the original civil suit was a sham since "the victim of the fraud (Sana-Bell) and the supposed perpetrator of the fraud (BMI on behalf of IRO) were the same." In other words, two Islamic investment companies established at two different times by two different persons, one Egyptian and the other Saudi, were engaged in a shell game so clever that the judge in the original case had also been conned into awarding some $2.3 million to Sana-Bell – which apparently never collected. Where did the money go? It was another mystery like that of the missing billions from the National Commercial Bank of Saudi Arabia, even if on a much more modest scale. There was only one reasonable explanation. The complex transactions and bitter lawsuit were simply to cover the transfer of money to terrorist organizations.

The allegations went further. Not only were Biheiri's Sana-Bell and BMI the same, both controlled by IRO, with the IRO in turn a front for the IIRO, but that institution in turn was a twin of the World Muslim League, which was itself a de facto arm of the Saudi royal family. Even worse, the FBI claimed to have discovered that secret sponsors and/or beneficiaries of BMI were Mousa Abu Marzouq, supposedly second-in-command of Hamas, Yasin al-Qadi, the notorious al-Qā'idah financier, and Mohammed Salah of Quranic Literary Institute fame, all Specially Designated Terrorists or Specially Designated Global Terrorists against whom the prior evidence was so overwhelming. Even more damning, the director of BMI also had business relations with Yousef Nada, head of the notorious Al Taqwa Group, which, as everyone knew, "has long acted as financial adviser to al Qaeda." And worse: it also became clear that Hamas, too, through Abu Marzouq, funnelled to Biheiri from its burgeoning coffers many millions for real-estate investments in the US with the intent to use the profits to fund terrorist actions against Israel.[15]

The feds gathered still more "credible" data to back up their affidavit. There was a CIA report, made public in response to a Freedom of Information Request, containing the considered judgment that, of more than fifty Islamic NGOs in the US, approximately one third either

supported terrorist groups or employed individuals suspected of terrorist connections. The report cited the well-documented ties between
Ramzi Yousef (architect of the 1993 World Trade Center attack) and
Usama bin Lāden (who stated quite openly he had no idea who Ramzi
Yousef was); it cited the well-known role of Usama's brother-in-law
Mohammed Khalifah in Manila-based plots to kill the pope and to
bomb a bunch of US airliners; it cited the equally well-known fact that
the IIRO put up a lot of the money for no less than six terrorist training
camps in Afghanistan.[16] There was information about the secret terror-
money trail that had appeared on the front page of the *New York Daily
News* and in other credible media. The agent who filed the court declaration in Biheiri's bail hearing made matters clear. "I know, based on
news reports, that the IIRO was banned in Kenya in September, 1998
following the bombings of the US embassies in Kenya and Tanzania in
1998 for suspicion of its involvement." What he perhaps did not know,
or forgot to tell the court, was that the Kenyan government, after an
investigation, had allowed its branch to reopen well before the affidavit
was filed.

There was more data of the same spurious quality. A former BMI
accountant suggested to the FBI that money the company may have
transferred overseas "may" have been used to finance the embassy
bombings.(Not only had the bombers not required outside funds but,
if all of the alleged financiers of that event had gathered all of the accumulated surpluses, they might have been able to cover the US balance
of trade deficit.) Further information came from another objective
source – Suleiman Biheiri's estranged wife, with whom he was then involved in a bitter custody battle.

With all of this evidence – spook leaks, *Daily News* reports, rumors
spread by disgruntled and frightened ex-employees, and the accusations of a woman scorned – it was no wonder that a federal grand jury
charged Suleiman Biheiri with three counts of immigration violations. Eventually found guilty of lying under oath, an offense carrying a maximum sentence of six months, the judge used against
Biheiri the same federal guideline that prosecutors later directed
against Dr Dhafir, namely that a judge can raise the sentence for a
non-terror offense if the crime was "intended to promote terrorism."
Prosecutors claimed Biheiri had "done business" with people "designated" as terrorists. Hence the judge sent him up for a full year and
demanded that he forfeit citizenship and return to Egypt after serving his sentence.[17]

Despite these striking successes against the flow of terror-dollars through allegedly phony charities, us law enforcement refused to rest on its laurels. During 2004, at a time when the public's attention had long before been diverted from Afghanistan to Iraq, they struck at two links they had previously missed.

One was the Islamic American Relief Agency, formally designated a financier of terrorism in 2004, then subjected to the usual Treasury raids and media frenzy. Lest anyone think that unearthing another key terror-dollar link so late in the game was the sign of poor police work, the feds explained that they had just discovered that the charity had closer links to al-Qā'idah than they had previously assumed. Indeed, as their investigation proceeded, they were shocked to find that the charity had provided "direct financial support to Osama bin Laden" and that it was the centre of a "worldwide network." The raid followed from the interrogation of Mustafa Ahmed al-Hawsawi, a Saudi "financier" (aren't they all?) who was yet another of the masterminds-cum-paymasters of 9/11.

Another reason for the delay was how well IARA had disguised its terrorist activities. In the late 1990s it even received State Department funding for relief work in Mali and the Sudan. It was finally cut off, over State Department protests, shortly after us missiles took out that chemical weapons facility in Khartoum that had somehow disguised its nerve gas production as if it were making animal vaccines while hiding the product in ibuprofen bottles. However, actually closing the charity had to await serious evidence of complicity in 9/11.

Khalid al-Fawwaz was one of many Saudi dissidents living legally in London from where they propagandized against the regime. He had helped Usama bin Lāden establish the Advice and Reformation Committee, another publicly operating anti-Saudi group, in the days when bin Lāden had been living in the Sudan. After bin Lāden returned to Afghanistan and began issuing increasingly violent diatribes, al-Fawwaz still circulated his communiqués and offered to arrange interviews for visiting reporters. Soon after the 1998 embassy bombings, he was accused of running bank accounts for bin Lāden and arrested at us request. Since the us denied al-Fawwaz the right to question anonymous witnesses who had provided its evidence, the British government refused extradition – but kept him locked up anyway.[18] In the meantime the British were smart enough to freeze his London bank account and proudly proclaim that they had taken £23.19 million out of the terror-dollar circuit. In fact the bank account held £23.19, about half the sum required for a taxi from central London to Heathrow airport. Al-Fawwaz, in preventive custody, found himself promoted from a "suspected bin Lāden ally" to the chief of the al-Qā'idah network in Britain. This effective action on both sides of the Atlantic was cheered publicly by the usual "anti-terrorism experts" in taxpayer-funded Washington institutes who had been trying to warn the feds of the dangers of Islamic charities for years.[19]

Yet another late target was the Islamic Center of Springfield, Missouri. Prior to its opening, local Muslims had only makeshift mosques like the basement of a doctor's office. But the proud new centre got caught in the aftermath of accusations against the Saudi-based Al Haramain Islamic Foundation, which, according to prosecutors, owned the Springfield mosque and its parent organization in Oregon. Prosecutors also insisted that there were "direct links between the US branch and Osama bin Laden." By the logic of the government claim, the anti-terror net could not only entangle every institution everywhere in the world to which the largest official Saudi charitable foundation had ever donated, along with local officers and other donors, but haul in every other organization to which the recipient charities had, in turn, donated. The government offered no evidence to back charges that the centre was used to solicit and contribute funds for terrorism. As a Springfield physician, one of the main officials of the mosque, aptly commented: "It's tough to be Muslim these days."[20]

THE BIG CHILL

In some ways the outcome of Islamic charity trials was irrelevant, except, obviously, to the defendants. The simple fact of the accusations, with or without formal charges, sent a chill deep into the hearts and wallets of potential donors in North America and beyond. The problem went beyond simply closing a charity under contrived circumstances. As economic conditions worsen across North Africa and the Middle East, as governments are forced by plummeting revenues and IMF demands to slash publicly funded social services and subsidies for food and fuel, more of their people are driven below the poverty line leaving mosques and Islamic charitable foundations to take up the slack. Mosques provide monthly stipends to the poor and ill and to the families of those jailed or killed by the government. They provide special emergency aid such as distribution of blankets in winter, food packages during Ramadan, or school supplies at the start of the academic year. They run health clinics and educational services, provide vocational training and loans, and help with garbage collection and the provision of clean water. A few have their own income-generating arms; but for the most part they rely on private philanthropy and contributions of cash, time, and expertise. Much of philanthropy comes from local individuals; but as the middle classes, too, are squeezed, there is a greater dependence, which can only grow over time, on remittances and charitable distributions based on contributions from abroad. Yet, if and when institutions smeared as part of the bin Lāden network (or as financiers of Hizbullāh or Hamas suicide bombers) are permitted to reopen, their reputations are probably damaged permanently. Not only will Muslims in the US fear to donate, lest they be charged with giving material support to terrorism, but headlines about how "top U.S. companies gave to charity linked to al-Qaeda" in, for example, the Benevolence International case would ensure that big corporations would in the future be shy about donations to any Muslim charity.[21]

The campaign in the US reached well above the level of the poor Muslim immigrant to affect the wife of Bandar ibn Sultan, the Saudi ambassador, a long-time crony of the Republican Right and a willing participant in enterprises like the Iran-Contra scam. In 1998 she received a letter from the Jordanian wife of a Saudi man living in San Diego, pleading for help with medical bills. In response she began to send $2,000 per month. The woman who received the money endorsed one check to the wife of another man who lent two of the future accused hijackers cash to rent an apartment – this was two years before anyone, including Mohammed Atta, had a clue about what was going to happen.[22] Apparently the post-9/11 climate held guilt to be not just by various degrees of indirect association but also by failure to exercise telepathic and clairvoyant skills.

In such an atmosphere, remaining Muslim charities in the US reported dramatic drops (some by 50 percent) in contributions. One in New York, for example, which operated a soup kitchen that had fed regularly four hundred people, found donations cut so far that it could only handle 150. Another, KinderUSA, formed early in 2002 specifically to fill the gap left by the forced closure of others, despite filing all required forms and communicating openly with the authorities, found itself under so much FBI scrutiny that it wrapped up voluntarily rather than subject its donors to police harassment. Far from thawing as the post-9/11 hysteria began to recede, the donor chill was accentuated early in 2004 when the Senate Finance Committee asked the IRS for confidential tax and financial records including the donor lists many Muslim charities in the US – guaranteed to shake further confidence of donors and dry up funds even more.[23] Nearly two years later the Senate Committee reported that it had found nothing "alarming" in the financial records of nearly two dozen Muslim groups it reviewed for terrorist connections.[24]

15

Chasing Green Herrings – The Netherworld of Terror Meets the Underworld of Crime?

The war on terror-dollars had three objectives. First, close the channels through which money moved to terrorist plotters. That required better monitoring of financial flows, including closer scrutiny of charitable institutions. Second, locate and freeze hoards before the money could find alternative routes. Third, stop fundraising at the source to prevent replenishment or replacement. This was the trickiest, particularly with money of criminal origin, which, by definition, begins life underground before proceeding through hidden channels, making it a double challenge.

Criminal money deployed for terrorist purposes seemed to be particularly abundant. Once law enforcement overturned the rock under which Al-Qā'idah and fellow-travellers-of-terror were hiding, the world was shocked to find, or at least to be told, that they had insinuated themselves into everything from financial fraud to drug smuggling, from peddling fake brand-name merchandise to wholesaling counterfeit currency, from bootlegging tax-free cigarettes to trafficking in conflict diamonds.[1]

ROUNDING UP THE OBVIOUS SUSPECTS

Among the worst moral aftershocks of 9/11 was the possibility that terrorist associates had used advanced information to short the stock[2] of afflicted industries like airlines, New York real-estate trusts, and insurance companies.[3] The fear spread to Europe. The Belgian Minister of Finance suspected that British markets (but not his own) had been manipulated; and the governor of Germany's central bank noted odd movements in oil and gold before 9/11.[4] After the US Justice Department set up the Capital Markets Task Force to investigate, the spotlight fell on a San Diego short-seller with the suspicious name Amr Ibrahim el-Gindy (later changed, wisely but sacrilegiously, to Anthony Abraham Elgindy). This covert plotter, it seems, had not only been telling anyone who checked his public website that the Dow would crash to three thousand but had also called his broker on 10 September 2001 to liquidate a trust fund held for his daughter.

El-Gindy was no stranger to controversy. He was arrested at age eighteen for assault with a deadly weapon, but the charges were dropped. In 1995 he confessed that he and other brokers had accepted bribes to manipulate shares – he was granted immunity in exchange for information. But in 2000 he was convicted and briefly imprisoned for accepting disability payments from an insurance company while still working. By then he had set himself up as an online financial guru. With his website, chat room, and eletter, he set out to expose overvalued equities and fraud by small, publicly traded companies. Some rivals suggested he really just located lightly capitalized, thinly traded firms, then spread negative information to move their shares down. Some suspected him of passing on to the FBI and SEC rumors to hasten action that would make the stock drop. He was certainly a reasonable target for securities investigators. But, if he was really an al-Qā'idah sleeper agent, he must have been slumbering for a long time – he had migrated to the US from Cairo at the ripe old age of three.[5]

Out of his arrangement to trade information for immunity grew a scheme to work in reverse – a FBI agent passed to el-Gindy tips about pending investigations, which el-Gindy used to extort cheap or free stock from company insiders in exchange for a pledge not to spread the story. In 2002 he and his FBI partner were arrested and charged with stock fraud and extortion, but not with plotting with bin Lāden to profit off the joint collapse of the Twin Towers and the Dow Jones Average. That did not prevent the government from trying to use the more mediagenic accusations for other purposes. In the bail hearing, the prosecution, backed by the coordinator of the Capital Markets Task Force, argued for denial on the grounds that el-Gindy was a dual Egyptian-American citizen, travelled extensively in the Middle East, and had made $700,000 in wire transfers to Lebanon shortly after 9/11, a sign he was preparing to flee with his ill-gotten gains. The defense countered that el-Gindy had not only denounced the architects of 9/11 on his website but had issued a call for short-sellers *not* to take advantage. The $300,000 trust that he had asked his brokers to liquidate on 10 September was not sold until markets reopened on 18 September, by which time he had lost considerable money. And the $700,000 had been used to buy a Beirut condo rather than a black-market mini-nuke.

Still, the other major charge against him – trading while Muslim – did not appear on the indictment papers. Although he had grown up in the United States and was married to a Louisiana native, he was an active supporter, along with his brother and father, of Islamic institutions. Perhaps most suspicious, el-Gindy's father had formed in Chicago in 1998 an umbrella organization of Muslim groups to defend Mohammed Salah, the much harassed volunteer at the Quranic Literacy Institute. Hence the FBI was careful to seize from el-Gindy possible instrumentalities of terror – his house, bank accounts, tens of thousands in cash and gold coins, plus his Bentley, Jaguar, and Hummer SUV, should he decide to crash them into the Pentagon. In 2004 he was convicted and faced a potential ten to fifteen years plus loss of his assets.[6] As to other Islamic profiteers, despite lurid accounts from conspiracy buffs, every effort to find some unusual pattern of short-selling in shares of vulnerable corporations came to naught.[7]

TOURISM FOR TERRORISM

In 2003, a scene rivalled the one in upstate New York during the raid on Dr Dhafir's clinic, after a three-year investigation involving the FBI, the DEA, the Central Florida Organized Crime Task Force, Customs, the IRS, the Orange Country Sheriff's Office, the INS, and the Florida Highway Patrol, agents brandishing assault rifles rushed the house of Jesse Issa Maali and rounded up the Palestinian immigrant's family, including his pregnant daughter-in-law. They followed with raids on thirteen of his businesses and offices. These included not a sleazy shish kebab joint full of men puffing hookahs but the Ponderosa with the world's top retail turnover.[8]

The federal prosecutor announced that Maali had "ties" to violent groups; the FBI elaborated that he dabbled in drugs and extortion from businesses along the tourist strip to raise money for terrorism; the DEA claimed that his "crime family" had tried to kill a government witness; an informant elaborated that this Maali Mafia had acid-bombed his apartment. Small wonder that the local Fox affiliate, eager to get to the bottom in at least one sense, dubbed the case "Tourism for Terrorism" and superimposed Maali's face next to that of bin Lāden.[9]

Yet Maali's behavior seemed odd for someone sponsoring suicide bombers. He had left a violence-wracked Palestine for Venezuela, where he married a local Palestinian, moved to the Bronx, where he opened a grocery business, and ended up in Orlando because it seemed a safer place to raise a family. There his businesses, which varied from fast-food franchises to selling T-shirts to tourists, thrived. This ought to have made him a true US success story. Instead banks and suppliers cut off his credit and his businesses crumbled once the government announced its decision to charge him with material support for terrorism.[10]

The basis for the charge was a $50,000 check Maali had written to the Society of In'ash al-Usra, a UN-endorsed human-rights group providing emergency assistance (food, clothing, and medicine) to Palestinian victims of Israeli occupation. The problem for Maali was that the society deposited the money in Al Aqsa Islamic Bank in Palestine, which the US (on instructions from Israel) had deemed a front for Hamas. The problem for the government was that Maali had written the check 2.5 years before the government made that designation, while the informant on whose stories the Maali-Mafia tale was based turned out to be a liar with a grudge.

Finally, the government charged Maali with hiring illegal workers and "laundering" the money to pay them through the books of his companies, like just about every construction company, corporate farm, or tourism-service business in Florida. The illegals were handled mainly by Maali's business partner, who advised them to get their papers in order if they wanted to keep their jobs. Some who failed to do so were fired. One of the dismissed workers turned informant, giving the government something to cover up its fiasco on terrorism-support charges. Maali had the distinction of being the first of 635 local cases of businesses hiring illegal labor to face a criminal rather than a regulatory charge.

SMOKING 'EM OUT!

Nothing better demonstrates the depths of deceit to which terrorist groups will go than the efforts made by Lebanon's Hizbullāh to raise money in the United States. It was so intent on creating a good cover story that it set up as fronts throughout the disadvantaged parts of

Lebanon dozens of clinics, hospitals, schools, irrigation and drinking-water supply stations, and housing cooperatives. But all of that was just a smokescreen to hide its "real" objectives: terrorist attacks on Israeli soldiers whose only offense was to have inadvertently wandered with their armor and air force into Lebanon in 1982 and been unable to find their way home.[11]

Formed among the poor Shi'a in 1984, Hizbullāh soon became one of the strongest forces articulating Lebanese nationalism and the most effective in harassing the occupation army. However by far its most important work is done through Jihad al-Bin'ā, its construction and social-affairs agency. Originally established to provide flood relief at a time when the government had no funds, after Operation Grapes of Wrath, a 1988 Israeli military rampage through 147 towns and villages, the agency provided aid for hundreds of thousands of displaced people then moved in to repair the damage. In the Beirut slums it opened schools, pharmacies, and clinics; it dug wells, repaired sewers, and, for a time, moved three hundred tons of garbage a day (until a private company could take over). In the countryside, apart from construction and agricultural development projects, it provided water and electricity to deprived areas, plus schools, dental clinics, pharmacies, rehabilitation facilities for people maimed by Israeli bombs and missiles, and hospitals, including rebuilding some destroyed by Israel. It extended interest-free loans to newlyweds and start-up capital to small businesses to help the Shi'a population assert independence of the traditional Christian and Sunnī elites. With its help citizens created bakeries, fish-packing plants, and clothing manufactories that exported to Lebanese traders around the world. In addition it set up commercial radio and television stations broadcasting to a sufficiently large audience that, to the ire of Israel, US corporations began to buy advertising time.

Far from a fundamentalist pariah, Hizbullāh cooperated with international institutions including the YMCA and the United Nations Development Fund; it had joint projects with the Lebanese Department of Agriculture; its charitable arms were/are officially registered with the government, which also licensed the clinics, hospitals, and schools; and it has several representatives in Parliament.[12]

All of this costs money. There are four main sources: subsidies from Iran; charitable donations collected at mosques; reinvestment of profits from successful businesses; and gifts from well-to-do émigrés. Those who object to Hizbullāh activities could do little about Iranian subsidies or local contributions, and not much about the profitable

investments beyond the occasional Israeli bomb or missile. But donations from the émigré population were easier targets.

In West Africa, Lebanese were (in some places still are) prominent in
the retail trade; a few amassed wealth in diamond-dealing – sometimes
legal, sometimes illegal – in competition with Israeli smugglers. In
Latin America the main businesses were, and are, import and distribution of consumer goods. In Canada, which encouraged the influx of
(often French-speaking) Lebanese, numerous Shi'a drive taxis and run
family restaurants. In the US, Lebanese expats were/are similarly engaged in the retail trade. That, after 9/11, caused US law enforcement
to raise the green flag and led to the disconcerting discovery of a
Hizbullāh "cell" in North Carolina.[13]

In July 2000, more than two hundred cops (FBI and local) raided
homes and businesses in Charlotte, North Carolina, then filed criminal
complaints against eighteen local residents of Lebanese origin for immigration violations, cigarette smuggling, and money-laundering, with
weapons offenses tossed in for good measure. The court affidavit contained other allegations, including suspicion that profits may have
gone to Hizbullāh, but these did not figure in the early set of charges.
In fact the list of offenses initially went down – handguns seized by the
police had been legally acquired and fully registered (odd behavior for
terrorist plotters). Nor at first was there much attention to the
Hizbullāh claim. Apart from accusations that some of the accused had
cooked up marriages to secure green cards, the matter seemed to be a
routine case of cigarette bootlegging, hardly worth the energy of all
those boys in blue.

It seems that in 1996 Mohammed Yousef Hammoud (dubbed the
ringleader), his brother, and a group of others, noting the big tax dif-
ferential between North Carolina and Michigan, where many recent
Arab immigrants live, began to buy cigarettes from a local wholesaler to
haul in their own vehicles for sale in and near Detroit. As business pros-
pered they added more vehicles and more suppliers. Yet as smugglers
they were sloppy – getting stopped several times by state troopers. They
also found they could buy more with credit cards. So they applied for
cards in false names. Despite the later charge of credit-card fraud, the
false names were not to cheat the credit card companies (the debts
were repaid from the proceeds of cigarette sales) but to disguise their
identity from the wholesalers. Using credit cards to buy cigarettes and
pay for gasoline was actually the mark of amateurs – the credit record
made it easy for law enforcement to trace their movements and to

calculate the amount of their transactions. Because the brothers sold 1.5 million packs at a profit of about seventy cents each, they collected about $1 million in gross profit over four years, out of which they paid operating expenses for themselves and sixteen "associates."

The feds claimed that the case was another brilliant success for their anti-money-laundering measures – i.e., cash deposits of greater than $10,000 working as "red flags." But that was news to the bank involved. All the required Currency Transaction Reports had been filed, and the bank had never written a Suspicious Activity Report for the good reason that "there was nothing unusual or out of the ordinary with the way these accounts were opened." The feds began investigating not on the basis of bank transactions but because of a report of a car with out-of-state license plates loading unusual amounts of cigarettes at a wholesaler. Then they requested that the bank check Mohammed Hammoud's account.[14] This is precisely what would have happened in a routine search for evidence even if no anti-money-laundering laws had existed.

Since penalties for (and public attention generated by) a minor bootlegging operation would be small, the prosecutors were eager to nail whomever they could for "terrorist financing." That would work, much like adding money-laundering charges (which also figured in the case) on top of minor crimes to greatly hike penalties. In March 2001, nearly a year after the original charges, the prosecution brought down a new indictment accusing nine of the smugglers of membership in a Hizbullāh "cell." It contended that the cigarette smuggling was to generate money to buy sophisticated weapons for Hizbullāh.

The indictment followed the pattern typical of cases involving charges of criminal "conspiracy." A series of separate transactions are cobbled together with enough scotch tape and imagination into a grand unified plot with a single or sometimes collective directing mind, be it Usama or "the Mafia" or, in this case, Hizbullāh – which, according to the carefully researched indictment, was also known as the Party of God (the literal translation), Islamic Jihad (a completely different group), Islamic Jihad Organization (a splinter and competitor of the previous), and Islamic Jihad for the Liberation of Palestine (again different, and Sunnī on top). In fact, the indictment asserted, at various times Hizbullāh was also known as the Revolutionary Justice Organization, the Organization of the Oppressed on Earth, the Organization for Right against Wrong, Ansar Allah, and the Followers of the Prophet Mohammed. Most of these names had popped up following particular actions when someone called

the media to claim responsibility; and they could have been used by almost anyone, including terror squads working for the Israeli, US, Syrian,
Saudi, or Lebanese intelligence services.

The alleged grand plot went as follows: the culprits were recruited in
Lebanon by Hizbullāh; sent to the US; instructed to infiltrate an open
and welcoming society with fake marriages; told to execute criminal
acts to generate money; then ordered to spend it to obtain sophisticated military equipment – night-vision goggles, GPS systems, aviation
antennas, mine- and metal-detection equipment, video recorders, computer equipment, advanced aircraft analysis and design software, stun
guns, hand-held radio receivers, cellphones, naval radar equipment,
and so forth.[15] That was quite an order for a handful of Lebanese mis-
fits trying to make ends meet running cigarettes. Just why Hizbullāh
would order electronic equipment in the US when much the same stuff
is available cheaper in Dubai, for example, was somewhat odd. Nor for
that matter was there any reason given why an organization routinely
denounced for receiving military equipment for free from Syria and
Iran would bother buying it anyway. (Nor indeed did officialdom feel
impelled to ask why all that neat stuff was so easily available in the US.)

Inevitably, too, came claims of "ties" to suicide bombers in the form of
a plot to get life insurance for thirty Hizbullāh members who were "going to go for a walk and never come back." It is doubtful if in its entire
history Hizbullāh had thirty suicide bombers in its inventory of human
resources. And the chances of the family of a Hizbullāh martyr applying
to a US insurance company for survivor's benefits seem rather low, to put
it mildly, particularly since no US insurance company would pay.

There was, of course, another interpretation: that the defendants fled
repeated acts of Israeli brigandage in Southern Lebanon; came to the
US in desperate circumstances; married as legitimately as most people in
poor neighborhoods where many people are recent immigrants fearful
of INS harassment and use quick marriages to try to remain in the US;
scrambled to make ends meet with menial jobs; saw their chance to
score some money running cigarettes; and, as they would no matter
what the origin of their income, sent some zakāt contributions to a foundation that provided assistance to family members back home in an area
where Hizbullāh runs just about everything. But that scenario was too
far-fetched to be taken seriously. After all, the prosecution presented in
evidence videos watched by the conspirators as they gathered regularly
(as do many Lebanese Muslims) on Thursday evening. These nasty
movies glorified the exploits of Hizbullāh guerrillas against the Israelis.

If the accused were really innocent, surely they would have spent their Thursday nights watching the *Terminator* series.

The most important piece of evidence, though, was the one that tied together the cigarette bootlegging with the plans to purchase military equipment. While some people involved in the cigarette end had been picked up on wiretaps talking about weapons, neither Mohammed Hammoud nor his brother were so heard. The smoking gun, so to speak, came with the testimony of Said Harb, the accused whose name popped up most often in the arms-deal discussions. He turned state's evidence in exchange for a greatly reduced sentence (cut from potentially sixty years to a maximum of six to eight) and a US promise to fly his family out of Lebanon. Harb testified that Mohammed Hammoud had given him personally $3,500 to take to a military commander of Hizbullāh. Leaving aside the fact that Harb had already stolen $12,000 from Mohammed Hammoud, who was unlikely to entrust Harb with another $3,500, if an officer of a militia with thousands of militants receives $3,500 from a cigarette smuggler in the US it might seem more like a personal payoff than an official transaction – although apparently not to the judge, prosecutors, or jurors in the case, or the media who gushed over it.[16]

As further proof, the prosecution produced a "receipt" for $1,300 from Mohammed Hussein Fadlallah, long identified as the spiritual leader of Hizbullāh.[17] Actually Sheikh Fadlallah is one of the main spiritual leaders of the whole Shi'a community in Lebanon and never had any operational association with Hizbullāh – although that did not prevent the CIA in 1985 from attempting to murder him with a massive car bomb that killed eighty and wounded two hundred innocent people.[18] Nor did anyone see fit to question why a devout Muslim like Mohammed Hammoud, who is supposed to contribute to charitable causes anonymously, demanded a receipt. Perhaps for US income tax purposes? Yet more "proof" came from claims of people like Matthew Levitt, the ex-FBI "terrorism expert" who had found a much more lucrative and politically comfortable career writing anti-Arab screeds and peddling his testimony in anti-Islamic cases.[19]

Against all this there seemed little the defense could do. One of the biggest problems it faced is that anyone accused of aiding a designated "terrorist organization" does not have legal standing to question the validity of the designation. Therefore the fact that military activity (in this case against an illegally occupying foreign power) was only a sideline for Hizbullāh and that any donated money from the Hammouds, trivial in relation to Hizbullāh's total needs, was likely swallowed up in bona fide charitable work, was irrelevant. Besides, merely to invoke the Hizbullāh name was to recall to judge and jury the myth that Hizbullāh was behind the 1983 suicide bombing of the Marine barracks in Beirut. This was an event heralded in the media as "the most fatal hour for US troops since Pearl Harbor" while the FBI spoke in awe of the most massive non-nuclear explosion on Earth since World War II. Yet Hizbullāh did not even exist when the bombing (along with a similar one against a French barracks) took place. Incidentally, Sheikh Fadlallah, its supposed spiritual guide, always denounced suicide attacks (and airplane hijackings) as unIslamic.[20]

With all this evidence against him, Mohammed Hammoud was given a sentence of 155 years, while the feds exulted in their first-ever victory with the 1996 material-support-for-terrorism law.[21] Since no evidence had been introduced that he had conspired to provide weapons or explosives or assisted the planning or execution of a terrorist act even on the promiscuous US definition, the sentence did raise some eyebrows. But as the prosecutor gravely noted, "We're not going to make a distinction between terrorists and those who fund terrorists."[22]

That such a sentence was possible can be explained by the timing. The cigarette-bootlegging and immigration charges were brought down in 2000. The escalation to a charge of material support for terrorism occurred in March of 2001. But the trial took place while post-9/11 hysteria was still near peak. In a subsequent unsuccessful appeal, one dissenting judge noted that, without the Hizbullāh brouhaha, the maximum sentence for Mohammed Hammoud would have been fifty-seven months. Another insisted that the government had demonstrably failed to prove its case against Mohammed Hammoud, that the only serious evidence against him was provided by a turned witness described during the trial as "untrustworthy, manipulative, a liar and an exaggerator." But the majority concurred with the original sentence, and Mohammed Hammoud was locked up effectively for life – for evading some cigarette taxes (he paid the North Carolina ones, but not the higher Michigan rate) and peddling without a license.[23]

The cigarette companies leaped joyfully on the case. Previously their refrain had been that high taxes led to an "organized crime" takeover of the smuggling business, neatly sidestepping the fact that all over the world tobacco smuggling is really run by the Virginia Cartel – the five big US and UK cigarette manufacturers. In the campaign to cut tobacco taxes, it was much more effective to claim that high taxes fed the coffers of Arab terrorists.[24]

Success in nailing the "Charlotte Hezbollah cell" led to other cases. This time it was the turn of the Treasury's Bureau of Alcohol, Tobacco and Firearms, perhaps the least glamorous of the federal law enforcement arms to vie with the FBI, DEA, and Customs for the media spotlight. Announcing a national crackdown, its assistant director crowed: "The deeper we dig into these cases, the more ties to terrorism we're discovering."[25]

The tobacco case was only one, albeit dramatic, part of a post-9/11 pan-US investigation of small Arab- and Muslim-owned businesses that, the authorities claimed, produced "tens of millions of dollars a year" for terrorist groups.[26] The United States, as everyone knows, is the land of terrorist milk, if not honey, and what better places for Arab terrorists to draw their goat's milk and the occasional jar of Yemeni honey than from corner grocery stores run by poor immigrants with large extended families to support? The new sweep, seeking those who, for example, steal and resell baby formula, came because US agents realized they had spent too much effort looking for "big rats" while they had let slip through "thousands of ants" – an allegorical improvement over "cockroaches" or "lice," phrases used by Israeli politicians and senior officers when speaking of Arabs.[27]

Thus, the FBI insisted that "$20 million to $30 million" raised annually in scams throughout the US constituted "a substantial portion of the estimated hundreds of millions of dollars that Middle Eastern terror groups raise and spend annually." One source was retail-coupon fraud. Apparently terrorist supporters were sifting through garbage piles and pilfering from recycling centres to get newspapers containing retail-coupon inserts, a heinous act that also took away support from welfare mothers and street people. The gangs then made deals with corrupt store owners to split the profits by cashing in coupons without genuine sale of merchandise. The result is that, of $3.5 billion in retail coupons redeemed in the US annually, "nearly 10 percent" (!) is fraudulent, and, according to "the experts," "at least several millions" ends up in the hands of "terrorists."[28]

OPIATES FOR WHOSE MASSES?

Nicotine is, of course, intensely addictive. But other things are worse, as al-Qā'idah understood only too well. As a result of Usama's reputed success in cornering the Afghan opium crop, his followers were said to peddle heroin across Europe. Sometimes that required alliances with local organized crime. For example, al-Qā'idah worked hand in glove with Bosnian traffickers along the Balkans Route, using drug profits to buy arms, with so much success that, according to intelligence experts, Bosnia "became an off-the-shelf model for fundraising and recruitment" used by al-Qā'idah elsewhere – Kosovo, Albania, and Chechnya, for a start.[29]

For a long time the US was relatively indifferent – little or no Afghan opiates reached its shores. But late in 2002 came electrifying news that the FBI and the DEA had joined forces to smash an operation that had planned to sell heroin and hashish, then use the money to finance the purchase of anti-aircraft missiles for al-Qā'idah: another scheme to use cocaine to buy East Bloc arms for South America was broken almost simultaneously. John Ashcroft, not formerly known for poetic sensitivities, laid before the press a string of colorful images linking steamy Latin American jungles to rugged Afghan mountains to arid Arabian wastelands. Flanked by the DEA director, the nation's first lawyer exulted, "We have demonstrated that drug traffickers and terrorists work out of the same jungle, they plan in the same cave, and they train in the same desert ... the war on terrorism has been joined with the war on illegal drug use," Thus the case threw a bone to Drug Warriors worried about losing pride of place to Terror Warriors. When Ashcroft characterized the arrests as a reminder "of the toxic combination of drugs and terrorism and the threats they can pose to our national security," the US prosecutor present at the extravaganza concurred that "Drugs are the currency of terrorists. This is the medium of terrorism in the 21st century."[30]

Perhaps. But if Ilyas Ali told the truth, what really happened was that the FBI and DEA conned a naive and desperate immigrant from India and two Pakistani confederates – none of whom had ever wandered through a rainforest, trekked the Hindu Kush, or ridden a camel off into the desert sunset – into believing that, if they could score some drugs back home, they could trade them to the undercover agents for Stinger missiles. As Ali explained it, he used to run a grocery store in St Paul, Minnesota. After the store was robbed of $100,000 worth of merchandise and goods, he found himself suddenly befriended by two undercover FBI agents – one claimed to be a drug dealer, the other a weapons specialist. They outlined the scheme for Ali and associates to obtain the drugs and missiles. They paid him to fly twice to Pakistan, once to Hong Kong to meet his two future confederates – all three were arrested and sent to the US.[31]

In other words there was no terror-dollar trail – the agents said they would finance the whole affair. There was no drug connection – Ali was a total neophyte. There was no al-Qā'idah waiting to take delivery of nonexistent missiles. It was from start to finish the kind of entrapment that for generations courts refused to accept, until law-and-order conservatives took over. With the media gushing over a "remarkable undercover investigation by daring FBI agents" helped, of course, by "legal reforms" under the Patriot Act, two of the three pled guilty to conspiring to distribute six hundred kilos of heroin and five tons of hashish and to provide "material support" to al-Qā'idah.[32]

Some drug schemes were even more insidious. In what was dubbed the largest-ever bust of a methamphetamine ring in North America, the DEA arrested one hundred people in ten cities, revealing "close ties" between Mexican drug-trafficking organizations and a brand-new threat on the US crime scene. It had been bad enough to deal with the Italian Mafia, the Chinese Triads, the Japanese Yakuza, the Colombian "cartels," Nigerian scamsters, then the Russian Mafyya. But now there was "Arab-American Organized Crime" not only intent on peddling drugs but also on sending profits to Hizbullāh – a claim suggesting that DEA analysts had been sampling some of the stuff the agency had seized.[33]

GETTING THE GOODS ON USAMA

There was growing realization that al-Qā'idah, and its partners like Hizbullāh and Hamas, had made not just key infrastructure like the World Trade Center but the US economy itself the target of their holy war.[34] Allegedly they were both probing for a soft underbelly where "the sword of Islam" could strike with maximum effect and searching for operating funds. One way to jointly accomplish both ends was product counterfeiting. Sale of fake consumer goods could be lucrative and, if conducted on sufficient scale, could erode customer confidence in the high-tech marvels of modern US industry – something to which any Indonesian worker toiling twelve hours a day for minimal pay in a Nike sweatshop could readily attest. Such a crisis of confidence might even threaten the recovery program enunciated by Vice-President Cheney when, in the aftermath of 9/11, he advised Americans to respond to the assault on their values by more shopping.[35]

For many years particular firms had complained about counterfeit goods. But for a long time the issue was not regarded as significant for the US economy as a whole.[36] However, by the 1980s, an increasing share of world trade depended on brand recognition, along with protection of trademarks, patents, and industrial designs; and ever more production was outsourced to places that offered the contradictory combination of virtual slave labor to enhance profits for US firms and a lax attitude towards "intellectual property rights" to threaten those same profits.

Hence by the 1990s the US, backed by an ever-faithful Britain, led not a worldwide campaign against sweatshop working conditions and appalling pay scales in poor countries but a global War on Counterfeiting. This was a remarkable example of selective amnesia. For centuries Britain had protected its industries with high tariffs and subsidies while destroying those of other countries through economic warfare and military conquest. Then, when its manufacturers had built up sufficient lead, it launched a crusade to sell the virtues of free trade to the rest of the world. Similarly the US in the nineteenth century openly copied from other countries industrial designs and technologies and enticed away their skilled craftsmen while molding its own intellectual property laws to preclude legal recourse.

When the US suddenly got free-trade religion, its main problem was that not only did much of the world resist its entreaties for a "level playing field" but, even inside rich countries, so-called intellectual-property crime was regarded by the public, and often by police and prosecutors, as a minor offense, if an offense at all.[37] True, with food and pharmaceutical products, some people were poisoned by fakes. However, laws already protected the afflicted consumer as distinct from the affected holder of the patent or trademark. Anyway, something like bogus Rolex watches does not pose the same threat as contraband prescription drugs. Nor is it clear how much they actually dampen the market. People willing to shell out $4,000 for a watch are hardly likely to buy a $40 replica. In at least some cases the main thing protected is the social pretensions of an elite of consumers upset when a plebe can sport for a tiny fraction of the price something that, on a quick view, yields the same social status as their own exorbitant acquisition. Furthermore it is at least arguable that the real fakery is not the imitation but the con job by the legitimate companies against clients foolish enough to pay full price – which makes product counterfeiting just a rip-off of a rip-off.

As to how big the problem is, in 1995 the International Anti-Counterfeiting Coalition, with about two hundred US corporate members, claimed annual losses of $200 billion. Yet *Forbes* magazine, hardly a place to find a radical critique of capitalist institutions, put the real loss at about $10 billion per year. To get the $200 billion figure, the IACC apparently took an estimate of the total number of counterfeit items sold (how it got *that* number is a good question), then multiplied by the full retail price of genuine articles on the assumption that people able to divert $40 from their welfare checks for a fake Rolex would, if the copy were not available, spend $4,000 on the real thing. Based on this, the IACC computed 210,000 lost jobs. Thus industries that had for decades outsourced in order to attack wages and working standards inside the US now cited job losses from counterfeiting to get governments to further entrench their monopolies – when the real question was not whether US jobs would be sacrificed but whether US corporations or Asian counterfeiters would profit.

Lack of solid evidence that the problem is either very extensive or much of a threat has not prevented counterfeiting from becoming a rising priority for action, international and domestic. Against some countries the US imposes trade and credit sanctions; while inside the US anti-counterfeiting laws have become increasingly draconian. Originally handled as a regulatory or civil matter, in 1984 the Trademark Counterfeiting Act imposed for the first time criminal as well as civil remedies. For industry, criminalization was a brilliant stroke – civil suits meant much of the proceeds ended up in the pockets of lawyers, while criminal cases shifted onto the public sector the cost of actions whose main objective was to protect the industry from competition and raise its profitability.

Then in 1996, following hyped IACC claims, came the Anti-Counterfeiting Consumer Protection Act, its Orwellian name befitting its Clintonian origins. This permitted the owner of a trademark to get an injunction to stop use of any trademark that diluted the distinctive quality of the owner's mark, strengthened provisions for seizure and disposal, and increased both civil and criminal penalties. The new law permitted a maximum civil penalty up to the retail value of the merchandise seized. However, in a bizarre twist of logic, that penalty was set at a "retail value" based on the manufacturers' list price for the genuine merchandise rather than on how much the counterfeit might have reaped. This meant that seizure, for example, of a fake "luxury" watch that cost a few dollars to manufacture, could make whoever was caught with the goods liable for thousands of dollars per watch, payable to the allegedly aggrieved party.

No matter how tough laws may be, they are useless if police agencies refuse to take them seriously. Historically collaring counterfeit goods lacked the sex appeal of chasing Commies or crack dealers; while judges balked at imposing stiff fines and long sentences whose principal impact was to raise the share price of companies that made the "real" article. The industry response came in three phases.

First, a clever lobbyist drafted a bill, passed first by the Georgia legislature, to permit police to keep 70 percent of any assets they grabbed in commodity-counterfeiting cases. The assumption was that, as with drug-money seizures, the police would be delighted to find a new way to flesh out their budgets at the expense of the "bad guys."[38]

Second, industry discovered "organized crime." At the end of the 1980s and on into the early 1990s, the media retailed tales of Triads, sometimes in league with China's People's Liberation Army, trafficking fake goods. This campaign culminated with the spectacle of a Vietnamese-American gangster, busted in 1991 with a counterfeit Rolex and Cartier "factory" in his home, bragging over the airwaves about his multiple millions from fake-watch sales.[39]

Third came 9/11 and the realization that behind so much product piracy stood Usama and his minions. Consumers who purchased these goods, and merchants who sold them, were no longer just greedy and shortsighted; they were complicit in high treason and mass murder. A formerly victimless crime now had victims in spades.[40]

This farce was aided and abetted by Interpol, the Paris-based organization that serves as a information clearing house for police forces around the world. Interpol had originally been created in Europe after World War I; then, its primary duty was to combat counterfeiting of currencies of recently emerged, financially weak states. Now, under its new Secretary General, a former senior official of both the US Treasury and Justice Department, Interpol again became proactive in a War on Counterfeiting, this time worldwide and focused on brand-name goods. The Secretary General, in the first-ever address of an Interpol boss before Congress, informed the legislators that "intellectual property crime is becoming the preferred method of funding for a number of terrorist groups."[41] Allegedly a "suspected al-Qaeda member" once sent a crate of counterfeit cosmetics from Dubai to Copenhagen, perhaps en route to the US. "It is possible," the Secretary General also noted, "that the funds generated were remitted to al-Qaeda indirectly through zakat-based ... giving." (It was also possible that they were remitted to the US Treasury directly though quarterly tax installments.) In addition bin Lāden's many supporters in Australia were supposedly implicated in counterfeiting Louis Vuitton bags. If so, they had lots of company in the region. Once the Louis Vuitton outlet in Pusan, South Korea, had to bribe a street peddler to clear the sidewalk in front of the store where he was offering cheap knockoffs to prospective clients.[42]

Of course, not all of the problem was caused by al-Qā'idah, Hamas, or Hizbullāh – nor was the US the only country to suffer. The Secretary General noted IRA involvement in contraband cigarettes and the actions of ethnic-Albanian extremist groups in Kosovo, where a "significant proportion" of consumer goods were fakes. Furthermore, in 2000, the Russian Federal Security Services shut down a counterfeit CD "plant," claiming it was run by a Chechen "organized crime" group that earned $500,000 to $700,000 per month for "terrorism." Still, the US was the prime target and had been for many years. The first World Trade Center attack way back in 1993 had been partly financed by the sale of fake T-shirts.[43]

Others concurred with the Interpol chief that the world had witnessed "a steady increase in counterfeited brands since Sept. 11, 2001," which had "created a deep concern among intelligence agents who fear many of these criminal organizations are tied directly to al-Qaeda."[44] Meanwhile, energized by the counterfeit-terror connection, the FBI finally got busy. It "estimated" that in the year 2002 fake goods cost US businesses $200–250 billion per year (suspiciously similar to the previous IACC counterfeit number with a suitable seven-year inflation factor built in). If true, that was a fair chunk of a world total of $450 billion worth of fake goods supposedly traded each year, amounting to a whopping 9 percent of world trade.[45]

Representatives of industry told Congress that the very success of the anti-terror effort in drying up funding in the Middle East had driven terrorists into counterfeit goods. To prevent these groups from recouping, it was time, the affected industries felt, for the world's law-enforcement agencies, prosecutors, and judges to take the threat from intellectual property crime more seriously.[46] Interpol's Secretary General made the connection quite clear: "In general law enforcement does not treat IPC [intellectual property crime] as a high priority crime … In contrast, terrorist financing is regarded as a high priority for law enforcement agencies."

With that in mind, the long arm of US law reached deep into South America. The target was the notorious Triborder Region, where Brazil, Argentina, and Paraguay meet, a hotbed of Islamic militancy with a growing Arab population and a freewheeling market in bootleg pharmaceuticals, pirated electronic goods, and brand-label counterfeits, along with, reputedly, cocaine and weapons. Not only was it already a major operations centre for Hizbullāh and Hamas, but local intelligence services suggested that, because of so many well-placed blows against his money-raising apparatus, Usama himself was about to transfer his financial headquarters there. Further research produced the alarming result that Khalid Sheikh Mohammed, one of the many purported masterminds of 9/11, had visited the area in 1995.[47]

The Triborder Region had been no stranger to smuggling long before Middle Eastern expats relocated there. The local capital, Cuidad del Este, Paraguay, had been founded by the old dictator, General Alfredo Stroessner, as a place where his senior officers could rent airstrips and sell protection to smugglers running US consumer goods (whiskey, blue jeans, electronics, and especially cigarettes) into protected markets like Argentina and Brazil. In fact local observers in the 1960s and 1970s were convinced that the notorious *contrabandista* system had actually been invented by the Virginia Cartel, the clique of US and UK tobacco companies that dominate world trade, legal and illegal, in cigarettes.[48] Into this smuggling Mecca (or, as the popular press preferred, Casablanca on the Parana) later came Lebanese exiles along with some Egyptians. With them, too, came tales about crazed jihādists collecting massive amounts of terror-dollars. Egypt's Gamā'at al-Islāmiyya ("linked to al-Qaeda") alone was reputed to be earning no less than $500 million per annum – not bad for a group that until then had financed itself by holding up the occasional Coptic jewellery store or printing the odd batch of fake Egyptian currency.[49]

Even before 9/11, US pressure had prompted the Paraguayan police to raid a wholesale electronics store owned by the reputed local Hizbullāh financial boss. Assad Ahmed Barakat (that name again!) had already fled to Brazil, but he somehow "forgot" to take his documents, videos, and literature. These allegedly included CDs containing "terrorist propaganda" and bank records showing $50 million transferred to Hizbullāh since 1995. As the Lebanese ambassador to Paraguay and Argentina tried to explain, a small amount of money was raised by zakāt among the entire Lebanese Shi'a expat community in the area and used by one of the Hizbullāh-linked charities in Lebanon to assist war orphans.[50]

Among those to see green, so to speak, when the Triborder Region was mentioned was General James Hill, newly appointed head of the US military's SOUTHCOM, and therefore in charge of Latin American military relations. Being capo of SOUTHCOM used to be the sexiest of regional commands. Whoever had the post also held the portfolio for "narco-terrorism," a connection between cocaine trafficking and leftist insurgency invented by Republican spinmeisters during the 1980s at a time when one of the main pipelines running drugs into the US was the

alliance of secret police agencies and right-wing terrorist groups cobbled together by the CIA to fight "communism" in Central America.[51]
But 9/11 shifted US attention to the Middle East and Central Asia.
That was something no self-respecting commanding officer was going
to accept without a fight.

Early in 2003, in a speech at Georgetown Institute of Strategic Studies, General Hill drew his line in the rainforest when he declared that
radical Islamic groups were getting hundreds of millions of dollars a
year from criminal networks in Latin America. When he warned his
audiences, including readers of the Sunday Edition of the *Miami
Herald*, that "The fastest-growing religion in Latin America today is Islam. We think that there are between 3 and 6 million people of Middle Eastern descent in Latin America," he forgot to mention that the
greatest part of that Arab population is made up of third-generation
Syro-Lebanese Christians, most of whom had forgotten their Arabic at
least one generation back. "As if narco-terrorist violence were not
enough," the general explained further, "extensions of Middle Eastern terrorism have crept into the area. There are radical Islamic
groups associated with that population that are using it to create lots
of money for their organizations." He cited specifically Hamas,
Hizbullāh, and "Islamiyya al Gammat." (Arabic grammar was not the
general's strong point.) In addition, there were support cells to provide logistics and personnel "extending from Trinidad and Tobago to
Margarita Island off Venezuela to the triborder areas of Paraguay, Argentina and Brazil." As to what they were up to, "Islamic radical
groups and narco-terrorists in Colombia all practice the same business
methods" generating "millions of dollars every year via their multiple
illicit activities."[52]

To meet the threat, in early 2005 the US sent in weapons, planes, and
five hundred crack troops to bolster an existing small airbase that, coincidentally, was near one of the most important fresh-water storage ba-
sins in the world and well-located to keep an eye on restless Bolivia,
whose natural gas reserves were second largest on the continent. But,
of course, the timing, just before Bolivia's presidential election (which,
as Washington feared, put an anti-free-trade aboriginal in power) was
purely coincidental. The real job was anti-terror in the Andes. Nor was
Bolivia the only concern. No less an authority than Pat Robertson of
the Christian Coalition insisted that after 9/11 Venezuela's César
Chavez, in his effort to build a Communist-Islamist anti-US alliance,
had donated $1.4 million to al-Qā'idah for "relocation costs."[53]

SUPERDOLLARS AND NONSENSE

Despite any success the US had in blunting a terror assault on the fake-goods front, the much greater danger was that al-Qā'idah and its supporters, aided by rogue states, would try to destroy confidence in the world's ultimate brand name, the US dollar. It would not be the first time hostile elements had tried to use phony money as a weapon of war. The British had issued fake Continental Bills in an effort to sabotage the Revolution. During the Civil War, Confederate agents attempted to flood the Union with phony greenbacks. The Bolsheviks after World War I had plotted to infiltrate bogus US notes into European banks to subvert the USA's emerging superpower status. The Nazis had a massive counterfeiting operation in place during World War II. But, according to the special Republican Party Task Force On Terrorism and Unconventional Warfare, the real inspiration for al-Qā'idah to wage numismatic warfare came from a scheme concocted in the 1980s by Iran and Syria and implemented by terrorist organizations under their control.

While the US $100 bill had long been a prime target for counterfeiters around the world, the "supernote" discovered in London in 1989 was declared almost perfect. According to the Task Force On Terrorism and Unconventional Warfare, which drew on the stellar research of Yousef Bodansky, the "supernote" emerged during the Lebanese civil war when the right-wing Christian Phalangists, short on money and weapons, linked up with Armenian printers to counterfeit US large-denomination notes. Although the results were not very impressive, Phalangist officials took a few suitcases abroad to buy weapons. Sometime in the 1980s, Syria's military intelligence took control and linked up with Iran.[54] At that point the plot thickened, as the USA's most inveterate enemies in the Middle East made common cause, drawing on infrastructure inadvertently provided by the US during better days.

As the Republican Task Force further reported, during the last years of the monarchy, the Shah of Iran had harbored ambitions for Iran to be the Gulf region's banking and financial centre, and for its currency to be the most trusted. Hence he bought the best US equipment. With his overthrow, the equipment fell into the hands of a mob of mad mullahs frothing with hatred against the "Great Satan." With "plates" thoughtfully provided by East Germany, the Iranians churned out bogus $100 notes, then flew them to Damascus, where Syrian intelligence arranged for distribution through Lebanese drug-trafficking networks. By the early 1990s they had together flooded the world with at least

$10 billion worth. The poorest quality went to developing countries to buy political support and to finance terrorism or, after 1991, to ex-Soviet Republics. In Russia itself the job was subcontracted to the Sicilian Mafia, which used its connections with Russian mobsters to buy up privatized businesses, loot raw materials, and acquire black-market nuclear arms. In this emerging terror-crime nexus, the Colombian "cartels" also had a role. Corrupt banks under their sway accepted counterfeit money mixed with massive deposits of drug dollars to pass on to unsuspecting people. Other notes, somewhat better, were used in the Middle East to pay for anti-Israel and anti-US terrorist acts. The very best, of course, were destined for the good old USA. If this act of numismatic terrorism ever succeeded in undermining faith in the US currency, Third World banks and leaders would shed their dollar holdings in favor of gold or other currencies, and the world financial system would downgrade drastically, if not repudiate completely, the central role of the US dollar.

In addition, the Iranian-Syrian enterprise aimed to undermine Israel's heavily dollarized economy and give the perpetrators the means to shop for an off-the-shelf, ready-to-use nuclear weapons system. The Task Force chillingly reported that: "… Syrian military representatives have been travelling in Czechia, Slovakia, and the Ukraine with some $800 million in cash trying to buy strategic weapons, including nuclear warheads and high performance weapons systems for immediate delivery." If the Task Force needed more proof, it came from two Lebanese drug dealers jailed in Massachusetts in 1992. They were eager to repent their former misdeeds by revealing details about the supernote project before throwing themselves on the mercies of the court.[55]

On the other hand, there was some debate over just how super the "supernote" was. To US Secret Service agents, it was full of visible flaws. But, to the US media, the only thing it lacked was Abe Lincoln's fingerprints. Equally contentious was its origins. Like most species of flu, it seems to have surfaced first in China before spreading to Europe. Nor was it clear why Eastern European countries with nuclear arsenals would be any keener than those of Western Europe to promote proliferation, particularly if their reward came in crates of US counterfeit. The Task Force also failed to explain how Syria persuaded the fanatically anti-Syrian Phalangists to fold their counterfeiting networks into the emerging Irano-Syrian one, and to permit the Syrians to export counterfeit through the port of Junieh, which was the scene, during much of the late 1980s and early 1990s, of a bitter shooting war between the Syrians and the Christian factions controlling the port. Nor was it immediately apparent how spreading low-quality fake money was likely to win friends and influence leaders in developing countries or ex-Soviet republics where Iran was attempting to raise its political profile. Parenthetically it was equally unclear why Sicilian Mafiosi or Colombian cocaine barons would cooperate in a plan to destroy the US financial system on which the security of their own reputed billions depended unless they, too, had secretly converted to militant Islam.

Anyway Iran's printing machines had been acquired not from the US, as the Task Force claimed in its highly idiosyncratic version of events, but from the Swiss firm De La Rue – Giori, the world's principal manufacturer of intaglio presses, which was to create a complete printing plant, install the equipment, and train the staff, until the revolution intervened. For years afterwards, the equipment sat incomplete and unopened; while Iran, desperate for new bank notes, was forced to overprint old ones to remove the Shah's head and emblazon them with revolutionary slogans.[56] At the very time the Iranians were supposedly pumping out US currency, their own economy was awash with fake notes that were apparently easy to counterfeit because the printing facilities used in Iran were so primitive.[57]

As to the purported effects on the US financial system and on the international role of the dollar, by the time the "supernote" surfaced, (real) US currency in circulation outside the USA's borders totalled around $400 billion, much to the delight of US Treasury officials. What happens by monetary magic is that the US gets to print a $100 bill for three cents a copy, then spends it to acquire the full $100 worth of foreign goods, services, or assets. If it borrowed the same amount of money that it prints, and had to pay interest on the borrowed funds, the cost to the US Treasury would have been $15–25 billion per year.

Furthermore, despite the undoubted popularity of US currency, the world's elites were more likely to keep their savings in US dollar-denominated securities rather than in cash stuffed in socks under their beds. To carry out financial transactions, the world monetary system relied not on the attaché cases filled with bank notes – that is more the province of Republican Party bagmen – but on trillions in dollar-denominated interbank transfers. If there really were a crisis of confidence in the US currency induced by the discovery of massive amounts of counterfeit, presumably the main losers would be drug dealers and tax evaders caught counting their cash rather than people who had already managed to deposit their money safely in obliging banks.

Still, there was no need to let facts get in the way, particularly since for many years US Treasury officials had been pressing the government for a radical redesign of the greenback to guard against not the plots of mad mullahs hovering over sophisticated intaglio presses but the antics of opportunistic Americans with access to the latest in color copiers that could mimic even the raised feeling of intaglio printing. Treasury officials were consistently stonewalled by Congressional fears that tampering with the comfortably familiar design of the US currency would cause a political backlash. However, public opinion surveys showed that the one thing that could get the public on side for a change was concern over the currency's security – and when it came to security who could pose a more credible threat than a Syro-Iranian, Russo-Mafia, terrorist-cocaine cartel coalition?

Then, with the successful redesign of the $100 bill and with a brief thaw in US-Syrian relations, the story changed. The new threat became a deal between North Korea and Iran to swap Iranian counterfeiting expertise for North Korean missile technology.[58] After 9/11, that variant was resurrected with a new twist. This time, North Korea printed the detector-defying $100 bills, while al-Qā'idah, through its global network of affiliates and its multitude of international black-market connections, put them into circulation. Once again, there were three purposes: to finance acquisition of weapons of mass destruction, to erode world confidence in the greenback, and, if the fakes could be circulated in sufficient amounts, to trigger hyperinflation in the US.[59]

Defying the skeptics, there was proof. After 9/11 the US Justice Department posted on its website an "al-Qaeda instruction manual" (it turned out to have nothing to do with Usama) that counselled the use of fake documents and currency. On the other hand, inside the US, while many would-be counterfeiters were arrested (everyone from high-school students using the facilities of their Graphic Arts Department Careers Center to night-shift workers at printing plants), the only "terrorist connection" anyone could find was a lone teenage Palestinian refugee who created some US notes using his home computer and ordinary paper. Even the local police dismissed early sensations about an al-Qā'idah connection.[60]

16

Conflicts of Interest? – On Bloody Diamonds and Tarnished Gold

A few years before 9/11, the world's curiously selective conscience was shocked by images from the little West African country of Sierra Leone. There, an insurgent group fond of hacking off hands and feet with machetes funded its war by exploiting slave labor in diamond fields, smuggling gemstones via complicit dealers (Lebanese, naturally) to Liberia, then onto world markets. To horror stories from Sierra Leone (and Liberia) were soon added those from Angola, where the government was locked in a protracted battle with the UNITA guerrilla movement (created and long sustained by the CIA), and from the Congo (AKA Zaire), on which neighboring countries descended in a multisided scramble for spoils after the death of its US-sponsored president-for-life. What to do about African "conflict diamonds" became one of the hottest topics discussed by the New York cognoscenti as they puffed contraband Cuban cigars and sampled poached Russian caviar while seated at tables made from illegally cut Brazilian big-leaf mahogany in dining rooms embellished with looted Egyptian, Greek, and, more recently, Iraqi antiquities. Thus, conflict diamonds (later reincarnated as "blood diamonds," when the original images started to lose their shock value) were already high on the international agenda before the conveniently timed discovery that behind the trade could be found the evil hand of al-Qā'idah.[1]

ROUGH AND TUMBLE

The "conflict diamonds" story actually began in Sierra Leone after World War II, when native soldiers who had been with British Special Forces returned home to find a country still under colonial rule and its leading industry still in the grip of a British monopoly. Most diamond mines produce a majority of industrial-grade stones, but in Sierra Leone almost all were (are) gem quality and in widely dispersed alluvial fields rather than concentrated in deep mines where security is easier, as in South Africa or Botswana. Initially the main problem was in company-run areas where miners would steal stones to sell to local merchants who would then pass them on to smugglers. But by the early 1950s more native diggers ventured into fresh territory. While the British regularly sent the police and Army to try to clear illegal diggings, the miners applied skills they had learned in irregular warfare to evade capture. For every informer kept by the company in the illegal mining camps, the miners seemed to have one in the local police.

Illegal production required a covert marketing channel. That was the role of Lebanese traders. The initial wave of Lebanese immigration into West Africa around the turn of the twentieth century had been mainly Christians fleeing economic crisis or Ottoman oppression. Their first destination was usually Marseilles, from where they hoped to move to the United States. Some unable to get to a New World whose streets were reputedly paved with gold ended up in West Africa, where, a little later, they found alluvial fields genuinely seeded with diamonds.[2] Initially prominent in retail commerce and real estate, with some smuggling as a sideline, during a post-World War II diamond boom, Lebanese traders advanced digging equipment and supplies, then arranged to move the diamonds to Liberia, which had low taxes and a US dollar-based financial system.[3] The traffic threatened the tight control over the world rough-diamond market held by the British/South African corporation De Beers Consolidated. Apart from feeding newspapers with claims that smuggling was sufficient to threaten the British balance of payments when the country had still not fully recovered from World War II, De Beers tried two other tricks.

The first was for "John Blaize," a self-proclaimed undercover agent for the International Diamond Security Organization, the De Beers private policing affiliate, to approach a former Naval Intelligence officer: Ian Fleming, who had already published *Diamonds Are Forever*, in which the dashingly decadent James Bond foils international smugglers working on behalf of Terror International. Who better to write the "true story" of the underground diamond trade than someone with the right political credentials and a proven capacity to concoct fantasies with the desired political spin?[4]

The problem De Beers faced was that existing methods to control trafficking in West Africa were failing. Within its own mining concessions, it had traditionally relied on X-rays to stop miners from stealing stones. But, as John Blaize explained to Fleming, "You can't go on X-raying men, even if they're black." Another technique consisted of planting irradiated stones, then trying to pick them up with Geiger counters as miners passed the turnstiles or to trace them to buyers. That, by definition, caught only the irradiated stones – of little use if large numbers of miners lifted large numbers of gems. Nor could the company irradiate en masse – stones had to be found before they could be so treated. And presumably there might be fears of a skin-cancer epidemic among the blushing brides who were its primary clientele. In the alluvial fields outside direct company control, the problem was worse. Here the company's most important technique was to plant its own agents to outbid the illicit buyers. While that permitted the company to control the output, it drove up the price and encouraged more illegal production. For a time the company combined that strategy with a buy-and-bust approach. But judges kept throwing out the cases – most of those entrapped were amateurs, with no previous history, who were lured into the traffic, then arrested in a blaze of publicity to try to scare away others. So John Blaize appealed to Fleming's patriotic, literary, and, undoubtedly, financial sentiments to help them publicize "the biggest racket being operated anywhere in the world."[5]

According to the story, the Evil Empire (at that time Atheistic Communism rather than Islamic Terrorism) ran the traffic for two purposes. One was to obtain industrial diamonds (in the face of a NATO embargo) to aid the Soviet nuclear weapons program. John Blaize assured Fleming that "our man in East Berlin" reported that the diamonds were distributed thus: the USSR and China each taking 25 percent, the rest going to various places in Eastern Europe, "all presumably for the various armaments industries."[6] This was some accomplishment given that stones from Sierra Leone were overwhelmingly gem quality, and that the USSR was already producing so many diamonds of its own that De Beers had entered a secret agreement to sneak them onto Western markets in violation of anti-Soviet sanctions then in force.[7]

The second purpose, so the account went, was to use gemstones to finance Arab "terrorist" activity in Syria (recently free of France), Iraq (which was shaking off the British), and Algeria (where the first shots of an insurrection against French rule had been fired). Reports of the Soviet-WMD/Arab-Terrorist plot sent a shudder through the British spook agencies, who endorsed a covert program, jointly with De Beers, to use British secret intelligence funds to infiltrate Lebanese smuggling rings, snare traders, and, where necessary, assassinate ringleaders.

Therefore, apart from alerting the public to these early conflict diamonds, De Beers arranged for Sir Percy Sillitoe, former head of Britain's MI-5, where he had made a reputation as a Commie-hunter, to be hauled from a pleasant retirement selling chocolates to spearhead the counterinsurgency. He soon realized that the real point was to permit De Beers to consolidate its monopoly with the British taxpayer picking up the tab. Not only had the Soviet Union already discovered enormous supplies of natural diamonds, but it was at the forefront of world synthetic-diamond research. The notion that it would buy black-market diamonds to fund guerrilla groups made no financial sense. The only traceable flow of smuggled diamonds into Arab hands ran from Christian traders of West Africa to Lebanon, then across the ceasefire line into Israel in defiance of the Arab League embargo against the Zionist state.[8] Nonetheless De Beers hired a Lebanese storekeeper who put together a gang of thugs and petty criminals to ambush convoys of smugglers, steal their diamonds, and collect a reward of one third their value.[9]

Despite this, rising nationalism and more smuggling made the company's position increasingly difficult. Eventually its holdings were opened to state-licensed miners and buyers. After the outbreak of civil war in Lebanon in 1975, the established Lebanese traders in Sierra Leone were joined by more Shi'a and by an influx of Israeli smugglers, eager to find a way, independent of De Beers, to feed Israel's enormous diamond-cutting business. For a time Sierra Leone became a scene of coup and countercoup in which Israel, South Africa, Iran, and the US manipulated clients.[10] For De Beers the problems were complicated by developments in other alluvial producers whose rising output threatened the system by which it had long controlled the market.[11]

Historically De Beers acted as buyer of last resort. With cooperation from the major producers, it took off the market surplus rough stones, including (by keeping its own buyers in black-market centres) smuggled material, then resold to selective cutters when particular subsets of the market began to heat up. (Any broker or manufacturer not on the

De Beers "sight" list had to obtain their stones off the secondary market in Antwerp or create direct links to producers, legal or illegal.) The key to control was the company's ability to carry a stockpile of several billion dollars "worth" – which also enabled it to dump selected types at strategic times to undermine any producer who tried to strike out on its own. Most major cutters were content to participate: the arrangement offered the security of steadily rising prices; and they could profit indirectly from the De Beers effort to convince the buying public that diamonds were "forever."[12] But throughout the 1980s and into the 1990s, this strategy became harder to implement.

For a long time the diamond market had been a duopoly. De Beers purchased Soviet stones to comingle with others in a market-rigging ploy from which both sides profited. But in 1991 the Soviet Union disappeared, replaced by a Russia chronically short of foreign exchange and eager to establish itself as a major gemstone cutting and polishing centre. New producing frontiers opened in Australia and then Canada, in neither of which De Beers held significant direct ownership interest. Alluvial mining spread farther in Central and West Africa, much of it in areas controlled by rebel movements and regional warlords who were harder to deal with than corrupt or thuggish governments. Meanwhile the world economy shifted from a generally inflationary post-World War II to a low- or zero-inflationary post-Cold War environment. In that context the De Beers stockpile ceased to be a good investment and became a drag on the company's share price. Just when things looked blackest, along came the uproar over conflict diamonds.

In 1998 the UN imposed sanctions on purchase of diamonds from the UNITA guerrilla movement in Angola. Hitherto all diamonds from Angola were to be accompanied by government-issued certificates of origin. This had the happy effect of creating work for skilled forgers and an opportunity for corrupt functionaries to comingle UNITA's with official stones. Citing difficulties of separating real from fake certificates, De Beers shut down all its buying in Angola. A short time later the UN imposed sanctions on Sierra Leone's gemstones, too. Zaire, wracked by civil war, was next. Ambitious NGOs kept up the pressure while the diamond trade scrambled to placate consumer countries.

The campaign had an important public sponsor. When the Canadian government heard the word "diamonds," its eyes began to sparkle, thanks to the conviction that Canada might soon account for 15–25 percent of the world's supply of gem-quality diamonds, all, of course, certifiable as "conflict free." In some ways it was a replay of the Apartheid era, when Canadian (and Australian) gold-mining firms led demands to embargo South African gold, while the Canadian government, whose Maple Leaf gold coin was the main international competitor to South Africa's Krugerrand, heartily seconded the motion.

The last pockets of resistance to controls on conflict diamonds crumbled when, in 2002, the world learned that behind the traffic in "the world's most precious gemstone" stood the intensely ascetic Usama bin Lāden. Apparently al-Qā'idah had not simply been profiting from the traffic, but had rushed, after 9/11, to convert its assets into more easily hidden forms, including rough diamonds. Soon the UN demanded the ban not just of "conflict diamonds" but of all "illicit" stones. Member states and the diamond industry began negotiating conventions to shut out of the market not the 3 percent of the world's gemstones that came from conflict-ridden areas of Africa but the 15–30 percent (depending on the definition) that bypassed official marketing agencies. Smiling broadly in the wings was De Beers.[13]

To the extent that the bans actually worked, their immediate impact was to open space for De Beers to unload onto the market identical stones from its own stockpile. That stockpile, long a drag on its finances, shot up in value, the shares of the company along with it. The drive to eliminate stones that had bypassed formal government monopolies (which almost always marketed through De Beers) enhanced the company's power. The changes in international rules came, quite conveniently, while De Beers was drastically revising its marketing strategy.[14] Instead of just specializing in the control of rough stones to the wholesale market, it decided to sell cut and polished ones to the retail trade. Instead of spending money to advertise diamonds for the market as a whole, it decided to promote its own brand name. It began to microprint diamonds for retail with its own logo and ID numbers as a supposed guarantee that the stones were "conflict free." The claim was bogus – once cut, there is no way to confirm a stone's origin. But it gave De Beers an edge over competitors, few of whom would ever handle a "conflict diamond" but even fewer of whom would to be able to convey the same assurance. The logo also promised to sooth a market spooked by the spread of sophisticated fakes, synthetics, or simulates. Not least, by downplaying the market stockpile business, De Beers hoped to ease its long-difficult relations with the United States, whose antitrust laws were a constant threat.[15] These changes in commercial strategy were cemented into place once reporters hungry for a scoop in alliance with NGOs eager for the spotlight began to market the "al-Qaeda"-meets-conflict-diamonds fable.[16]

This is not to suggest there was no "evidence." For one thing there was the discovery by the BBC that a twenty-eight-year-old al-Qā'idah "member" named Mohammed Khalfan, arrested in Africa for involvement in the 1998 embassy bombings, was a leading shareholder of a Congolese diamond mine. The actual shareholder turned out to be Kamal Khalfan, a man in his sixties – the BBC publicly apologized and paid £500,000 in damages to his company.[17] But that was not the end of such evidence. There were also abundant stories about a couple of Lebanese Shi'a diamond dealers "linked to" al-Qā'idah – somehow they had missed the fact that at the time they were financially supporting bin Lāden, his Tāliban allies in Afghanistan were engaged, allegedly with the help of Arab auxiliaries, in massacring that country's Shi'a population.

The Lebanese dealers later claimed (probably correctly) that rumors of their bin Lāden association were spread by business rivals seeking to discredit them. Just who those rivals might be can perhaps be inferred from the fact that the UN found a group of ex-Israeli Air Force pilots moving smuggled diamonds from Angola, Sierra Leone, and Liberia and that one of the first acts of a post-conflict government of Sierra Leone was to arrest Israeli Reserve-Colonel Yair Klein. Klein, who had won undying fame in the late 1980s for training narco-militias on behalf of Colombian drug lords, had arrived in Sierra Leone to sell "security services" to Israeli diamond traders trying to recover territory lost to the Lebanese Shi'a in an earlier round of diamond wars.[18]

There were a few other problems with the Usama-sells-conflict-diamonds story. For one thing, how did an organization supposedly spearheaded by a Saudi "Wahhābī fundamentalist" make a breakthrough into an area where most of the population in the trade was Shi'a Muslim from Southern Lebanon? True, those intent on peddling the tale about al-Qā'idah peddling conflict diamonds could resurrect the "link" between al-Qā'idah and Hizbullāh. But even that begged a few questions. It was never clear from any of the sensationalist stories if Hizbullāh was supposed to be actually running "cells" of diamond dealers or just getting contributions from time to time from members of the Lebanese Diaspora who made money in diamonds, or real estate, or selling powdered milk and cans of tuna. Furthermore Hizbullāh was never a serious presence in West Africa. To the extent Lebanese Shi'a in the region have any consistent political preference, it would be not for the radical Hizbullāh but the far more mainstream and rival AMAL movement, whose leader, senior Lebanese politician Nabih Berri, was born in Sierra Leone.

In any case, participation would be interspersed in a matrix of undercover activity that would be almost impossible to unscramble. The diamond begins its commercial life in mines rife with theft; crosses borders in smugglers' pouches or, what is often the same thing, diplomatic luggage; comes briefly into daylight again in cutting and polishing centres whose practitioners, more often than not, grant themselves a general tax exemption; re-enters underground freight channels via informal bourses where deals have traditionally been done in cash and sealed with a handshake; sneaks again across borders to dodge import duties or excise taxes; then finally arrives in a retail marketing network replete with commercial fraud. En route the diamond might pass through the hands of impoverished diggers and backwoods traders, career criminals and corrupt functionaries, spies and insurgents, counterfeiters and money-launderers, and investment sharks and telemarketing scam artists before coming to rest around an especially elegant neck or a languorously beckoning finger – at least until some enterprising jewel thief thinks differently.

In addition, only cut and polished diamonds are really effective as capital flight vehicles. Even the most adroit trader in rough finds it difficult to guess a stone's ultimate value – amateurs usually lose their shirts. If, just before 9/11, al-Qā'idah had really shifted its supposed assets from traceable forms into things like diamonds that were nicely anonymous and easy to move, its financial experts made a dumb move. During the latter part of 2001, a glut drove down prices of some leading categories by 30 percent.[19] In that case, the involvement of al-Qā'idah in conflict diamonds is presumably something the world's anti-terror experts ought to welcome, for it would work faster than investments in Sudanese agribusiness to deplete Usama's fabled fortune.

Not least, the entire "conflict diamonds funding terrorism" tale misses a key point about the structure of the underground diamond business. Rarely do insurgent groups actually control diamond mining. As with virtually all other forms of contraband, they control the areas in which production occurs or across which traffic runs. Their major gain comes not from direct participation, though particular individuals might do so on their own account, but from taxation. Rebel groups manage through military power (which neither al-Qā'idah nor Hizbullāh could possible muster in sub-Saharan Africa) to impose import and export duties, license fees, transportation surcharges, and, in some cases direct bribes for particular officers. In other words, the insurgents form the quasi-public infrastructure within which the diamond trade is run by experts and industry insiders much as before any indigenous guerrilla group takes over, something that neither al-Qā'idah nor Hizbullāh could ever in their (or CNN's) wildest dreams hope to accomplish.[20]

Nonetheless the campaign was a great success. The NGOs, peddling a mishmash of half-truths, unsubstantiated rumors, and spook disinformation, got their certification schemes, which gave officials of corrupt and repressive governments a pretext to knock out independent miners and turn concessions over to kin and cronies.[21] De Beers had its market power confirmed. The reporter who first broke the story won laurels and a book contract.[22] National security types got to reinforce their bin Lāden myth. And the US took advantage of the tale to assign a Treasury official to work with banks in the Sahel region of Africa to disrupt terrorist operations in diamonds and in gold.[23] On the other side, innocent people were smeared with association with terrorism and anti-Arab stereotypes further entrenched. But that was just more unfortunate collateral damage of the sort that any war, including one on terrorism, inevitably produces.[24]

WHEN USAMA GETS BLUE

The anti-conflict-diamond campaign was so successful, with one country after another stumbling to sign on, that it refused to rest on its diamond-studded laurels. The next target was the latest gemstone rage to sweep the United States. Tanzanite is a blue variant of zoisite, a hydrous aluminum and calcium silicate. As a member of the epidote family, it is quite soft (6.5 on the Mohs scale) for a gemstone. Although known by gemstone insiders for decades, its fame is quite recent and reflects not the inherent brilliance of the stone but that of the PR campaign mounted by Tiffany & Co., particularly after the stone played a starring role in the Hollywood blockbuster *Titanic*. That most "tanzanite" on the market is actually common green zoisite artificially turned blue by heat treatment – supplemented more recently by totally synthetic material, made in the West then snuck into the mining area to pose as the real stuff[25] – is a trade secret big retailers seldom share with their trend-dazzled clientele.

Named after its (so far) sole geological location, a five-square-mile area of Tanzania, rough tanzanite is mined and sold under the same conditions that prevail in most of that country's not inconsiderable gemstone mining ventures – independent prospectors turn over their output to dealers based in the city of Arusha who, in turn, arrange to smuggle much of it, using Massai tribesmen (along with complicit civil servants, cops, and Customs officers) who can cross the Kenyan border with impunity to Nairobi and usually on to India for manufacture. In the illicit gemstone business, the big money goes to those who arrange sales to cutters. Therein lies the problem. Historically that end of the business was run by Kenyan Indians, members of the clan that has historically dominated gem dealing and manufacturing in India. Then the miners, Massai and Muslims of Afro-Arab descent, began agitating for a larger share of the revenues. On top of that conflict was superimposed another. The largest legal producer of tanzanite was African Gem Resources (AfGem) of South Africa, a firm long suspected by the independent miners of harboring an ambition to monopolize production. A final interested party was the Tanzanian government, worried about loss of revenue from smuggling to Kenya and India and hoping to create an indigenous cutting industry.[26]

The issue of who mined, exported, cut, and polished tanzanite was of interest to only a fairly arcane subset of gemstone investors – until the trial of persons accused in the 1998 bombing of the US embassies in Nairobi and Dar es Salaam. Out of it came electrifying evidence of an al-Qā'idah connection. A couple of intrepid reporters for the *Wall Street Journal* got hot on the trail. Suddenly tanzanite was in the headlines, along with accusations that the trade was full of Muslim extremists trying to fund terror cells, that a fanatical Tanzanian "sheik" who trafficked in tanzanite had told his followers to sell their stones only to fellow Muslims as he preached holy war from his sparkling new tanzanite-financed mosque, and that the traffickers were pioneering new routes via Mombassa ("a stronghold of al-Qaeda") to the smuggling and money-laundering hotbed of Dubai. All this was based on impeccable sources – a senior official of the Tanzania Mineral Dealers Association (TAMIDA), a Kenyan gem dealer who was also a teacher at the guilty mosque, and the "sheik" himself, a man named Omari.[27]

As with even the most rigorously conducted investigation, there were a few problems with the story. The Tanzanian official swore an affidavit that he had never conversed with either of the reporters; the head of the mosque (whose name was Mudir Omar Suleiman) pointed out that he was not a sheikh (a tribal leader or respected religious scholar), had never traded tanzanite, and presided over a pile of corrugated iron and old timber that could, with everyone holding their breath, hold no more than thirty people. He, too, claimed he had never talked to the reporters. As to the final witness, the teacher, no one at the mosque had ever heard of him, and a search by TAMIDA failed to locate him.[28]

Most independent miners had long-term relations with established members of the International Colored Gemstone Association, almost all from India, Israel, and the US. There was minimal scope for independent Muslim-fundamentalist gem traders. And almost all smuggling is handled via Kenya by a contraband network working out of Jaipur in the Indian state of Rajathstan, where gem dealers are overwhelmingly Jain, not Muslim, by religion.

Still, shocked at the revelation that their clients might have unwittingly financed the World Trade Center attack, big US retailers began to suspend further sales of tanzanite. First QVC pulled it off the market. Then came a startling ABC-TV special with conclusive proof: a close-up shot of notebooks, with numbers scribbled in them apparently indicating large sums in tanzanite sales, belonging to an "al-Qaeda terrorist" named Wadih el-Hage (with a withered arm and jailed for life after the embassy bombings trial).[29] So Tiffany and Zale followed suit. Later, it was revealed that the notebooks contained not sales data but telephone and fax numbers: ABC had covered the words "fax" and "phone" with other documents during the filming.[30]

Nonetheless AfGem sternly announced that it would follow the De Beers lead and laser-microprint its own squeaky-clean production – few independents could afford to do the same. That the US State Department publicly announced there was no evidence of tanzanite used to finance terrorism did not prevent Tanzania from making a pilgrimage to the annual Tucson meeting of the American Gem Trade Association.[31] The result was the Tucson Protocols, a certification program like that already agreed by diamond merchants. Back home, the Tanzanian government seized the occasion to force miners to sign declarations that they were not funding terrorism; and, just to show it meant business, it banned the export of uncut tanzanite, something that, if enforceable, just might stimulate the development of its own gemstone cutting business, while further consolidating the position of AfGem.[32]

Much as with conflict diamonds, the "evidence" of the al-Qā'idah connection was a fatuous extrapolation from a flimsy factual base fed by political and commercial interests. Wadih el-Hage, supposedly Usama bin Lāden's "personal secretary" and the man in charge of setting up the East Africa "cell," was so badly remunerated by his super-rich boss that he had tried to support himself and his family with a Nairobi car-leasing business. When that failed, he, like so many others in Nairobi, tried his hand at gemstones. He had to borrow money from friends to complete his only business trip abroad. When he was caught up in the bombing investigation, the authorities seized not bomb-making materials but a few hundred dollars of equipment used to identify and classify gemstones whose thermodynamic qualities he apparently preferred to those of gelignite. From this the al-Qā'idah-tanzanite legend was born.[33]

GREEN GOLD?

Since bin Lāden showed such a propensity for precious stones – perhaps a reflection of his need to appease multiple wives – naturally he was also interested in a substance in which to set them. Gold could function even better than diamonds as a covert means to make financial transfers and as a source of speculative underground profits. The same intrepid investigators who had fed the frenzy over "blood diamonds" were on the job to strip the cover from the "critical yet mysterious" al-Qā'idah gold flows. While, of course, no one could define exactly how much was involved, there was no doubt, the experts warned the world, that gold was a "huge factor in the moving of terrorist money."[34]

Gold, the experts claimed, became entrenched in the al-Qā'idah financial apparatus during its Afghanistan heyday. Since there was no dependable local currency, gold was "the preferred financial instrument."[35] The Tāliban, it seems, collected taxes from the "trucking mafia" and from opium growers in gold and made payments in the same stuff. Obviously all those onsite who claimed to have seen truckers pay protection fees and kickbacks in Pakistani rupees were no more observant than those who had commented with bemusement on the habit of the Tāliban chief, Mullah Omar, in making official government disbursements in bundles of crumpled bank notes taken from a beat-up metal box.

However, gold allegedly had a second role. Because Afghanistan lacked a formal banking system, gold was, along with the underground hawāla system, the preferred mechanism for international receipts and remittances. In fact the two were inseparable, for the hawāla system throughout central Asia was intimately linked to gold movements.

Here there was an element of truth. The fulcrum for both gold and hawāla in the Gulf region, and one of the primary targets of us post 9/11 attention, is the little sheikhdom of Dubai. Although part of the United Arab Emirates, Dubai has little oil. Formerly much of its income came from the pearl industry, which was ruined, first by the Great Depression, then by the Japanese invention of the cultured pearl, then by massive oil pollution of the Gulf waters. Now its wealth comes principally from trade and from the blessings of geography. With the best harbor within striking distance by small boat of Iran, Pakistan, and India, Dubai became a regional smugglers' supermarket, its warehouses stuffed with watches, synthetic fabrics (in the past restricted in India to help the local cotton and jute industry), electronics, auto parts, whiskey, perfume, cigarettes, pornographic movies ... and gold, virtually all in the tiny bars fashioned explicitly (i.e., rounded to avoid injuring the delicate parts of a courier's anatomy) for the Indo-Pakistan market.[36]

It is all out in the open. The Dubai government issues trading licenses only to the minority of residents actually born there. But recipients can sell those licenses to Indian and Pakistani merchants. Those merchants then purchase gold (and silver) from local branches of the big Swiss and British banks using capital (both legal and illegal in origin) from various local and foreign investors who typically have their risks spread across several voyages. The chances of being caught are relatively low – those who run the gold have ample experience, the infrastructure to receive it on the other side is well developed, and there is widespread bribery of Customs and police in India and Pakistan.

While some gold goes by plane, carried by couriers or hidden in baggage or cargo, historically most has crossed by dhow. With interiors easily converted to haul almost any kind of cargo, and drawing little water, these little ships can go almost anywhere along the Arabian, African, and South West Asian coasts. They can alternate between motor and sail as the respective need for speed and distance demands. The technology is very simple, making for low maintenance costs and ease of recruitment of crew, who work for very little. As a result they ply the region with cargoes of everything from whiskey (for dry areas like Saudi Arabia), to ivory (smuggled out of East Africa for eventual delivery to Hong Kong carving shops), to qāt (the recreational drug of choice in the Horn of Africa), to gold to feed the voracious Indo-Pakistani demand.[37]

The hawāla operators run a complementary financial circuit. In India and Pakistan, gold is retailed for rupees. In Switzerland and Dubai gold is wholesaled for dollars. The problem was how to bridge the currency gap since, until fairly recently, Indian and Pakistani rupees were legally inconvertible.

Sometimes gold was purchased with hard currency picked up on the black market in India or Pakistan from tourists or smugglers. More important was phony invoicing of trade accounts – merchants would report to the exchange-control authorities that imports cost more, or exports yielded less, than they did, with the excess stashed abroad and used, among other purposes, to finance gold imports. Another technique was to smuggle out from India, and to a lesser degree, from Pakistan, antiquities, rare animal skins, silver, and gemstones.[38] Yet another commodity that could be used to balance the gold trade was heroin. Not only were Pakistan and India major transshipment centres for Afghan opiates, but India is one of the world's largest producers of legal opium, some of which could be diverted into heroin production. But of all the techniques available, none has been as important as the Indo-Pakistani "underground banking system."[39] Émigré workers from India and Pakistan turn their hard currency earnings over to gold traders (who are often hawāldars simultaneously). The hard currency buys gold. The gold is smuggled and sold for rupees in the subcontinent. And the rupees are used to settle accounts with the families of the émigré workers. Much the same mechanism could serve, via Pakistan, to handle gold movements in and out of Afghanistan, if there were any. The difference was that Afghanistan's émigré population was largely huddled in refugee camps drawing relief rations, not working in the Gulf depositing tax-free salaries in bank accounts.

Given this supposed central importance of gold, when the US assault on Afghanistan began, al-Qā'idah and the Tāliban jointly sent "waves of couriers with bars of gold and bundles of dollars" into Pakistan.[40] Apparently Usama and his friends had been too busy with their meticulous planning of the details of 9/11 to have had time to work out a financial exit strategy and therefore had to improvise when the bombs started to fall.

The gold was allegedly shipped to Karachi, then sent to Iran and Dubai. After all, the experts insisted, "smuggling gold by sea from Karachi into Iran and Dubai is also a centuries-old activity."[41] (That must have been a surprise to all the dhow operators who had mistakenly assumed they had been smuggling gold in the opposite direction for so many years.) But those were not the final destinations. With the aid of Iranian clerics, who set aside their anger at the Tāliban murdering their diplomats and harassing the Shi'a, some of the gold was flown to safety on Iranian airplanes. The final destination was no surprise. Usama's gold, in "large quantities," was heading for safety in the Sudan, now re-emerging as a world financial epicentre for terrorism, even though the National Islamic Front had been ousted some years before in a military coup supported by the US and Egypt. All this was enough to send reporters scurrying around the Dubai gold bazaar asking prominent bullion merchants about their relations with al-Qā'idah.[42]

The audacity of al-Qā'idah's gold-market machinations did not end there. Some of its supporters also planned to smuggle gold into the US to raise money, probably for local operations. Fortunately Customs had shifted NIPS (the Numerically Integrated Profiling System), its supercomputer program, away from tracking drug money flows to exposing commercial transactions that might serve as a cover for terrorist finance. One thing onto which the computer supposedly honed was discrepancies between the amount of gold imported into the US and the amount of jewellery sold – the difference was presumably diverted to black-market sale. That led to Florida's Intrigue Jewelers – if the name itself was insufficient indication of nefarious intent, the fact that its owner was Pakistani was more than enough "probable cause." The firm had imported considerably more gold than it had reported as sold in its seventy-five licensed kiosks located across seven states. The records – bills, computers, bank statements, receipts, etc. – were seized; and over a dozen kiosk owners were detained, including a former US Army mechanic. He was grilled for hours about his knowledge of al-Qā'idah and bin Lāden. Once the hype was stripped away, the real reason for the raid turned out to be not information spat out by the Customs supercomputer but that the mechanic, some time before 9/11, had taken a photograph of the World Trade Center. True, tens of thousands of others had done likewise, but how many of them had a name like Tariq Hussain?[43]

17

Striking Out! – Al-Qā'idah Cells
in the Global Petrie Dish

After 9/11, Middle Eastern militants seemed poised to strike repeat-edly across the world. Some plots took place to terrible effect. Others, potentially as lethal, were fortunately caught beforehand. Some others were real, but the work of bungling amateurs or psychotics like Richard Reid, the "shoe-bomber." Yet others were sting operations to entrap the naive, the foolish, or the confused to permit the authorities to proclaim another "victory" in their Terror War. Either that or, as in the case of José Padilla, the "dirty bomber" who never had a nuclear device, never tried to get one, and never had any instructions from "al-Qaeda" to do so, the nature of the threat supposedly posed could change with re-markable alacrity depending upon the story the authorities wanted to feed the media on any particular day.[1]

What the plots had in common was not just that their architects were supposedly committed Muslims – some of whom drank booze, smoked dope, and seemed to prefer topless bars to mosques or madrasas.[2] Rather, by invoking the spectre of al-Qā'idah, some governments hoped that no one would be inclined to peek too closely at what they were try-ing to sweep under a very broad, sometimes quite old, carpet. Once stripped of hype, each incident became explicable largely or sometimes entirely by local conditions and local actors. While no doubt there were on occasion informal associations between local perpetrators and vari-ous other individuals or scattered grouplets around North Africa, the Middle East, and Central Asia, while there might even be the odd transfer of funds, none of these was evidence of some grand, hierarchical conspiracy. In all the plots that genuinely existed, "links" to al-Qā'idah or bin Lāden varied from the peripheral to the completely contrived. Yet all were stuck together in a great ball of misinformation that, as it rolled downhill picking up momentum, soon crushed justice and common sense.

THE BENEFITS OF HINDSIGHT

At home, the US saw three major antecedents to 9/11. The first occurred early in 1993, when a van loaded with homemade explosives and compressed hydrogen-gas tanks blew up in the underground garage of the World Trade Center in New York, killing six people. The trail initially led to the man who had rented the suspect truck (in his own name) and who was so security conscious that he went back to the agency to try to get his deposit refunded, claiming that the vehicle had been stolen; to another genius (whose business card was found in the possession of the first) who reputedly acquired the chemicals and left faxes claiming credit for the bombing on his office computer; to another, accused of helping to mix the explosives, who was picked up with remarkable ease in Egypt; and finally to the mastermind, Ramzi Yousef, who had apparently skipped the class at his "terrorist training camp" in which attendees were taught to wear gloves to avoid covering their handiwork with fingerprints.[3]

Yousef managed to hightail it for Pakistan and eventually the Philippines, from where he was extradited back for trial two years later. Sentenced to 240 years in prison, he became a star again with the post-9/11 discovery of his "ties" to al-Qā'idah. He had an "uncle" in Pakistan named Khalid Sheikh Mohammed, later promoted to central planner of 9/11, who became the first of a succession of "number 3 in al-Qaeda" types that the US collared.[4] In 1992 KSM had wired a cash-short Yousef, then living in New York, $660 dollars. Since KSM was an ex-mujahideen, obviously he was passing Usama's money to Ramzi Yousef to pull off al-Qā'idah's first major operation on US soil.

There were only five problems with the story. One was that Khalid Sheikh Mohammed fought during the anti-Soviet war not with an Arab group "linked to" bin Lāden but with the Pashtun, Abdul Rasoul Sayyaf – not a great surprise since both KSM and Yousef Ramzi were Baluchis. And Abdul Sayyaf was an ally of Ahmed Shah Mas'ud, whom bin Lāden allegedly helped the Tāliban assassinate.

A second was that, when KSM wired money to his needy nephew, KSM was not hatching bomb plots in Afghanistan or helping Usama count his billions but working in Qatar for the government department of electricity and water. KSM's path apparently only crossed that of bin Lāden after the embassy bombings, which came five years after the original WTC plot.

There were three other oddities. Yousef issued communiqués in the name of the rather unIslamic-sounding Liberation Army, Fifth Battalion.[5] Although Yousef was caught with the business card of bin Lāden's brother-in-law, Mohammed Khalifah, then running Islamic charities in Mindanao, he got it from someone with no connection to terror plots who simply suggested Khalifah as a contact if Yousef needed help finding his way around the Philippines. Furthermore Usama, who had no problem declaring in interviews when he knew accused plotters, stated categorically that he had never met Yousef.

On the other hand, the US had ironclad proof – from Khalid Sheikh Mohammed himself, after the CIA abducted his two sons (aged seven and nine) and held them hostage until he agreed to talk, a decision no doubt facilitated by periodic immersions in a tub of water until he was on the point of drowning.[6] The fact that the government refused to allow the defense in the trial of Zacarias Moussaoui, the alleged twentieth hijacker, or of another accused man in Germany, to call KSM as a witness could be taken as either a desire to keep "pumping" him for more vital intelligence or as a fear of having the circumstances of his confession subjected to public scrutiny.[7]

Ramzi Yousef was no shrinking violet. He told his captors that, if he had had more money, he would have pulled off a bigger operation; his computer hard drive contained plans to hijack and blow up twelve US airliners; one of his friends with a pilot's license was reputed to have schemed to crash a plane into CIA headquarters; and with another buddy Yousef dreamed of bumping off the pope on a Philippines visit. But he comes off less as a vital cog in a transnational terror machine than as a largely solitary homicidal maniac with a political grudge and a huge ego.[8]

Much the same expost-reconstructionism typified claims that conspirators in the Landmark Plot to bomb five major New York City targets were agents of the infamous Usama. Actually the operation, rolled up shortly after the first World Trade Center attack, was a sting. Its biggest catch was Sheikh Umar Abd al-Rahman, the almost-blind and diabetic Egyptian who was variously identified as the "spiritual leader" of

Gamā'at al-Islāmiyya and as a CIA agent who recruited for Afghanistan. Since the alleged plotters attended Al Farouq Mosque in Brooklyn, where Abd al-Rahman had preached, since Abd al-Rahman was caught on tape stating that US military installations overseas were legitimate targets, and since Abd al-Rahman during the Afghan war had crossed paths and no doubt on occasion cooperated with bin Lāden, that sufficed to make the Landmark Plot also an al-Qā'idah operation even though it would be another five years before US prosecutors got around to inventing the concept. The indictment did cite bin Lāden as a co-conspirator; but it so cited dozens of others and attached no particular significance to any of them. That the sheikh was ultimately found guilty not of the acts per se but of "conspiracy" on the basis of statements elicited from informants who had made deals for reductions in charges and sentences did not alter the justice of it one iota.[9]

A similar example of wisdom after the fact could be found with the so-called Millennium Plot. It was really two distinct plans by independent operatives – one was to bomb tourist sites in Jordan; the other targeted Los Angeles Airport. However, lumping them together as a grand, unified plot greatly enhanced the fear factor so useful for advancing political-cum-prosecutorial ambitions and improving television ratings.

On the Jordanian side, the spectre of Usama was invoked even before the trial. Khalil al-Deek, a Palestinian with US citizenship, had gone to Pakistan to help run a computer store that, according to the US government, shared a bank account with "a major al-Qaeda operative." Late in 1999, Pakistan arrested al-Deek and flew him, despite his US citizenship, to Jordan to be held without charges or access to a lawyer for sixteen months. As a US diplomat later confessed, "In the U.S. Deek would have been out of jail in about 30 seconds."[10] Yet he was finally released for lack of evidence; he subsequently vanished from view.[11] Some might consider that a sensible precaution, given his former treatment. But it also allowed the experts to later accuse him of everything from producing an electronic terrorist encyclopedia to conspiring to finance al-Qā'idah with the profits from a company exporting Yemeni honey.[12]

Another of al-Deek's alleged sins was recruiting Raed Hijazi. Born in the US to Jordanian parents, then raised abroad, Hijazi returned to the US to work for eighteen months as a Boston cabbie and security guard. According to the prosecution, he headed back to Jordan with his savings, part of which he used during a stopover in Britain to buy chemicals and detonator devices. Others did likewise. Even if that story is correct, it was only after the plot was hatched, the funds raised, and the equipment assembled that some members of the cabal went to Afghanistan to learn to use explosives properly. Before they could put any plan into action, Jordanian intelligence, which had been listening in to their phone conversations, busted it up.

Afterwards came a show trial (on both sides) of fifteen defendants, with another thirteen tried in absentia. Held behind bars even in the courtroom so that audiences could see how dangerous they were, the fifteen kitted themselves in Afghan robes and ostentatiously read from the Qur'ān during proceedings. All admitted to supporting armed struggle but denied belonging to al-Qā'idah or planning the Jordan attacks. Defense lawyers dismissed the evidence as largely hearsay or as the product of informants who had been offered deals or as the government simply settling outstanding scores.[13] Although the judges gave most defendants life sentences and imposed on a few the death penalty, they acquitted all twenty-eight of membership in a banned organization.[14] That detail seemed to have slipped past much of US media, particularly since al-Qā'idah's Millennium Plot supposedly had an even more dangerous component at home.

RETURN OF THE BARBARY PIRATES?

Actually the US was an odd target for Algerians intent on exporting their country's political violence. For decades anger had been focused on the former colonial master, France. In 1830, France had conquered the supposed pirate haven of Algiers – which had virtually no Navy and was lauded by contemporary travellers as perhaps the best regulated city in the world.[15] The real objective was to control trade in the southern Mediterranean. As France extended its hold, Algerians were pushed into marginal areas while prime land was taken over by French farmers. Until the French arrived, Berber and Arab communities had a legacy of intermarriage and common struggle against outsiders. But the French tried to cultivate Berber nationalism to counter to the tendency of those denied economic equality or civil rights to define themselves as ethnically Arab – privileged Berbers had their children attend the same school system as French settlers while Arabs were relegated to a distinctly inferior one. While the strategy did leave some legacy of tension, it failed to dampen growing political dissent – Berbers played a central role in the emerging nationalist movement.

In the late 1950s, Algerian veterans of the French Army, inspired by the success of the North Vietnamese in winning independence from

France, launched their own insurrection.[16] France fought back bitterly. Algeria held a million French settlers and supplied most of France's oil needs in the face of an UK/US stranglehold on the Middle East. Although over a million Algerians were killed, eventually the French fled. The victorious Front de libération nationale took power, then refused to budge. Major sectors of the state-run economy became private fiefdoms of senior FLN veterans. Growing corruption coexisted with rising unemployment and a high birthrate. During the 1970s, many Algerians sought work in the Gulf; during the 1980s, when oil prices collapsed, more fled to economic exile in Western Europe, particularly in France, where they moved into sprawling urban slums; some joined the Islamic Brigade in Afghanistan. By the 1990s, with the "socialist" model (and secular nationalism) discredited, political initiative shifted to Islamists.

The Islamist opposition first tried the democratic route. But in 1992, with the support of France, the Army blocked an election that would have delivered the biggest block of seats to the Front Islamique du salut (FIS). The result was the formation of a number of radical insurgent groups. Some contained Afghan vets.[17] Most of the recruits, however, were strictly local, the result of the mass migration of displaced peasantry to the cities and the rising levels of urban unemployment. While some groups took to calling themselves salafi, they had little in common with the Saudi variety. Their objectives were not to launch worldwide Islamic revolution but to purify their own society and to protect it from French recolonization – under IMF pressure, the government had begun to sell off state assets to big French corporations, a program that in the mid-1980s led to the destruction of 200,000 jobs, most of which had required skilled and educated people.[18] Out of all this came attacks on government and Army targets and a parallel campaign of economic warfare. One technique was to threaten the country's tax collectors on the rationale that under Islam zakāt is the only permissible form in which revenues could be raised.[19]

The Algerian civil war(s) became notorious for wholesale massacres. Yet most seemed to occur in areas that had voted heavily for the FIS. From the safety of exile, former Army and intelligence veterans denounced government complicity. The police, Army, and intelligence services had kept an eye on returning Afghan vets and may have turned some to undermine sympathy with the FIS. Rumors existed, too, that, to discredit peaceful Islamists, some violent factions were created by the Army just before the 1992 electoral coup. It became clear that some, while spouting radical rhetoric, took the civil breakdown as a pretext to loot, sometimes with a de facto license from the regime and the Army.[20]

Along with perhaps 150,000 dead came massive internal displacement. Many thousands more ended up in prisons without charges while, on the other side, radical Islamists began to target foreigners. Even in such cases there were doubts about the true architects. For example, one notorious incident that claimed the lives of seven French monks might have been an Army operation that got out of control. But the atrocities permitted the French government to whip up public anger against the Islamists and to back, with money, arms, and intelligence, efforts by the FLN government to crush them.[21]

Contrary to tales of bin Lāden billions, the Algerian rebels (of which there were always several competing factions) never needed serious outside financial aid. They sometimes controlled roads to levy tolls on passing traffic. In urban centres they shook down businesses for contributions. Money from abroad ran through networks of sympathizers, particularly in France. Sometimes Islamists solicited "donations" from Algerian businessmen in Europe under threat of reprisals ranging from disrupting their businesses to threatening families back home. Another alleged source was the traffic in fake luxury watches and brand-name clothes to supply flea markets and street vendors in Marseilles and Paris. Occasionally there were armed robberies of Muslim-owned businesses, possibly the work of ordinary criminals posing as Islamists to throw police off track. Some exiled radicals peddled drugs – naturally French police blamed the entire drug supply on "jihādist" elements. Allegedly cash from criminal sources then went to purchase black-market arms, although most rebel weapons were likely stolen or purchased from corrupt Army officers.[22] While radical Islamists certainly had sympathizers in places like the Gulf who would wire money, it was never clear that this was "organized" as opposed to largely entrepreneurial. Furthermore with so many other sources of funds, and abundant weapons at home, there was no simple, one-for-one connection between any such transfers and the course of the insurrection(s).

Thus, not only was bin Lāden nowhere in sight, but his mythical megabucks would have been largely irrelevant. When Algerian newspapers blamed the violence on bin Lāden, the country's top anti-terrorist cop snorted: "Our terrorists don't even know who Osama bin Laden is."[23] In fact of the seven groups operating when the violence peaked in the early part of the millennium, only one, the Groupe salafiste pour prédication et combat, was ever seriously accused of having "ties" to bin Lāden – and no real evidence was forthcoming. Indeed, its links to the ruling regime might be closer than any ties to outside radicals. Still, claiming that the insurrection was part of the general problem of the

rising Islamintern gave the regime a means to attract support from
France and the US and to dampen criticisms of its own crimes, incompetence, and corruption.

If the bin Lāden connection to the Algerian insurrection was largely
chimerical, it was equally so when Algerians were implicated in terrorism abroad. In fact in such cases the perpetrators usually had only the
loosest links, if any at all, even to insurgent groups back home.

That was true of Ahmed Ressam, who attempted to bomb Los Angeles
Airport, the US side of the so-called Millennium Plot. Like most young
Algerians, he had heard tales of the insurrection against French rule –
his father had been an honored member of the resistance. His family
was moderately devout, but not oppressively so. What set him on the
path that eventually led to his arrest at the Canada-US border was a mis-
diagnosed illness that forced him to miss many classes in high school,
blocking his admission to university. He was still in Algeria when Afghan vets began to return, some determined to turn their guns on the
regime and its Soviet-inspired economic system. Yet he had nothing to
do with them. On the contrary; he drank wine, smoked hashish, and
tried to pick up girls in nightclubs, while the returnees and their local
imitators tried to purge cities of intoxicants, Western music, and vice.
Certainly there was no encouragement to radical activity in his house –
his father regarded the new militants as "terrorists." With prospects so
poor at home, in 1992 he took off to France, where he worked off-
the-books at menial jobs. There, too, he had nothing to do with Islamic radicals. Caught with a fake passport, he was scheduled for a
deportation hearing but lit out for Canada, where, on the basis of a
story of being tortured in Algeria, he applied for refugee status. The
application was rejected; but the government of Canada was in no
hurry to deport him.[24]

US journalists later depicted Ahmed Ressam as blowing money from
his ample welfare checks in nightclubs and haberdashers. This would
imply a level of generosity of the Canadian welfare system that no other
recipient had noticed. In fact, when his welfare money ran short, he
turned to shoplifting, then to stealing from tourists. If he collared a
passport, he might sell it to Fateh Kamel, an Afghan veteran and black-
market operator who had fled to Montreal after French police broke
up his gang in Paris. That was Ahmed Ressam's introduction to "jihād."

Ressam was caught by the cops; but Canada was slow to toss him in
jail for petty nonviolent crimes. So he remained at large, hobnobbing
with his new Islamist friends. He himself dreamed up the LAX plot; of

the four original conspirators, only he went to Afghanistan to learn to improvise bombs. However he obviously learned nothing about security requirements in a modern urban environment – perhaps because his instructors were more concerned with places like Kashmir or Tajikistan than the US. During the trial of a confederate, he explained how rigorous was the training in such matters:

COURT: So you did take a course in counterintelligence, didn't you?
WITNESS: Not as a course, but as a warning.
COURT: There were lectures on that, is that right?
WITNESS: Yes. They told us not to trust everybody.[25]

Having contracted malaria in Afghanistan, Ressam was sweating as he crossed the Canada-US border. A perceptive Customs officer pulled him over. The discovery that his vehicle was full of explosives led to open season on Muslims in the US – wiretaps, surveillance, and mass detentions – in a dress rehearsal for the post-9/11 scene. Apparently his Afghan instructors had also failed to teach him the importance of loyalty. He made a deal to cut his sentence in half by ratting out everyone else, and then some. He told tales of terrorist camps in Afghanistan training "thousands" in chemical warfare techniques with the same verve that big catches in the Drug War show when relating before televised Congressional hearings how they had hauled cocaine in thousand-kilo lots, then managed billions of the resulting money.

Among those caught in the backwash was Mokhtar Haouari, a career fraudster to whom for a while Ressam had sold ID cards from stolen tourist luggage – Haouari used the IDs to produce fake credit cards. After Ressam returned from Afghanistan and Haouari needed someone to pretend to be his employer for a credit-card application, they linked up again. Once Ressam concocted the LAX plan, he asked Haouari to recommend someone in the US who could help with "important and dangerous business" without mentioning what it was. Given Haouari's career path, that phrase could easily have meant a particularly audacious financial scheme, and Haouari recommended not a Qu'rān-quoting black-market explosives dealer but a bank-fraud artist. Despite efforts of the prosecution, it proved impossible to pin on Haouari direct knowledge of the plot. However, Haouari, the jurors claimed, on top of being guilty of bank, credit-card, and document fraud, had "consciously avoided" confirming the plot's details. Yet, as the foreman stated, "he should have known, given the reputation of the people he was dealing with."[26] In effect Haouari was found guilty of being a financier of terror, not because of what he knew or did but because of what he ought to have known about what others were planning to do.

At almost the same time the LAX plot was afoot, so was a plan by a group of Strasbourg-based Algerians, allegedly to bomb the Notre Dame de Strasbourg Cathedral and the nearby Christmas Market, using materials acquired, once again, with fake and stolen credit cards. In December 2000, German police, who had the gang's hideout wired, arrested four men with bomb-making equipment, false passports, and $14,000 in cash.[27]

When the trials began, al-Qā'idah was very much in the air. The plotters were supposedly affiliated with the Groupe salafiste pour prédication et combat, which in turn was "linked to" bin Lāden. They all admitted going to Afghanistan but denied any association with such groups. Although the British police insisted that the operation had been planned and financed from Britain by contributions from Abu Doha, a British-based Islamic radical, in fact the gang had largely financed themselves from petty theft and peddling Afghan hashish.[28] Eventually the prosecutors dropped the charges of belonging to a foreign terrorist organization.

There was even some question about just what they had plotted. At the trial most denied any plan to bomb the cathedral or the market, insisting that the real target had been an empty synagogue nearby. Only one stated that the market, with the prospects of a swathe of indiscriminate death and destruction, was the objective; interestingly, he received a somewhat lower sentence. Nor were any of them veterans of the anti-Soviet struggle. They were, like Ahmed Ressam, a younger generation of refugees from the Algerian civil war, radicalized subsequent to seeking asylum abroad.[29] For example, Salim Boukhari came from a middle-class family that wanted him to study engineering abroad. Originally he had no particular political views or any real interest in religion. Even when the military government cancelled the 1992 elections, he reacted to the subsequent insurgency by going to university in France. Encountering police harassment and public racism, he joined the exodus of Algerian youth to Britain, where they were freer (until after 9/11) from such treatment. In London, Boukhari was drawn to mosques whose imams preached fiery sermons – in at least one notorious case, with the complicity of Britain's MI-5 domestic intelligence agency.[30] Perhaps more importantly, he began to pay attention to televised scenes of Palestinians beaten, deported, and murdered by Israelis along with images of the Russian bloodbath in Chechnya. Without those events he, and undoubtedly many like him, would probably never have connected Islamic rhetoric with practical action. Next stop, Afghanistan, to learn to manufacture bombs from easily obtainable materials. Since he had studied electronics, he was particularly adept. He returned to London eager to enlist for Chechnya, only to learn that getting there was nearly impossible. Frustrated, he linked up with the Frankfort plotters, but, as he continued to insist, the real target had been the empty synagogue with no intent to kill anyone.

By the time of the Strasbourg trial, Britain had been shaken by the discovery that, using another group of compliant Algerians, al-Qā'idah had planned to poison London citizens en masse with ricin, a toxic substance extracted from castor beans. This WMD first achieved notoriety during the Cold War when a Bulgarian dissident living in exile in London was stabbed in the back with the point of an umbrella dipped in the stuff. Since then, alleged ease of manufacture and deadly impact had made ricin the stuff of legends.

This particular plot was unveiled when Kamal Bourgass, an Algerian resident in London, killed a police officer. That led to the inadvertent discovery in his apartment of a "ricin lab" with castor beans, processing chemicals, and written instructions based on an "Al Qaeda training manual," a copy of which had been first found in a raid in Manchester two years before. Some ninety Muslim men were arrested. Bourgass and a few "trained in Afghanistan" accomplices were stuffed away in a special British maximum-security facility awaiting trial. The story was picked up by Colin Powell, who, in his February 2003 presentation to the UN, in which he was desperately trying to justify the pending US invasion of Iraq, revealed the ricin plot as another joint venture of bin Lāden and Saddam Hussein, with Abu Musab al-Zarqawi, supposedly Usamah's Iraq-based lieutenant, ready to disseminate the stuff. That the plot was a farce only became clear two years later after the US/UK military assault had already reduced much of Iraq to ruin.

There had been no ricin in Bourgass' apartment, just some castor beans. And the notes were not copied from an alleged "Al Qaeda Training Manual"; the document in question had been produced for pro-US mujahideen forces during the anti-Soviet war, then given the "Al Qaeda" label on the US Department of Justice website when Attorney General John Ashcroft was whipping up support for the Patriot Act. True, it had a section on homemade poisons. But the Bourgass notes followed a different formula, originating from a US survivalist, that got passed around Armageddon-is-coming circles. Bourgass ultimately found it through a Yahoo search. Anyway, ricin is hardly a weapon of mass destruction; it can be used only for solitary poisonings, as in the Bulgarian affair two decades before.[31]

After a six-month trial, Bourgass, already convicted of murder of the police officer, was also found guilty of ... conspiring to cause a public nuisance. Four other suspects were acquitted; police dropped charges against the remaining four. Nonetheless the head of Britain's anti-terrorist police claimed that the poison plot was "hugely serious."[32] To make sure that the public was protected, Britain shortly after ordered the deportation of seven men designated as threats to national security, including some who had been cleared in the ricin trial.[33]

AVENGING THE RECONQUISTA?

Probably nowhere in Europe did fear over an Islamic resurgence run so deep as in Spain. Just across the Straits of Gibraltar lay Morocco, principle refuge for hundreds of thousands of Moors stripped of their homes and properties and forced into exile in the fifteenth century. Reference to the "tragedy of Andalous" even figured in one of bin Lāden's broadcasts. Worse, Spanish enclaves on the south side of the Mediterranean were surrounded by enemy territory. Hence no country besides the USA itself was so zealous after 9/11 in hunting down, jailing, and prosecuting Islamic militants – even if most charges were the handiwork of Balthazar Garzón, an investigating magistrate with a reputation for high-profile, low-substance cases whose main purpose seems to have been to build up his public image in preparation for a bid for high office.[34]

Among his prize catches was Tayseer Alouni, the reporter for Al Jazeera who had scooped the world and outraged Washington by being the first to interview bin Lāden after 9/11. From Afghanistan, where he reported on the carnage caused by the US/UK bombing, Alouni moved on to tell about civilian death and destruction in Iraq. An exile from Syria with Spanish citizenship, when Alouni returned to his new home, he found himself on a terror list of thirty-five Spanish citizens of Arab extraction. Garzón claimed that Alouni had used coded conversations in his reports and phone conversations to help Mohammed Atta plan his attack and that Alouni had obtained $4,000 from a top executive of al-Qā'idah in Britain to pass to the supposed chief of al-Qā'idah's Spanish subsidiary. Hence Alouni was charged with supporting, financing, supervising, and coordinating criminal activities on behalf of al-Qā'idah. Out on bail, Alouni went back to work, reporting from the scene when Islamic militants struck at Spain in a bomb attack on the Madrid railway station.[35]

The government, fearful that, in the run-up to an election, the public might interpret the attack as payback for Madrid's (unpopular) participation in the Iraq war, claimed the blasts to be the work of ETA, the military wing of the Basque separatist movement, while the opposition successfully used the al-Qā'idah bogeyman to help win power. But the Madrid attack turned out to be the autonomous work largely of locally resident Moroccans whom the authorities, several years later, acknowledged had no connection whatsoever to Usama and his minions – although the official version of events still insisted that they were "inspired by" al-Qā'idah, whatever that is supposed to mean.[36] Furthermore, if there were any precedents to Madrid, they took the form not of the successive World Trade Center attacks in the US but of a string of suicide bombings in Casablanca.

Morocco is unusual in that its king can trace his lineage back to the Prophet Muhammad, which gives him a claim to theological as well as political leadership. The country also has several strong Islamist currents with quite different political stances. The mainstream Party of Justice and Development accepts the monarchy as an institution but agitates for a more Islamic policy path. There are also those who sport Afghan-type dress and spout salafī theology, but they, in deference to their Saudi sponsors, are largely apolitical. The status quo is further bolstered by Saudi Arabia pouring in money to support the Moroccan Army and government and to build religious institutions, while Saudi princes invest in luxury homes and businesses, including the burgeoning (and distinctly unIslamic) tourism sector. However, two other types of Islamic political activism are more problematic for the regime. One is the Justice and Welfare movement, which shuns cooperation with the state, articulates the aspirations of the urban poor, and openly criticizes the monarchy. The other comprises groups of Islamist political radicals.[37]

In 2003, twelve suicide bombers hit simultaneously five locations in Casablanca: a five-star hotel, Spanish and Italian restaurants, the Alliance Israelite community centre, and a Jewish cemetery and empty community centre.[38] The toll was forty-five dead, including ten of the bombers, another one hundred injured. Inevitably came stories that behind the bombers was the Moroccan Islamic Combat Group, a local "affiliate" of al-Qā'idah, and that the money came from al-Qā'idah via its most dangerous new recruit, Abu Musab al-Zarqawi.[39] If so, bin Lāden must have done a remarkable recruiting job from his Pakistani or Kashmiri hideout – thousands were rounded up and imprisoned.

As in the US after 9/11, the government was happy to capitalize. The attacks reduced (temporarily) the popularity of legal Islamists. They allowed the king to enhance his own religious credentials. They deflected attention from the fact that, as in Algeria, Morocco under World Bank pressure had begun to privatize state-owned industries, which meant selling them cheaply to French companies in exchange for French diplomatic and military support, a program that attracted angry denunciation from nationalist and Islamist leaders.[40] And, in a response that even John Ashcroft would have envied, two days after the events, the state proclaimed a new anti-terror law that granted the security services sweeping powers of arrest and preventive detention and increased the range of offenses for which the death penalty was mandated. Mass trials, sometimes with fifty defendants at a time, followed. Of course, the police did obtain some confessions when, so defense lawyers claimed, detainees had broken bottles shoved up their anuses, rags soaked in noxious liquids stuffed in their mouths, or were subjected to homosexual rape.[41]

After the initial confusion, the stories began to change. The Abu Musab al-Zarqawi connection vanished when it turned out that a much-vaunted bank transfer to local al-Qā'idah recruits was really some small charitable donations to families of Moroccans who had fought in Afghanistan. Those responsible for the bombings apparently emerged from the sprawling slums around Casablanca where clean water rarely flows but crime, drugs, and misery abound and where radical Islamists sought purification through violence against a state whose legitimacy they reject.[42] The actual perpetrators were identified as "members" of several marginal groups whose organization was largely spontaneous, one of which had actually called for the assassination of Usama bin Lāden on the grounds that his politics were too moderate. Any funds they needed came from credit-card fraud or, so the police said, peddling hashish, although this is odd given that the groups were notorious for patrolling the slums to kill drug dealers. The attacks were amateurish, several bombs failing to explode or missing their targets. And the targets (except the Jewish ones) were chosen not because they were Western but because they represented booze and prostitution. No doubt more information could have been gleaned from the alleged ringleader, but he happened to die while in the custody of the security services.

Both the grievances that led to and the perpetrators of Casablanca were basically local, whatever the indirect contribution of Afghan vets. The same could be said in 2004 when ten bombs tore through four trains at the Madrid railway station, killing 191 people and wounding over one thousand. While no doubt those responsible for the carnage rationalized their acts by the usual convoluted notions about striking back at enemies of Islam, the choice of targets likely had more to do with the frustrations of a handful of psychopaths drawn from the large North African underclass in Spain.

The highly tenuous position of that underclass was captured starkly in February 2000 in the town of El Ejido, where a mob of thousands smashed shops, wrecked cars, and firebombed immigrant workers' shanties while chanting "Out with the Moors!" Until the 1970s, the area, in the heart of old Arab Andalous, was one of the poorest in Spain – and the source of heavy out-migration. Then came agricultural development (fruits and vegetables) for export, the so-called Almeria miracle, whose secret ingredient was cheap North African labor. Over a thousand Moroccans are reckoned to drown each year trying to cross the Straits of Gibraltar in small boats to find menial work with scanty pay but abundant harassment on the other side. While some regularized their positions, most remained illegal, receiving half the pay of legals (itself hardly generous) and living in hovels that provided about 4.5 square metres of space per person, usually without running water or electricity.[43]

Morocco was in no position to protest – remittances, as much as $2.5 billion annually, were the largest source of foreign exchange in a country with half its children under fifteen below the official poverty line. Nor was its monarchy likely to care very much about the treatment of its surplus population abroad – it was more likely delighted to be rid of them. True, Morocco's relations with Spain were not exactly rosy towards the end of the twentieth century. After Morocco refused to renew a one-sided fishing deal that had given hundreds of Spanish trawlers access to its territorial waters without limits on their catch, Spain retaliated by closing ports to Moroccan ships. Just before the El Ejido riots, a convoy of trucks with Moroccan fruit and fish en route to European markets was attacked by 1,500 club-brandishing Spaniards, the produce dumped in the sea. Then there was the problem of the old Spanish Sahara. The area had been taken by Spain from the former Moroccan Empire in the seventeenth century. After it was forcibly reincorporated by Morocco in the 1970s, the Polisario guerrilla movement rose in rebellion. In 2000, Spain raised pension payments to former employees of its colonial administration living in Polisario-run refugee camps, even though Morocco protested that the money would just feed the rebellion. Spanish Prime Minister José Aznar followed with a public visit to Melilla and Ceuta, two enclaves in Morocco conquered by Spain in the sixteenth century. No doubt the eagerness with which Aznar joined George Bush II's invasion of Iraq further soured some opinion among Islamic radicals. But it is unlikely that the presence of a few Spanish troops in Iraq or offhand comments in bin Lāden's speeches or even historically based nationalist affronts had much to do with the Madrid bombings.[44]

Nor did the perpetrators have any need for Usama's fabled terror treasury. The central conspirator, Sarhane Ben Abdelmajid Fakhet, had lived in Spain for eight years, studied economics, and been financial officer for the largest mosque in Madrid before he took up a career in real estate. He had never gone to Afghanistan. Nor had his apparent right-hand man, who trafficked in hashish and used part of the proceeds to buy dynamite off the local black market.[45]

Inevitably the bombings further soured the atmosphere for Arabs living in Spain, particularly those arrested in the post-9/11 roundup. With the judges under heavy pressure, most defendants were found guilty of something or other. Yet despite all the claims about al-Qāʾidah's "deep roots" in Spain, defendants accused of direct participation in 9/11 went free. The most that could be secured for others was the vague charge of collaborating with a terrorist group of which those on trial were the main constituents. In other words, they, including the Al Jazeera reporter, were guilty not just by association but by association with themselves. Afterwards major Spanish newspapers denounced the 9/11 connection as a "flight of fancy."[46]

SINAI DESERT STORM?

In 2004 a bomb blast shook the Egyptian tourist centre of Taba in the Northern Sinai, rekindling terrible memories of Luxor. Tourism by then was generating 12 percent of Egypt's GDP and employing nearly two million in a country where industry had largely collapsed under the impact of "liberalization," land aggrandizement and foreign imports had devastated traditional agriculture, the Army had been effectively dismantled as a safety valve for the rural unemployed, and population growth still accelerated. Credit for the blast was quickly claimed by the

Abdullah Azzam Brigade – Al Qaeda in Egypt.[47] Usama, it seems, had forgotten his earlier criticism of Egyptian Islamists for launching local attacks. Yet Egyptian security forces had a different idea. They rounded up thousands of "suspects" from local Bedu tribes. That response reflected a conflict in the Sinai, which had nothing to do with militant Islam versus secularism, or with the machinations of Usama bin Lāden.

The indigenous peoples of the Sinai are from the same tribes who wandered the deserts of Jordan and Saudi Arabia until forcibly settled. Relations between them and Egyptians from the Nile Valley have historically been tense. That helped Israel, during its occupation of the Sinai, build networks of Bedu informants. When the Sinai was returned, Egypt was blocked from full control of areas close to the Israeli border (drug traffickers had better weapons than Egyptian soldiers and police) and forced to strike deals with Bedu sheikhs to provide security. It also decided, on advice from the World Bank, to open the area to mass tourism. Since the Bedu historically had limited concepts of private property, Egyptian developers were able to force them out of choice areas. Because ordinary Bedu were usually too proud to take menial service jobs, almost all employment opportunities went to Nile Valley Egyptians.

The Taba investigation exacerbated tensions. Although Bedu chiefs were supposedly in charge of security, as tourism grew, the state had reduced them to auxiliaries that could be bossed and tossed.[48] Sheikhs were forced by threats of reprisal to denounce tribe members – Egypt got some sacrificial lambs to placate the tourism industry while the sheikhs stood accused of violating the tribal code of honor, further weakening their positions from within. Less than a year later, the day before the State Security Court was to begin hearings about the suspects corralled after Taba, came the Sharm al-Sheikh bombing.

Taba had been amateur hour, the work of a Palestinian with some Bedu accomplices. And most tourists killed were Israelis. But Sharm targeted rich Egyptians and Gulf Arabs and involved three distinct bombs: one at a major hotel; one in a taxi parked just outside and timed to catch people who fled the hotel; and a third at the Sharm Old Market, probably because the bombers were caught in traffic on their way to their intended target. Like Luxor, this attack came at the height of the tourist season. The bombers managed to get into Sharm – showcase of the Egyptian tourism industry, where surrounding roads were dotted with checkpoints – with at least five hundred kilos of explosives hidden in vegetable trucks. Either the security forces were unusually lax or the bombers were guided along unmarked tracks by local Bedu – or both.

The same Abdullah Azzam Brigade – Al Qaeda in Egypt, which had surfaced after Taba, claimed credit. So, too, did the Mujahedi Masr (Holy Warriors of Egypt) and the Defense of the Honor of the Sinai Communities. Some suspected (as they had after Luxor) the handiwork of Israel seeking to disrupt the Egyptian tourist industry. Others put the blame on the complex internal dynamics of Egyptian politics.

Under Gamal Abd al-Nasir, Egypt, like Algeria after independence, had adopted a state-led model of economic development with import restrictions and state-owned industrial complexes. Then came Anwar Sadat and "liberalization" – the country was flooded with imports financed largely by remittances from émigré workers in the Gulf. Next came the World Bank "development" plan that led to a massive sell-off of public assets and promoted tourism as the key to Egypt's economic future. Among its key boosters was Gamal Mubarak, the son and would-be heir of the president, rumored to have big personal investments in Sharm al-Sheikh.

There were many opponents: Bedu traditionalists trying to defend their way of life from further desecration; nationalists loyal to the al-Nasir legacy who were angry over the dismantling of state infrastructure and happy to discredit the waiters-and-bedmakers model of "development"; and Islamists repelled by the spectacle of drunken foreigners revelling nude on Sinai beaches. But there were also people inside the security services who were threatened by the prospect of reform or repeal of Egypt's Emergency Law, passed after the 1981 assassination of Anwar Sadat.

In Egypt the normal criminal justice system had long before collapsed.[49] That left an open field for the police, particularly the investigative branch, and the security services. They took bribes from drug smugglers crossing both the Sinai and Libyan deserts; they arrested people on phony charges to strip them of cash and valuables; they operated as private law-enforcement agents for those who needed a court judgment enforced, or not, as the case may be; they used their regulatory powers over business to extort protection payments; they accepted payoffs from corrupt businessmen to enforce illegal or unfair contracts or to raid a competitor's warehouses, claiming to find shoddy or smuggled merchandise; they peddled information gained under "duress" for purposes of blackmail; and they got on the payrolls of people smuggling consumer goods into Egypt and antiquities back out.[50] (In one particularly notorious case, a senior security officer of Alexandria Airport was caught in 2005 helping a member of a French underwater archeological team smuggle out artefacts and ancient gold coins.) The most lucrative rackets were run by senior officers hand-picked from well-to-do and well-connected families. As the ultimate defenders of the regime, they were also arbiters of Parliamentary "elections" – bosses of businesses, legal and illegal, sought Parliamentary seats both for the immunity from prosecution and for easier access to state resources.[51]

With the breaking of Gamā'at al-Islāmiyya and Al Jihad, the immediate threat from political Islamists faded. Pressure mounted to reform or repeal the Emergency Law – until Taba and Sharm. The more conspiratorially minded suggested that the bombs might have been a plot hatched by old-line nationalists in league with radical Islamists, managed on the ground by disgruntled Bedu and abetted by the security forces in the Sinai, who, right after the attack, flung wide open the routes out of Sharm with the result that the bombers could dissolve among the panicked mass of humanity attempting to flee. On the other hand, Sharm could have been the act of a handful of schemers who got lucky. Still, the notion that state security services and/or military intelligence could have covert relations with and benefit from the actions of underground Islamic paramilitary groups cannot be dismissed out of hand. It was long suspected in Algeria. And it was a possible factor in two other major post-9/11 bomb attacks, in Istanbul and in Bali.

RESTORING THE CALIPHATE?

In late autumn 2003, truck bombs ripped through two synagogues in Istanbul, killing twenty-seven people: some were inside the synagogues, but most victims were Turkish bystanders. The Islamic Great Eastern Raider's Front (a radical "salafi" group whose objective is to re-establish the Caliphate) claimed authorship; but the government dismissed it as incapable of such a job. Five days later, bombs went off at the British consulate and a British bank, killing thirty more, including the consul general, nine consulate employees, three bank staff, with, once again, most victims Turks who just happened to be there.[52] Everyone had their favorite candidate. To the US and some in the Turkish government, al-Qā'idah was responsible, if not directly then "in spirit." To Israel, it was Syria; while Islamists in Egypt and Pakistan countered that it was Mossad or the CIA punishing Turkey for refusing to send troops to Iraq. However DNA samples suggested that the likely suicide bombers were from a run-down area of Turkish Kurdistan where unemployment topped 70–80 percent and where the most thriving industry consists of smuggling heroin from Iran. That raised the real possibility that the culprits were members of the Turkish Hizbullah (quite distinct from its Lebanese or Saudi namesakes), whose existence owed nothing to the anti-Soviet war in Afghanistan or bin Lāden's Terror International but a great deal to Turkey's internal struggles.[53]

Turkey, the southern cornerstone of NATO, was (is) a country confused over three national identities. The official ideology, created after the end of the Ottoman Empire, emphasizes a Western secular society. But it coexists with a sense of Islamic community that pulls the country closer to the Middle East, and with the concept of a pan-Turkic entity spanning central Asia to China. Pan-Turkism formally entered the political arena in 1960, when a military government purged from cabinet several extremist officers who then founded the Nationalist Action Party.[54] For a time it represented only a neofascist fringe. But in the 1970s a land-reform program alienated big landlords who swung against the government just as the political left took up arms. In the ensuing chaos, the Nationalist Action Party created the Bozkurtlar (Gray Wolves), a paramilitary force established, in the words of the party leader, to "defend Turkey against Communism."[55] In practice that meant unleashing the Gray Wolves against Turkish leftists and Kurdish independence activists. Initially dependent on big landlords for support, the Gray Wolves were soon financially autonomous. They drew money from extortion rackets and, aided by sympathizers in Customs, from running contraband for the drugs-and-arms mafya.[56]

The violence of the 1970s provided the pretext for a 1980 military coup. Afterwards the military government (selectively) banned extremist groups, including the Gray Wolves. Over the next few years, most leftist factions were neutralized or liquidated. The challenge from the urban political left was replaced by a growing insurrection in Kurdistan spearheaded by the Kurdish Workers Party (PKK). A brutal Army counterinsurgency campaign killed, imprisoned, and tortured thousands of people and emptied hundreds of villages, allegedly on strategic grounds. The economy of the region virtually collapsed. In this effort to destroy the PKK, the Army had a curious ally.

During the late 1970s, the Army, despite its reputation as staunchly anti-Islamist, had encouraged the spread of Islamist groups who were both antagonistic to the political left and prone to stress Islamic unity over ethnicity, therefore offsetting the appeal of Kurdish nationalism. Although the PKK claimed to be the principal voice of Kurdish aspirations, its Marxism alienated Kurdish religious and tribal leaders along with local landlords in a very conservative area – they probably supported the emerging Hizbullah. While the top brass of the Army and intelligence services left Hizbullah alone as long as it was useful, local commanders of military and police units may have covertly shared intelligence and supplied weapons. Certainly Hizbullah, while rhetorically committed to overthrowing the secular order, in the early years avoided direct confrontation with the state. Instead it engaged in a number of grizzly tortures and murders of Kurdish independence figures, leaders of rival Islamist groups, critics of the Army, and nosy reporters. The emergence of Hizbullah helped weaken the Kurdistan independence movement up to its collapse in the late 1990s. Following the 1999 capture of PKK leader Abdullah Öcalan, Hizbullah, poised to fill the void, became a serious threat. The military and intelligence forces, now free to concentrate on the Hizbullah, struck a series of heavy blows that killed its leader (possibly because he knew too many things potentially embarrassing to the political elite) and dismantled much of its infrastructure, while revelations of its gory methods led to a collapse of support. It seems as if Hizbullah, too, had seen its day.[57] Then came the Istanbul bombings, a sign either of military revival or, more likely, of political desperation.[58]

BRAND-NAME LOYALTY

Meanwhile, just south of Turkey, the US was sinking into Iraqi quicksand. If the notion of a link between Usama and Saddam Hussein had been useful for selling the invasion, the US soon learned that the resulting resistance, too, could be laid at the doorstep of al-Qā'idah. The secret was Abu Musab al-Zarqawi (Ahmed Fadl al-Khalayleh), who soon bore the same price tag ($25 million) as Usama himself. Allegedly this one-legged Palestinian "top al-Qaeda operative" and Afghan vet had been instrumental in orchestrating the Millennium Plot in Jordan, then fled back to Afghanistan to be reunited with his boss, then turned up in Iraq to pledge allegiance to Saddam (whom bin Lāden despised) and, after Hussein's fall, to head the Iraqi terrorist forces opposing the transition to democracy. The Pentagon gave him credit for organizing 50 percent of the attacks on "coalition" forces.[59]

Poking a little below the surface, a rather different story appears. Not at all a Palestinian, Abu Musab al-Zarqawi was from the Beni Hassan, a prominent Bedu family, and was raised in a grimy Jordanian industrial town where he earned an early reputation as a not-very-bright, poorly educated, inarticulate street tough with a passion for drinking and brawling and for getting himself plastered with tattoos, a practice frowned upon by Islam. After a brief jail term for sexual assault, he headed for Afghanistan, arriving only in 1989 after anti-Soviet war was pretty much over – and he spent the next while as a reporter for a small Islamic magazine, following around the true veterans and soaking up vicarious glory from their tales of derring-do. Back then he had a favorable view of Americans, whom he praised as fellow believers. On his return to Jordan, he initially had no great ambition to enter politics – in fact he once considered opening a vegetable stand. But he soon ran afoul of the law again – he was caught with assault rifles and bombs in his house and tried to explain that he found them by accident! In prison, he threw himself into three activities – studying the Qur'ān, pumping iron, and intimidating his fellow inmates. True, he also began to gather like minds, but his was only one of many theopolitical groups ("cells"?) in that prison. On his release and the victory of the Tāliban, he headed back for Afghanistan. His absence was a great benefit to the Jordanian authorities, who could then blame him for the Jordanian end of the great Millennium Plot, secure from the danger of contradiction. Two years later they also credited him with the assassination of a US diplomat. Early in 2006 they managed to sentence him to death in absentia for supposed conspiring with a group of local plotters to have suicide bombers drive trucks loaded with explosives and chemicals into the grounds of the Jordanian intelligence services in Amman.[60]

By then the United States had caught the spirit. When Colin Powell made his preposterous pitch to the UN to try to win approval for war on Iraq, complete with phony tales of covert purchases of uranium yellowcake, the Secretary of State claimed al-Zarqawi to be the key link between Saddam and bin Lāden, a link forged when al-Zarqawi went to Baghdad after the Afghan bombing to have a wounded leg removed. (Secretary Powell forgot to mention whether al-Zarqawi shared a room with Abu Nidal.) In fact, although there had been a training camp in Afghanistan under al-Zarqawi's control, it was distinct from and competitive with any run by bin Lāden or the other jihādist wannabe-leaders assembled there. Furthermore while bin Lāden was based in the Pashtun heartland, al-Zarqawi's operating headquarters was near the westernmost city of Herat, which permitted him to escape via Iran when US bombs started to fall.[61]

From Iran he did seem to have made his way to Iraq. However, he turned up not in Saddam's palace but in Iraqi Kurdistan, a part of the country kept autonomous from Baghdad by US and UK air power.[62] There his hosts were apparently members of Ansar al-Islam. This was an out growth of the former Islamic Movement of Kurdistan, which had been the third most powerful force in the area but which soon broke up into dissident parts. Eventually some small breakaways merged into the Islamic Unity Front, which then became Jund al-Islam, which then became Ansar al-Islam, a sternly puritanical movement that attacked vices and Sufis with equal zeal and was the bane of the two main factions running the region on behalf of the US. The United States claimed that Ansar al-Islam was receiving seed money in the hundreds of millions plus weapons and Toyota Land Cruisers from bin Lāden – remarkable for a group that never numbered above a few hundred. A more likely scenario was that Ansar got help from Saddam's secret service in exchange for creating political divisions in Kurdistan, from Iran for doing likewise to weaken the appeal to Iranian Kurds of a similar separatist venture, and from smugglers who benefited from the resulting freer borders. In fact the only confirmed account of financial aid to Ansar came from witnesses who saw Kurdish police donate part of their US-supplied salaries to its bagmen.[63] As to the al-Qā'idah connection, once Ansar was again busted up into tiny grouplets by military pressure and internal splits, informants revealed that, while members loved to watch al-Qā'idah videos and tried to act and dress like the people around bin Lāden, there was no organic connection.[64] It was a little like the spectacle in New York in the 1980s, when police wiretaps would pick up conversations between Italo-American gangsters imitating the lines and the slang from *The Godfather.*

Not that the breakup of Ansar seemed to bode badly for al-Zarqawi who was, after the US invasion, proclaimed by the Bush administration head of the new al-Tawhid wa al-Jihād group supposedly spearheading resistance to US rule. Surely no one could doubt that foreign Islamic fighters were causing the trouble. After all, what had the Americans done to incur the anger of genuine Iraqis? True, in the course of fifteen years they had indiscriminately slaughtered thousands of hapless conscripts during Gulf War I; bombed the country for the next twelve years, destroying the infrastructure and water, power, and medical facilities, opening the country to malnutrition and epidemics of cholera; spread powdered depleted uranium, causing cancer rates to soar; slapped on sanctions that may have killed a million more, half of them children under five; subjected the country to another brutal bombing campaign and then a mass invasion; dismissed the Army and civil service at a time when unemployment already topped 60 percent while those still employed earned well below subsistence; brought in masses of cheap labor from places like Bangladesh into a country with probably more engineers and technicians per capita (almost all jobless) than the US; imposed a gangster regime of discredited exiles; stood around while government buildings were burned and the cultural heritage sacked; rounded up people en masse for incarceration and torture; launched Israeli-style mass reprisals against the civilian population by uprooting ancient date, orange, and lemon trees; allowed US soldiers to steal gold, cash, and valuables with impunity while engaged in "counterinsurgency" operations; and turned loose well-heeled US evangelicals to attempt to convert the desperate population.[65] Yet Saddam was gone; so there could be no serious cause for complaint.

Within six months of George II's famed photo op jet-landing, when he declared major combat operations over, groups who claimed responsibility for attacks on US and quisling targets, included: remnants of Saddam's Fidayin paramilitary force; another al-Ansar group, this one made up of Ba'th party militants; grouplets of Iraqi Afghan vets; the Jerusalem Brigade created by Iraqi Military Intelligence during the second intifāda; the National Front for the Liberation of Iraq, comprised of secular and religious members of the Republican Guard; the Popular Resistance for the Liberation of Iraq; Awda (the Return), a collection of ex-security men and demobilized soldiers with cells across the major Sunnī cities; Muhammad's Army; the Iraq Liberation Army; the Organization of the Jihad Brigades of Iraq; the New Return; the Snake's Head Movement; the Islamic Movement in Iraq; Martyr Khattab Brigade; the Mujahideen Battalions of the Salafi Group of Iraq (supposedly inspired by the late Abdullah Azzam); the Muslim Youths; the Islamic Armed Group; Islamic Jihad; the Islamic Liberation Party; the Armed Vanguards of Mohammed's Second Army; the Masri Brigade; Wakefulness and Holy War; the Islamic Armed Group of al-Qā'idah; the Black Banner Organization; National Iraqi Command Front; the Iraqi Resistance Brigades; the Unification Front for the Liberation of Iraq; the General Secretariat for the Liberation of Democratic Iraq; and the Anbar Armed Brigades of the Iraqi Revolution. There were also the Badr Battalions of the Supreme Council for the Islamic Revolution and the Imam Mahdi Army of Muqtada Sadr, causing trouble of their own. Not to be forgotten were assorted bands of looters and smugglers whose main interest was just to keep the security situation volatile.[66] To be fair, sometimes foreigners did seem to be causing the trouble – for example when two British SAS commandos were caught in Arab dress with a jeep full of explosives. When they were arrested by the Basra security services, British tanks staged a dramatic prison break to ensure they would not be questioned. The theory was they were planning to plant bombs at a Shi'a religious festival just to keep the intercommunal pot boiling.

Nonetheless, the official line was that the real trouble came from Zarqawi's al-Tawhid wa al-Jihād, especially after it was rechristened, so to speak, Tanzīm al-Qā'idah fi al-Bild al-Rāfidayn (al-Qā'idah Jihād Organization in the Land of the Two Rivers). In addition to "spearheading" the attacks, al-Zarqawi was held personally responsible for the videotaped beheading of an American hostage – even though the person who did the hacking was overweight (almost unknown in Iraq after years of sanctions), right-handed (while Zarqawi was a lefty), wore a gold ring (a most unIslamic affectation), and seemed to do rather well on two legs. Although there was evidence to suggest that the entire "beheading" was faked, its shock value had a useful diversionary effect, coming as it did just as the revelations began about sexual humiliation, torture, and murder in Abu Gharib prison.

The al-Zarqawi legend had further uses. When the US decided to attack Fallujah, then the most important centre of resistance, it announced that the intent was to root out al-Zarqawi and his hordes, who were holed up there – a curious place for an alleged Islamic purist to pick as his headquarters, given that Iraq's city of mosques is also its historic centre for Sufi orders.[67] To save the city, it was necessary to destroy it – along with thirty-six thousand homes, 8,400 commercial establishments, sixty-five mosques, and sixty educational institutions. Thereafter al-Zarqawis peregrinations could be cited, much like those of Ayman al-Zawahiri in Pakistan and Afghanistan, as an excuse for dropping bombs at will.

This is not to suggest that the stories about al-Zarqawi were simply US fabrications. US forces were paying informants up to $10,000 for tip-offs, and got the same kind of results the police do when they employ such tactics: an assortment of crooks and con artists came forward to tell Military Intelligence what it wanted to hear. This mishmash of hearsay and invention was passed on to the Pentagon and to the White House, sometimes with qualifications and warnings that were then stripped away; and the "intelligence" then became the basis not just for public rationalizations of political and military actions but, worse, for formulation of future policy.[68]

Perhaps the most interesting use made of al-Zarqawi was when one of the paid informants sold to the USA a letter supposedly from al-Zarqawi pledging allegiance to bin Lāden, who ostensibly then appointed his former rival as his Iraqi lieutenant, along with a memo ostensibly issued by al-Zarqawi in the name of al-Qā'idah calling for a civil war between Sunnī and Shi'a Iraqis.[69] To bin Lāden (whose religious evocations seemed to bear elements of Sufi and Shi'a belief) the most important thing had always been for Muslims to patch up their internecine quarrels and unite to face the external enemy. However the idea of exacerbating the religious or ethnic divide in Iraq certainly occurred to others. For the US, playing off Kurd, Sunnī, and Shi'a became the only effective way to diffuse the opposition to US occupation, while Israeli strategists had long discussed plans to partition Iraq into ethnoreligious subdivisions, much as Israel had attempted to do in Lebanon two decades before.

Despite the insistence by those in the know that the al-Zarqawi story was largely fabricated, and the man himself may have been killed early in the war, the legend grew, with the US reporting a string of second- and third-in-commands killed or captured that threatened to rival their record of success against Usama's upper management in Pakistan and Afghanistan.[70] By the end of 2005, faced with the growing list of the resistance groups, US intelligence solved the problem neatly by declaring that they had all become affiliates of al-Zarqawi's new Terror International, which "now has two dozen terror groups scattered across almost 40 countries, creating a network to rival Osama bin Laden's."[71] Al-Zarqawi was reputed to have taken his jihād worldwide on the basis of a seven-stage plan: first, awaken the Muslim world through massive operations like 9/11; second, develop a mass movement inside Iraq; third, shift focus to Syria, Jordan, and Turkey; fourth, totally defeat Western-backed regimes in the Muslim world; fifth, declare a caliphate; sixth, mobilize Muslims for worldwide armed confrontation; and seventh, achieve total victory over the Judeo-Christian side. If the world needed more proof, it came with word that al-Zarqawi's version of al-Qā'idah had spilled over into Southern Afghanistan probably en route to the Far East, where countries competed to see whose "al Qaeda regional affiliate" was most dangerous.[72]

THE EAST IS GREEN?

That prize seemed to go to Indonesia, particularly after two bombs in Bali, one in a discotheque, the other in a nightclub, killed two hundred people, including dozens of Australian tourists. The US administration, the CIA, and the serving head of Indonesia intelligence had no doubts: responsibility lay with bin Lāden, who had sent $74,000 to his regional affiliate, the fanatically anti-Christian Jemmah Islamiyah.

Originally dismissed as a "back office" for bin Lāden, after Bali, Jemmah Islamiyah was promoted variously to "an important financial centre for Al Qaeda" or to a group with an autonomous terror capacity with aims to create a Southeast Asian caliphate similar to the one Ugandan intelligence claimed that Usama was building across Africa or the one that Abu Musab al-Zarqawi was supposedly conniving from Iraq. Fears that Jemmah Islamiyah was on the march subsequently served well the governments not just of Indonesia but of Singapore, Malaysia, the Philippines, Thailand, and even Cambodia as a pretext to round up the usual suspects; while, the US government's index of forbidden organizations soon bulged with Southeast Asian charitable and commercial bodies supposedly funding al-Qā'idah or Jemmah.[73] In fact by some accounts the two had merged in a way that paralleled the earlier union of al-Qā'idah and Ayman al-Zawahiri's Al Jihad. Indeed, some experts gave Jemmah Islamiyah priority over al-Qā'idah, dating its "very sophisticated and complex" organization to the late 1980s. After the "Allied victory" in Afghanistan, it was Southeast Asia (especially the parts of Indonesia infested by Jemmah and areas of neighboring Philippines haunted by closely linked Moro guerrilla groups) that started to host "terrorist training camps."

The similarities went beyond the organizational to the financial. Jemmah Islamiya allegedly extorted zakāt contributions, skimmed from Islamic charities, earned money through gold and gemstone smuggling and from petty crime, conducted ransom kidnappings, and ran guns. The money was moved around by cash courier, via the top-secret hawāla system, or through corporate fronts.[74]

Proof seemed ample and persuasive. When the CIA captured a notorious terrorist named Omar al-Faruq, he reported under what was later described as "no-holds-barred CIA-backed military interrogation" that he was an operative for al-Qā'idah who had been instructed to provide arms and money to Jemmah Islamiyah to murder Indonesia's president, blow up the US Embassy, and carry out attacks against local Christians. Naturally this top-secret information was splashed over *Time Magazine*.[75] The only sour note was sounded by the former chief of Indonesia's State Intelligence Coordinating Board, who insisted that al-Faruq, a Kuwaiti who had married a local woman, was really a CIA agent recruited to infiltrate Indonesian Islamist groups and act as an agent provocateur to discredit them.[76] Unfortunately it was not possible to ask Omar al-Faruq for clarification – he managed to escape from US custody at Bagram Air Force base in Afghanistan, from a facility where even the cockroaches were probably subjected to a retinal scan coming and going. On the other hand, so much of its military stores, along with computer flash-drives with secret information, ended up for sale openly in the sprawling bazaar just outside the base: maybe his escape was not so difficult.[77]

Although Indonesia is the world's most populous Islamic country, it was an odd choice from which to try to create a new Caliphate. Its Islam is remarkably loose to start with and further watered down by customary beliefs and relics of the country's Buddhist and Hindu past. Primary loyalties are based on tightly knit family structures and village-based communities closed to outsiders, in which nothing functions without clan assent. In that context pan-Islamism is as indigenous as ham sandwiches. In the twentieth century decolonization struggle, the Islamic party, whose doctrines were heavily infused with Javanese mysticism, was a distant third to the Communists and to Achmed Soekarno's Partai Nasional Indonesia. Once the Dutch were ousted and Soekarno needed something else to hold together the sprawling country with its many ethnic divisions, he created an indigenous ideology that was a (rather clever) combination of traditionalist beliefs, bits and pieces of Islam, and odds and ends from Karl Marx. True, during the second decade of his long presidency, he so outraged pious Muslim opinion with both his governance and his personal lifestyle that in the late 1950s there was a brief Islamist insurrection in Sumatra. However this would likely not have occurred without choreographing by the CIA – which objected to Soekarno's close relations with China and the USSR and to his efforts, together with India's Nehru and Egypt's al-Nasir, to create the Non-Aligned Movement.[78] When, with US aid in the mid-1960s Mohammed Soeharto organized a bloody coup and murdered up to 500,000 "Communists," he secured support from Islamists by a promise to replace Soekarno's pseudo-socialism with an Islamic regime. Instead, with enthusiastic backing from US resource corporations, he created one of the most corrupt systems of grab-and-run capitalism to disgrace the region or the world. Disenchanted once again, Islamists took to the streets to proselytize among the displaced and disadvantaged.

There were already very large grass-roots organizations. The Nahdalat Ulama was founded in the early twentieth century and represented the mystical form of rural Javanese Islam. By the time its leader,

Abdurrahman Waheed, succeeded Soeharto as president of Indonesia, it had at least twenty-five million members. The second, the Muhamaddiyya, emerged in the 1920s with a more urban orientation. Today it has about the same size membership. Both have long had representatives in Parliament, were and are committed to peaceful change, and have a liberal view of Islamic practice that would have driven the Taliban into a state of apoplexy. What was new in the crisis was the emergence of groups like Jemmah Islamiyah.

Jemmah Islamiyah's roots stretch back to 1967, when Abu Bakir Bashir (like the bin Lāden family, originally from the Hadramawt region of Yemen) began anti-government agitation over a local radio station, then, a few years later, opened an Islamic school. Arrested frequently, in 1979 he was sentenced to nine years, but got out in three.[79] In 1985, when the Indonesian Supreme Court reinstituted the original sentence, he fled into exile, from where he denounced the government and rallied volunteers for Afghanistan. At the time the Soeharto government was engaged in another crackdown on the radical Islamist opposition, which helped to provide recruits. In Afghanistan, they, along with volunteers from elsewhere in the region, were trained in camps run not by bin Lāden but by Abdul Rasoul Sayyaf.

After the great Asian financial crisis of 1997 and the subsequent fall of Soeharto, Bashir returned home to again take up the theme that the regime was unIslamic and corrupt and to rebuild Jemmah Islamiyah. Soon he was surrounded by people attracted by his message about building a new society based on equal economic opportunity, social justice, and piety. The group's links to outside organizations were largely incidental and personal – men later prominent with Jemmah Islamiyah had met in Afghanistan activists from other countries. Senior figures made no secret that they knew bin Lāden but denied any organizational or financial link. In fact Jemmah Islamiyah needed little money. What it required for welfare activities and schools came mainly from contributions to mosques and small charities by its largely working-class supporters.

However, there was a shadier side. During the chaos of the immediate post-Soeharto era, the Christian elite of the Maluccas, and, later, central Sulweisi, organized massacres of Muslim newcomers from elsewhere in Indonesia. This led Jemmah Islamiyah to form a paramilitary wing. After the Maluccas and central Sulweisi clashes came bomb attacks on churches and assassination attempts on priests. While Jemmah Islamiyah obviously claimed no role in them, with any militant organization living at least partially in the shadows, it is difficult to separate the main body from more fanatical individuals or small groups who may operate in the name of the whole. Money for these guerrilla raids came not from Jemmah's official budget but from credit-card fraud and robberies, particularly of Chinese goldsmith shops. Even that choice was more practical than racial or religious – goldsmith shops and jewellery stores are full of cash and easily negotiable valuables, and much more poorly guarded than banks; and in Indonesia virtually all are Chinese-owned. In the subsequent efforts to portray Jemmah Islamiyah as a Southeast Asia al-Qā'idah, there were even stories that its operations chief, Riduan Isamuddin (better known as Hambali), was, like bin Lāden, a wealthy patron of terror. His arrest in Thailand in 2003 was celebrated by the US government as a crippling blow against al-Qā'idah. The reality was that Hambali, the son of a poor farmer with eleven children, was a nobody until 9/11 set the US and its national security industry on a worldwide hunt for al-Qā'idah "cells."

The really big news after the anti-Muslim riots was not Jemmah Islamiyah but the newly emerged Laskar Jihad. It went on to function as an auxiliary force for the Army in suppressing a rebellion in the oil-rich Aceh province and to spearhead anti-vice campaigns in the cities – its followers smashed up gambling dens, brothels, and bars. Its prominence moved George Bush II to refer to the group as "international jihadists" and Colin Powell to label it another affiliate of al-Qā'idah. There were breathless reports that it trained hundreds of non-Indonesians, including al-Qā'idah operatives, in its "jungle camps." Yet Laskar Jihad is almost exclusively Java-based; and there is scarcely enough jungle left on that island (an ecological disaster zone of one hundred million people interspersed with rice paddies) to hide an orangutan, let alone a military camp. Laskar Jihad's boss, Jaffar Umar Thalib, an Afghan vet, scorned bin Lāden as a spiritually empty lightweight void of religious knowledge and denounced bin Lāden's attitude towards Saudi Arabia, which Jaffar Umar Thalib regarded as a model Islamic state. True, Thalib had no kind words for the US, but the sole interest of Laskar Jihad was to create an Islamic state in Indonesia, in the meantime fighting regional separatists and purging cities of vice. In fact Laskar Jihad was so worried over the possible effects of the Bali bombing on its public support that, like Egypt's Gamā'at al-Islāmiyya after Luxor, it publicly renounced paramilitary action – although what it continued to do in private is another matter.[80]

Bali was the epicentre of the Indonesian tourism industry; and the bombs caused the same sort of mass cancellation that they did in

Egypt.[81] Yet neither Laskar nor Jemmah, both of which had informal but positive relations with senior government and military figures, had an interest in destabilizing the Indonesian economy. Granted that a good Muslim might be outraged at the way Australian youths came to Bali to drink, do drugs, and pick up local prostitutes, not to mention at its growing popularity with European gays. But Bali is 95 percent Hindu; and Islamic purists were far more concerned with cities in Muslim-inhabited islands. One possible motive was revenge for Australia's support for the independence of East Timor, linked to Australia's growing greed to control mineral and petroleum resources in its neighborhood. But, if so, the suspects would have to include Indonesian nationalist groups of all ideological stripes, along with the Army and intelligence services. Abu Bakir himself claimed that Islamic militants had meant to explode only a small device to scare off drunks and drug-addled tourists, and that Israel, the us, and Australia had planted a larger one responsible for most of the deaths. Even if that was fantasy, one senior Pakistani diplomatic (an ex-commando and explosives expert) who inspected the main crater insisted that it had been produced with military-grade explosive. Nor did it escape notice that, prior to the bombing, Indonesia had been understandably reluctant to sign on to Washington's War on Terror. Within days after the event, resistance crumbled.[82]

Of course the Indonesian government, as had others, quickly turned the situation to advantage by pushing through a severe new anti-terror law. While its real target was regional separatists, under the terms of the new law, the Bali bombers were quickly rounded up, tried, and sentenced to death. However, their trial never established a direct connection to Jemmah. Iman Samudra, leader of the cabal, was fully open about spending time in Afghanistan in the 1990s and teaching for a while in a school run by Abu Bakir Bashir. But he took full responsibility – he did the planning, secured the materials, then chose the time and place. As to financing, he got the money in the usual way, from holding up a Chinese jewellery store.[83] Abu Bakir Bashir plus eighteen other members of Jemmah had also been arrested. Ultimately the court cleared him of all the major charges, ruling that there was no proof he had planned or mobilized others to act. (It helped the defense that the us refused to allow either Hambali or Omar al-Faruq, before his remarkable escape, to testify for the prosecution.[84]) Bashir was convicted only of one charge under the old criminal code, effectively that he had met and encouraged one of the bombers before the event. His sentence of 2.5 years was later reduced on appeal.[85] Others facing death or long

sentences were suddenly reprieved when one defendant successfully appealed on the rather logical grounds that the new anti-terror law under
which they had been convicted had been passed after the bombing –
the Indonesian constitution barred use of retroactive legislation.[86]

When about three years later bombs again ripped through a Bali bar
and restaurant just as the tourist business was beginning to recover,
fingers pointed once more to Jemmah acting on behalf of al-Qā'idah.
However it turned out to be a copycat operation by a small gang upset
at the "moral pollution" of terrorism, with no connections to any
major organization.[87]

The grand al-Qā'idah/Jemmah Islamiyah merger had supposedly
meant that Usama's reach could also extend much further into Asia,
for example, into Cambodia, an overwhelmingly Buddhist country,
with a weak and isolated Muslim community making up a mere 6 percent of the population. Cambodian Muslims received special attention from the Khmer Rouge, which had desecrated mosques, banned
prayers and use of the local language, forced people to eat pork, and
murdered religious and village leaders. After the Khmer Rouge was
ousted, the community reached out to the Islamic world, especially to
Saudi Arabia, which provided money for schools and community rehabilitation. But then, by the end of the decade, amidst fears of Islamic militancy throughout the region, came a crackdown. Once the
FBI got hot on the trail of a Saudi charitable foundation called Umm
al-Qura Foundation, which had sponsored an Islamic school in Cambodia, Cambodian authorities raided the school, claiming it was a
front for the transfer of $50,000 to Jemmah Islamiyah for attacking
US targets.[88]

It turned out that one teacher had been holding a bag of cash on behalf of a courier (possibly the notorious Hambali). There was no connection to either the Saudi charity or the school, apart from that teacher.
Jemmah itself received no help from Saudi charities – which poured
funds into the officially recognized, mainstream Islamist groups in Indonesia. Yet the school was closed, several teachers were held for months
without charges, and the rest of the staff was deported.[89]

Similarly, the wily Saudi was blamed for the Muslim insurgency on
the Philippines island of Mindanao through his support for the notorious Abu Sayyaf Group. In reality Moro aspirations to autonomy or
independence date back centuries. In modern times, the initial Moro
rebels had been trained in the late 1960s by the Philippines Army to

spearhead a covert invasion of the resource-rich neighboring island of Sabah, part of Malaysia. They had taken up arms against their former sponsor after the Philippines Army was suspected of working on behalf of logging and mining companies to murder Muslim villagers in order to chase them out of their lands.[90] Subsequently a number of Moro factions emerged with different agendas. Some wanted more autonomy and protection of ancestral land from Christian settlers; some wanted an independent Islamic state. The Abu Sayyaf Group wanted neither. It was founded in 1991 by an Afghan vet who had fought, as its name proclaimed, with Abdul Sayyaf, not with bin Lāden. Of marginal significance in the Moro struggle, it had probably been encouraged by the Philippines Army to discredit more serious groups. Then it began a campaign of freelance ransom kidnapping and extortion. After 1998, when the police killed its leader, it fractured into several pieces.[91] Nonetheless the Philippines government was probably delighted when, after 9/11, the US government upgraded the group's status to local affiliate of al-Qā'idah. That served to rationalize $50 million in extra US military aid for Manila's "counterinsurgency" operations plus an equal sum in economic assistance. It also brought US troops back to the Philippines to support a renewed crackdown on Moro aspirations. The resulting bombings of villages triggered massive flights of refugees that helped to continue the demographic transformation intended to marginalize the Moros in a historic homeland for which they had fought in succession Spain, the USA, and the Manila government.[92]

So, too, in the very heartland of Asia. When George Bush also listed as a terrorist organization the East Turkistan Islamic Movement, no doubt every blue-blooded American was relieved to find that such a threat to their right to life, liberty, and pursuit of a second SUV had been skewered, although they might also have paused to ask why, if the movement was so dangerous, the CIA had supported it with arms and money before bin Lāden was born.

The roots of the revolt by the Uighurs, a Turkic-speaking minority in Xinjiang go back to the eighteenth century, when China crossed the Gobi desert to conquer the area, formerly an independent khanate. Subsequent attempts to regain independence culminated in 1944 in a brief Republic of East Turkistan. After the Communist victory in the Chinese Civil War, the central government reasserted control. The result was a low-level guerrilla campaign in which the CIA for probably the first time provided logistical and financial aid to a Muslim insurgency. When in the early 1950s the rebellion collapsed, the CIA flew the leader, along with his treasury of gold bars, to exile.[93]

Although China began to flood the area with Han settlers, they were located well away from most of the Uighur population: hence the area remained relatively quiet. Then, during the Afghan war, China encouraged Muslim religious leaders to recruit volunteers. Some returned convinced that, since they had defeated the Soviet Union, they could do the same to China. After the fall of the Soviet Union, West Turkistan had re-emerged, even if in the form of five independent republics. So why not East Turkistan?

China was determined to hold firm. Xinjiang contained most of China's gold, plus 70 percent of its oil and coal, and it is also the logical route for a pipeline to haul the Kazakh oil, on which China's future economic strategy depends. Hence the authorities closed mosques and Qur'ānic schools, forcibly "re-educated" imams, and arrested, imprisoned, and shot dissidents. Previously "fundamentalism" was almost unknown, and the Uighur leadership could probably have been placated by regional autonomy. But China's actions led to radicalization. As bomb attacks multiplied, China began denouncing first the Tāliban then bin Lāden for aiding the rebels.

For a time the US government took the events as just an opportunity to berate China for political repression and religious persecution. Then came 9/11. Once the US bought permission from the government of Uzbekistan to set up military bases by labelling the Islamic Movement of Uzbekistan a terrorist organization, China saw its chance. And the US, anxious to stop the spread of Chinese missile technology to Pakistan and Iran, agreed to a trade. Thus was a new al-Qā'idah affiliate born.[94]

STRIKING OUT

Each attack – Tunis, London, Paris, Amman, etc. – became the occasion for authorities in afflicted countries, seeking to cater to Washington and/or to advance a local agenda, to sound the al-Qā'idah alert, therefore giving the brand name a credibility it would otherwise have lacked. That helped create a global reign of fear beyond the wildest dreams of the reclusive Saudi, who was probably awestruck at his own success, or simply having a good laugh.

For example, in June 2002 a car bomb exploded outside the US consulate in Karachi – a city that US-supplied weapons had turned into a free-fire zone – and killed twelve people. Washington declared bin Lāden the prime suspect, while CNN asked if this was the start of an al-Qā'idah comeback after the stunning Allied success in Afghanistan.[95] Pakistan's Minister of the Interior took up the chorus: "We know Al Qaeda was behind it. We have credible information that Al Qaeda financed it." It was the price that Pakistan was paying, its officials claimed, for supporting the international community in the War on Terror. Of course, when pressed, the US acknowledged that it had "no evidence." The real architects remain unknown.[96]

Even though Saudi Arabia had cleared bin Lāden in the 1995 Riyadh and 1996 Khobar attacks, the regime, to set the stage for a crackdown on internal dissent, again invoked the al-Qā'idah threat in 2003. The initiating event was a suicide bombing in Riyadh against Vinnell Corporation. Heavily staffed with ex-Military Intelligence and CIA personnel, its job was to train and, to a large degree, control, the Saudi National Guard on which the regime depends for its survival. Although the US had already announced the pending withdrawal of its forces from Saudi Arabia, Vinnell, as a "private" corporation, was excluded.[97] That made the company the obvious target for any internal dissident group, of which there were ample with no "links" to bin Lāden other than occasionally invoking his name. A short time later came a blast at a Riyadh residential compound, killing seventeen people, mainly foreign Arabs. Immediately imputed to al-Qā'idah, it was likely the work of local religious figures angry that the state permitted licentious behavior by foreign and Saudi playboys in a pleasure ground into which the Saudi religious police were forbidden to enter.[98]

Even international organizations got into the spirit. For many years the International Maritime Board had tried to draw attention to piracy, particularly in and around the Straits of Malacca, the busiest shipping lane in the world. There, cargo ships and tankers were sometimes boarded by armed gangs that made off with the crew's valuables, sometimes cargoes, and occasionally the ships themselves – to be repainted, reregistered, and resold. Following release of a supposed bin Lāden tape praising a suicide attack on a French tanker off Yemen, the IMB warned of a possible al-Qā'idah plot to hijack a tanker full of liquefied natural gas (gas explodes while oil just burns) and crash it into another ship, a refinery, or a crowded port. Curiously, the warning came when the IMB's own data showed a reduction in the number of attacks over the previous two years.[99]

When, a year later, the *MV Superferry 14* out of Davao caught fire and one hundred passengers died, an anonymous caller claimed credit on behalf of a suicide bomber deployed by the Abu Sayyaf Group, allegedly al-Qā'idah's Philippines affiliate. The initial diagnosis was an accidental paint-room fire. But three weeks later, prompted by the need to justify more US aid, the president announced the capture of four Abu Sayyaf Group militants and a cache of explosives, pre-empting, she claimed, a Madrid-style attack; and she demanded the Marine Board of Inquiry to reopen the *MV Superferry 14* inquiry; it eventually obliged with a report that the accident was really a terrorist attack.[100]

It did not require the spectacular impact of bombs for countries to hitch their political horses to the "blame Usama" bandwagon. In the Middle East and North Africa, he seemed to be everywhere. After a US marine was killed in Kuwait in 2002, the government claimed that it found a video identifying the incident as an al-Qā'idah operation – although it later admitted that, apart from a tape of rather dubious provenance, it had no evidence the attack was ordered from outside.[101] In Algeria, in 2003, following a dramatic escalation in the civil war when one group of guerrillas killed nearly fifty elite paratroopers, an embarrassed government insisted that it must have been the work of bin Lāden, who was variously accused of financing the insurgents, directing military operations, and running guns via Mauritania and Mali.[102]

In 2004, following demands from the IMF to cut its budget deficit, Jordan announced tax and price hikes of the type that, in the past, had always led to demonstrations, riots, and bombings. Simultaneously it released stories of al-Qā'idah conspiracies and pictures of a truck loaded with explosives supposedly smuggled in from Syria. While security forces fanned out across the country looking for al-Qā'idah cells, the Islamic Action Front denounced the moves as a charade to distract public attention from the tax and price increases and to discredit Islamist opposition to them.[103] Then al-Qā'idah, or rather the new, improved al-Zarqawi version, supposedly struck again with the bombing of three hotels in Amman; the one would-be bomber who survived because of a malfunctioning suicide vest turned out to be a woman driven to the act by the killing of her three brothers by the Americans in Fallujah.[104]

Nor was al-Qā'idah absent from Occupied Palestine. At a time when the Israeli Army had hermetically sealed Gaza, while further uprooting farmers from the villages and hamlets near Jewish settlements in the West Bank, Palestinians began receiving phone and email messages from supposed bin Lāden's recruiters offering money and other assistance. The security forces of the Palestinian Authority traced them back to Shin Beit, Israel's internal police and intelligence arm, which apparently figured that if it could entrap Palestinians into signing up even for a bogus al-Qā'idah, Israel could sell to the US the notion that the secular authorities of Palestine, seduced by Islamic fundamentalism, were unfit for self-government, and that the region was not ready for an Israeli Army withdrawal.[105]

Nor was Europe spared, although one tragedy was pre-empted by the neat work of the Macedonian police. The Minister of the Interior proudly announced the foiling of a plot by a bin Lāden-inspired group of Albanian-Muslim guerrillas to attack the US, British, and German Embassies in Skopje. What really happened was that two months after 9/11, ministry officials decided to cause a backlash against the Albanian minority. That would give the government a pretext to reverse civil-rights concessions won a couple years before. The police chief contacted an alien smuggler who obligingly led six Pakistanis and one Indian to a spot where a specially formed anti-terror squad was waiting. The seven were kidnapped, held for a few days at the home of the Minister of the Interior, then taken away to be murdered. Afterwards the police dressed them in uniforms of the (Albanian) National Liberation Army and planted Qur'āns and weapons. A few hours later the minister appeared before a TV crew outside the US Embassy to claim proof of links between Albanian insurgents and al-Qā'idah. Alas, his men had done a sloppy job. One gun shoved into the pants of a dead "guerrilla" covered four bullet holes. Another body hosted fifty-three gunshot wounds. On others the planted weapons were new and unfired. The truth emerged only after the government changed and former Albanian guerrillas demanded an investigation as part of their price for participating in a new coalition.[106]

Fortunately, even though the US was surely the country most menaced by al Qā'idah, it would never resort to any such debasement of decent standards in its criminal justice system to meet that threat. Or would it?

18

Securing the Home Front – The USA's Hunt for the Enemy Within

The events of 9/11 led to a minor revolution in US jurisprudence. In normal criminal procedures the prosecution must prove beyond reasonable doubt commission of an offense and (in most but not all cases) intent to commit it. In standard civil procedures the burden of proof is much lower, merely a balance of probabilities; and there is rarely a need to establish intent, although proof of malice may help to squeeze out a juicy settlement in a tort case. However, in the post-9/11 atmosphere of growing Islamophobia, it became up to the accused to prove innocence, not just on a balance of probabilities, not just beyond reasonable doubt, but with sufficient force to drive any possible suspicion from the minds of a dozen righteous citizens more psyched up by administration propaganda and media sensationalism for duty with a lynch mob than with a jury – assuming the accused was not simply "disappeared" into a secret military holding facility or, more benignly, held incommunicado in an immigration pen until deported on the basis of secret "evidence." Then there was the additional problem posed by judges and prosecutors ready to sacrifice a few Saracens in a Crusade for higher office.

Worse, court procedures functioned through an evidentiary perpetual-motion machine. The police or prosecutors fed "tips" to reporters they could trust to put the right spin on the story; and the ensuing newspaper accounts were read by cops or prosecutors into the court record as independent evidence, particularly in things like bail hearings, where the use of hearsay and gossip is commonplace. Lurid media stories also colored the attitudes of jurors, who were hardly unaware of former Attorney General Ashcroft's habit of pronouncing verdicts before trials ended, or sometimes began.

As with organized crime cases, those dealing with organized terror often turned on testimony from informants paid by cash, reduced sentences, or freedom from deportation proceedings. But all's fair in love and Terror War, particularly when the US was engaged in a desperate hunt to locate "sleeper cells" before their alarm clocks rang.

COUNTERFEIT JUSTICE

Less than a week after 9/11, the FBI went to a Detroit apartment to pick up Nabil al-Marabh, suspected of being instrumental in the attacks. Born in Kuwait of Syrian parents, al-Marabh had trained in Afghanistan, entered the US illegally, been deported, then returned. He had some $22,000 in a Kuwait bank account, odd for someone who appeared to be living at the margins; and he allegedly communicated regularly with people involved in both 9/11 and the previous Millennium Plot. The feds did not find al-Marabh at his last-known address; but they did find three other Arab men, along with a pile of fake passports, visas, social security cards, and alien registration certificates. A fourth man was picked up shortly after.

Initially the feds were not particularly excited. The Detroit Four were charged with possession of false documents and put in preventive detention pending immigration hearings, while the hunt for al-Marabh continued. A couple days after the Detroit raid, they located him working part-time in a Chicago-area convenience store. The feds strutted, the media exulted, and the public breathed a sign of relief – one more rag-head nailed and jailed. Yet in al-Marabh's version of events, he comes across not as a Muslim fanatic working for a Saudi ringmaster of terror but as a reincarnation of Joe Btfsplk – the *Li'l Abner* comic strip character who walks around with a black cloud permanently over his head and goes from one inadvertent disaster to another.[1]

According to al-Marabh, his bad luck began in Boston in 1989 while he worked briefly as a cab driver. A customer with whom he had a dispute told the FBI that al-Marabh was a mad bomber. The FBI determined that the story was bogus, then tried to recruit al-Marabh as an informer on Arab community activists – he claims that he refused. Unemployed, he volunteered to work in Pakistan for the World Muslim

League, a charitable foundation that distributed food, medicine, and money to Afghan refugees. According to the FBI, he also trained in Afghanistan in how to handle small arms. Since al-Marabh had an uncle in Toronto, he later moved there to work in a family print shop while he tried to get refugee status; but his term with the World Muslim League attracted the attention of CSIS, and he was refused. Hence he snuck back into the US and used false papers to try to find work. In 1998 Raed Hijazi, a young man al-Marabh had met in Afghanistan and to whom he had sent some money, moved into his apartment. But they quarrelled; and Hijazi was kicked out. Three years later, Hijazi was sentenced to death in Jordan for plotting to bomb a hotel – in his "confession" he fingered al-Marabh as an "al-Qā'idah agent." Meanwhile, early in 2001, facing a six-month suspended sentence for stabbing another roommate (judgement about roommates does not seem to have been al-Marabh's strong point), al-Marabh fled to Canada again, tried to sneak back to the US, and was arrested and charged in Canada with possessing false documents. Released from jail after his uncle posted bail, he succeeded in entering the US on a phony passport, then moved into the ill-fated Detroit apartment while he studied for a commercial truck driver's license. Later he managed to get a part-time job at the convenience store in a Chicago suburb where he was arrested in a blaze of post-9/11 publicity.

Since al-Marabh had once worked in a print shop, he was accused of producing false IDs for the 9/11 hijackers; since he had once lent money to Hijazi, he was accused of financing not just the Millennium Plot but 9/11 as well, thus joining a list, which had started to take on the dimensions of the Cairo or Riyadh phone directories, of supposed financiers of the event. The government claimed that his telephone records showed frequent conversations with the hijackers. Even worse, he had secured his license to transport hazardous materials – a sign of likely intent to detonate a truckload of explosives in the some public place. All this, of course, was broadcast far and wide as the government made its plans to bring al-Marabh to justice before an unbiased jury of his peers. Meanwhile he was kept in solitary in several detention centres including one in Brooklyn, where, he claims, he was stuck in a tiny, almost unheated cell, strip-searched and beaten by guards, and deprived of legal representation for the first eight months – during which time he went on a series of hunger strikes to try to better his conditions. His guardians finally provided him with an Arabic-speaking cellmate who, in return for having some criminal charges watered down, informed the FBI about the contents of their conversations.[2]

In the final analysis al-Marabh was in fact charged – for a border violation. Since he had already spent eleven months in confinement and the
offense carried a maximum of eight months, he was released – into the
waiting hands of immigration agents who deported him to Syria. Originally the prosecutors rationalized their about-face by the claim that to
prosecute him for terrorism would compromise intelligence sources.
Then, in announcing al-Marabh's release into INS custody, the US attorney in charge of the case simply commented, "We are not making any
claims of terrorism to do with this charge." Why bother? The mass media
had already done a splendid job of spreading those claims far and wide.[3]
In the meantime the al-Marabh saga spun out two subplots.

Hassan al-Mrei was of Syrian origin but raised in Saudi Arabia, where
his father, a member of the Muslim Brotherhood, had fled to political
exile. Caught up in the spirit of the Afghan war, in 1990 he went to Pakistan on the usual subsidized air fare for volunteers – which permitted
Saudi Arabia to keep tabs on who was coming and going. From 1995
to 1997, he travelled between Yemen and Pakistan trading honey, a
profession that would later come under scrutiny once the US decided
that a Yemeni owner of a honey-trading company had been the brains
behind the attack on the *USS Cole* in Aden harbor.[4] When al-Mrei returned to Saudi Arabia, he found that the Saudis were rounding up,
interrogating, and jailing Afghan volunteers. In 1999, visiting Canada
on a bogus passport, he sought refugee status but censored his Afghan
experiences out of his application. In Canada his main offense seems
to have been an assault on the culinary sensitivities of the upscale den-
izens of Toronto's trendy Yorkville district, where he ran an Eata Pita
franchise. Far from being able to finance terrorism out of its huge cash
flow, he soon found himself $10,000 in debt. When his friend Nabil al-
Marabh needed to get a false passport to visit his sick mother in Kuwait
(where she died of a stroke while al-Marabh was in custody), al-Mrei located one. Shortly after 9/11, when the US added two Yemenite honey
producers to its list of financiers of terrorism, al-Mrei was arrested by
the Mounties and held while they plotted with the United States to
send him to Syria for a proper interrogation. The only thing saving the
pita peddler from that fate was the previous deportation of Maher
Arar, a computer engineer and long-time Ottawa resident of Syrian
origin, who had been kidnapped by US immigration agents in New
York, then turned over to Syria to be locked into a coffin-sized cell
where he was beaten regularly for nearly a year, even though Canadian
consular officers dropped in for the occasional chat.[5] When the Syrians finally allowed Arar to go home, the uproar prevented al-Mrei

from sharing that fate. Instead he was kept in solitary in Toronto, year after year, with the "evidence" against him kept secret.[6]

Meanwhile, once Nabil al-Marabh, their big fish, had assumed the dimensions of an embryonic zooplankton, US authorities turned their sights on the other bunch of "conspirators" who had been fortuitously arrested in his old apartment. A year after their original indictment for false documents, the Detroit Four faced a new set of charges, this time of providing material support to terrorism. Among the evidence seized by the FBI in the original raid were some incriminating videos, plus a day-planner supposedly containing references to a US Air Force base in Turkey, to the "American foreign minister," and to a military hospital in Jordan, along with what seemed to be a diagram of an airport flight line, aircraft, and runways. They were actually written by a Yemeni acquaintance who, by the time of the raid, had committed suicide. But the prosecution argued that the conspirators persuaded the deceased to interpose himself to better hide the trail.[7]

Central to the government's case was the testimony of a Moroccan illegal immigrant named Youssef Hmimssa, who had briefly shared the apartment with three defendants. He had been arrested on charges of credit-card fraud in mid-September 2001. At that time the boys in blue had other things on their mind and made sure that so did Hmimssa. They told him that they had proof of his association with a suspected terror cell. Facing up to eighty-one years in jail for just the credit-card offenses, and far worse if the feds decided to go for terror charges, he decided to play along. In exchange for a drastic cut in sentence – no more than forty-six months for credit-card offenses and no reference to terrorism – he performed to order. He declared that the defendants were Islamic fanatics. (Defense witnesses countered that only one of the accused had shown any real interest in religion.) He testified that one of the Detroit Four had told him about possible attacks a month before 9/11, with Las Vegas and Disneyland among the targets. He stated that the men had scouted Detroit Airport looking for security lapses and that they wanted to acquire Stinger missiles to shoot down planes. It was great stuff, but there was one minor problem.[8]

Hmimssa had a string of charges (stolen watches, faked documents, even currency black-market transactions) and a few arrests in North Africa and Central Europe before he arrived in the US on a phony French passport. Some jurors afterwards claimed that they had trouble believing him. But they were patriots in the Britney Spears mold. ("Honestly," she gushed, "I think we should just trust our president in every decision he makes and should just support that, you know, and be faithful in what happens."9) Hence they apparently figured that, if the government said the defendants were guilty, it must be true. Furthermore the witness' credibility problems were alleviated by John Ashcroft, who called the convicted fraud artist a shining example of a cooperative witness.

Of the four defendants, one was acquitted; one was founded guilty of document fraud; the other two were also nailed on that, plus terrorism support. The government heralded the results as its first post-9/11 anti-terror victory. The sole defendant found not guilty had a slightly different and more prophetic interpretation: "This case is a lie."10

It later turned out that the US assistant attorney in charge of the prosecution had not exactly played straight. He had tried to get court employees to dig up confidential information to discredit a witness who had testified that Youssef Hmimssa was lying; he had made a deal with a drug trafficker for a reduced sentence in exchange for the trafficker going underground to collect information about and steal mail from others of Arab origin living in the area; and he had withheld a letter from a former cellmate of the star prosecution witness explaining how Hmimssa had bragged about fabricating the story he told in court. According to Milton "Butch" Jones, a local gang leader, Hmimssa "get to telling me how he lied to the FBI, how he fool'd the Secret Service agent on his case."11 When the full texts of Hmimssa's debriefings were examined, it was clear that what he had to say evolved over time in response to prodding by prosecutors. Furthermore surveillance footage of New York, California, and Las Vegas found in the apartment turned out to be amateur footage from a university student's trip.12 The trial judge eventually overturned the convictions.13 Indeed, early in 2006 the prosecutor himself later faced a criminal indictment, although he may have had a point when he claimed that he was a scapegoat to cover up the government's own mismanagement.14

However, the denouement was not all bad for the government. The government filed new charges of insurance and mail fraud – since the three defendants were Arabs they had to be guilty of something. Meanwhile the drug dealer who had lied to, stolen mail from, and spied on Arab-Americans in the Detroit area decided that his life was in danger and, with the assistance of the US government, left for an undisclosed foreign location.15

Yet the feds had not exhausted all the leads thrown up by their careful investigation of Nabil al-Marabh, despite the less than inspired conclusion of the case. Indeed, it highlighted the danger of Arabs getting access to hazardous materials and helped the feds bag someone else as dangerous as al-Marabh.

Ali Alubeidy was a refugee from Iraq who had spent five years in a refugee camp in Saudi Arabia before being admitted to the US, where he and a friend ran a Pittsburgh used-car sales and repair business. When he injured his back changing tires, he decided to apply for a commercial driver's license – the work involved less physical strain. Since he had been a truck driver in the Iraqi Army, he seemed qualified. But his English was not yet good enough to pass the test. So, with the help of a corrupt bureaucrat in the state licensing agency, he got a friend to pass it for him. His business partner did likewise. The two spread the word about the scam to other Iraqi refugees. But in 2000 the Pennsylvania government opened an investigation of its license bureau. Then came 9/11. Information from Pennsylvania was passed to the FBI, then engaged in its first major roundup of Arab males, with inevitable results.[16] In citing Ali Alubeidy in a press conference just after the events, John Ashcroft proudly announced: "our investigation has uncovered several individuals ... who may have links to the hijackers, who fraudulently have obtained or attempted to obtain hazardous-material transportation licenses."[17] With his name all over the news, Alubeidy's business was burned down. Finally he was cleared of all serious charges and given three years probation for bribing the state bureaucrat. He managed to open another car-repair business, this time under an Italian name.[18]

NO LACK OF WANNABES?

Even before the US determined that the Detroit Four were far more than just immigration law violators, the FBI had nabbed the Lackawanna Five, named after the town near Buffalo where they lived. This set of arrests, which came fortuitously just after the first anniversary of 9/11, was such a prize catch that Bush added the Five in his State of the Union address to his list of successfully broken al-Qā'idah cells. (Unfortunately for Lackawanna's mass-tourism ambitions, its name lacked the media cachet of Hamburg, London, Paris, etc.; so the Five were renamed the Buffalo Cell.) Governor George Pataki of New York, as a re-election stunt, crowed before fourteen cameras: "These arrests send a very important message: Terrorism is real, and not just in major cities." A Buffalo city councillor who had gained notoriety for claims that a new mosque in the city was a terrorist training centre was sufficiently

vindicated for his boosters to call for a boycott of Arab-American businesses on the grounds that they were probably funding al-Qā'idah.[19]
Back in Washington, John Ashcroft gave the team that "cracked" the
case his department's top award. The result of the arrests, he claimed,
was to send "an unambiguous message that we will track down terrorists
wherever they hide." That all five were US citizens, four born in the US,
that four were married, three with children; that all had regular jobs,
and that prior to their arrests they had gone about their lives quite normally, might seem an odd way to "hide." But at least the case against
them was open and shut – the only thing missing was a serious crime
with which to charge them. However when it came to protecting the US
public, the government was not going to let a detail like that stand in its
way. After all, the five were of Yemeni descent.[20]

Children born to Yemeni parents in Lackawanna, like so many immigrant offspring, often felt split between two worlds. Hence some young
men were susceptible when Kamel Darwesh, himself an American of
Yemeni origin, preached in their local mosque that it was their duty to
defend the faith. Since Darwesh claimed to have fought in Bosnia, his
words carried weight. Early in 2001, he mobilized several men to go to
Afghanistan. Not only was this before 9/11, but the US was engaged in
dialogue with the Tāliban, and it was still legal for Americans to visit Afghanistan. There they were taught basic weapons and survival skills –
no one trained them on flight simulators or taught them how to cultivate anthrax spores. True, part of their education consisted of indoctrination in Islamist causes; but some form of brainwashing about virtue
and duty, and the perfidy of the other side, is routine in military
courses, and in Sunday sermons by US Christian "fundamentalist" pas-
tors. Perhaps the only thing remarkable was that the recruits, to their
surprise, were apparently favored with a visit by Usama himself.

One of the youths, Sahim Alwan, panicked over what he was hearing
and decided to leave early. The others followed him shortly after. Interestingly, bin Lāden had no problem with young Americans (of questionable Islamic fervor) quitting and heading home – he even offered
to help Alwan with passport problems. On their return to the US, they
agreed on a cover story – that they had been in Pakistan to study Islam.
Then came 9/11.

Sahim Alwan knew that trouble might be brewing. He had already
been in touch with a local FBI agent on a different matter. So he
phoned the agent to volunteer his help. The agent asked him to report
anything amiss. Then the FBI got an anonymous tip that some local

men had trained in Afghanistan and were involved in drugs and cigarette smuggling. It began to poke around. So did others.

Just as the US military used 9/11 to invoke the doctrine of preventive
war, i.e., the notion of knocking out places just in case they might at
some point in the future decide to become a threat, so the Justice apparatus decided to proceed to arrests and prosecutions not to solve
terror-related crimes but to anticipate them. Moreover domestic law enforcement was no longer the exclusive preserve of the police – the CIA
found 9/11 an excellent pretext, sanctified in the Patriot Act, to conduct more domestic espionage. Soon eleven different agencies were
monitoring email and voice communications to and from the Five, with
twice daily reports to the president. The FBI decided that Kamel Darwesh, the original recruiter, was "a card-carrying member of Al Qaeda" –
evoking glorious memories of the agency's Commie-hunting days. After
Mukhtar al-Bakri, one of the Five, departed for Bahrain to get married,
the CIA determined that chit-chat about the planned wedding and an
upcoming soccer game at home was code for a pending attack. Hence
its conclusion that the Lackawanna Five constituted "probably the most
dangerous terrorist group in the United States."

With the first anniversary of 9/11 drawing close, there were two possible courses of action. The Defense Department wanted the Five declared illegal combatants who could be whizzed off to one of its secret
facilities, then eventually hauled before a military tribunal before which
the government would not have to reveal sources or methods. But that
would deny the Bush administration the PR that only a public trial
could generate. The prosecutors thought they could secure a conviction for material support. But that required establishing that the youths
had actually been training in Afghanistan, rather than reading the
Qur'ān in a Pakistani madrasa.

After Mukhtar al-Bakri's wedding in Bahrain, local police burst into
the happy couple's hotel room, hauled him out of bed, and took him
to headquarters, where an Arabic-speaking FBI agent was waiting. The
young man was frightened into confessing to the Afghan escapade.
The FBI agent, of Egyptian parentage, saw al-Bakri simply as just a
scared kid who loved all things American, including junk food and
football, but who, out of fear of getting himself in trouble, had gotten
in deeper. However, to the prosecutors, his confession was the key to
open criminal proceedings. Shortly after, Sahim Alwan also admitted
to his Afghan visit. The next day the Deputy Attorney General announced the disruption of "a Qaeda-trained terrorist cell on American

soil." Yet the defendants were not remotely anti-US; they were not actually planning anything; their sole offense was to visit a training facility in Afghanistan at which bin Lāden made a speech; and once home their lives were so innocent even the prosecutor refused to refer to them as a terrorist cell.

In the final analysis the prosecution made the Five an offer – plead guilty to assisting al-Qā'idah by training in Afghanistan and face prison terms of up to ten years, or face charges of training with weapons, which could carry a term of thirty years. Against the advice of their lawyers, they agreed to the lesser charge. In their plea bargain, they parroted the party line. Not only had they received pep talks directly from Usama, but once he turned up with no less than Ayman al-Zawahiri in tow to announce that the two had joined forces. Reputedly bin Lāden explained further (to a medley of young and confused foreign recruits) that he provided the money and the global network while al-Zawahiri provided the operational skill. The government and police were jubilant. "We were looking to prevent something. And we did," the lead FBI agent said. "Obviously nothing happened. So we all did our job."[21]

The decision of the Wannabe Five to cop a plea was probably the coup de grace for Mohammed Abdullah Warsame. He hardly matched anyone's stereotype of a terrorist suspect. A Somali who had migrated to Canada in 1989 to claim refugee status, he had worked odd jobs there, married a local Somali girl, then he headed to Afghanistan. However his inspiration was hardly religious. In fact the imām of his mosque in Toronto had told him that he was nuts to go. Subsequently he enrolled to study electronics in a Minnesota college. His stint in Afghanistan, along with the fact that he had once shared accommodation with Zacarias Moussaoui, the alleged twentieth would-be hijacker, sealed his fate.[22] He became the object of a mega-investigation led by the FBI in which every conceivable agency (Homeland Security, Bureau of Immigration and Customs Enforcement, US Marshals Service, Minneapolis Police Department, St Paul Police Department, Hennepin County Sheriff's Office, the Minnesota Department of Public Safety, etc.) except the local dogcatcher was able to claim a share of the credit. He was arrested initially as a material witness against Moussaoui, then accused of attending an al-Qā'idah terrorist training camp.[23] That accusation was hardly a revelation – when FBI agents first approached him in December 2003, he volunteered the information, down to and including his training camp "alias" of Abu Maryam. Such a suspect alias was sternly reported in the court documents filed against him.[24]

Yet all it means is "father of Miriam" – it is commonplace in Arabic-speaking countries for people to adopt for popular use names derived from those of their children. Although Afghanistan probably had no more private military training facilities than Michigan, the one Warsame attended was different. Once again bin Lāden was "said to have visited the camp during the time." Hence Attorney General Ashcroft warned the public, "The charge [of material support] against Warsame is a grim reminder that al-Qaeda, aided by agents and cells in this country, continues its shadowy efforts to destroy the lives and freedoms of the people of the United States."[25]

MISFIRE?

The beauty of the "material support" concept is that just about anything anyone did involving any association, even inadvertent, with a designated "terrorist organization" could be so construed. Combining it with "conspiracy" made it even more elastic. However "material support" had a downside. It was much less sexy as a public-relations gimmick than weapons charges, for example. That is why Hemant Lakhani was such a godsend. Here was a case of "material support" that also came with sensational revelations about gunrunning, notably fearsome shoulder-fired anti-aircraft missiles whose legend the US had promoted during the anti-Soviet war in Afghanistan. Even better, it also involved "conflict diamonds" and the notorious hawāla banking system.[26] That the arms dealer was a blundering amateur conned into the operation by a paid government informant, that the diamond dealer was running money with no idea of where it came from or where it was ultimately going, that the "hawāla" aspect with purported secret codes was totally contrived by the cops, and that the entire plot would not have existed without the energetic efforts of the combined intelligence services of the US, Russia, and Britain (who apparently, in all the global terrorism scare, had nothing better to do with their time and resources) did not in the least detract from this "incredible triumph" (according to the prosecuting attorney) in the War on Terror.[27]

It began more or less simultaneously in Pakistan and India, where, quite independently, two businessmen in the garment trade faced difficult times and decided to deal with them in dubious ways. When Muhammed Habib Rehman found that the family textile business in Pakistan was collapsing, he tried to make ends meet by dabbling in drugs, but he was caught and turned into an informer by the Pakistani police. When gangster associates began to threaten, he hightailed it to the US with his family and hired on to do a similar job with the DEA and FBI. Meanwhile in India, Hemant Lakhani, a member of the community that has long dominated Mumbai's textile industry, had been losing money in everything he tried – with one exception. His investment in rupee-denominated debt owed by India to the ex-Soviet Union had produced a fair return and introduced him to business in the Ukraine. He managed to broker a sale of Ukrainian armored cars to Angola. The deal was small and took three years to consummate. But it pointed to the potential of the arms business for his financial salvation. Then fate intervened to bring Rehman and Lakhani together.[28]

When Lakhani shuttled between Mumbai and Angola, he passed via Dubai. There he bumped into an old acquaintance: a Mumbai gangster who had fled to Dubai (from where Mumbai smugglers run much of their business) after he became a suspect in a series of bomb blasts that had rocked the Mumbai financial district in 1993. With Lakhani looking for more arms business, the gangster gave him Rehman's name in the US as a possible contact. Once Lakhani made his initial pitch, Rehman phoned the FBI, who told him to set up the sting.[29]

Lakhani's enquiry had come at the perfect time for Rehman, who had against him six court judgments in four states totalling $700,000 (mainly for his children's medical bills). On top he owed $9,000 in back taxes. So he was happy to again be of service to the FBI. It told him to pose as a member of a Somali terrorist group in the market for shoulder-fired anti-aircraft missiles. Rehman asked Lakhani if he could get his hands on something like the US Stinger. When Lakhani said yes, in any quantity, Rehman took the news back to the FBI and added a few embellishments. He depicted Lakhani as a major arms trafficker who also dealt in drugs and embargoed Iraqi oil and who was probably worth in the vicinity of $400 million. At the time Lakhani was living in a modest semi-detached London house in danger of being foreclosed by the mortgage company, while trying to manage a failing clothing store. Rehman also subtly Islamized Hemant Lakhani, a practicing Hindu, by referring to him in conversations with his cop handlers as Hamed.

After Rehman informed Lakhani that his clients required twenty to fifty missiles plus two to three hundred anti-aircraft guns, Lakhani tried to mobilize his contacts in the Ukraine. Russia's Federal Security Bureau was soon on the case. After consulting with the FBI, the Russians permitted Lakhani one sample of their Igla-S portable missile, disabled and useless. Lakhani showed his catch to Rehman, who announced that the weaponry would be used in a Holy War against the US. Lakhani got into the spirit, praising bin Lāden for taking some of the stuffing out of US pretenses to grandeur and offered the suggestion that his customers use the missiles fifty at a time for maximum impact.[30] At other times he offered his new friend tanks, armored personel carriers, radar systems, and a "dirty bomb." While the prosecution seized on such statements to portray Lakhani as a fanatic, an alternative explanation is that he was a buffoon desperately trying to impress would-be clients. He had also boasted of friendships with Mu'ammar Qadhaffi and fugitive Jewish billionaire Marc Rich, and he claimed to have lunched with Tony Blair at Ten Downing Street. Even his lawyer characterized him as an "idiot."[31]

Most genuine arms-dealers are closed-mouthed – their professional and physiological lives depend on it. But Lakhani bragged that the Tamil Tigers approached him for arms – he turned them down because he only sold to governments. After his arrest, the Indian press came up with another story. In 1999, so the tale went, the Indian Army lost several artillery pieces to Pakistani fire and wanted better radar to locate enemy batteries. Refused aid by the US, which had slapped an embargo on both Pakistan and India after their nuclear tests, India allegedly asked Lakhani to get Ukrainian stuff. But the deal was aborted when the arms embargo lifted. At that point he supposedly got into shadier operations, including a plot with a notorious East African-based Indian arms-dealer to sell weapons to Sierra Leone in the face of a world embargo. That led inevitably to stories of his involvement in arms-for-conflict-diamonds deals, and with al-Qā'idah.[32]

In April 2005 Lakhani was found guilty of arms trafficking and material support, with money-laundering tossed in for good measure. The US announced triumphantly that it had broken up another plot to use anti-aircraft missiles to bring down US passenger jets. Yet Lakhani had no contacts in the Ukraine or Russia that could have provided him with missiles; he had no record of criminal arms trafficking (his sole weapons deal was legal); and all the meetings had been arranged by the US government, which put up the money, then carefully recovered it by forfeiture proceedings. Thus US cops took credit for cracking a conspiracy that they themselves had invented and financed. Nonetheless the timing was excellent – it rekindled fears over the safety of civilian aircraft and helped the FBI, which had taken considerable flak over 9/11, regain public confidence. Even better, sentence was handed down the day after the fourth anniversary of 9/11, a fact the prosecutor did not forget to point out in his public preening over the outcome.[33]

Lakhani did not take the fall alone. Also arrested was Moinuddeen Ahmed Hameed, an Indian living in Malaysia, where he was held without bail on the frightening charge of conspiring to operate an unlicensed money-transmitting business. Arrested as well and charged with the same, plus money-laundering, was his boss, Yehuda Abraham, who ran a New York gem company. Their role had been simply to covertly move abroad $30,000 of FBI cash that Rehman had provided to Lakhani to make a down-payment. Both pleaded guilty.[34] That was triple coup for the feds. First, the cops had been trying to mount a high-profile case against the gemstone industry since 1990 – when undercover agents had called on fifteen New York gem dealers and discovered that thirteen of them were willing to accept "criminal money," to operate under false names, or to avoid completely the legal reporting requirements for cash transactions. Second, newspapers were full of stories about hawāla, and the FBI wanted the public to know that they were on top of it – even if the actual incident was a cop invention. Third, the case gave the feds a chance to test new Patriot Act powers against unlicensed money changers and to demonstrate that its provisions requiring gem-dealers and jewellers to implement anti-money-laundering programs were going to be enforced.[35]

Others were equally delighted. Officials in Washington and Moscow announced that the case represented a "breakthrough" in their relations.[36] Bible John was even more exuberant. "This investigation shows that all agencies of the federal government and our international allies will work together tirelessly to keep innocent people safe."[37] Just how a con job pulled on a bankrupt old textile broker using one useless missile was supposed to "keep innocent people safe" when thousands of genuine shoulder-fired missiles were trafficked regularly on the world black market was not immediately evident. On the other hand, when George Bush II described the case as "a pretty good example of what we're doing in order to protect the American people," he was undoubtedly right. Certainly a prominent sheikh from Yemen would be inclined to agree.

CHARGES THAT REALLY STICK

Right after 9/11 the US had slapped an asset freeze on twenty-seven individuals and groups "associated with" al-Qā'idah. The next month it targeted second-tier "supporters" and front companies. Among the thirty-nine new names were those of a bakery, some sweet shops, and a couple of Yemeni honey exporters (Al Nur Honey Press and Al Shifa Honey Press). It was quite a breakthrough. After 9/11 officials had been frustrated over their inability to unscramble the massive apparatus by which bin Lāden moved his mega-millions. But then a Yemeni informant named Mohammed Alanssi denounced a former business partner who was later charged with trying to send $140,000 to Yemen hidden in a consignment of honey for the Middle East. Soon multiple criss-crossing trails attracted feds like flies to the honey.

Yemen, where al-Qā'idah was supposedly particularly strong, produces the world's finest honey; during Usamah's Sudan exile, trading in honey had been among the many flourishing enterprises that drained him of his assets; and, of course, honey was almost tailor-made to be manipulated by Islamic terrorists. Arms (or drugs or cash) could be wrapped in (hopefully leak-proof) plastic and buried in two-hundred-litre containers whose smell threw off contraband-sniffing dogs and whose viscosity discouraged manual search. Furthermore the enormous profits could be a source of direct terrorist-financing, while manipulating the prices at which honey was traded internationally was a possible way to shift funds covertly from place to place. Shortly after 9/11, two Florida university professors who, for years, had been tantalizing US Customs with tales of money-laundering via phony invoicing, discovered huge price discrepancies in the honey-trade data and collected a $2 million grant to study the honey-money problem.[38]

This did not exhaust the evidence. The owner of one of the targeted honey-trading companies was involved with the Islamic Cultural Institute of Milan, described by the US Treasury with its usual measured language as the main al-Qā'idah "station house" in Europe. Furthermore central figures in al-Qā'idah, including Abu Zubeidah, its "minister of external affairs," and Khalid al-Deek, jailed in Jordan in connection with Millennium Plot, but freed for lack of evidence, were alleged to have at various times dipped their fingers into the honey pot. Honey also helped al-Qā'idah move agents – presumably disguised as managers or traders rather than wrapped in plastic and immersed in the tubs. Perhaps suspicions were further aroused because one of the honey companies, Al Shifa, had the same name as the "chemical weapons" facility Usama had supposedly owned in the Sudan. The other one (Al Nur) had an owner who was not only Yemeni but had been one of the first Arabs to fight in Afghanistan – that, to the USA's national-security experts, was enough to clinch the case.[39] Not only was there so much proof that Usama used the honey business to stick various of his cells together, but the honey-money trail also crossed the terrorism path from another direction.

Ownership of the honey companies seemed to change as often as the identity of 9/11 "financiers." But at one point Al Nur Honey Press was supposedly owned by Abd al-Rahim al-Nashiri, allegedly the man who plotted the attack on the uss *Cole*. And al-Nashiri, so the story went, had as a senior aide a certain Yemeni sheikh who, in time off from running an orphanage and a food-for-the-hungry project that between them took care of eight thousand people, collected money for al-Qā'idah and Hamas.[40] According to no less an expert than John Ashcroft, Sheikh Muhammed Ali Hassan al-Mouyad, in addition to serving as bin Lāden's "spiritual advisor," managed to raise during a single whistle-stop at Brooklyn's Al-Farouq Mosque some $20 million. Not a bad haul from a mosque serving a distinctly low-income clientele. After the sheikh and his principal assistant were arrested in Germany, Ashcroft could reassure a testy Congressional hearing into his Terror War performance that at least one major terror-dollar channel had been closed.[41]

Certainly the charges against al-Mouyad seemed serious. He had been caught on tape lauding bin Lāden and telling a prospective contributor that his $2.5 million would be used to finance military action against the us.[42] Yet the government of Yemen reacted with disbelief. Back home the sheikh was both a senior leader of the Al Islāh party – the legal Islamist movement that cooperated with the government – and consultant to the Ministry of Religious Endowments. So Yemen lobbied Germany for his return. There were also public demonstrations in his support led by those who had benefited from his charitable activities. Germany itself seemed less than overwhelmed by the us claims, initially insisting that the evidence was inconclusive. Although Germany eventually cleared the two men for extradition to the us, its courts also stated that the sheikh had been tricked by us agents. And therein lies a strange tale.[43]

It seems that the fbi had sent Mohammed Alnassi, its original honey-money informant, to Yemen with the task of coaxing the sheikh to leave the country on a double pretext – meet a potentially big donor to his charitable centre and obtain much better treatment for his asthma and diabetes than was available at home. Alnassi arranged for the sheikh and his assistant to be picked up at Frankfort Airport in a limousine that was already wired and to check into a room at the Sheraton with hidden microphones and cameras. Then he introduced them to the potential donor, a black fbi undercover agent who claimed to be a member of the Black Panthers. The sheikh wanted money for his charity. But Alnassi had apparently told al-Mouyad that, since the man wanted to contribute $2.5 million to arm and train Islamic fighters, the only way the sheikh could get the funds was to play along. Even then the sheikh talked primarily about feeding the poor and about the work of his charity centre. Finally when asked directly by the FBI agent-cum-donor if the money would finance a jihād, he said that, God willing, he would "work in these fields, as they are my fields." That, along with words of praise for bin Lāden and empty boasts (designed to impress the donor) about his previous success as a jihādi fundraiser, was enough to justify his arrest by German police (directed by the FBI) and subsequent extradition, his assistant along with him.[44]

Back in the US, Ashcroft wanted to connect them to at least one concrete terrorist action in order to press for life sentences. Hence the FBI filed trial affidavits claiming that the sheikh hosted a wedding reception in Yemen during which a leader of Hamas gave a speech praising an operation in which five Israelis (but no Americans) had been killed.[45] That settled the issue. Another problem was to provide proof that the sheikh intended the money to go to al-Qā'idah – nothing on the tapes pointed specifically in that direction. However the sheikh, who ran a large bakery, did refer to his "oven," which, according to prosecutors, was a code word for terrorist activity – as was, they claimed, the sheikh's frequent use of the term "charity."

One potentially major hitch in the prosecution case came when Alnassi, in protest against his treatment by the US government, set himself on fire in front of the White House. He had complained that the FBI promised him loads of money, but, himself suffering from diabetes and heart trouble, he could not afford to pay his medical or drug bills. He complained further that the feds had impounded his passport and prevented him from visiting his wife, who was seriously ill with stomach cancer back in Yemen, and that they had neither protected his identity (thus opening his family to threats back home) nor given him permanent residency in the US. He described his decision to cooperate as a "big mistake" that "destroyed my life and my family's life."[46] But the prosecution got the judge to admit the tapes without the government having to face the potential embarrassment of the Alnassi himself appearing in court – where he might have had to answer questions about how often and how blatantly he had led the sheikh into the trap.

Finally in the summer of 2005 justice was done. The judge decreed that the coaxed statements were "chilling." The most serious was a tape of the sheikh at prayer saying of Jews and Americans, "Dear God, strike them dead with earthquakes [not hijacked airliners], put them in their coffins, abandon them and defeat them" – sentiments probably milder than those that ring out in southern "praise temples" with Muslims and Arabs rather than Jews and Americans as the subject. The judge sentenced the sheikh to seventy-five years for supporting Hamas and for conspiracy to support Hamas and al-Qā'idah. As he was led away, a perplexed Sheikh al-Mouyad asked in Arabic, "Your honor, what have I done?"[47]

Someone else probably asking the same question was Abad Elfgeeh, the Yemeni owner of a Brooklyn ice-cream parlor whom Mohammed Alnassi also delivered to the FBI during their crackdown on hawāla operators. It was no great feat of criminal investigation to hone in on Elfgeeh, who, over the course of several years, had wired to Yemen many millions on behalf of fellow émigrés. The funds all went through his regular bank account. But when Alnassi wandered in to ask not for a double scoop of pralines-and-cream in a sugar cone but for Elfgeeh's help in sending $100,000 to al-Mouyad, Elfgeeh asked him the source of the funds. When Alnassi, who looked like a street felon, could not give a coherent reply, Elfgeeh told him to go to Western Union. A second visit from Alnassi led to the same response. A year later the FBI arrived without a warrant – and Elfgeeh, who felt he had nothing to hide, allowed them free access to his records. Those records revealed that although the shop generated less than $200,000 per annum, over six years it had allegedly wired over $20 million, mostly to Yemen but also to Thailand, China, and Italy. Although the money was from recent immigrants to the US wanting to remit to their families or to buy houses or support businesses back home, Elfgeeh was publicly portrayed as a key link in the terror-dollar trail, responsible for funnelling millions to Hamas and al-Qā'idah. Once the publicity had done its job, the charges were reduced to running an unlicensed money-changing business and structuring bank deposits to evade the $10,000 reporting ceiling. He was found guilty on all counts.[48]

VIGILANTE ON PROZAC?

While the most publicized actions took place in major cities like New York, all over the United States the forces of order had mobilized to protect the public. On announcing his resignation in November 2004, John Ashcroft proudly cited 211 criminal charges, 478 deportations, and $124 million in frozen assets.[49] Yet there had been only one actual terrorism conviction – of Richard Reid, the shoe-bomber who tried to hotfoot it across the Atlantic. Ashcroft's fanciful total included: four US-born workers who omitted to mention prior drug convictions or other crimes when they applied to do construction work at an airport; five Mexican citizens who stole cans of baby formula from store shelves and (the real offense) sold them to a man of Arab descent for resale; two Pakistanis who had sham marriages to permit them to continue to work in a convenience store; and two New Jersey men (Arabs, naturally) who operated a small grocery store, convicted of receiving hundreds of boxes of stolen breakfast cereal, a crime that took place sixteen months before 9/11. (But, of course, terrorists had first to raise money by selling the cereal before they could make other things go snap, crackle, pop.) The cases also included one in which a Moroccan sold fake IDs to immigrants from Algeria, Eritrea, France, Palestine, Pakistan, and Morocco – all of those convicted of buying his IDs were added to terrorism list. Probably the greatest proportion of convictions were ordinary immigration offenses. And the median sentence was two weeks.[50]

Even those numbers represented a distortion upwards. In normal times, many of the charges for banal offenses would never have been laid; and if they had been, the defendants would have often been able to beat (minor) raps. But in the post 9/11 context, fear on the part of the defendants, exacerbated considerably by the threat of being declared an enemy combatant, led to guilty pleas on trivial charges. These permitted the government to claim resounding blows against terrorism while leaving people whose offense might have been welfare fraud or violation of visa restrictions with a lifelong taint of "terrorist activity."[51]

When reporters queried these oddities, a federal prosecutor responded: "Bona fide terrorism is a matter of semantics. I don't think you can draw conclusions based on what a person is convicted of." Indeed. In a further explanation of the inner workings of the justice system, he noted: "We charged them with readily provable offenses ... rather than what they might actually have done." In other words, the public ought to be aware that behind each person successfully prosecuted for driving under the influence might be a power-drunk Islamic terrorist plotting to explode a truckload of ammonia fertilizer in a traffic tunnel. After all, the prosecutor continued: "if we've disrupted one part of what might have developed into a cell, we've done something important in prevention."[52]

The Justice Department concurred. One of its spokesman observed that, "Today, in order to protect the lives of Americans at the earliest opportunity, the government may charge potential terror suspects with lesser offences to remove them from our communities." This was not unprecedented. The US had once, so the mantra went, "prosecuted Al Capone for tax evasion to remove him from the streets."[53] A better analogy would be if the US had decided to curb bootlegging in the 1920s by charging everyone with an Italian surname with vagrancy, then locking them up on Ellis Island.

The data were also misleading on another level. As soon as a prosecution started, the government could scarcely not lose no matter how a judge ruled or a jury decided. That was well illustrated with the case of Sami Omar al-Hussayen, son of a former Saudi Minister of Education, who had come to the US in 1995 for graduate studies.[54] Between working on his PhD and taking care of his growing family, he had volunteered at the Islamic Assembly of North America. There he set up a website to promote study of Islam. Among the many links was one to another website established by a group the US subsequently designated a terrorist organization. Another link went to a site where, among a large volume of postings, were four short documents written by radical clerics discussing the wars in Chechnya and Palestine – one of those postings sanctioned suicide attacks, although without endorsement from the operators of the site. First al-Hussayen was charged with material support; then the government added claims of visa violations. As a foreign student he was not allowed to work; and somehow volunteering time at a religious and educational institution constituted "work." He spent 1.5 years in jail before a federal jury acquitted him in 2004.[55] On the surface that might seem another embarrassing failure. But it succeeded in demonstrating to Muslim males that the Justice Department had the power to destroy their lives. Prior to his legal vindication, al-Hussayen's wife and children were deported; his studies were interrupted, rendering his previous work useless; his friends were scared off; his reputation was ruined; and, of course, he had spent eighteen months under lock and key. Ultimately the government agreed to drop the immigration charge, too, if he in turn agreed not to appeal his deportation order.[56]

The handling of cases involving Muslim males contrasted sharply with the one involving Dr Robert Goldstein. After his wife phoned the cops to say that Goldstein had threatened to kill her, they searched the house but found nothing unusual – just forty weapons, including handguns, 50-calibre machine guns, armor-piercing rockets, more than thirty explosive devices, including hand grenades and a five-gallon gasoline bomb with a timer and a wire attached. They also found a list of Islamic worship centres in the area with a drawing of one of them, the Islamic Society of Pinellas County, along with instructions on how to conduct an attack and what to wear during it. Goldstein insisted that, to make a statement for "his people" against Arabs and Muslims, he was planning "kill all the 'rags' at this Islamic Education center." To achieve what he called "ZERO residual presence," the plan was to bomb the building, then shoot or stab any survivors.

Goldstein had help. His dentist allegedly wanted to hone his skills at extracting diseased tissue; while the machine guns were provided by a fellow member of Goldstein's synagogue. Yet no one talked of a Pinnellas County Jewish Terror Cell. With high-paid legal counselling, Goldstein made a deal – he pleaded guilty to plotting to blow up a mosque, conspiring to violate civil rights, planning to damage religious property, and possessing unregistered firearms, but not to terrorism or even attempted murder. That seemed perfect fair since, as Dr Goldstein noted frequently at his trial, he was in a precarious state of mental health requiring a number of prescription drugs, including Prozac. As his attorney commented, the end of the trial "will help Dr. Goldstein put behind him an extremely tumultuous, troubling and stressful time in his life." Apparently the tumultuous, troubling, and stressful time faced by the Islamic centres in Florida and elsewhere was not worth mentioning.[57]

Epilogue

By popular consensus – how that was shaped is another matter – the font of Islamic Evil today is (was?) Usama bin Lāden. His cloven hoof-prints can be found at the scene of a series of ugly acts, whether actually perpetrated or narrowly averted, in East Africa, the Middle East, Europe, and Asia. Before the US and its closest allies could circle the wagons, bin Lāden attacked the very heartland not only to wreak death and destruction but, so he hoped, to bring the United States itself trembling to its economic knees – hence the World Trade Center as his most outstanding (in all senses) target.

After 9/11 the US, both its government and its general public, waited with bated breath to see how and where Usama would strike next. Would it be a supertanker burning in New Orleans harbor; a dirty bomb going off on New Year's Eve in Times Square; a truckload of ammonia fertilizer exploding in the Lincoln Tunnel at rush hour; another passenger plane crashing, this time into the Three Mile Island or the Los Angeles Library Tower?[1] Bin Lāden could hide among his wild followers in the Afghan-Pakistan border region or maybe in Kashmir before issuing orders through ultra-sophisticated channels that intelligence experts were unable to monitor. (Carrier pigeons perhaps?) Meanwhile the rest of the world could do little but hunt frantically for would-be perpetrators of more tragedies like Bali, Madrid, Casablanca, Sharm al-Sheikh, and London, and for the money that made these events possible.

Although Usama's schemes reputedly required megabucks, there seemed ample sources – secret funding from his fabulously rich family and from other sympathetic "oil sheeks," profits from his thriving enterprises in places like the Sudan, the take from rackets ranging from drug dealing to currency counterfeiting to trafficking in conflict diamonds, etc. This money had to be moved, hidden, then made available where and when he and his Islamic Brigade required. The usual co-conspirators in offshore banking were eager to aid and abet, as were more esoteric types like hawāla operators. However, the most important technique was Islamic charities pretending to be doing relief work around the world.

Thus, the US mobilized not just on the military but also on the financial fronts. The government escalated a worldwide program against money-laundering put in place during the Drug War and added new measures specifically to go after the Islamic terror-dollar, while private citizens joined the battle with massive lawsuits designed to bankrupt the financiers of terror. The targets included not just al-Qā'idah but also its main affiliates, well-known ones like Palestine's Hamas and Lebanon's Hizbullāh, along with less publicized but potentially just as threatening groups such as Somalia's al-Ittihād al-Islāmiyya or Indonesia's Jemmah Islamiyah. All in all, it was a chilling story with only one flaw – virtually everything in it was false.

The role of bin Lāden in recent terrorist outrages is not only grossly exaggerated, in many instances it is completely fictional. This is not to suggest he is/was a nice guy – he preached a violent and retrograde ideology, exhorted and encouraged at least some of the crimes imputed to him, and applauded them after the fact. There were/are probably plenty of raps on which to haul him before a genuine court of justice (by definition, outside the US). But for a variety of reasons it was/is convenient to give him credit for actions in which he had at best a peripheral role, frequently none at all. Blowing bin Lāden metaphorically out of all proportion before blowing him physically off the face of the Earth is consistent with a US tradition of personifying infamy by inventing supervillains with whom superheroes do battle, inevitably to a victory that, if not real, is certainly loudly and publicly declared. While the practice may be politically expedient (and profitable for the infotainment industry) in the short run, it obscures understanding and therefore impedes sensible action in the long.

Similarly with al-Qā'idah. The original construct was built on myths about "criminal organizations" as large-scale, transnational, centrally run entities, which were extrapolated from the criminal justice to the "national security" fields. Just as crime is almost always the preserve of individuals or of loose ad hoc associations without serious long-term staying power, so, too, with "terrorist" groups. To the extent that relationships ever do exist between various militant factions beyond the merely rhetorical, they are temporary alliances of convenience among those with essentially local grudges rather than the result of those groups (usually guided by men with huge egos) being departments or subsidiaries of some hierarchically controlled international conspiracy. Under these circumstances to attempt to combat them using measures created to deal with either countries (with a geophysical existence) or organizations (with a supposedly corporate one) is like furiously throwing lethal punches in the air and hoping there are not too many innocent bystanders, or at least no independent witnesses, in the general vicinity. Even worse, by effectively creating, then advertising, an al-Qā'idah brand name, the US and the West at large gave local groups a global significance they otherwise would not likely have had, guaranteeing further sets of imitators in the future.

The notion that an emerging Islamintern targeted the economic foundations of modern industrial civilization is equally silly. The World Trade Center was chosen – probably by Mohammed Atta – not because it was the throbbing heart of US capitalism, but because it was obvious, dramatic, and vulnerable, and the object of a previous attempt.[2] In fact attacking World Trade Centers seems almost a reflex action for insurgent groups – a unit of Sri Lanka's Tamil Tigers bombed the Colombo namesake four years before 9/11. Yet once politicians and the media ran amok with the al-Qā'idah threat to the world economy, it was easy for radical groups to crank up the fear factor – for example, by threats against oil installations in the Gulf States that they probably never had the wherewithal to carry out.[3]

As to the idea that bin Lāden hoped to force the US to waste precious resources on its military, therefore bringing the country to the point of bankruptcy as he had the USSR, not only is that a caricature of what led to the breakup of the Soviet Union (and an absurd inflation of bin Lāden's significance in the anti-Soviet struggle in Afghanistan), but it suggests on the part of US elites a reluctance to lavish on the Pentagon tax money (little of it theirs), which is difficult to discern in recent history even before bin Lāden leaped onto the world stage. If anything, the reverse is true – the military and their sponsoring industries were chafing at the bit for another round of spending hikes (and more opportunities for the usual types of graft) just when Usama fortuitously came along.[4] It was no accident that General Peter Schoomaker, the US Army's chief of staff, announced that the 9/11 attack had "a huge silver lining."[5]

Nor did the 9/11 attacks drive the US into a recession – technically speaking, it was already in one. In fact the US agencies who monitor the business cycle announced the recession officially over less than two months after the destruction of the Twin Towers, suggesting that bin Lāden might deserve more credit for ending than starting a downturn. But blaming, for example, the stock market's dismal performance on bin Lāden was a great way to divert public attention from a series of corporate scandals. And the story about the enormously negative impact of 9/11 provided an excellent pretext to bring in an emergency tax-cut package to stimulate not the US economy in general but the investment portfolios of well-heeled Republican supporters of the Bush administration.

Furthermore, far from a harbinger of a coordinated global terror challenge, 9/11 looks like a lucky hit. Despite recurrent tales of how such a sophisticated attack must have had the help of a major intelligence agency, all that was required was four committed individuals with some basic knowledge of how to fly, fifteen dupes who were just along for the ride, so to speak, and publicly accessible airline schedules, plus the freak occurrence of airlines actually running on time. Even Mohammed Atta seems to have been winging it, no pun intended. About a year and a half before the attacks he tried to get a US$650,000 government loan to buy a small plane to convert into a crop duster. No matter how much pesticide it might hold, it would hardly make a dent in the World Trade Center. To make sure he would remain unnoticed, he threw a temper tantrum when the Department of Agriculture official in Florida told him that he had to be a US citizen to qualify.[6]

Most other recent attacks by Islamist militants have been amateur hour, when not simply broken up by police and intelligence services who tracked the plotters using traditional means. When successful outrages do occur, rather than a manifestation of rising Islamic hordes, they are (or, at least, were) more symptoms of the opposite, of the fact that the violent Islamist current had already peaked before 9/11. Losing public support as Islamic activists shifted attention from political confrontation to social struggle through educational and charitable work, the remaining hardcore militants tried to reaffirm their importance by spectacular efforts that were actually counterproductive. As with the 1997 Luxor massacre, grotesque crimes do far more to alienate local populations than to cause them to rally to the side of the militants. Similarly 9/11 would probably have knocked much of the remaining wind out of the sails of radical political Islam if the US (faithfully backed by Britain) had not decided to put it on life-support through a series of outrages of its own.

Since there is no grand, hierarchical transnational "organization" plotting atrocities like 9/11 (or Bali or Casablanca or Madrid or London), there is no collective treasury. At most what happened is that someone would show up in Afghanistan to receive a nod of approval and perhaps some pocket change, then go off to finish a job already started. Yet in much the way law enforcement routinely produces wild guesstimates of the financial resources of its godfather-of-the-month – the legendary hoards of Colombian narco-baron Pablo Escobar were pinpointed at between $3–14 billion – so bin Lāden's personal wealth was grossly inflated. Even the Congressional 9/11 Commission eventually agreed.[7] And most allegations about "al-Qaeda" rackets have turned out to be fatuous. Instead, "Islamic militants" (who are almost always motivated by wordly political concerns) follow the norms of insurgent groups throughout history – fundraising is largely opportunistic and localized; it is tailored to meet particular short-term needs; it is based mainly on petty crime, minor-league scams, or donations, sometimes voluntary, sometimes coerced, from people in the general geographical, theological, or anthropological vicinity; and it may also involve minor trafficking on local or regional black markets that are themselves of marginal significance in the overall scheme of economic life.[8]

In any case, horrendous acts do not require humungous sums. Materials for the 1993 World Trade Center attack, which killed six people and did about $500 million in damage cost $400 to assemble. The only outside funding came a full year before the attacks, when Khalid Sheikh Mohammed, then not affiliated with any known radical group, out of his legal salary sent $660 to his nephew Ramzi Yousef – because Yousef was strapped for cash.[9]

Since there are no great terror treasuries, the idea of huge sums of terror-dollars washing through the global financial system is equally chimerical. The role of things like hawāla, the "underground banking system" that operates openly with witnesses and records, is grossly misrepresented; while Islamic banks and charities are smeared and caricatured.

The assault on Islamic charities, which have had their accounts frozen, their principals jailed, and their contributors frightened off, is particularly problematic. With cutbacks in government services across the Middle East and North Africa, often the result of pressure from Western creditors, no other institutions can provide essential services to alleviate extreme poverty. In the Gulf States, the biggest international source of Islamic charitable funds, there have been recent moves to turn the charitable donation into a tool for tracking individual finances, as if it were simply the equivalent of the regulatory-and-reporting requirements now common in the West. Not only is that a religious insult (since only Allāh is supposed to witness acts of charitable giving), it can be interpreted as part of the grand design of the neocon artists running US foreign policy to "reform" Islam by making the shopping mall rather than the mosque the place in which the holiest rites are performed.

Of course, if and when possible, sums of money in the hands of those who can be genuinely suspected of planning terrorist outrages (as opposed to those whose objectives are simply regarded by various authorities as politically inconvenient) should be frozen. But neither fact nor logic suggest that this makes sense as a *primary* preventive strategy. And the very notion of combating terrorism (however opportunistically the concept is defined and however selectively the resulting definition is applied) by chasing the money can be a delusion and a diversion. For several years prior to 9/11, the US Treasury and the CIA pursued the alleged bin Lāden billions. Yet their earlier efforts did nothing to stop the carnage. Possibly the reverse – the effort might simply have served to dissipate investigative resources by chasing green herrings. Nor is the post-9/11 practice of declaring freezes on the basis, it seems, of names drawn from a fez likely to produce better results in the future.

None of the trials of alleged al-Qā'idah personnel showed evidence of generous packages of external aid. Even those identified as the 9/11 hijackers lived by low-wage jobs, petty scams, or begging money from their families. Once Mohammed Atta and a fellow pilot in the World Trade Center attack got to Florida for flying lessons, they stayed in cheap motels, did their own washing at coin-operated laundromats, and bought groceries so they could avoid restaurant bills.[10]

If the sums involved are relatively small, tracing and then seizing them is tactically very difficult – the smaller the sum, the bigger the problem. This is all the more the case given that "terror money" (unlike, by definition, criminal money) is largely of legal origin. The elaborate reporting apparatus was conceived to detect (even if it usually does not) funds that are inherently suspect, for example, sums not commensurate with the normal business activity of a financial institution's customer. With money destined for terrorist operations, those considerations will rarely apply. And obviously a freeze only works to prevent money from leaving a financial institution. If a sum deemed suspicious because of its origins comes into a bank, there may be time to activate appropriate procedures. But if money of quite legitimate origin arrives, rarely if ever will anyone have the information to invoke a freeze until after it has left the institution and been employed in some nefarious act – at which point even US Treasury and Customs sleuths would have trouble rationalizing a freeze-and-seize order.

In any case, even if war chests are occasionally grabbed, their very small size makes them easy to replace – whereas people ready and able to undertake the deeds are, under normal circumstances, rare indeed. Ultimately the principal asset of those carrying out terrorist acts is not money but commitment, and commitment cannot be frozen in a bank account. However it can be renewed, almost indefinitely, when the US engages in mass incarcerations and torture of innocents, incinerates villages, flattens cities, and insults and degrades the cultural and religious heritages of other peoples in the name of its War on Terror.

Still, that was not the official conclusion. If there were difficulties finding the terror-dollar trail, that was taken as proof not of the absence of great hoards of terror-dollars in the hands of great hordes of Muslim fanatics but that the terrorist-financing links created by bin Lāden were "elusive and impenetrable"[11] and that "terrorist financing links in the United States are more pervasive than … previously thought."[12] Hence the call for ever stronger measures and more resources until the battlefield becomes so littered with the financial equivalent of unexploded ordnance that for decades to come it will be a perilous place indeed onto which any ordinary citizen might inadvertently wander.[13]

Indeed, the notion of a global financier of terrorism has proven marvelously adaptable. In the US, when the drums of war began sounding again in 2005, this time directed towards Iran, Condoleeza Rice proved herself a worthy successor to Colin Powell as Secretary of State. To the lies he told about Iraq's fabled weapons of mass destruction, she not only added tales of Iranian ones but went on to describe the country as "in effect, the central banker of terrorism."[14]

Of course, all the hype over the money trail has another purpose, which it serves admirably, namely to give politicians, police, and prosecutors a weapon with which to go after people whose opinions and actions, even if legal and nonviolent, are politically unwelcome. Take, for

example, the case of Sami al-Arian, a tenured University of South Florida computer science professor who was for years harassed by the FBI
and the media as a reputed kingpin of Palestine's Islamic Jihad, fired
after 9/11, then charged, along with three other Palestinians who had
taken refuge in the land of the free, for "material support" as well as
for running an organized crime ring. Al-Arian, the indictment claimed,
"directed the audit of all moneys and properties of PIJ throughout the
world." Once the case came to trial, the usual "national security experts"
plus a bevy of Israeli spooks descended on Tampa to bolster the case.
And the prosecutor, no slouch when it came to detecting what might
turn on a jury, even referred to the defendants as the equivalent of
Mafia dons. But the prosecution must have done a lousy job of screen-
ing potential jurors – at least some managed to notice that the government never managed to draw a line between the raising of the
money and its arrival in the hands of PIJ gunmen. With the jury
divided, the prosecution case failed against all defendants. Not to
fear, the government decided to just deport them anyway – and presumably leave it to Israel to mete out "justice" once they were back in
Occupied Palestine.[15]

If the conventional version of events, and of how to prevent repeti-
tions, is fatally flawed, it is important to know why myth and legend
have so overwhelmed fact and common sense. Part of the problem derives from that fact that anti-terrorism stands on the cusp between law
enforcement and intelligence domains, each with their own mindsets,
methods, and agendas. Police tend to believe that they are facing a
wave of crime-run-amok – abetted by corrupt lawyers, shrugged off by a
complacent public, and condoned in the breach by ignorant or unprin-
cipled politicians. Although to drive home the problem, police in the
West may embellish liberally, it is uncommon (although, alas, far from
unknown) for them to resort to total fabrication. More likely they just
massage the evidence or accidentally lose something that might point
in a contrary direction. Furthermore, they are subject to checks and
balances. Not only might they face an occasional well-informed defense
attorney, but many mainstream reporters have learned through bitter
experience to take what the police say (at least in criminal cases) not
with just a grain of salt but with the whole shaker.

By contrast, it is part of the duty of intelligence officers to lie, generally with impunity. They are largely immune from courtroom cross-
examination; and the media reflexively swallow their tales, particularly
when patriotism is invoked. Thus the phrase "intelligence agencies

suspect" becomes a stamp of veracity rather than a warning of the converse, when even a casual glance at the record might suggest taking any such story not with just a grain of salt, not even with the whole shaker, but with an option on the output of all the world's salt mines.[16]

Worse, intelligence agencies fool even skeptics by feeding stories through NGOs and tax-exempt "think tanks" stuffed with out-of-office types, future government-post aspirants, political hangers-on, and ex-spooks put out to greener pasture. The media then cite these "objective" sources, and politicians can use the resulting public response as justification for predetermined initiatives. The consequent difficulty in separating fact from fable, news from newspeak, and accidental misinformation from spook-sponsored disinformation inevitably affects both diagnosis of cause and, more to the point, prescriptions for dealing with the consequences.

The problem goes far beyond deliberate invention. What appears to have happened is that recent US administrations, unsure of how to respond to a new (but predictable) threat, even one of their own creation, began looking for a shorthand description to make it both readily explicable to the public (and to themselves) and seemingly amenable to control through existing methods. These methods were partly military, partly legal – the first evolved from the Cold War, the second largely from the Crime War, both of which had their own self-sustaining myths. This occurred at more or less the same time that bin Lāden, too, discovered the magic of the media and the advantages of inventing and embellishing stories about his own accomplishments – although, compared to spokespersons for the US government, he was the epitome of honesty. In effect the two sides began to play off against each other. Then other interested parties began to hitch their own agendas to the al-Qā'idah bandwagon, which soon had enough momentum to roll on its own. Much as with the Mafia legend during the twentieth century, eventually there were too many individuals and institutions, in government and in academia, writers of police reports, and composers of fiction with too much at stake in the prevailing belief structure to let go. To do so would draw down on their heads the same sort of ridicule as undoubtedly accompanied those in late medieval Europe who suggested the Earth might not be flat after all.

Some of the uses to which the al-Qā'idah legend were put are simply foolish. Elements have been used, for example, to try to reduce the world supply of gemstones outside the control of the diamond cartel by spreading fear over "conflict diamonds" and, by the world's luxury-goods manufacturers, to try to protect their pretense and profit from cheap copies by claiming Islamic terrorists benefit from their sale. Zealots leaped on stories about al-Qā'idah flooding the world with narcotics to ensure that Drug Warriors did not lose their place in the limelight to Terror Warriors. In fact the two were subtly merged; US warships now seize vessels in international waters claiming that they are looking for drug dealers working for Usama.[17] More recently animal-rights activists have tried to blame al-Qā'idah (along with Colombian drug "cartels") for trafficking in endangered birds.[18]

Some uses of the tales have been more serious in terms of their long-term damage. Witness the alacrity with which the anti-money-laundering industry and the law-enforcement apparatus leaped on the terror-dollar bandwagon to advance their agenda. So, too, the intelligence agencies seeking a strongly reinforced and hopefully (for them) permanent mandate to expand espionage at home and abroad without even the minimal pre-9/11 constraints and to build and access giant, multifunction databases.[19]

Some critics of US action decry the direction of the War on Terror on the grounds that it is not only immoral but counterproductive to true US national interests· on the geopolitical, financial, and economic planes. This is an illusion. There is no such thing as "national interest." Policy is the result of the to-ing and fro-ing of coalitions of vested interest groups. Even if losses to society as a whole egregiously exceed benefits, the point is that those who lose are quite distinct from those who gain – who put their own interests first.

Certainly the myths and misconceptions about the terror threat have had political advantages to those at the top of the power ladder. Scrambling the jets, launching the missiles, and sending in the Marines are the easiest and most dramatic ways for a leadership, caught with its proverbial pants around its ankles or its nose in children's stories about pet goats, to be seen doing something serious. Furthermore 9/11 provided a perfect pretext for the Bush administration to shift the main focus on the Terror War from the Clinton era's use of legal initiatives backed by covert action and the occasional air strike to the current method of waging total war.

More than that, there is obviously *some* truth in the accusation that the military bureaucracy and its corporate camp followers (some might invert the positions) were eager to seize the occasion to reverse a decade or more of post-Cold War budget cuts and mission shifts. The Pentagon abhors a vacuum as much as does nature. For a time the generals pinned hopes on the Drug War – they spoke gravely about how Andean countries represented a Ho Chi Minh Trail for pushers, while arms makers advertised the adaptability of their equipment to the new challenge of drug interdiction. But neither the Drug War nor a series of Orwellian War-for-Peace skirmishes in the Clinton era could suffice. Hence the alacrity with which the Pentagon responded when the opportunity appeared once more to confront the Empire of Evil – which had conveniently changed its colors from Red to Green. To counter Islamic militants in Toyota Land Cruisers, it rationalized the weaponization of space. To deal with suicide bombers in crowded urban areas, it proposed a new generation of tactical nuclear arms along with the doctrine of preventive warfare.[20] To respond to the apparent proliferation of al-Qā'idah cells worldwide, the assistant to the Joint Chiefs of Staff warned Americans to expect a "long war" of at least twenty years, akin to the old Cold War on which the military-industrial complex had waxed so fat. Not surprisingly, 9/11 was followed not only by a series of sharp hikes in the military budget but by a dramatic acceleration of sales pitches by US arms manufacturers eager to use the new world assertiveness of the US military to get the drop on their international competitors.[21]

Any roundup of the usual suspects generally puts the US and UK oil companies, too, in the dock. With them the issue is rarely guilt or innocence, merely how long the indictment papers ought to be. Today the oil barons stand accused of plotting a lunge for the Earth's dwindling hydrocarbon resources, a lunge that took, among other forms, plans for gas pipelines across Afghanistan and schemes to take over the state-owned and state-managed oil reserves in Iraq, places that were, by the oddest coincidence, the first and second declared fronts in the military part of the War on Terror.

Of course, neither the control of nor the commercial benefits from oil depend on actually owning fields or operating wells. Moreover the less the oil pumped through the pipelines and in and out of tankers, other things equal, the higher the prices and the greater the profit margins. In that case, logically, the worse the job the Marines do of guarding oil wells in Occupied Iraq for example, the happier the oil companies ought to be. That the rate of discovery of new oil has probably peaked and, as a result, fresh supplies are lagging behind the currently rapid growth of worldwide demand as geological realities overtake oil company accounting fantasies, that after two decades of glut the balance of market power is shifting to the producer countries, that producers are heavily concentrated in the Islamic world, and that emerging great powers like China and India are eyeing the Middle East and Central Asia to accommodate their own burgeoning needs combine to form a rather obvious incentive for showing the flag. Oil is the equivalent of the Holy Grail to Western industrial "civilization," and most of it happens to be located in the same general area that inspired past Crusades – even if the oil companies (and their corporate allies in banking and oil service) are eventually found guilty more as ex post profiteers than as ex ante conspirators.

Nor is it possible to ignore the pro-Israel lobby in all its manifestations – from AIPAC (the America-Israel Public Affairs Committee) to the ADL (the Anti-Defamation League of the B'nai Brith), from the numerous and often thinly disguised Political Action Committees to a series of tax-exempt "think tanks" like the Jewish Institute of National Security Affairs.[22] Various constituents work sometimes in tandem, more often simply by shared consensus, so that it may be misleading to think of it as a lobby at all in the traditional sense. Nonetheless that collective set of pro-Israel institutions has been eminently successful in placing friends in positions of great influence in successive US governments, in guaranteeing for Israel a rich stream of economic benefits at taxpayer expense, in securing for the Israeli military open access to US arms and military technology, and in steering US policy in directions that complement and enhance Israeli strategic objectives, while smearing its critics as "anti-Semites."[23]

Once again a qualification is necessary. It is foolish to present the US as a victim of a tiny state with a population of seven million, no matter how many nuclear weapons or captive Congressmen that state possesses. The Israel-made-us-do-it school of US nationalism not only shifts responsibility for US actions off the US government but substitutes simple-minded conspiracy theory for the hard work of understanding just how policy is conceived, formulated, legislated, implemented, and assessed. Ultimately the pro-Israel lobby stands fairly accused only of doing effectively what it is supposed to do – responsibility for the results ultimately rests with the society that permits these results to occur.

Nonetheless it is important to give credit where it is really due – and the pro-Israel lobby does its job remarkably well. Not least of its accomplishments is to react to every crisis or pseudo-crisis by agitating the US mind with calumnies about Muslim zealots and Arab fanatics.[24]

Understanding acts of terror, the motives of the perpetrators, and the constituents of a sensible response are clouded not merely by the extent to which vested interest groups manipulate events to advance their own agendas but by the fact that in their hands language itself is a weapon. The terms used (repeatedly) define the parameters of both official discourse and public understanding and are selected not to elucidate but to provoke an emotional response. Few are so effective in foreclosing sensible debate than "terrorist organization." Simply put, there is no such thing as a "terrorist organization." Terrorism is not an objective of political action but one of several means that might be employed by the dangerous, the devious, or the merely disenfranchised to advance political ends.

Furthermore the term "terrorist organization" functions much like "organized crime" to shift attention away from exploring political, social, and economic conditions that breed the acts, and therefore away from attempting to understand what motivates the perpetrators or what they seek to achieve. Thus it pre-empts a possibly inconvenient or embarrassing answer. Instead the focus is on the evil inherent in the actors (and, by inference, in others of similar genotype). This strategy in turn automatically biases instruments with which to respond toward the tools of repression rather than the means of remediation. The consequence is a "War on Terror" conducted in such a way that its trail of dead bodies far exceeds those produced by the acts that initiated the cycle, thus assuring its perpetuation.

Notes

1 See, for example, "Sept. 11 Showed Chinks in US Economic Armor," Stratfor, *Global Intelligence Report*, 11 September 2002. This theme continued to be stressed by analysts for years after. See, for example, Don Van Natta Jr and Leslie Wayne, "Al Qaeda Seeks to Disrupt US Economy, Experts Warn," *New York Times*, 2 August 2004.
2 See the comments of Michael Chertoff, then assistant US attorney general and soon to be Secretary of Homeland Security as reported in *Financial Times*, 10 September 2002.
3 This is essentially the case against bin Lāden posted by the British government on its official website, 5 October 2001, under the title "Responsibility for the Terrorist Atrocities in the United States, 11 September 2001." At least the British government had the decency to state that the document "does not purport to provide a prosecutable case against Usamah Bin Laden in a court of law." Similar caricatures produced by the US government contained no such disclaimer. See *New York Times*, 5 October 2001. Much the same story won a Pulitzer Prize in 2002. See also Steven Engleberger's "One Man and a Web of Violence," *New York Times*, 14 January 2001, with "research" contributed by Judith Miller.
4 *Knight Ridder Washington Bureau*, 25 September 2001.
5 Still the best work making these points is Jason Burke's *Al-Qaeda: Casting a Shadow of Terror* (London, 2003). Probably its only serious flaw was its

prediction that 9/11 was the beginning of a mass terror movement by thousands of disaffected Muslim youth.

6 Some of the sources are diagnosed in Karen Armstrong's *Holy War: The Crusades and Their Impact on Today's World* (New York, 1988).

7 Paul Robinson, "The Good News about Terrorism," *The Spectator*, 4 February 2005.

8 The Center for Strategic and International Studies examined Saudis heading for Iraq to fight the US and discovered that almost all were radicalized by the US invasion. (Reuters, "Iraq Invasion Radicalized Saudi Fighters: Report," *ABC News*, 19 January 2005).

9 This was long the opinion of French investigating magistrate Jean-Louis Brugière, dean of Europe's anti-terrorism judges. In sharp contrast to the US party line, he stressed that groups "micro-finance" rather than act from some central treasury.

10 See especially Malise Ruthven in *Fundamentalism: The Search for Meaning* (Oxford, 2004).

11 For a reasoned explanation, see Mahmood Mamdani, *Good Muslim, Bad Muslim: America, the Cold War and the Roots of Terror* (New York, 2004), 47–50. For a critical examination of the translation of jihād as holy war, see Rudolph Peters, *Islam and Colonialsm: The Doctrine of Jihād in Modern History* (The Hague, 1979), 3–4, and Bruce Lawrence, "Reconsidering Holy War (Jihād) in Islam," *Islam and Christian-Muslim Relations*, vol. 1 (1990), 261–8. The term was used in many different ways in many different contexts, and acted upon accordingly.

12 See, for example, David Ray Griffin, *The 9/11 Commission Report: Omissions and Distortions* (Northampton, MA: 2005) for a compilation of questions and enigmas about the events and their causes, some of which are useful and on target, some of which are off the wall. For an attempt to weave it all into a grand conspiracy, see Michael Ruppert, *Crossing the Rubicon: The Decline of the American Empire and the End of the Age of Oil* (Vancouver, 2004).

13 A work that pioneered much of the discussion of the use of "crime control" measures as a disguised form of foreign policy is Ethan Nadelman's *Cops across Borders: The Internationalization of US Criminal Law Enforcement* (University Park, PA: 1993).

14 Robert Allison, *The Crescent Obscured: The United States and the Muslim World 1776–1815* (Oxford, 1995), 57. For a detailed examination, see R.T. Naylor, "Ghosts of Terror Wars Past? Crime, Terror and America's First Clash with the Saracen Hordes," *Crime, Law & Social Change* (forthcoming).

15 For a review of the history and logic, see R.T. Naylor, *Patriots & Profiteers: On Economic Warfare, Embargo-Busting and State Sponsored Crime* (Toronto, 1999) or *Economic Warfare: Sanctions, Embargoes and Their Human Cost* (Boston, 2002).

16 This is one of the main themes in R.T. Naylor, *Wages of Crime: Black Markets, Illegal Finance and the Underworld Economy* (Montreal and Ithaca, NY: 2002, 2004).

17 Widely reported, for example, see "Batman Takes Aim at Osama," *ABC News*, 14 February 2006, abcnews.go.com/Entertainment/story?id=1616836&page=1.

18 This is not just a US phenomenon. Britain with its Belmarsh prison for the indefinite detention of terrorism suspects, some of whom have been driven mad, is hardly an model alternative. See Tariq Ali, "The Logic of Colonial Rule," *Guardian*, 23 July 2005.

CHAPTER ONE

1 Drought causes famine in Afghanistan. FAO, 13 June 2001; www.fao.org/NEWS/GLOBAL/gwo105-e.htm. For a personal account of the famine, see Mohsen Makhmalbaf's account of "dying people covering the streets like carpets" in "The Buddha Was not Demolished in Afghanistan; It Collapsed out of Shame," www.facets.org/asticat?function=web&catname=facets&web=features&path=/directors/makhmalbafmohsen/thebuddhacollapses.

2 www.whitehouse.gov/news/releases/2001/11/20011117.html.

3 After reporters could view the actual scene, major media networks quickly dropped the high-tech fantasies but without any public retraction. See Éric Laurent, *La Face Cachée du 11 Septembre* (Paris, 2004), 35–9.

4 For the 1998 negotiations following the embassy bombings, see United States Department of State Memo (Secret State 220495 281515Z) of 28 November 1998 declassified and released on 10 March 2005. These negotiations were aborted, then renewed in 2001 virtually up to the eve of the US invasion.

5 One of the more comprehensive books on the anti-Soviet war is Steve Coll's *Ghost Wars* (New York, 2004).

6 For a comprehensive overview of the US strategy, stretching back decades, to cultivate radical Islam as an anti-Communist tool, see Robert Dreyfuss, *Devil's Game: How the United States Helped Unleash Fundamentalist Islam* (New York, 2006).

7 Afghan history was largely neglected in the West, except for some British Colonial Office-supported work with its own agenda, until after World

War II. Even then it was fairly superficial – by contrast, the most detailed work was done in the Soviet Union. An older excellent work in English drawing on much Soviet research is Vartan Gregorian, *The Emergence of Modern Afghanistan* (Stanford, 1969). Since the 1980s there has been a deluge of works in English. Among the best general recent histories is Angelo Rasanayagam, *Afghanistan: A Modern History* (London, 2003). It is marred by some quicky post-9/11 add-ons. A good work with a focus almost entirely on more modern political developments is Ralph Magnus and Eden Naby, *Afghanistan: Mullah, Marx and Mujahid* (Boulder, CO: 2000).

8 One of the better ethnographic studies is Sayed Askar Mousavi, *The Hazaras of Afghanistan* (Richmond, UK: 1998).

9 See Azmat Hayat Khan, *The Durand Line – Its Geo-strategic Importance* (Peshawar, 2000).

10 In addition to the general histories noted above, there are three excellent backgrounders on Afghanistan and its recent troubles. Ahmed Rashid's *Taliban: Militant Islam, Oil & Fundamentalism in Central Asia* (New Haven, 2001) is the work of one of the most experienced journalists to cover the region; Michael Griffin's *Reaping the Whirlwind: The Taliban Movement in Afghanistan* (London, 2001), while lacking the immediacy of Rashid, has a stronger sense of historical depth. Both can be supplemented by the Afghan material in Dipi, *Hiro's War Without End: The Rise of Islamist Terrorism and Global Response* (London, 2002).

11 John Griffiths, *Afghanistan* (New York, Washington, and London, 1967), 42–9, notes that the US replied with some megaprojects largely for show, while the USSR assistance, in the form of long-term programs, was far more effective.

12 Allende's death during a military coup was later claimed by the military to have been a "suicide." Moro, after repeated warnings from the US, was kidnapped and murdered by the Red Brigades, a far-left terrorist group later revealed to have been infiltrated and manipulated by the ultra-right, including by the Italian military intelligence service.

13 For a detailed examination of the political currents, see Sam Noumoff, "Reflections on the Afghan Revolution," *Bangladesh Institute for International Strategic Studies*, vol. 6, no. 1, 1985.

14 Rasanayagam, *Afghanistan*, 70.

15 Coll, *Ghost*, 42; there is a good summary of events in William Blum, *Killing Hope: U.S. Military and CIA Interventions since World War II*, Updated Ed. (Monroe, ME: 2004) 338–51.

16 *Wall Street Journal*, 7 January 1980.

17 Edward Mortimer, *Faith & Power: The Politics of Islam* (New York, 1982), 392–4.

18 The pipeline is described by Brigadier Mohammed Yousaf (the Pakistani general in charge of the supply operation) and Major Mark Adkin, *The Bear Trap: Afghanistan's Untold Story* (London, 1992), 36. The figures on leakage were always controversial. The CIA insisted that the loss rate was "only" 20 percent. (*Washington Post*, January 1985), the US Senate Foreign Relations Committee put it between 30 and 50 percent, while admitting it was just a guess (*New York Times*, 24 March 1987). Others have put the diversion at 65 percent and even higher. On the role of the Afghan arms pipeline in the world arms black market, see Naylor, *Wages of Crime*, chapter 3.

19 Kurt Lohbeck, *Holy War, Unholy Victory* (Washington, 1993), 183–4.

20 *Washington Post*, 1 May 1987.

21 *New York Times*, 23 October 1987; *Wall Street Journal*, 8 December 1987; *Christian Science Monitor*, 21 December 1987; *The Middle East*, October 1991. These diversions are denied or minimized by Mohammed Yousaf, *Bear Trap*, 102.

22 For an overview of Pakistan's role, see Marvin Weinbaum, "War and Peace in Afghanistan: The Pakistani Role," *Middle East Journal*, vol. 45, no. 1, 1991.

23 *Washington Post*, 6 May 1987; *La Presse*, 31 December 1988; *Far Eastern Economic Review*, 22 February 1990.

24 Cooley, *Unholy Wars*, 81–91; Coll, *Ghost*, 83–4.

25 *New York Times*, 15 May 1987; *Herald*, August 1986; *Far Eastern Economic Review*, 6 June 1991, 31 October 1991.

26 *Far Eastern Economic Review*, 5 March 1987; *Financial Times*, 6 July 1989.

27 Coll, *Ghost*, 152.

28 Mohammed Yousaf (*Bear Trap*, 104–5) claims that the distribution was strictly according to military prowess, while virtually everyone else insisted that most weapons went to factions that Pakistan found politically reliable and that some avoided combat with the Afghan government and the Soviet military to preserve their strength for settling accounts with their resistance rivals. (Weinbaum, "War and Peace," 79; *Washington Post*, 26 March 1989; *Financial Times*, 1 June 1989; *Guardian Weekly*, 12 March 1989).

29 *Times of London*, 11 January 1989; *Jeune Afrique*, 19 March 1990; *New York Times*, 16 February 1990.

30 *New York Times*, 1 December 1987; *Far Eastern Economic Review*, 6 June 1991; *Observer*, 3 May 1992; Fullerton John, *The Soviet Occupation of Afghanistan* (Hong Kong, 1983), 59. Mas'ud also collected taxes on gemstones mined in his area and smuggled to Peshawar for sale.

31 Paul Eddy and Sara Walden, *Hunting Marco Polo* (New York, 1991), 47.
32 *Christian Science Monitor,* 2 January 1989.
33 *Middle East Times,* 31 May 1987; *Financial Times,* 19 January 1989, 6 July 1989; *Times of London,* 25 September 1989.
34 See the excellent early investigation by Lawrence Lifschultz, "Inside the Kingdom of Heroin," *The Nation,* 14 November 1988.
35 For a good summary of the evidence see Alan Kuperman, "The Stinger Missile and U.S. Intervention in Afghanistan," *Political Science Quarterly,* vol. 114, no. 2, 1999.
36 For this neglected aspect of the "Iran-Contra scandal," see Naylor, *Economic Warfare,* chapter 18.
37 *Financial Times,* 27 April 2002; Coll, *Ghost,* 11–12.
38 This is the tale told, for example, by PBS. See www.pbs.org/wgbh/pages/frontline/shows/binladen.
39 An early account by Salamat Ali ("Cause and Effect," *Far Eastern Economic Review,* 27 May 1991) presents al-Qā'idah forces as being badly mauled during the battle. It is also perhaps the first account to begin the process of exaggerating the size of Usamah's loyalist group and of inflating his personal financial contribution.
40 *Financial Times,* 3 October 1988; *Far Eastern Economic Review,* 19 February 1987; *Wall Street Journal,* 25 August 1988.
41 These stories actually began at least a decade before 9/11. See for example "Trail of Arab Zealotry Leads Back to Kabul," *Sunday Times,* 5 July 1992.

CHAPTER TWO

1 See James Clay, "The US and the Bin Laden Bogey," *Middle East International,* 10 March 2000. This excellent early dissection of the US falling into the "Bin Laden" trap makes the essential points that evidence of his direct involvement in various attacks was minimal, his wealth was exaggerated, his role was largely symbolic, and the US was making a big mistake by blowing him out of all proportion.
2 Shortly after 9/11, Prince Bandar ibn Sultan, then Saudi Ambassador to the US, ventured what seems to have been a common opinion: "I didn't think he could lead eight ducks across the road" (*Frontline,* 11 October 2001).
3 For a polemical view of corruption in the Bush-Cheney administration, see William Hartung, *How Much Are You Making on the War, Daddy?* (New York, 2003); a more detailed examination of some aspects is in Dan Briody, *The Iron Triangle: Inside the Secret World of the Carlyle Group* (New York, 2003) and

The Halliburton Agenda: The Politics of Oil and Money (New York, 2004). None of these prove that corruption is actually more extensive, just perhaps more blatant, than in earlier administrations.

4 *New York Times*, 28 October 2001; Mary Anne Weaver, "The Real Bin Laden," *New Yorker*, 24 January 2000. Saudi dissidents, with no love of either the regime or bin Lāden, tried in the early post-9/11 days to point out that the Usama bin Lāden gezillions did not exist (*Financial Times*, 24 September 2001). In vain.

5 Milton Bearsden, the CIA station chief for Pakistan, 1986–89, who oversaw much of the military aid, never met him. Nor did he hear anything about bin Lāden to make the Saudi seem exceptional. "There were a lot of bin Ladens who came to do jihad."

6 An interesting portrait is by veteran Middle East correspondent, Jonathan Randal, *Osama: The Making of a Terrorist* (New York, 2004), although, surprisingly in light of Randal's record in Lebanon, it seems to take some rumors and unsubstantiated stories at face value.

7 *Far Eastern Economic Review*, 23 May 1991.

8 Coll, *Ghosts*, 164, 204.

9 Cooley, *Unholy Wars*, 81–97, 223, 243.

10 See, for example, "Bin Laden camps trained 70,000 in terror," *Financial Times*, 15 November 2001.

11 This was the estimate Abdullah Azzam's son-in-law, who told writer Lawrence Wright that most were drivers, secretaries, and cooks, that the fighting was done overwhelmingly by Afghans (*New Yorker*, 16 September 2002).

12 Coll, *Ghosts*, 157, 200. In all the hype about bin Lāden's importance, it was never explained why Saudi Arabia would tolerate Usama raising money to establish facilities competitive with factions Saudi Arabia itself sponsored.

13 *Globe and Mail*, 29 August 2005, 6 September 2005.

14 Cited in Anthony Shadid, *Legacy of the Prophet* (Boulder, CO: 2002), 87.

15 Randal, *Osama* 79, 86; Coll (*Ghost* 222–3) accepts without question claims of the Saudi intelligence chief that bin Lāden revealed radical personality changes on his return. In other words, he had gone nuts, and that explains everything.

16 *Middle East International*, 10 June 2005.

17 For an insightful attempt to clarify the concepts, see Gabriel Almond, R. Scott Appleby, and Emmanual Sivan, *Strong Religion: The Rise of Fundamentalisms around the World* (Chicago, 2003), 10–11.

18 See Wael Hallaq, *A History of Islamic Legal Theories* (Cambridge, 1997), and *The Origins and Evolution of Islamic Law* (Cambridge, 2005).

19 On this, probably the most powerful and influential dissection is by Olivier Roy, *The Failure of Political Islam* (Cambridge, MA: 1994), who grounds their actions not in the concept of jihād but in the terror tactics of "recent European, radical, ultra-leftist and Third Worldist movements." Another interpretation, also stressing the fundamental break of radical political Islam with Islamic tradition, is given by Gilles Kepel, *Jihad: The Trail of Political Islam* (Cambridge, MA: 2002) and *The War for Muslim Minds: Islam and the West* (Cambridge, MA: 2004).

20 Hiro, *War without End*, 79.

21 "Those who are twisted of mind look for verses equivocal seeking deviation and giving them interpretations of their own but none knows their meaning except God" (sura 3, verse 7). "Woe to them who fake Scriptures and say 'This is from God' so that they might earn some profit thereby, and woe to them for what they fake, and woe to them for what they earn from it" (sura 2, verse 79).

22 An excellent summary is in Roger Hardy, "Saudi Arabia: Violence and Reform," *Middle East International*, 23 January 2004.

23 See Haneef James Oliver's *The 'Wahhabi' Myth: Dispelling Prevalent Fallacies and the Fictitious Link with Bin Laden*, privately published, 2002 (www.thewahhabimyth.com).

24 Randal *Osama*, 55–6.

25 For a detailed examination of the corruption surrounding Saudi arms purchases, see especially Said Aburish, *The Rise, Corruption, and Pending Fall of the House of Saud* (New York, 1996).

26 *Sunday Times*, 21 October 2001; *New York Times*, 4 November 2001.

27 In his May 1998 interview on PBS's *Frontline*.

28 *Time*, 6 May 1996.

29 In June 2001 the US issued a formal indictment against fourteen Saudis who were all identified, but for one Palestinian John Doe, as members of Saudi Hizbullāh. Only three years later did the 9/11 Commission suggest that bin Lāden "may" have helped them by "possibly" providing explosives etc., but it gave no basis for the claim.

30 There is a huge literature on the Muslim Brotherhood. A concise account is in Edward Mortimer, *Faith & Power: The Politics of Islam* (New York, 1982), 251–9. Anthony Shedid's *Legacy of the Prophet* (Boulder, CO: 2002), 55–60, is also excellent. Hiro, *War without End*, 60–109, gives much detail about the Brotherhood and its offshoots.

31 An insider account is by Montasser al-Zayyat, *The Road to Al-Qaeda* (London, 2004). A former militant, al-Zayyat was also a lawyer who

defended many of the Islamists. He also seems to have set himself up as *the* source on whom most Western reporters rely.

32 Cited in Wilhelm Dietl, *Holy War* (New York, 1984).

33 Cooley, *Unholy*, 37.

34 Economist Intelligence Unit, *Egypt, Country Report*, no. 3, 1992; *Middle East Times*, 5 November 1997. Gizya (or jizya) applies only to able-bodied non-Muslim males of military age – women, children, the poor, hermits the disabled, and the elderly are all exempt.

35 Al-Zayyat, *Road*, 78.

36 *Middle East International*, 26 September 1997, 24 May 1998.

37 See Susan Sachs, "An Investigation in Egypt Illustrates Al Qaeda's Web," *New York Times*, 21 November 2001. What the newspaper did, typically, was present all the material as fact for the first few paragraphs, which is all that most readers peruse, then later let out the information that the testimony might be tortured out of the informants.

38 For an interesting discussion that follows quite closely the conventional line but provides some fascinating details, see Lawrence Wright, "The Man behind Bin Laden," *New Yorker*, 16 September 2002.

CHAPER THREE

1 "Address to a Joint Session of Congress and the American People," Office of the Press Secretary, The White House, 20 September 2001.

2 The language used to describe presumed terror operatives, too, was replete with organized-crime jargon. For example, when Khalid Sheikh Mohammed, one of many designated paymasters-planners-managers of 9/11, was arrested in Pakistan in early 2003, us authorities expressed delight that they had captured "the kingpin of al-Qaeda." (*New York Times*, 2 March 2003.)

3 Among the best descriptions of conditions in the slums was Herbert Asbury's *The Gangs of New York* (New York, 1927), not to be confused with the movie that shares little but the name; also its sequel, *The French Quarter* (New York, 1936).

4 One of the best overviews is Michael Woodiwiss, *Organized Crime and American Power* (Toronto, 2001). For a more conventional view see, for example, Stephen Fox, *Blood and Power: Organized Crime in Twentieth Century America* (New York, 1959).

5 Pino Arlacchi's *Mafia Business: The Mafia Ethic and the Spirit of Capitalism* (London, 1986) argued that the wealth of the heroin trade in the late twentieth century transformed the old Mafia into something much more

modern and entrepreneurial. But this view was challenged, for example, by Diego Gambetta's *The Sicilian Mafia – The Business of Private Protection* (Cambridge, MA: 1993).

6 For a overview of the politics of crime in Italy, see Judith Chubb, *The Mafia and Politics: The Italian State under Siege* (Ithaca, NY: 1989).

7 The pioneering works in English dispelling the myths were Humberti Nelli's *The Business of Crime: Italians and Syndicate Crime in the United States* (New York, 1970) and Joseph Albini's *The American Mafia: Genesis of a Legend* (New York, 1971). This was followed by Dwight Smith's *The Mafia Mystique* (New York, 1975), which examines in depth the interplay between fiction and reality.

8 See Harry Anslinger and Will Oursler, *The Murderers: The Story of the Narcotics Gangs* (New York, 1962). He claimed that by the 1930s the Mafia had taken over from the Chinese the business of supplying the United States with opiates.

9 Cited in Woodiwiss, *Organized Crime*, 239. He later shaved it down to a more modest "criminal standing army" of half a million.

10 Woodiwiss, *Organized Crime*, 184–9.

11 Woodiwiss, *Organized Crime*, 198.

12 This is dissected in William Howard Moore, *The Kefauver Committee and the Politics of Crime* (Columbia, MS: 1974), 32–3, 200–1.

13 Cf. Craig Bradley, "Racketeering," 215, where he notes that the fundamental bureaucratic principle is that failure is success; if the alleged problem the institution was created to combat continues to expand, that ensures the continued existence of the institution whereas "success" does the opposite.

14 Moore, *Kefauver*, 79, 116–19, 120–2, 131–2.

15 Robert F. Kennedy, *The Enemy Within* (New York, 1960), 160. See also Gordon Hawkins, "God and the Mafia," *The Public Interest*, no. 13, Winter 1969.

16 Kennedy, *Enemy*, 252.

17 See especially Victor Navasky, *Kennedy Justice* (New York, 1971), which takes Kennedy's crime-out-of-control rhetoric at face value.

18 Bradley, "Racketeering," 242–6.

19 Bean, *Court TV*, op. cit.

20 For a general survey, see Jeff Atkinson, "Racketeer Influenced And Corrupt Organizations," *The Journal of Criminal Law and Criminology*, vol. 69, no. 1, 1978. For early criticism, see Alan Block, "The Organized Crime Control Act, 1970," *The Public Historian*, vol. 2, no. 2, 1980. For a recent critical assessment see Carlo Morselli and Lila Kazemian "Scrutinizing RICO," *Critical Criminology* 12, 2004.

21 Peter Maas, *The Valachi Papers* (New York, 1968). In the foreword, Rudolph Giuliani, then the ambitious attorney for the Southern District who already had his eye on higher office, states, "Valachi exposed the Big Lie. He confirmed the existence of a secret organization of so-called Families engaged in a wide range of criminal activities." (x) He also comments that, "The passage of the racketeering act commonly called the RICO statute was made possible largely because of Valachi's confessions" (xi).

22 For a critical dissection of the Valachi revelations, see Gordon Hawkins, "God and the Mafia," *The Public Interest*, vol. 14, Winter 1968, and Albini, *American Mafia*, 222–47.

23 Albini, *The American Mafia*, 236.

24 Jay Albanese, "What Lockheed and La Cosa Nostra Have in Common," *Crime & Delinquency*, April 1982, 227.

25 Hawkins, "God and the Mafia," 43.

26 This point is made very well in Carlo Morselli & Lila Kazemian "Scrutinizing RICO," *Critical Criminology* 12, 2004.

27 The Republic of the Philippines versus Ferdinand Marcos et al, Case No. CIV 86–3859 MRP (Gx).

28 There was a deluge of publicity leading up to Noriega's trial, but a remarkable silence after. The silence was broken by Noriega himself, working with Peter Eisner, in *America's Prisoner: the Memoirs of Manuel Noriega* (New York, 1997).

29 This history is summarized in Naylor, *Hot Money*, chapter 12, and *Economic Warfare*, chapter 15.

30 There are a number of critical works on the Noriega era in Panama. Two by insiders have to be treated with a certain amount of caution. See Luis Murillo, *The Noriega Mess: The Drugs, the Canal and Why America Invaded* (Berkeley, 1995), and R.M. Koster and Guillermo Sanchez, *In the Time of the Tyrants: Panama 1968–1990* (New York, 1990). See also Frederick Kempe, *Divorcing the Dictator* (New York, 1990), and John Dinges, *Our Man in Panama* (New York, 1991).

31 *New York Times*, 12 June 1986.

32 "Drugs and Money Laundering in Panama," Hearing Before the Permanent Subcommittee on Investigations of the Committee on Governmental Affairs, United States Senate, 28 January 1988.

33 For the economic pressure tactics, see Naylor, *Economic Warfare*, chapter 15.

34 Eisner, *Noriega*, introduction, xiv-xv. The invasion was not an easy sell. Opponents included Admiral William Crowe, chairman of the Joint Chiefs of Staff, and General Fred Woerner, the Panama-based head of SOUTHCOM. Both were dismissed, with Crowe replaced by Colin Powell, who was

suddenly jumped from staff aide to the highest military rank. For Powell it was excellent preparation for a future career of pandering to and lying on behalf of those with real power. Also among the dissenting voices were a number of Noriega fans in both the CIA and the DEA. But they were over-ridden by the demands of the State Department.

35 The Stealth bomber, for example, had its debut in Panama, and garnered enough media attention to mount a successful defense against the threat posed by Congressional budget-cutters. See the congratulatory piece in *Time*, 8 January 1990.

36 As one of the DEA agents responsible for stringing together the case after-wards commented: "We had no evidence, so we had to do our duty and convict him anyway" (Eisner, *Noriega*, 235).

37 Eisner, *Noriega*, introduction, xix–xx. He notes: "After sifting through the Noriega trial, reviewing trial testimony, interviewing lawyers, witnesses and investigators, intelligence sources and Noriega opponents, I found the drug case against Noriega to be deeply flawed and wholly circumstantial." Interestingly, R.M. Koster, author of a highly critical anti-Noriega book, whom Eisner savages, concurs completely with the description of the trial as a fraud and a disgrace. See R.M. Koster "Noriega – Panama," *Escape from America Magazine*, vol. 6, no. 3, March 2004.

38 On the other hand, every US senior military, intelligence, or police officer who wanted to testify in Noriega's favor was ordered not to do so. For more on the dubious nature of the evidence, see Michael Massing, "Noriega in Miami," *The Nation*, 2 December 1991.

39 *Miami Herald*, 22 January 1990; Eisner, *Noriega*, 194.

CHAPTER FOUR

1 See, for example, Stratfor's Global Intelligence Report, "A Coming Offen-sive in the Sudan," 30 June 2003.

2 There is a very thorough compilation of the sequence of political events by the European Sudanese Public Affairs, "The Peace Process: A Chronologi-cal History" (London, 2002).

3 *Middle East International*, 25 July 1997.

4 For an excellent survey, see Riad Ibrahim, "Factors Contributing to the Po-litical Ascendancy of the Muslim Brethern in Sudan," *Arab Studies Quarterly*, vol. 12, nos 3 and 4, Summer/Fall 1990. On the parties and their sect-family allegiances, see *Africa Confidential*, 12 March 1986.

5 *Middle East Report*, November-December 1989. See also Abbashar Jamal, "Funding Fundamentalism," *Middle East Report*, September-October 1991.

6 See Marthan Wenger, "Sudan; Politics & Society," *Middle East Report*, September-October 1991.

7 Mohamed Suliman "Civil War in the Sudan: From Ethnic to Ecological Conflict," *The Ecologist*, vol. 23, no. 3, May-June 1993; *Middle East International*, 5 April 1985.

8 *Africa Confidential*, 29 April 1988, 17 November 1989; *AfricAsia*, February 1985; *Middle East International* 17, 31 May 1985.

9 *Middle East Reporter*, 25 June 1983, 31 March 1984; *Africa Confidential*, 22 May 1985, 12 November 1986. In fact some of the auxiliary units and local allies of the SPLA took their enthusiasm for other people's livestock across the border into Kenya, a move that almost lost the SPLA the support of the Kenyan government, which had provided it with fuel as well as arms.

10 *Middle East International*, 13 April 1990; *Africa Confidential*, 28 July 1989, 20 April 1990.

11 *Africa Confidential*, 9 November 1990, 25 January 1991, 12 July 1991.

12 *The Independent*, 17 September 1993.

13 *New York Times*, 21 September 1998; *The Times* (London), 22 September 1998.

14 Agence France Presse, 21 July 1998; *Africa Confidential*, 3 March 1995; "The Crisis in Sudan," *Hearings before the Subcommittee on Africa of the Committee on International Relations*, House of Representatives, 22 March 1995; *New York Times Magazine*, November 1997.

15 Milton Viorst, "Sudan's Islamic Experiment: Fundamentalism in Power," *Foreign Affairs*, vol. 74, no. 3, May-June 1995. As a result Islamic radicals distrusted al-Turabi and the NIF.

16 Randal, *Osama*, 125.

17 Burke puts it well: "This can be seen as either an astonishing lapse of security or an indication that bin Laden genuinely saw himself as nothing more than a devout and legitimate businessman who financed Islamic activism" (*Al-Qaeda*, 132).

18 See Ruddy Doom and Koen Vlassenroot, "Kony's Message," *African Affairs*, January 1999; *Los Angeles Times*, 1 April 1996.

19 See, for example, Amnesty International, *Uganda;* "Breaking God's Commands," AFR 59/001, 18 September 1997; and Human Rights News, *LRA Conflict in Northern Uganda and Southern Sudan*, 2002.

20 www.mapinc.org/drugnews/v01.n1806.a05.html, *WorldNetDaily*, 13 October 2001. There was nothing new about the use of drug propaganda in the struggles in the Sudan. See *Geopolitical Drug Dispatch*, April 1997.

21 *Middle East International*, 19 December 1997.

22 Joseph Wheelan, *Jefferson's War: America's First War on Terror 1801–5* (New York, 2003), 35.

23 *Washington Post*, 1 August 1998, 23 December 1999, 26 February 2002; *New York Times*, 27 April 2001; *The Independent*, 26 February 2002.

24 *Observer*, 30 August 1998.

25 *Middle East International*, 4 September 1998.

26 *Boston Globe*, 22 August 1999; *Guardian*, 2 October 2001.

27 Randal, *Osama*, 146.

CHAPTER FIVE

1 Coll, *Ghost*, 325.

2 Olivier Roy, *Afghanistan: From Holy War to Civil War* (Princeton, 1995), 88.

3 A fascinating view of the consequences by someone with no political axe to grind is in Christopher Kremmer, *The Carpet Wars* (New York, 2002).

4 *Globe and Mail*, 2 January 2002.

5 *Village Voice*, 30 October 2001; *New York Times*, 4 November 2001.

6 Hiro, *War without End*, 2002, 193.

7 Malise Ruthven, *Fundamentalism: The Search for Meaning* (Oxford, 2004), 107–11.

8 For a fascinating account of the early oil frontier, see Essad Bey, *Blood and Oil in the Orient*, translated from the German by Elsa Talmey (New York, 1932).

9 An excellent analysis of the interaction of pipelines, politics, and military bases is in F. William Engdahl "Revolution, Geopolitics and Pipelines," *Asia Times*, 30 june 2005.

10 Apart from Rashid (who pioneered much of the analysis of the oil question in the region) in *Taliban*, chapter 11, see Michael Klare, *Resource Wars: The New Landscape of Global Conflict* (New York, 2001), chapter 4; James Dorian "Oil, Gas in FSU Central Asia, Northwestern China Await Development," *Oil & Gas Journal*, vol. 99, no. 37, 10 September 2001; and Lutz Kleveman, *The New Great Game: Blood and Oil in Central Asia* (New York, 2003).

11 Klare, *Resource Wars*, 90; Griffin, *Taliban*, 115.

12 *Globe and Mail*, 26 February 2002.

13 *Washington Post*, 25 January 2002; *Sunday Telegraph*, 14 December 1997; *The Independent*, 10 January 2002. A good summary of the Enron role is by Ron Callari in the *Fairfield County Weekly*, 7 March 2002.

14 *Geopolitical Drug Dispatch*, no. 34, August 1994.

15 *New York Times*, 22 October 2001; *Financial Times*, 14 October 2001; *The Scotsman*, 4 October 2001; Rashid, *Taliban*, 100–24.

16 *Geopolitical Drug Dispatch*, no. 30, April 1994.

17 *Geopolitical Drug Dispatch*, no. 44, June 1995.

18 Rashid, *Taliban*, 48.

19 Griffin, *Whirlwind*, 148–53; Rashid, *Taliban*, 118–19.

20 *New York Times*, 26 November 2001; *The Independent*, 14 February 2002.

21 *New York Times*, 5 October 2001; *Village Voice*, 27 October 2001.

22 See the excellent analysis by Alan Cullison and Andrew Higgins, "Inside al Qaeda's Afghan Turmoil," *Wall Street Journal*, 2 August, 2002.

23 Kleveman, *New Great Game*, 238.

24 There is a good summary in Griffin, *Whirlwind*, 121–7, 180–1. See also Coll, *Ghost*, 399–401.

25 Kremmer, *Carpet*, 143–5.

26 *Wall Street Journal*, 2 August 2002; "U.S., Taliban Bargained Over Bin Laden, Documents Show," CNN, 19 August 2005.

CHAPTER SIX

1 United States of America V. Usama Bin Laden et. al., United States District Court, Southern District of New York, 4 November 1998.

2 In fact bin Lāden's "Declaration of War against Americans Occupying the Land of the Two Holy Places" was not a fatwā, and its contents consisted largely of a denunciation of the sorry state of economic and political affairs within the kingdom.

3 On the absence of any serious proof behind the allegations, see Loren Jenkins "Is bin Laden a Terrorist Mastermind – or a Fall Guy?" *Salon*, 27 August 1998; *New York Times*, 5 November 1998; *Facts on File*, 12 November 1998; *Newsweek*, 11 March 1999.

4 en.wikipedia.org/wiki/Jamal_al-Fadl.

5 See, for example, Matt Bean, "Like a Kingpin: Prosecuting Osama bin Laden under RICO," *Court TV*, 28 November 2001; Marc Levin of the American Freedom Center, "Guilt by Association Needed to Nab Terrorists," *Political USA*, 16 October 2001; Ron Carrico, "The Trial of Osama bin Laden," *San Diego Daily Transcript*, 18 December 2001.

6 See the comments of Alan Dershowitz, "Bin Laden Trial," CourtTV.com, 10 November 2001. He disagreed with using RICO criminally – on the grounds that al-Qā'idah was more like a holding than an operating company and that its purpose was not to make money per se. But he heartily endorsed civil suits.

7 See www.cnn.com/LAW/trials.and.cases/case.files/0012/embassy.bombing/ for the testimony.

8 For a reasoned explanation, see Mahmood Mamdani, *Good Muslim, Bad Muslim: America, the Cold War and the Roots of Terror* (New York, 2004), 47–50.

9   Bay'a was presented a little more accurately elsewhere in the trial, for example, the testimony of FBI Agent John Anticev on defendant Odeh.

10 Thanks to Professor Issa Boullata of the McGill University Islamic Studies Institute for this clarification.

11 The result was a series of books with chilling titles like *The Octopus* or *The Merger*. The pioneer was the late Claire Sterling who made her name with *The Terror Network* (New York, 1981), then climbed on the organized-crime bandwagon with *Thieves World* (New York, 1994).

12 See Griffin, *Reaping*, 136–7. Curiously Griffin seems willing to take it half-seriously even though noting some of the logical problems.

13 *Los Angeles Times*, 4 December 2005; *Associated Press*, 6 December 2005. The story is told in al-Masri's own words in *Los Angeles Times*, 19 December 2005.

14 Yet the story was presented as a matter of al-Fadl fleeing for his life only to walk "into the arms of American investigators" at a US embassy (*New York Times*, 13 February 2001).

15 "In return for his testimony, the United States gave him witness protection in America and hundreds of thousands of dollars. Many lawyers at the trial believed al-Fadl exaggerated and lied to give the Americans a picture of a terrorist organisation they needed to prosecute bin Laden" ("Jamal al-Fadl," Wikipedia; this is a "free encyclopedia" written by thousands of volunteers, so any information it presents needs to be treated with suitable skepticism – nonetheless this story does ring true).

16 CNN.com, 3 May 2004.

17 *Globe and Mail*, 6 November 2001.

18 For the mini-nukes saga, see Peter Hounam and Steve McQuillan, *The Mini-Nuke Conspiracy* (London, 1995).

19 *WorldDailyNet*, 2 October 2002.

20 *Globe and Mail*, 6 October 2001, 20 September 2005; *Canadian Press*, 2 June 2004.

21 For a backgrounder, see *PBS Frontline*, 12 September 2001. Given the timing of the program – just after the trial – this was quite balanced.

22 *Newsweek*, 14 January 2002.

23 Curiously, part of the agent's questioning had nothing to do with the bombing or bin Lāden but rather with el-Hage's attitudes towards Middle Eastern politics, especially his anger over Israeli behavior in Palestine and the conviction of himself and his ex-Sudan confreres that US support kept repressive governments in power (US District Court, Southern District of New York, *United States versus bin Laden et al* S(7) 98 Cr. 1023, 22 March 2001).

24 CNN, 16 April 2001. Re: the perjury charge, he had denied any communication with bin Lāden "associates" after he left Khartoum; but phone records along with business documents rebutted his claim.

25 In that interview he worked himself into quite a lather, contending further that "Our religion is under attack. They kill and main our brothers They compromise our honor and our dignity and dare we utter a single word of protest against the injustice, we are called terrorists ... The whole Muslim world is the victim of international terrorism, engineered by America at the United Nations."

26 John Miller, ABC interview with bin Lāden, May 1998.

27 This is particularly strong in his August 1996 "fatwā," published in Al-Quds al-'Arabi and translated shortly after in www.pbs.org/newshour/terrorism/international/fatwa_1996.html, 4.

28 Full text translated in *Observer*, 24 November 2002.

29 Full text translated in *BBC News/Middle East*, 16 April 2001.

30 This fundamental notion of reciprocity is stressed in Diane Perlman's insightful "Misinterpreting Osama's Message," *Alternet*, 21 November 2002. For example, "Our acts are a response to your own acts."

31 Full text translated in *Al Jazeera*, 30 October 2004.

32 *Associated Press*, 20 October 2004.

33 While Dershowitz agreed that the tapes prove nothing factual, he thought they might influence a jury (*National Post*, 15 December 2001). No kidding!

34 Second quote from text translated in *Observer*, 24 November 2002; the first appears in his 2004 pre-election speech.

CHAPTER SEVEN

1 See *New Yorker*, 24 July 2005.

2 *Middle East International*, 15 January 1999, 26 February 1999, 12 November 1999; See also Hiro, *War*, 317; Mary Weaver, "The Real bin Laden," *New Yorker*, 24 January 2000, a well-researched piece by someone knowledgeable; and Kimberly McCloud and Adam Dolnik, "Debunk the Myth of Al Qaeda," *Christian Science Monitor*, 23 May 2002.

3 See the account by Alexander Cockburn and Jeffrey St Clair, "How Bush Was Offered Bin Laden and Blew It," *Counterpunch*, 10 November 2004.

4 Sunil Sainis, "Ahmad Shah Mas'ud," *Bharat Rakshak Monitor*, vol. 4, no. 3, November-December 2001.

5 Coll, *Ghost*, 11–12.

6 See the revealing memo by Richard A. Clarke to Condoleeza Rice: "Presidential Policy Initiative/Review – the Al-Qida Network," *National Security Council*, 25 January 2002.

7 Griffin, *Taliban*, 213; Coll, *Ghost*, 468–9, 502.

8 See, for example, "Taliban and bin Laden Network 'are as one,'" *Financial Times*, 28 September 2001.

9 *Financial Times*, 29 November 2001.

10 On black propaganda involving drugs see Edward Jay Epstein, *Agency of Fear: Opiates and Political Power in America* (New York, 1990).

11 *New York Times*, 11 and 16 November 2001. The original story was by Judith Miller, whose credibility as a serious journalist has been called into question.

12 For the technical background, see Frank Barnaby, *How to Build a Nuclear Bomb* (London, 2004). For a sensible view that deflates much of the hysteria, see Rensselaer Lee III, *Smuggling Armageddon: The Nuclear Black Market in the Former Soviet Union* (New York, 1998).

13 Kremmer in *Carpet Wars*, passim, describes illiterate and virtually innumerate Talibān finance officials bossing terrified civil servants of the old regime kept on because they alone could tally the figures.

14 *New York Times*, 26 February 2002, 23 March 2002.

15 *New York Times*, 28 October 2001.

16 See also the military puff piece "Afghan Food Drop Underscores Bush's Humanitarian Pledge" by Master Sgt Randy Mitchell in *American Forces Press Service*, 9 October 2001.

17 *Financial Times*, 27 April 2002. Although in theory the battery packs on the Stingers were only supposed to be good for five years, some claimed they could be extended to last ten. And of course the batteries could be replaced. On the black-market spread of the Stingers, see Ken Silverstein, "Stingers, Stingers, Who's Got the Stingers?" *Slate*, 2 October 2001.

18 On the impact of the cluster bombs, see Carlotta Gall "Farmers in Afghanistan Face Fields of Bombs," *New York Times*, 9 October 2002.

19 *Irish Examiner*, 10 October 2001; *The Independent*, 9 October 2001; Laura Flanders, "Killer Food Drops," Workingforchange.com, 10 September 2001. *New York Times*, 4 January 2002; "Agencies Question Afghan Aid Drops," CNN.com, 9 October 2001; "Operation Bombs and Bread." ABCNEWS.com, 9 October 2001; Nathan Ford, "Chaos in Afghanistan: famine, Aid, and Bombs," *The Lancet*, 3 November 2001, vol. 358, no. 9292; Russ Kick, "Food-Drop Fiasco: Humanitarian Aid for Afghanistan Doomed from Start to Finish," *Abuse Your Illusions* (New York, 2003).

20 See especially the summary by Geov Parrish, "Where the Bodies Are," *AlterNet*, 23 October 2001. Also *Globe and Mail*, 3 November 2001; *New York Times*, 2 December 2001, 27 May 2002, 21 July 2002.

21 See especially Cees Wiebes, *Intelligence and the War in Bosnia 1992–1995* (Hamburg and London, 2003). See also *The Spectator*, 12 September 2002, and *Guardian*, 22 April 2002.

22 Eric Margolis, *Toronto Sun*, 9 September 2003.

23 Brendan O'Neill, "Al-Qaeda: Blowing Up the Numbers," *Spiked-Online,* 23 June 2004.

24 "Operation Anaconda: Questionable Outcomes for the United States," *Stratfor,* 11 March 2002; Dexter Filkins, "Flaws in U.S. Air War Left Hundreds of Civilians Dead," *New York Times,* 21 July 2002.

25 "Ground War Strategies," *Stratfor,* 14 November 2001.

26 *Asia Times,* 26 August 2003.

27 See Jonathan Landay, "New Taliban Proves to Be Formidable Foe," *Knight Ridder,* 21 August 2005.

28 *New York Times,* 6 January 2002.

29 Robert Fisk, "Afghanistan Is on the Brink of Another Disaster," *The Independent,* 14 August 2002.

30 Rory Stewart, "The Looting of Turquoise Mountain," *New York Times Magazine,* 25 August 2002.

31 *The Independent,* 13 November 2001; *Village Voice,* 15 November 2001; *New York Times,* 19 November 2001, 6 January 2002, 21 May 2002.

32 See Eric Margolis, "U.S. Caught in Kabul," *Toronto Sun,* 12 December 2004.

33 *Associated Press,* 9 October 2003.

34 Juan Cole, *Informed Comment,* 10 January 2006, www.juancole.com.

35 *The Independent,* 15 November 2005; *Asia Times,* 1 January 2006; "Taliban's Omar Calls for Jihad against U.S.," *Japan Newswire,* 9 January 2006; "Time to Talk: us Engages the Taliban," *Asia Times,* 22 November 2005.

36 *Forbes,* 5 January 2006. This in fact may have been one reason for the us to escalate its war of words with, and, in all probability, covert attacks on Iran, using as a pretext accusations Iran was building nuclear weapons.

37 Risen, *State of War,* 154–5.

38 *The Independent,* 14 February 2002.

39 *Associated Press,* 7 September 2003.

40 For hints about high level corruption, without naming names, see *The Telegraph,* 5 February 2006.

41 *New York Times,* 26 November 2001, 5 May 2002; *Newsday,* 7 September 2003; *The Independent,* 23 September 2005.

42 *The Independent,* 3 October 2005; *Observer,* 5 February 2006.

43 *Asia Times,* 16 November 2005; *Globe and Mail,* 21 January 2006.

44 *Asia Times,* 3 September 2005.

45 *Asia Times,* 22 December 2005.

46 *New York Times,* 7 December 2002.

47 Listarchives.his.com/intelforum/intelforum.0204/msg00022.html.

48 James Risen and David Rohde, "A Hostile Land Foils the Quest for bin Laden," *New York Times,* 13 December 2004.

CHAPTER EIGHT

1 *San Francisco Chronicle*, 16 December 2001; *New York Times*, 4 December 2002; *BBC News Online*, 21 December 2001. Richard Boucher of the State Department explained: "We've always made it clear that we felt that Somalia and the situation that existed there made it a potential haven for terrorists" (CNN.com, 10 January 2002). This continued to be a neocon theme for years after. See Stratfor, *Geopolitical Diary*, 1 February 2004.

2 *Globe and Mail*, 28 March 2002.

3 There is an excellent summary of Barre's career in an obituary in *The Independent*, 3 January 1995.

4 Initially Saudi Arabia, almost surely with US assent, paid Egypt's Anwar Sadat to ship his old Soviet weapons to Barre to help him break free of the USSR. But later the US made a deal with the USSR to stop supporting Barre if the USSR stayed out of Rhodesia-Zimbabwe (Cooley, *Unholy Wars*, 27).

5 There is a good summary of the political history in George Archer and Paulos Milkias, "The Second Scramble for Africa," *Horn of Africa*, vol. 2, no. 3, 1978. See also Michael Maren's *The Road to Hell: The Ravaging Effects of Foreign Aid and International Charity* (New York, 1997).

6 *Middle East International*, 19 August 1983. By the end of his regime, Barre had received some $3 billion worth of weapons from the USSR and the US (*Guardian Weekly*, 20 September 1992). A UN arms embargo was therefore an absurdity (*Middle East International*, 6 March 1992).

7 See Alex De Waal's excellent survey, "The Shadow," *Africa Report*, March-April 1993.

8 *Geopolitical Drug Dispatch*, no. 16, February 1993; *Toronto Star*, 11 December 1992.

9 Qāt can also be dried and smoked or made into a beverage or kneaded into a paste, but chewing is the most popular; *Africa*, no. 147, November 1983.

10 For a general history, see Lee Cassanelli, "Qat: A Quasilegal Commodity," *The Social Life of Things: Commodities in Cultural Perspective*, Arjun Appadurai, ed. (New York, 1986). For the medical impact see Michael Griffin, "Pleasure or Peril?" *National Geographic*, April 1988; Peter Kalix, "Chewing Khat," *World Health*, June 1986, and "Khat: Scientific Knowledge and Policy Issues," *British Journal of Addiction*, vol. 82, 1987.

11 See especially Shelagh Weir, "Economic Aspects of the Qat Industry in North-West Yemen," *Economy, Society & Culture in Contemporary Yemen*, B.R. Pridham, ed. (London, 1985), and *Geopolitical Drug Dispatch*, no. 65, March 1997. For more recent government policy, see *Middle East International*, 18 June 1999.

12 *Geopolitical Drug Dispatch*, no 21, July 1993; no. 92, June 1999; no. 93, September 1999.

13 This absurd notion was articulated with respect to the Yemen trade in Richard Labévrière, *Les Dollars de la terreur* (Paris, 1999), 18: "A Yémen, Oussama Bin Laden contrôle les principales routes du qât." Peter Bergen (*Holy War*, 32) remarks that the author must have been chewing the stuff when he wrote that passage. But the story persists. See Kim Sengupta, "The Rise of Khat," *The Independent*, 23 August 2005.

14 *Middle East International*, 19 August 1983.

15 EIU Country Report No. 3, *Ethiopia*, 1989, 29.

16 *The Montreal Gazette*, 2 September 1990; *Africa Confidential*, 8 September 1989, 21 December 1990; *Economist Intelligence Unit, Somalia*, no. 4, 1988; no. 1, 1989.

17 *Middle East International*, 19 April 1983; *Economist Intelligence Unit, Somalia*, no. 3, 1987; no. 4, 1988; no. 2, 1989; *Africa Confidential*, 3 April 1992.

18 *Financial Times*, 28 August 2004.

19 See the four-part series by Peter Symes, "The Banknotes of Somalia," www.pjsymes.com.au.

20 They included the United Somali Front (Iise), Somali Democratic Alliance (Gadabursi), United Somali Party (Dulbahante), Somali Democratic Movement (Rahanwayn), and Somali National Front (Mareehaan).

21 *The Times (London)*, 16 September 1992. Much as had happened in Lebanon or Iraq during their periods of maximum social disintegration, bandit groups also engaged in wholesale plundering of the country's infrastructure – entire factories were dismantled (there were not many to begin with) and sold off as scrap.

22 On the role of US agricultural surpluses, see Dan Morgan, *Merchants of Grain* (New York, 1979), 98–102, and Maren, *Road to Hell*, passim.

23 One of the most dramatized instances came when a tank (in some accounts three) was (or were) used to take over the port, shoot at UN military observers, and stand guard while thirty-five trucks hauled off three huindred tons of supplies. *New York Times*, 1 December 1992. See also *Financial Times*, 6 November 1992; *Globe and Mail*, 3 September 1993; etc.

24 *The Times (London)*, 29 August 1992; *Sunday Times*, 30 August 1992.

25 *Los Angeles Times*, 18 January 1993.

26 Maren sums it up well: "Billions of dollars and several hundred thousand foreign nationals were involved in a global operation to settle what was, at its core, the politics of dysfunctional families" (*Road to Hell*, 257).

27 "We dislike being interfered with without our consent," he said prior to the arrival of the United States (*New York Times*, 6 December 1992).

28 *New York Times*, 24 August 1993, 2 September 1993.

29 *The Independent*, 1 December 2004.

30 Blocked from using the port of Muqdisho by an alliance of his two former allies, Aideed tried to recover his financial base by arranging for two Italian companies to refurbish an old port to the south and to pay him a fee for every crate of fruit they hauled out. Meanwhile Ali Hassan Osman and Ali Mahdi opened their own competing port further north.

31 *Wall Street Journal*, 28 November 2001.

32 *Africa Confidential*, 2 February 1983, 31 October 1984, 29 April 1989; Robert Kaplan, "The Loneliest War," *Atlantic Monthly*, July 1988.

33 *Al-Ahram Weekly*, 27 December 2001 to 2 January 2002.

34 BBC Africa, 26 September 2001; Randal, *Osama*, 124.

35 CNN.com, 23 April 2001.

36 *Sunday Times*, 30 August 1992.

CHAPTER NINE

1 "Executive Order on Terrorist Financing" Office of the Press Secretary, The White House, 24 September 2001.

2 *New York Times*, 19 December 2001.

3 *Financial Times*, 29 September 2001.

4 Leonard Levy, *Jefferson and Civil Liberties: The Darker Side* (Chicago, 1963), 114, 120–5.

5 For a review of the history and logic, see Naylor, *Patriots & Profiteers* and *Economic Warfare*.

6 There is an excellent discussion in Cassel, *Civil Liberties*, 12, 90–1.

7 *Forward*, 30 December 1994.

8 See "The FTO List and Congress: Sanctioning Designated Foreign Terrorist Organizations," Congressional Research Service, *Report for Congress*, 21 October 2003.

9 For a dissection of the laws and their impact, see Leonard Levy, *A License to Steal: The Forfeiture of Property* (Chapel Hill and London, 1996).

10 This is one of the main themes in Naylor, *Wages of Crime*, chapters 4 and 6.

11 *New York Times*, 20 September 2001; *Money Laundering Alert*, October 2002, states: "The money laundering portion of the Patriot Act ... was largely a collection of bills that had been pending in Congress for several years."

12 For example, a provision amended immigration and naturalization law to block entry of any alien whom any consular officer or the Department of Justice had reason to believe had engaged in money-laundering or intended to enter the US to so engage. *Money Laundering Alert*, vol. 13, no. 3 (January 2002).

13 *Money Laundering Alert*, vol. 13, no. 3 (January 2002). The publication dryly observed that "U.S. enforcement and intelligence agents will now have information sources they never had before."

14 See Patti Waldmeir's critique in *Financial Times*, 21 March 2002.

15 *Money Laundering Alert*, vol. 13, no. 1 (November 2001); *Money Laundering Alert*, vol. 13, no. 2 (December 2001); *Money Laundering Alert*, vol. 13, no. 3 (January 2002).

16 Although a shell bank could still get a US correspondent account, it would have to operate through one foreign bank that would have to set up a correspondent account in yet another foreign bank that, in turn, would open a correspondent account with a US bank. In principle this would not only increase the cost and inconvenience but also act as a red flag to alert the participating banks – who would be fearful of becoming themselves the target of retaliatory measures (John Moscow, "The Fight against Money Laundering after September 11," *Address to the Second International Conference on Money Laundering*, Brussels, 23 April 2002).

17 *Money Laundering Alert*, vol. 13, no. 2 (December 2001).

18 *Ottawa Citizen*, 17 September 2003.

19 *Money Laundering Alert*, vol. 13, no. 4 (February 2002).

20 Some Congressmen wanted to make it a crime simply to take more than $10,000 in cash in and out of the country (*Financial Times*, 6 October 2001).

21 *Money Laundering Alert*, vol. 12, no. 12 (October 2001).

22 *The Q: A Private Newsletter*, no. 31 (September 2003).

23 Some Congressmen demanded a law to *require* the Treasury to forbid dealings with banks in any country where secrecy laws prevent cooperation with a US investigative agency (*New York Times*, 5 October 2001).

24 See, for example, *eWeek Enterprise News and Reviews*, 29 July 2002, for a virtual Big Brother "compliance" software to automatically file SARs, follow ongoing cases, and disperse notifications when investigations need to be escalated.

25 Hilary Russ, "Credit Card Companies Close Muslim Accounts," *AlterNet*, 15 April 2003.

26 *Providence Journal*, 28 February 2006.

27 Cf. Michael Levi and Bill Gilmore, "Terrorist Financing, Money Laundering, and the Rise and Rise of Mutual Evaluation," *European Journal of Law Reform*, vol. 4, no. 2 (2002).

28 *The Independent*, 2 November 2001.

29 In his Congressional testimony of 5 June 2003 (*New York Times*, 6 June 2003).

30 For example, its use in a Seattle case involving importing marijuana from British Colombia (*Seattle Times*, 30 July 2004).

31 *The Q: A Private Newsletter,* no. 31 (September 2003).

32 *New York Times,* 12 November 2003; *Boston Globe,* 15 December 2003; *Associated Press,* 15 December 2003.

33 *Financial Times,* 15 September 2004.

34 *Money Laundering Alert,* April 2004.

35 See US Customs Service, Office of Investigations, "Green Que$t: Finding the Missing Piece of the Terrorist Puzzle," Washington, October 2002.

CHAPTER TEN

1 Its other members were Thomas Biersteker, David Cohen, W. Bowman Cutter, Stuart Eizenstat, Michael Fenzel, Rick Small, Maurice Sonnenberg, Joan Spero, Todd Stern, and Jonathan Winer, along with ex-FBI chief, William Webster.

2 Report of an Independent Task Force, *Terrorist Financing,* Council on Foreign Relations, New York, 2002.

3 At the same time he warned about excessive optimism: "While the Mafia is a shell of what it once was [others might argue that it is exactly what it always was], we haven't stamped it out yet," (*New York Times,* 10 December 2002). No, indeed. It is much to useful to lose.

4 See "Testimony by Lee Wolosky Concerning the Second Report of an Independent Task Force on Terrorist Finacning Sponsored by the Council on Foreign Relations," *US Senate,* Committee on Governmental Affairs, 15 June 2004.

5 "Greenberg and Sons," *Fortune,* 21 February 2005.

6 *New York Times,* 12 April 2005.

7 See, for example, *New York Times,* 3 October 2001.

8 Task Force *Report,* 15. This claim was followed by a discussion revealing that their top-quality state-of-the-art information had been derived from a recent story in the *New York Times* – which in other stories quoted the Task Force approvingly.

9 *New York Times,* 5 November 2001.

10 See Richard J. Mangan, "The Southeast Asian Banking System," DEA *Quarterly,* Winter 1984, for a law-enforcement perspective. This study is ostensibly classified, though copies circulate freely throughout the research community. It is not clear if it was classified because the DEA thought it contained significant information or because the contents are so foolish. For an insightful rejoinder, see William L. Cassidy, "Fei-Ch'ien Flying Money: A Study of Chinese Underground Banking," address before the 12th Annual International Asian Organized Crime Conference, 26 June 1990.

11 A sketch of the rise of the Chinese entrepreneurial Diaspora is in Sterling Seagrave's *Lords of the Rim* (New York, 1995).

12 The Templars can also be creditted as architects of the moral antecedents of bank secrecy laws. They acted as discreet custodians of the wealth of noblemen who ventured forth to rescue the Holy Sepulchre (and any gold or silver they could find) from the Saracen hordes. And they defended such wealth against efforts by rival nobles or the Crown to exercise a sort-of medieval right of asset seizure. See Alain Demurger, *Vie et mort de l'ordre du Temple* (Paris, 1989), part 4.

13 See, for example, Phillip Curtin, *Cross-Cultural Trade in World History* (Cambridge, 1984). On the modern spread see Joel Kotkin, *Tribes: How Race, Religion and Identity Determine Success in the New Global Economy* (New York, 1993).

14 Sometimes the Hindu term, hundhi system, is used interchangeably, although, properly speaking, hundhi refers to a promissory note or a bill of exchange while hawāla derives from an Arabic root meaning *transfer*. There actually is an important distinction in practice. Hawāldars essentially engage in remittance business, local or international (which would automatically involve them in foreign exchange transactions); while hundiwallahs can do that and more – they can provide credit for small-scale enterprises, handle trade financing, act as depository institutions on behalf of their clients. Thanks to Azfar Khan for these points.

15 See, for example, C.P.S. Nayyar, "Can a Traditional Financial Technology Co-exist with Modern Financial Technologies: The Indian Experience," *Savings And Development*, vol. 10, no.1, 1986; and Thomas Timberg and C.V. Aiyar, "Informal Credit Markets in India," *Economic Development and Cultural Change*, 1984.

16 *Times of India*, 22 June 1986.

17 See, for example, the account in L.C. Jain, *Indigenous Banking in India* (London, 1929).

18 Two good works on the Indio-Pakistani system are by Angelina Malhotra, "India's Underground Bankers," *Asia, Inc.*, August 1995; and B.V. Kumar, "Capital Flight Operations and the Developing World," *Money Laundering and Asset Forfeiture*, vol. 1, Baldwin and Monro, eds.

19 *Illustrated Weekly of India*, 10 November 1974.

20 For serious examinations of the phenomenon, see Nikos Passas, *Informal Value Transfer Systems and Criminal Organizations: A Study of So-Called Underground Banking Networks* Wetenschappelijk Onderzoek – en Documentaticentrum, the Hague, 1999/4; John Wilson, "Hawala and other Informal Payment Systems: An Economic Perspective," *IMF Middle Eastern Department*, 2002; Patrick Jost and Harjit Singh Sandhu, *The Hawala Alternative*

Remittance System and Its Role in Money Laundering, Interpol General Secretariat (Lyon, 2000); Roger Ballard, *A Background Report on the Operation of Informal Value Transfer Systems* (Manchester University, 2003) and *Hawala Transformed: Remittance-Driven Transnational Networks in the Post-Imperial Economic Order* (Manchester University, 2003); Samuel Maimbo, *The Money Exchange Dealers of Kabul: A Study of the Hawala System in Afghanistan*, Finance and Private Sector Unit, South Asia Region, World Bank, June 2003.

21 These points are particularly well made by Roger Ballard in *Background Report* and *Hawala Transformed*.

22 *New York Times*, 3 October 2003. Since they work mainly among kinfolk, most hawāla operators charge only a token sum for small movements, while making most of their money off large remittances arranged for the wealthy and from correctly anticipating exchange fluctuations.

23 Dexter Filkins "In Afghan War, Top Exiles Printed Themselves a Fortune," *New York Times*, 2 May 2002.

24 *Financial Times*, 14 October 2001.

25 *Financial Times*, 9 December 1999.

26 *Times of India*, 15 November 2004.

27 R.T. Naylor, "From Underworld to Underground: Enterprise Crime, 'Informal Sector' Business and the Public Policy Response," *Crime, Law & Social Change* 24, 1996, 98–105.

28 *Money Laundering Alert*, vol. 13, no. 4 (February 2002).

29 *New York Times*, 30 May 2003.

30 *Financial Times*, 27 May 2003; BBC News, 8 May 2003.

31 *La Presse*, 30 October 1993.

32 See the observations by Andrew Cockburn in *National Geographic*, July 2002.

33 *Financial Times*, 26 October 2001. See the accounts of the harassment of Somalis in the US in Tram Nguyen, *We Are All Suspects Now* (Boston, 2005), 34–5 et passim.

34 The Bank of Boston's 1985 scandal had (fortuitously, of course) smoothed the passage of the first US anti-money-laundering law. See R.T. Naylor, *Hot Money and the Politics of Debt*, 3rd ed. (Montreal, 2004), 289.

35 In fact the highest guesstimate of the *total* amount of Somalia-bound remittances handled by several different companies never topped $500 million, and that was pushing it; while Al Barakaat agents in various countries took 1 percent and the central organization about 3 percent more to cover costs plus profits.

36 *New York Times*, 10 December 2001.

37 *New York Times*, 8 November 2001.

38 *Financial Times*, 21 February 2002.

39 *Financial Times*, 8 November 2001.

40 *New York Times*, 30 January 2002.

41 *New York Times*, 8 November 2001, 30 January 2002; *Financial Times*, 29 November 2001, 21 February 2002; *Daily Telegraph*, 9 November 2002.

42 www.africaaction.org/docs01/somo111.htm.

43 *Financial Times*, 26 October 2001, 9 November 2001.

44 *New York Times*, 8 November 2001.

45 *Financial Times*, 21 February 2002.

46 ILO Mission to Somalia, Report – The Role of Remittances on Economy in Somalia, June 1998.

47 *Financial Times* 15 November 2001.

48 *Star-Tribune* (Minnesota), 19 November 2000.

49 *Daily Telegraph*, 9 November 2001.

50 *Money Laundering Alert*, vol. 13, no. 8, June 2002. In Canada it was properly licensed (*Globe and Mail*, 10 November 2001).

51 *United States versus Abdi*, United States Court of Appeals for the Fourth District CR–02–14–A, 3 September 2003.

52 *Washington Post*, 18 May 2004.

53 *New York Times*, 23 August 2002; *Africa News*, 9 September 2002.

54 *New York Times*, 13 April 2002.

CHAPTER ELEVEN

1 An enormous literature on "Islamic economics" has emerged since the 1970s. For an early treatise, see Anwar Iqbal Qureshi, *The Economic and Social System of Islam* (Lahore, 1979). For a more current one Mohammad Manzoor Alam, *Perspectives on Islamic Economics*, (New Delhi, 1996). Perhaps the biggest problem in practice has been reconciling Islamic principles with modern banking methods. See, for example, Muhammad Nejatullah Siddiqi, *Issues in Islamic Banking* (Leicester, 1983).

2 "It is He Who hath created for you all things that are on earth" (sura 2, verse 29). "See ye the seed that ye sow in the ground? Is it ye that cause it to grow, or are We the Cause?" (sura 56, verse 63). "It is We Who have placed you with authority on earth, and provided you therein with means for the fulfillment of your life" (sura 7, verse 10). "Whatever man possesses, therefore, is given to him by Allah" (sura 43, verse 32).

3 Sura 104, verse 2–9, theatens dire punishment for such behavior.

4 Thus: "O ye who believe! Devour not usury, doubling and quadrupling [the sum lent]. Observe your duty to Allah that ye may be successful" (sura 3, verse 130).

5 Maxine Rodinson, *Islam and Capitalism* (New York, 1973), 36–8. See also Benjamin Nelson, *The Idea of Usury from Tribal Brotherhood to Universal Brotherhood* (Chicago, 1969).

6 That is precisely the function of the Biblical Year of Jubilee, for example. See Exodus 21:2, 23:10–11; Deuteronomy 15; Leviticus 25–26. There are similar institutions in other societies. Thanks to Michael Hudson for these insights.

7 Athar Murtuza, "Analyzing the Contemporary Discourse about Riba Among Muslims," paper presented at the AMSS 32nd Annual Conference, Indiana University, Bloomington, IN, 26–28 September 2003.

8 One of the finest and most comprehensive works on this subject is Ibrahim Warde, *Islamic Finance in the Global Economy* (Edinburgh, 2000). He makes the important distinction that the shari'a recognizes the economic value of time – it just does not agree that the time value of money be predetermined in quantity and rate (21). See also Saeed Abdullah, *Islamic Banking and Interest* (Leiden, 1996) and Fuad al-Omar and Mohammed Abdel-Haq, *Islamic Banking: Theory, Practice and Challenges* (Karachi, 1996).

9 See especially Frank Vogel and Samuel Hayes, *Islamic Law and Finance: Religion, Risk and Return* (London and Boston, 1998).

10 *Financial Times*, 28 September 2001, 8 October 2001, 18 December 2001. See "War on Terrorism: Special Report," *Boston Herald*, 14 October 2001. This "special report" is a concoction of unsubstantiated aspersions. See also *Newsweek*, 11 November 2001, where much is made of "possible ties" from the fact that "the Dutch Bank ABN AMRO has a 40% interest in Saudi Hollandi Bank in Jidda, the largest non-Saudi-owned bank in the country. Saudi Hollandi has a relationship with the Sudanese Al Shamal Islamic Bank, said to have been founded by Osama bin Laden." It is interesting that such guilt by association also applies to major international banking institutions who process billions of dollars in transactions daily.

11 www.albaraka.com.

12 *New York Times*, 8 November 2001.

13 Some of these relationships are traced in Dan Briody, *The Iron Triangle: Inside the Secret World of the Carlyle Group* (New York, 2003).

14 See "Italy Freezes 'Terror' Funds," CNN.com, 29 August 2002; *New York Times*, 8 November 2001; *Washington Post*, 12 November 2001; *Newsweek*, 25 March 2002. *Newsweek* added the claim that the Bahamian banks managed the treasury (allegedly some $60 million) of Hamas, the main Palestinian resistance group (and an outgrowth of the Muslim Brotherhood). And it lauded the closing as "an important step in slowing down bin Laden's river of cash to a trickle." Incidentally another part of Al Taqwa's

unwritten rap sheet may be the fact that its board included the unpopular Ahmed Huber, a Swiss convert to Islam who is routinely described in the press as a "Holocaust denier."

15 "It is used to facilitate the movement of weapons, men and money across the world" (*Newsweek*, 13 November 2002).

16 This is not to suggest the blind sheikh is any innocent. (See Robert Friedman's excellent "The CIA and the Sheik," *Village Voice*, 30 March 1993.) Rather he seems to be simply another Islamic-clerical loudmouth who utters exhortations and leaves it to other deluded souls to actually plan and act. After the media had saturated the public, including jurors, with months of Islamophobia, he was convicted of various acts of "conspiracy," the usual way of nailing someone when there is little or no evidence of direct participation in actual acts.

17 Cited in Alam, *Perspectives*, 118.

18 For example: "Lo! Those who give alms, both men and women, and lend unto Allah a goodly loan, it will be doubled for them, and theirs will be a rich reward" (sura 57, verse 18). Some translations prefer "beautiful loan."

19 Thanks to Mehmet Karabela for these insights.

20 "If you do deeds of charity openly, it is well; but if you bestow it on the needy in secret, it will be even better for you, and it will atone for some of your bad deeds. And God is aware of all that you do" (sura 2, verse 271).

21 There is also fitrah, a special donation to the poor during Ramadan. Thanks to Homa Hoodfar for these points.

22 See the comments of Ambassador Edward Walker at the Middle East Institute's "Islamic Charity, the Concept of Zakat, and the Post 9/11 Environment," *Congressional Staff Lunch Briefing*, 30 June 2004.

23 See the eulogy to the Task Force report by Jeff Gerth and Judith Miller, "Report Says Saudis Fail to Crack Down on Charities That Finance Terrorists," *New York Times*, 17 October 2002.

24 See, for example, *US News & World Report*, 15 December 2003. This cover story was entitled "The Saudi Connection," the name obviously chosen to invoke a Hollywood-style criminal conspiracy.

25 *Washington Post*, 6 August 2002.

26 US Treasury Department, Office of Public Affairs, *Treasury News*, 9 January 2002. The move was presented as the Bush administration "continuing its assault on Osama bin Laden's financial network" (*New York Times*, 10 February 2002). Indeed, just as effectively and precisely as before.

27 *Los Angeles Times*, 16 October 2002. Indeed there is a possibility the causation actually worked in reverse. The US bought the captives sight unseen; assumed that, if they had been in Afghanistan, they had to be al-Qā'idah;

began to interrogate them; discovered they worked for several charities; and then added those two organizations to the list of terror-supporting charities.

28 *The Independent*, 14 October 2005.

29 *New York Times*, 21 December 2001, 22 December 2001.

30 Gul, *Unholy Nexus*, 114, 187–9.

31 *Los Angeles Times*, 26 September 2001.

32 *Newsweek*, 22 October 2001; *Boston Herald*, 14 October 2001.

33 See *Newsweek*, 22 October 2001.

34 "Bin Laden's money is not coming over to help the Abu Sayyaf. It's the other way around," *Gulf News*, 4 February 2002. The flow was supposedly "on a regular basis." Apart from the fact that "regular" transfers violate the most elementary rule of security in covert funds movements, this also raises the obvious question, where were the police and intelligence agencies when all this was happening on a "regular" basis?

35 "Bin Laden's Brother-in-Law Speaks," CNN.com, 24 November 2004. I am especially indebted to Jane Hunter, who interviewed Khalifah in 1995 during his tribulations with the US.

36 See, for example, *New York Times*, 13 October 2001. "Mr. Mahfouz and Mr. bin Laden were both born in Yemen, and are revered by many Yemenis. A U.S. probe into the terrorist attack there has been stymied by the Yemen government, which openly supports a 'holy war' against the U.S., and has vowed to provide sanctuary to jihad militants." This story is typical of the handiwork of Judith Miller.

37 *Forbes*, 18 March 2002.

38 *Arab News*, 1 March 2004.

39 *Guardian*, 26 September 2001.

40 *Chicago Tribune*, 16 October 2001.

41 *Beta News Agency*, Belgrade, 23 October 2004 (BBC Monitoring International Reports, 31 October 2004).

42 "Hotlink to Terror?" *ABC News*, 6 December 2002; *Newsweek*, 6 December 20–02; *New York Times*, 7 December 2002; *Forbes*, 6 December 2002. See especially the always delightfully delirious Rachel Ehrenfeld, "Dollars of Terror," *FrontPageMagazine*, 18 April 2005.

43 Oussama Ziade, to be exact. See "Terrorist Probe Hobbles Ptech," *Computerworld*, 17 January 2003. The company survived and continues to operate as PtechInc.

44 *Arab News*, 19 September 2002.

45 *New York Times*, 3 June 2004; *Financial Times*, 3 June 2004.

46 *New York Times*, 17 September 2003.

47 *Arab News*, 9 February 2005.

48 *Afrol News*, 22 January 2004; *New York Times*, 3 June 2004.

49 Edward Walker, "The Quiet Revolution," *Middle East Institute*, 14 January 2004.

CHAPTER TWELVE

1 There was subsequently an effort to whitewash the affair with the claim that the terrorist group warned the British of the bomb. This is true – by telephone, one minute before the blast. One part of the hotel was used as British administrative headquarters, which led to apologists saying that it was a military target. Obviously it was impossible to take out the military administration without also killing large numbers of innocent bystanders. The bombs were placed in the cafeteria used by everyone and designed so that any attempt to move them automatically triggered the explosion. Begin did not plant the bombs, but he gave the order.

2 See J. Bowyer Bell, *Terror out of Zion: Irgun Zvai Leumi, LEHI, and the Palestine Underground* (New York, 1977). This work is based overwhelmingly on recollections of Zionist activists with only token efforts to secure an Arab point of view.

3 For a recent examination of the mindset, see Jacqueline Rose, *The Question of Zion* (Princeton, 2005).

4 Mohammed Heikal, *Secret Channels: The Inside Story of the Arab-Israeli Peace Negotiations* (London, 1996), 16, 22.

5 On the early theopolitical debates see Israel Shakah, *Jewish History, Jewish Religion: The Weight of Three Thousand Years* (London, 1994).

6 An excellent dissection is in David Fromkin, *A Peace to End All Peace* (New York, 1989).

7 Chaim Weizmann, *Trial and Error* (New York, 1949), 173–4.

8 See his remarkable "Zionism versus Bolshevism," *Sunday Herald*, 8 February 1920.

9 Cooley, *Babylon*, 31.

10 The pre-World War II destruction of Palestinian peasant society is examined in Ilan Pappe, *A History of Modern Palestine* (Cambridge, 2004). Pappe is one of the leading "new historians" in Israel who have challenged the society's deep-rooted myths about its formation – and been harassed and threatened for their efforts.

11 The history is explained in Lenni Brenner's two studies, *Zionism in the Age of Dictators: A Reappraisal* (London, 1983) and *The Iron Wall: Zionist Revisionism from Jabotinsky to Shamir* (London, 1984). See also his recent compilation,

51 Documents: Zionist Collaboration with the Nazis (Fort Lee, NJ: 2002). See also Edwin Black, *The Transfer Agreement: The Dramatic Story of the Pact between the Third Reich and Jewish Palestine* (New York, 2001).

12 Peter Day, "Jewish Plot to Kill Bevin in London," *The Times* (London), 5 March 2006.

13 Stephen Green, *Taking Sides: America's Secret Relations with a Militant Israel* (New York, 1984), 47n.

14 See Wilbur Eveland Crane, *Ropes of Sand: America's Failure in the Middle East* (New York, 1980). Crane, who had a long and distinguished diplomatic (and perhaps espionage) career in the Middle East, recalls how harassment forced his own family to pack up and move from the area.

15 Although the account is fairly conventional, details about the "Kosher Nostra" can be found in Stephen Fox, *Blood and Power: Organized Crime in Twentieth Century America* (New York, 1989). See also an account of an Irgun fundraiser in the memoirs of Jimmy "the weasel" Fratianno – Ovid Desmaris, *The Last Mafioso* (New York, 1981), 32–3 – who stated "I've never seen so many Jewish bookmakers in one place in my life."

16 *New York Times,* 19 May 1944.

17 *The Times* (London), 25 July 1946, 14 September 1946, 16 December 1946; *New York Times,* 13 January 1946, 28 July 1946, 25 March 1947, 23 July 1947; Robert John and Sami Hadawi, *The Palestine Diary* Vol. II (New York, 1985), 340. Menachem Begin in his memoirs, *The Revolt* (New York, 1977), 80–1, brags of his role in the payroll train heist, claiming they were very careful not to hurt anyone – the credibility of this can be assessed by the fact that in the New York meeting attended by Jimmy "the weasel" Fratianno, Begin was quite forthcoming about his role in the King David Hotel bombing. The assembled mobsters in fact found Begin's history very attractive, including the fact that, like so many of them, he was on the lam. That may account in part for their willingness to contribute generously to his further activities.

18 Bell, *Terror,* 28–9.

19 Shamir later confessed to ordering, but not to commiting, the murder, claiming that his rival had "lost his mind." No doubt a bullet hole through his skull facilitated the process. On Shamir's career, see Brenner, *Iron Wall,* passim; *Le Monde,* 1 September 1983; *Toronto Star,* 2 September 1983; *Globe and Mail,* 2 September 1983, 8 October 1983; *Middle East International* 16, 30 September 1983. On Shamir's confession, see *Associated Press,* 14 January 1994.

20 *Times of London,* 23 September 1940, 23 January 1942, 9 November 1944, 4 December 1946; John and Hadawi, *Palestine Diary,* II, 298–9, 337. It was

not always clear which faction was behind the robberies, and in some cases they could have been the work of entrepreneurial robbers pretending to be terrorists to throw the British police off the trail. See, for example, *The Times* (London), 24 January 1946, 27 June 1946, 29 November 1946. Diamonds were also stolen by the Irgun, for example, during one of its post office robberies (Bell, *Terror,* 110).

21 Green, *Taking Sides,* 21, 55.

22 The most comprehensive account of weapons procurement and smuggling is by Leonard Slater, *The Pledge* (New York, 1970).

23 John and Hadawi, *Palestine Diary,* II, 86, 302. Properly speaking, it was the Jewish Agency that did the black market operations, then used the money to buy arms for the militia groups.

24 There are different accounts of just who was involved – Meyer Lansky, Mickey Cohen, or Moe Sedway, possibly all of them. See for example, Messick, *Lansky,* 276.

25 Slater, *Pledge,* 27 et passim; David Ben Gurion and Moshe Pearlman, *Ben Gurion Looks Back* (New York, 1965), 139.

26 On the early protests, see *Jerusalem Post,* 16 February 1988.

27 Stopping arms rackets was one of the central concerns of British military intelligence in the region. See, for example, *The Times* (London), 13 December 1943, 25 September 1945; Alan Hart, *Arafat: Terrorist or Peacemaker* (London, 1984), 72, 141; David Hacohen "Smuggling Arms for the Haganah," *Jerusalem Quarterly,* no. 9, Fall 1978.

28 Robert Lacey, *Little Man: Meyer Lansky and the Gangster Life* (Boston, 1991), 163; Hank Messick, *Lansky* (New York, 1973), 276.

29 Green, *Taking Sides,* 21, 55, 60–5; Andrew and Leslie Cockburn, *Dangerous Liaison: The Inside Story of the U.S.-Israel Covert Relationship* (New York, 1991), 14, 22–3, 108 et passim.

30 Bell, *Terror,* 110, 264, 312.

31 On the conduct of the ethnic cleansing, see especially Pappe, *Palestine,* 129–31, 136–41, and the account in *Ha'ir,* 6 May 1992. None of this was a closely held secret. In 1943 President Roosevelt sent a US general to assess on the situation in Palestine. He reported that the Zionist plan was clear and consisted of three parts: to establish a Jewish state in all of Palestine, including Transjordan; to transfer the Arab population en masse to Iraq; and to permit, as he put it, "Jewish leadership for the whole Middle East in the fields of economic development and control," General Patrick Hurley to President Franklin Roosevelt in United States, *Foreign Relations of the United States 1943: The Near East and Africa* (Washington, DC: 1964), 776–7.

32 Flapan, *Birth of Israel*, 88–96. See also Sami Hadawi, *Bitter Harvest: Palestine 1914–1979* (New York, 1979), especially chapter 7, for the recollections of a Palestinian who survived the events.

33 This was confirmed by neutrals at the time, but expunged from the mainstream historical record. On the correction of the record, see the work of the Israeli historian Benny Morris, *The Birth of the Palestinian Refugee Problem* (Cambridge, 1987) and *1948 and After: Israel and the Palestinians* (Oxford, 1990). Lest Morris be taken as a biased source and denounced in the same terms as "new historians" like Ilan Pappe, he took pains to make it clear that, while each time he researched the issue, he found more rapes, murders, and massacres, he approved wholeheartedly. To him the biggest mistake the Zionist movement had made was to not complete the job, leaving some areas inside the 80 percent of Palestine taken over in 1948 still populated by Arabs. In an interview with a leading Israeli newspaper, he put it simply: "You can't make an omelet without breaking eggs. You have to dirty your hands … If you expected me to burst into tears, I'm sorry to disappoint you. I will not do that" (*Haaretz*, 8 January 2004). Most of this pseudo-uproar over the sudden discovery by Israeli historians of the pattern of deliberate massacres is foolish – all they had to do was ask Palestinian survivors. But then, presumably Israeli historians are able to work with recently opened government and military archives, which are "objective," while Palestinian victims are untrustworthy. It would be interesting to see the history of the Holocaust similarly rewritten to eliminate personal accounts of victims and to rely purely on official Nazi files.

34 Interestingly, about the only properties ever returned were some of the Arab bank accounts frozen in Haifa, the commercial and financial centre of Palestine – in the future Israel would recruit Arab informants and spies by offering to release some of their impounded money. See Central Intelligence Agency, *Israel: Foreign Intelligence and Security Services*, March 1979, 22. A copy of this document was retrieved from the shredder during the takeover of the US Embassy in Teheran in 1979.

35 The story of the seizures and looting is told very well by Tom Segev, *1949: The First Israelis* (New York, 1986), chapter 3. See also Flapan, *Birth of Israel*, 100–1. Despite Ben Gurion's concerns, by the early 1950s more than one third of Israel's population was living in "absentee property."

36 Green, *Taking Sides*, 38–40, traces official complicity in the murder and in the escape of the perpetrators.

37 On conditions in Occupied Palestine, see Naylor, *Patriots & Profiteers*, chapter 9.

38 On the flow of US aid money, see *Wall Street Journal*, 19 September 1991;
Christian Science Monitor, 9 December 2002; Richard Curtis, "U.S. Aid to
Isrel: The Subject No One Mentions," *The Link*, vol. 30, no. 4, September-
October 1997; Thomas Stauffer, "The Cost of Conflict in the Middle East,"
Middle East Policy Journal, vol. 10, no. 1, Spring 2003; Clyde Mark, "Israel:
U.S. Foreign Assistance," *Congressional Research Service*, 1 April 2003.

39 There is an enormous amount of rumor and disinformation surrounding
the career of Abu Nidal. By far the best work is by Patrick Seale, *Abu Nidal:
A Gun for Hire* (New York, 1992) – it is flawed only by taking some of the exaggerated rumors about Abu Nidal's financial assets seriously. See also the
obituary by David Hirst in *The Guardian*, 20 August 2002.

40 Seale, *Abu Nidal*, 60–2, 66.

41 For the comic-book version of events, see the late Claire Sterling's *The Terror Network: The Secret War of International Terrorism* (New York, 1981); the
similar work by Ovid Demaris, *Brothers in Blood: The International Terrorist
Network* (New York, 1977) preceded it by several years but without the same
impact. Interestingly, Demaris transformed himself from Organized Crime
expert to Organized Terrorism guru; while Sterling did the opposite. Many
mainstream media accounts seem to have been copied from Claire
Sterling's *The Terror Network*, which Seale appropriately refers to as "comic
strip reports" (Seale, *Abu Nidal*, 52). David Yallop adds: "Outside the worlds
of Edward Lear and Lewis Carroll it would be difficult to find so much nonsense gathered between the covers of one book as that contained in *The Terror Network*" (Yallop, *Ends*, 535). For a summary of terrorist attacks imputed
to Abu Nidal, see *Wall Street Journal*, 15 October 1987.

42 Informed books on Carlos reflect both contemporary concerns and the
authors' special sources. The first was by Colin Smith, *Carlos: Portrait of a
Terrorist* (London, 1976). Written at the time the Carlos myth was still
growing, it was based almost entirely on Western police and security service information. (The same applies to the 1995 reissue.) Much of the material was called into question in David Yallop's *To the Ends of the Earth: The
Hunt for the Jackal* (London, 1993). Yallop spent years cultivating informants onsite and had unparalleled access to the PLO – which knew Carlos
better than anyone, except perhaps East Germany. The third book, by
John Pollain, *Jackal: The Secret Wars of Carlos the Jackal* (London, 1998), in
some ways harkens back to the first in that it is largely stripped of critical
political context – the heroes and villains are predictable. However the author had access to East Bloc archives and agents who dealt with Carlos and
the benefit of Carlos's extensive debriefing (to the extent the results can

be trusted) by the French authorities after his capture. It is useful to read the second and third together to get a balanced (although occasionally contradictory) view.

43 While the prevalent belief was (is) that the scheme was sponsored by Mu'ammar Qadhafi, in reality the "madman" ruling Libya regarded Carlos as a common criminal and played a major role in thwarting the operation. A more likely (but still improbable) suspect was Saddam Hussein. At the time OPEC was split between price doves (both Iran and Saudi Arabia favored a freeze) and hawks; and Saddam reputedly wanted extra revenue to prepare for war with Iran. The result was, by one theory, a plan to take over OPEC headquarters in Vienna, force the Austrian government to give the kidnappers a plane, hop from country to country discharging various oil ministers in a barrage of propaganda, then finish in Baghdad where the ministers of Saudi Arabia and Iran would be murdered – as if Saddam would be dumb enough to stage such a finale on his own turf. That would pave the way for another big price increase (Yallop, *Ends*, 377–9); Pollain (*Jackal*, 102) prefers the tale that it was Qadhafi's work, although he introduces Saddam as a co-conspirator.

44 Pollain (*Jackal*, 102) has Carlos actually pocketing much of the money although his information from East German sources is likely less reliable than Yallop's from the PLO.

45 Abu Iyad, the PLO's intelligence supremo, until his murder by the Abu Nidal terrorist group, told David Yallop: "Carlos is an empty drum … Carlos has no connection with the KGB … He is not even a leftist, just someone pretending to be of the left" (*Ends*, 214).

46 Cited in Pollain, *Jackal*, 215.

47 Smith, *Carlos*, 313–24.

48 Pollain interviewed one of the jurors after the trial. Interestingly, the juror found Carlos's revolutionary commitment decidedly unconvincing. "He seemed more like a gun for hire who had been abandoned by everyone" (*Jackal*, 264).

49 Cited in Pollain, *Jackal*, 262.

50 Adam Zagorin, "A House Divided," *Foreign Policy*, Spring 1983; *Middle East Reporter*, 30 August 1980; *Wall Street Journal*, 25 July 1986.

51 For a fair portrayal, see *Business Week*, 22 February 1988; see also *Wall Street Journal*, 6 July 2004, 20 April 2005, *Jerusalem Post*, 21 April 2005.

52 Most of the work dealing with the PLO finances is preposterous, largely based on recycled Israeli intelligence disinformation. See, for example, Edgar O'Ballance, *Arab Guerrilla Power 1967–72* (London, 1973); James Adams, *The Financing of Terror* (New York, 1986), part 2; and, perhaps the worst, Neil

Livingston and David Halevy, *Inside the PLO: Covert Units, Secret Funds and the War against Israel and the United States* (New York, 1990). As befitting a book with such a subtitle, its chapter dealing with finance is a clever amalgam of correct information that was already in the public domain regarding the PLO's fiscal position with assertions about an Arafat-controlled secret fund supposedly derived from skyjacking ransoms, drugs, and bank robbery. The authors fudge the distinction between various Palestinian groups and the PLO itself. Hijackings carried out by the Popular Front for the Liberation of Palestine, for example, are imputed to Arafat. Even those well known to be carried out by the Abu Nidal, who has probably murdered more PLO officials than the Israeli Mossad, are blended into the PLO activities.

53 Yallop, *Ends of the Earth*, 64, 91, 331, 357, 442.

54 For a summary, see Naylor, *Patriots & Profiteers* or *Economic Warfare*, chapter 8.

55 *Middle East Reporter*, 4 April 1981.

56 *An-Nahar*, 27 December 1982; *Wall Street Journal*, 19 October 1983; *Arab News*, 23 August 1983, 12 September 1983. The lower figure was an official estimate excluding Palestinian infrastructure, and the basis of a subsequent demand by the Lebanese government for war reparations. It referred only to capital losses, excluding any calculation of lost income. See the survey of the damage in Marwan Iskander and Elias Baroudi, *The Lebanese Economy in 1981–2* (Beirut, 1982).

57 See full text of his speech in *Aljazeera*, 1 November 2004.

58 Seale, *Abu Nidal*, 72–5, 99–100.

59 On his Polish career, see *Wall Street Journal*, 15 October 1987; *Middle East Reporter*, 12 March 1988; *New York Times*, 24–25 January 1988; *L'Express*, 31 March 1987. In fact his ability was greatly overrated – once he pocketed an $11 million commission and never delivered on the deal; and eventually Bulgaria shut him down and imprisoned some of his people.

60 Patrick Seale, *Asad: The Struggle for the Middle East* (London, 1988), 336.

61 *The Times* (London), 7 March 1983. According to the *Guardian*, 7 March 1983, the triggerman was also a colonel in Iraqi military intelligence, but no one else seems to concur.

62 Seale, *Abu Nidal*, 210–11.

63 *Middle East*, September 1982; *The Times* (London), 7 and 9 March 1983; *Guardian*, 31 October 1982, 7 March 1983; *Daily Telegraph*, 7 March 1983; *The Economist*, 9 October 1982; Seale, *Abu Nidal*, 143, 153–6, 243 et passim. Yallop (*Ends*, 164, 210) was first informed that Mossad had penetrated Abu Nidal's network by Austrian Chancellor Bruno Kriesky; and Yallop claims he himself received direct confirmation from his enquiries in Lebanon.

64 *Wall Street Journal*, 16 June 1993.

65 *Sunday Times*, 3 November 1991.

66 *Middle East International*, 26 March 1999.

67 *Telegraph*, 25 August 2002.

CHAPTER THIRTEEN

1 On fundraising in the US by militant Hindu groups, see Sabrang Communications, "The Foreign Exchange of Hate: IDRF and the American Funding of Hinutva," www.stopfundinghate.org/sacw/. For a summary, see *Financial Times*, 21 February 2003. The accuracy of this report has been challenged by Hindu groups, though most of their criticisms have consisted of personal attacks on the motivation of the authors rather than on the contents.

2 Some idea of how persuasive all the hidden evidence was can perhaps be garnered from the fact that, according to the Global Relief Foundation's lawyer, when FBI carried out raids in the United States, more than one agent admitted "they were appalled at what they had to do" (*New York Times*, 18 December 2001).

3 *New York Times*, 11 February 2003.

4 *Middle East International*, 7 November 1997. There is an excellent survey by Robert Sale, "Hamas History Tied to Israel," *United Press International*, 18 June 2002.

5 Yet see *The Economist*, 22 November 1997, re: Hamas. "Its finances are clouded in mystery; money is know to come from many sources, including western ones, mainly channelled from charitable organisations and Islamic foundations." Somehow the finances could be clouded in mystery, yet at the same time the sources and routes well known.

6 See Yakov Rabkin, *A Threat from Within: A Century of Jewish Opposition to Zionism* (Vancouver, 2005).

7 For excellent examinations of these trends, see Israel Shahak, *Jewish History, Jewish Religon: The Weight of Three Thousand Years* (London, 1994), and Israel Shahak and Norton Mezvinsky, *Jewish Fundamentalism in Israel* (London, 2004).

8 One of the earlier, but still excellent, overviews of the process is by Ian Lustick, *For the Land and the Lord: Jewish Fundamentalism in Israel* (New York, 1988).

9 See especially Grace Halsell, *Prophesy and Politics* (Chicago, 1986), and *Jerusalem Post*, 17 June 1984.

10 *Macleans*, 7 October 1996; *Knight Ridder Tribune News Services*, 21 September 1996. There is an abundance of documentation on his recent activities at www.stopmoskowitz.org.

11 Kahane's career is examined in the late Robert Friedman's *The False Prophet: Rabbi Meir Kahane from FBI Informant to Knesset Member* (New York, 1990).

12 "Many rich Jews give me a lot of money but they won't admit it openly." This and all other quotes from Meir Kahane come from two sources. One is Raphael Mergui and Philippe Simonnot, *Israel's Ayatollahs: Meir Kahane and the Far Right in Israel* (Atlantic Highlands, NJ: 1987); chapter 2 is an extended and very frank interview with Kahane. The second is Robert Friedman's "The Sayings of Rabbi Kahane," *New York Review of Books*, 13 February 1986. The exception, on weapons, comes from *Middle East International*, 10 February 1984.

13 *Jerusalem Report*, 17 December 1994.

14 See Nadav Shragan, "We're not Kach, but We Love Kahane," *Ha'aretz*, 18 December 2002.

15 "Everybody is mad at me ... because I have confronted people with the following contradiction: you can't have Zionism and democracy at the same time."

16 "Let me tell you what the minimal borders are, and which the rabbis agree upon, according to the description given in the Bible. The southern boundary runs up to El Arish, which takes in all of the northern Sinai ... To the east, the frontier runs along the western part of the East Bank of the Jordan river, hence part of what is now Jordan. Eretz Yisrael also includes parts of the Lebanon and certain parts of Syria, and part of Iraq all the way to the Tigris River ..."

17 "Zionism accelerates the coming of the Messiah ... To have this state is a miracle that comes from G-D ... We are living at the end of time ... The creation of the state of Israel only marks the beginning of the messianic era."

18 *Jerusalem Post*, 8 February 1991.

19 Yet in 2002 the man who assumed de facto leadership of Kach, along with many of his supporters, was formally integrated into the Herut Party, a long-time feature on the Israeli legal political scene and the vehicle which had projected the old Irgun boss, Menachem Begin, to power in 1977 (*Ha'aretz*, 18 December 2002).

20 *New York Times*, 13 November 1995; *The Jerusalem Report*, 9 May 1994, 14 December 1995; *New York Daily News*, 19 November 1995.

21 "The flood of increasingly sophisticated weapons originating from Egypt has reached large-scale proportions ... The weapons are given to Hamas mobsters with a nod and a wink from Arafat" (*Jerusalem Post*, 24 November 1994). Jewish terrorists, by contrast, got their weapons legally – from the Israeli Army.

22 The biggest problem the Israeli occupation authorities faced with Hamas or its alleged military arm was that, unlike the PLO, which was largely an alien import and increasingly despised for its authoritarianism, complicity, and corruption, Hamas was very much a part of the indigenous community; and informants were virtually nonexistent. Nor did those few who did exist have particularly long professional or physiological lifespans (*Haaretz*, 10 February 1993).

23 These statements appeared in *Jerusalem Post*, 24 November 1994, a newspaper whose main function is to convey a positive image of Israel to people (including most North American Jews) unable to read the much more honest Hebrew press. This particular article was the work of two people whose previous credits included hagiographies of Ariel Sharon and Meyer Lansky.

24 *National Catholic Reporter*, 10 February 1995.

25 See "A Look Inside the Radical Islamist Network," *New Republic*, 12 June 1995. The article was written by Steve Emerson, who speaks no Arabic but bills himself as an "expert" in Middle East "terrorist" groups.

26 AP, 7 October 2003; Islam-online.net, 10 July 2003.

27 Thanks to Jane Hunter for this information.

28 In Salah's 2006 trial, a world-renowned human-rights lawyer backed up defense claims by stating that he had interviewed hundreds of detainees in Israeli prisons who were tortured to force them to confess (Chuck Goudie, "Chicago Court Hears Chilling Tales of Torture," *ABC News*, 14 March 2006).

29 Several other Arab Americans who had tried to take money to families in Occupied Palestine reported on their return to the US that they had been arrested, accused of being couriers for Hamas, tied to chairs, shackled, hooded, blasted with loud music, and deprived of sleep for eighty hours. Thanks to Jane Hunter for this information.

30 Cassel, *Liberties*, 79.

31 Boim versus Quranic Literary Society et al. United States District Court Northern District of Illinois Eastern Division No. 00 C2905.

32 *New York Times*, 13 October 2001.

33 *Associated Press*, 9 December 2004; *United Press International*, 9 December 2004; *Muslim American Society*, 9 December 2004.

34 The same seems to apply even to Arab citizens of Israel. When an Israeli soldier, in protest at the closure of Gaza settlements, shot dead four unarmed Arab Israelis, the Israeli Ministry of Defense ruled that the four Arabs were not killed in an act of terrorism and therefore not entitled to compensation (Chris McGreal, "Jewish Gunman Was No Terrorist, Israel Rules," *Guardian*, 9 January 2005).

35 *New York Times*, 4 December 2001.

36 Supreme Court of the United States, *The Holy Land Foundation for Relief and Development v. John Ashcroft* No. 03–775; *Reuters*, 1 March 2004.

37 Department of Justice, "Holy Land Foundation, Leaders, Accused of Providing Material Support to Hamas Terrorist Organization," 27 July 2004; *Money Laundering Alert*, April 2002, August 2003.

38 United States Department of Justice, *Prepared Remarks of Attorney General John Ashcroft*, News Conference, 18 December 2002.

39 *Dallas Morning News*, 6 June 2004.

40 *New York Times*, 17 September 2004. This followed the actions of the previous month in freezing the assets of six reputed top Hamas leaders – who actually were so poor they had nothing to freeze. Still, the increasingly unpopular Arafat regime in Occupied Palestine accommodated the US by ordering a freeze on Hamas bank accounts and set off mass protests by people, especially Gazans, facing potential malnutrition from the cutting off of their sole means of support (IslamOnline.net 23 and 28 August 2004).

41 *New York Times*, 9 February 2005.

42 *Detroit Free Press*, 4 September 2004.

43 Global Relief Foundation Inc. Plaintiff v. Paul H. O'Neill, Colin L. Powell, John Ashcroft, et. al, Defendants, Case No. 02 C674 US District Court for the Northern District of Illinois, Eastern Division, 5 April and 11 June 2002.

44 *Chicago Tribune*, 12 June 2002.

45 Randal, *Osama*, 227.

46 *Michigan Daily*, 26 March 2004; *Metro Times*, 21 March 2004.

47 United States Attorney, Northern District of Illinois, "FBI Arrests Head of Chicago-Based Int'l Charity Organization," 30 April 2002; *USA Today*, 1 May 2002.

48 *Financial Times*, 19 November 2003.

49 *New York Times*, 10 October 2002.

CHAPTER FOURTEEN

1 See *Boston Globe*, 2 November 2001; *Daily News*, 10 April 2002; *Washington Post*, 21 March 2002; *Los Angeles Times*, 22 February 2003; *New York Law Journal*, vol. 231, no. 110, 9 June 2004. Thanks to Max Pomeranc for these references.

2 On hate crimes see Nguyen, *Suspects*, xxii et passim. The call for internment came from, among others, Jack Nicholson on 12 September 2001. See *Observer*, 25 February 2005. Some radical right-wing pundits recalled the mass

internment of Japanese during World War II and asked why not the same treatment for the new enemy who had just declared World War III similarly "without provocation"? See Michelle Malkin, *In Defense of Internment: The Case for "Racial Profiling" in World War II and the War on Terror* (New York, 2004).

3 Attacks and discriminatory actions are monitored by among others the Muslim Civil Rights Center: www.mcrcnet.org/index.htm.

4 See the excellent summary in Madeleine Baran, "The Terrorism Case That Wasn't," *NewStandard*, 29 February 2004, also reprinted in *Alternet*, 20 April 2004, and Jennifer Van Bergen, "New American Law: The Case of Dr. Dhafir," *Counterpunch*, 7 October 2905. Press coverage is compiled at www.jubileeinitiative.org/FreeDhafir1.htm.

5 United States Department of Justice, "Indictments Allege Illegal Financial Transfers to Iraq; Visa Fraud Involving Assistance to Groups That Advocate Violence," no. 119, 26 February 2003.

6 See Madlaine Baran, "As Help the Needy Charity Trial Nears, Case Further Politicizes," *The NewStandard*, 18 April 2004.

7 ABC News, "Iraq's Attack Network," 5 March 2003.

8 Michael Chertoff, the senior Justice official and future Secretary of Homeland Security, crowed "We will hunt from coast to coast, anywhere in the country, those who violate the laws that prohibit illegal transfer of money overseas ..." (*New York Times*, 20 December 2002).

9 *New York Times*, 21 March 2002.

10 The US also targeted Abdul Rahman al-Amoudi, founder of the American Muslim Foundation and the American Muslim Council, and former executive assistant to the president of the SAAR Foundation, who was charged with illegal financial transactions with Libya, money-laundering, misuse of a passport, perjury in his citizenship application, and failure to report foreign bank accounts. Indeed, he had the honor of being perhaps the first foreign national accused under that particular clause of the US anti-money-laundering laws. *Money Laundering Alert*, vol. 15, no. 1, November 2003; *Washington Times*, 29 October 2003.

11 Douglas Farah and John Mintz, "U.S. Trails Va. Muslim Money, Ties," *Washington Post*, 7 October 2002; Randal, *Osama*, 228.

12 This is Rita Katz of the "private" SITE (Search for International Terrorist Entities) Institute in Washington (*Washington Post*, 7 October 2002).

13 See Matthew Epstein and Ben Schmidt, "Operation Support-System Shutdown," *National Review Online*, 4 September 2003; a hyperbolic version of the story can be found in Steven Emerson with Jonathan Levin, "Terrorism Finance: Origination, Organization and Prevention," Testimony to

United States Senate, Committee on Governmental Affairs, 31 July 2003. There is remarkable similarity to the affidavit of David Kane cited in note 18 below.

14 Its last entry (May 1997) in the directory of American Muslim charitable organizations reads: "Your tax deductible donation ... brings a ray of hope through food and clothing distribution, agricultural and small business development; health care and educational programs, as well as special emergency aid – wherever and whenever it's needed!" This charity ran offices throughout the Balkans and in East Africa, Afghanistan, Cambodia, North Africa, the Middle East, ex-Soviet Central Asia, Palestine, and the Indian Subcontinent, focusing on health care as well as emergency food, clothing and shelter.

15 "Hamas – Coming to a Neighborhood Near You," *Jerusalem Newswire*, 28 March 2004.

16 See *us News & World Report*, "The Saudi Connection," 15 November 2003.

17 See David Kane, "Declaration in Support of Pre-Trial Detention," *United States of America v. Soliman Biheiri*, Case No. 03–365–A, United States Court for the Eastern District of Virginia. Kane was the same agent who claimed that SAAR was the world's biggest terror-finance operation. See also Matthew Epstein and Ben Schmidt, "Operation Support-System Shutdown: Who Paid for the 1998 East African Embassy Bombings?" *National Review Online*, 4 September 2003.

18 *New Statesman*, 5 November 2001; *Guardian*, 3 March 2003; *Financial Times*, 6 March 2003.

19 *Newsweek*, 20 October 2004. Rita Katz of SITE supposedly had tracked IARA "for years," eager to get the goods on this nefarious terror network.

20 *Associated Press*, 3 October 2004.

21 *Financial Times*, 31 October 2003.

22 *Newsweek*, 9 December 2002; *New York Times*, 24 November 2002.

23 *Washington Post*, 14 January 2004.

24 *Indianapolis Star*, 15 November 2005.

CHAPTER FIFTEEN

1 Not only in the US but also abroad there was a "vast criminal network ... that provides these groups with the financial revenue to buy military equipment ... It is narcoterrorism all intertwined with organized crime" (*New York Times*, 10 December 2001).

2 Selling on the market today for the current price but for future delivery in the hope that the price will fall before the contract has to be honored.

3 *Reuters*, 20 September 2001; *Wall Street Journal*, 21 October 2001; *Dow Jones Business News*, 20 September 2001; USA *Today*, 26 September 2001.

4 "Probes into suspicious trading," CNN, 24 September 2001; *San Francisco Chronicle*, 3 October 2001; *Daily Telegraph*, 23 September 2001; *Associated Press*, 2 October 2001.

5 *New York Times*, 8 June 2002.

6 *New York Times*, 25 May 2002; *Globe and Mail*, 20 May 2002. Once he was convicted, the government could proceed to forfeiture of his cars, cash, and financial assets (*San Diego Union-Tribune*, 25 January 2005).

7 *Dow Jones Newswire*, 29 September 2003. For examples of the wilder claims see David Ray Griffin, *The 9/11 Commission Report: Omissions and Distortions* (Northampton, MA: 2005), 52–7, and Eric Laurent, *La Face Cachée*, chapter 2.

8 *Orlando Sentinel*, 12 June 2005.

9 See the excellent investigation by Jeffrey Billman, "Malicious Prosecution," *Orlando Weekly*, 17 July 2003.

10 Bob Irvine, "The High Price of Bad Publicity," *Orlando Business Journal*, 11 July 2005.

11 One of the best works explaining the Hizbullāh phenomenon is by Hala Jaber, *Hezbollah: Born with a Vengeance* (New York, 1993); see also Anthony Shadid, *Legacy of the Prophet* (Boulder, CO: 2002), esp. 133–41.

12 *Daily Star* (Beirut), 5 April 1997.

13 Much of the hype over the case can be traced to Daniel Pipes, who runs a website that, among other things, urges people to denounce university professors who are critical of Israel in their classes. See *National Review*, 28 August 2000. In the North Carolina case, Pipes got himself steamed up about not just criminality itself but also the sheer contempt for US law shown by "a bunch of criminal aliens and political extremists."

14 *Charlotte Observer*, 21 September 2001.

15 The original indictment United States v. Mohamad Hammoud et al filed in the District Court, Western District of North Carolina, Charlotte Division, 3:00 CR-147-mu, 31 July 2000, was superceded by two others in March 2001 and March 2002.

16 It is interesting that another turned witness, Samir Debk, testified that he heard Mohammed Hammoud exclaim, "If someone lies and says I'm Hezbollah, they will deal with me in Lebanon" (*Daily Star*, 14 June 2002). Somehow this was taken by the court to imply that Hammoud was indeed a "member," whatever that means, of Hizbullāh, whereas most people might interpret it as a denial.

17 *New York Times*, 24 May 2002.

18 There is a problematic account in Bob Woodward's *Veil: Secret Wars of the CIA 1981–1987* (New York, 1987), 396–9.

19 See especially his "Hezbollah Finances: Funding the Party of God," Washington Institute for Near East Policy, February 2005, and his "Hezbollah: Financing Terror Through Criminal Enterprise," United States Senate, *Hearing of the Committee on Homeland Security*, 25 May 2005.

20 This attack and a similar one against the French forces was claimed by the previously unknown Islamic Jihad group. However this was really more a set of uncoordinated fragments than a formal organization; see Robin Wright, *Sacred Rage* (New York, 1985), 85. Another possible candidate was Islamic Amal, whose chief, Hussein Musawi, denied carrying out the attacks but, in a prelude to the kind of grandstanding for which Usama bin Lāden would later be famed, regretted the fact that he had not. William Dietl, *Holy War* (New York, 1984), 175.

21 *Money Laundering Alert*, vol. 13, July 2002.

22 *Charlotte Observer*, 1 March 2003.

23 *Herald-Sun*, Durham, 2 April 2002.

24 National Center for Policy Analysis, Daily Policy Digest, *Funding Terrorism*, 7 August 2002.

25 *Washington Post*, 8 June 2004. It has been since renamed the Alcohol and Tobacco Tax and Trade Bureau.

26 *Washington Post*, 12 August 2002.

27 The website FactsofIsrael.com graciously commented that, while "many Muslims are not involved in the financing or support of terrorism, it is clear that a certain number are." Therefore its advice to Americans: "Next time you buy your sixpack from your neighborhood Arab/Muslim convenience store, please don't: your money could be used to murder un-armed civilians, including babies and children" (www.factsofisrael.com/blog/archives/000272.html).

28 *Washington Post*, 12 August 2002.

29 *New York Times*, 10 December 2001.

30 *New York Times*, 7 November 2002; *Washington Post*, 7 November 2002. When asked if there were any actual evidence linking the Pakistanis to "al-Qaeda" the law enforcement officials declined to comment.

31 See United States District Court, Southern District of California, Indictment, United States v. Syed Mustajab Shah, Muhammed Abid Afridi, Ilyas Asi. July 2002.

32 Kurt Nimmo, "Inventing Crimes: The FBI-CIA Entrapment Tag Team," *Counterpunch*, 1 February 2003.

33 *Globe and Mail,* 12 August 2002. This time even the prosecution in the trial, as well as the RCMP on the Canadian side, disputed the claims about some grand terrorist connection.

34 See "Economy Vulnerable al-Qaeda Target," in *Omega Letter,* 4 November 2004, a Christian fundamentalist "intelligence" bulletin. "America's main vulnerability is its economy. The terrorists are well aware of it, and have zeroed in on it as its [sic] main target." The same kind of sentiments were expressed by Stratfor, the neocon fundamentalist "intelligence" service in, among its other rants, "U.S. – Economic Impact," 11 September 2002.

35 Cheney called for Americans to "stick their thumb in the eye of the terror-ists and ... not let what's happened here in any way throw off their normal level of activity." To be fair to Cheney, other political leaders expressed sim-ilar market patriotism (*Washington Post,* 23 September 2001). On Wall Street, with the stock market dipping, people were asked to show their pa-triotism by buying more shares (Aaron Task, The Street.Com, 9 September 2002). No one can say Cheney does not practice what he preaches. Right after Hurricaine Katrina devastated tens of thousands of homes in poor areas of Louisiana and nearby states he was himself busy shopping for a new $3 million mansion (*New York Times,* 7 September 2005).

36 An old but still useful general work is Jonathan Fenby, *Piracy and the Public* (London, 1983).

37 In Italy, for example, the highest court made clear the distinction between knock-off replicas for the knowledgeable mass market and exact reproduc-tions designed to defraud companies and their clients. In a precedent-setting case it ruled that there was not an offense to sell fakes provided no one was in real danger of being fooled, that is to say, if the price were well below the originals and the imitation obvious enough to be easily identifi-able as such. *Deutsche Press-Argentur,* 4 March 2000.

38 *Forbes,* 28 December 1998.

39 *New York Times,* 23 June 2002; United States Senate, Committee of the Judi-ciary, *Anticounterfeiting Consumer Protection Cct of 1995,* 28 November 1995.

40 One of the most absurd is Roslyn Mazer, "From T-Shirts to Terrorism: That Fake Nike Swoosh May be Helping to Fund Bin Laden's Network," *Washington Post,* 30 September 2001. This one appeared within a couple weeks of the 9/11 tragedy: it recycled several years of previously unsub-stantiated rumors to arrive at the dramatic conclusion: "The staggering economic losses to America's copyright and trademark industries – alarming unto themselves – now are compounded by the opportunistic trafficking in IP products to finance terrorism and other organized criminal endeavors."

41 The Interpol allegations were, naturally enough, seconded by US Customs, which had similar agendas to advance. See Kathleen Millar, Office of Public Affairs, "Financing Terror: Profits from Counterfeit Goods Pay for Attacks," *U.S. Customs Today*, November 2002.

42 *Far Eastern Economic Review*, 18 June 1992.

43 Ronald Noble, Secretary General of Interpol, "The Links between Intellectual Property Crime and Terrorist Financing," Testimony before United States Congress, House of Representatives Committee on International Relations, 16 July 2003.

44 See the remarkably named *Insight on the News*, 30 October 2003.

45 *New York Times*, 16 July 2003.

46 *Time*, 2 August 2004.

47 *Middle East Intelligence Bulletin*, January 2002.

48 For the rise of the system, see Evert Clark and Nicholas Horrock, *Contrabandista!* (New York, 1973).

49 See *Daily Star* (Beirut), 17 March 2003.

50 *New York Times*, 21 December 2002. See also *Middle East Intelligence Bulletin*, January 2002. This publication is the joint venture of Daniel Pipes, a pro-Israel militant, and the US wing of the Lebanese Christian-extremist party. Brazil seized on the post-9/11 crisis atmosphere to assert its power in the disputed region by claiming that Paraguay did not have the means to stop the spread of terrorist activity.

51 This connection was detailed by many investigators, although the accusations were often hyperbolic. See, for example, Leslie Cockburn, *Out of Control* (New York, 1987); Peter Dale Scott and Jonathan Marshall, *Cocaine Politics: Drugs, Armies and the CIA in Central America* (Berkeley, 1991); Gary Webb, *Dark Alliance: The CIA, the Contras and the Crack Cocaine Explosion* (New York, 1998); and an official, considerably more nuanced report, Subcommittee on Terrorism, Narcotics and International Operations, Committee on Foreign Relations, United States Senate, *Drugs, Law Enforcement and Foreign Policy*, Washington, 1988.

52 See General James T. Hill, "Colombia – the Way Ahead," Center for Strategic & International Studies, 10 September 2003; *Miami Herald*, 15 March 2003.

53 Benjamin Dangl "Fears Mount as US Opens New Miliary Installation in Paraguay," *Excalibur*, 10 October 2005; "Al-Qaida South of the Border," WorldNetDaily.Com, 16 February 2004; *The Australian*, 10 October 2005.

54 House Republican Research Committee, Task Force on Terrorism and Unconventional Warfare, "Iran, Syria and the Trail of Counterfeit Dollars," 1 July 1992. See also Frederic Dannen and Ira Silverman,

"The Supernote," *New Yorker*, 23 October 1995, and Robert Kupperman and David Andelman in *Washington Post*, 6 March 1994.

55 *Boston Globe*, 14 January 1993.

56 Murray Bloom, *The Brotherhood of Money* (Port Clinton, 1983), 37.

57 Of course the Iranians blamed the US, a charge that the Republican Task Force was ready, quite rightly, to fling back in their teeth, timing the release of its report, as the Task Force stated explicitly, exactly to counter the Iranian claim that it was being subjected to a concerted campaign by the US to destabilize its economy (*Los Angeles Times*, 2 July 1992).

58 BBC *Summary of World Broadcasts*, 30 April 1996; *New York Times*, 18 June 1997.

59 "Economy Vulnerable al-Qaeda Target," *Omega Letter*, 4 November 2004; *Time*, 3 March 2003. These stories continued for several years, heating up whenever the Bush administration needed another club with which to beat North Korea. See Martin Fackler, "North Korean Counterfeiting Complicates Nuclear Crisis," *New York Times*, 29 January 2006.

60 *Valley Morning Star*, 2 June 2004.

CHAPTER SIXTEEN

1 The first "investigation" to hit the headlines was by Douglas Farah of the *Washington Post* on 30 December 2001. The most influential was "For a Few Dollars More: How al Qaeda Moved into the Diamond Trade," by Global Witness, the NGO that had, since 1998, taken the lead in agitating for controls on the traffic in diamonds. See also Greg Campbell, *Blood Diamonds: Tracing the Deadly Path of the World's Most Precious Stones* (Boulder, CO: 2002), which takes much the same line.

2 R.W. Winder, "The Lebanese in West Africa," *Immigrants and Associations*, L.A. Fallers, ed. (The Hague, 1967).

3 See H.L. van der Laan, *The Sierra Leone Diamonds* (Oxford, 1965); Michael Harbottle, *The Knaves of Diamonds* (London, 1976); and Peter Greenhalgh, *West African Diamonds: 1919–1983* (Manchester, 1985).

4 Ian Fleming, *The Diamond Smugglers* (London, 1956).

5 Fleming, *Smugglers*, 18–19, 33, 37, 42.

6 Fleming, *Smugglers*, 148.

7 When Fleming raised the story of the Soviet diamond discovery, "John Blaize" assured him that "No one's ever seen anything to back that story up" (Fleming, *Smugglers*, 147).

8 The story is outlined in A.W. Cockerill, *Sir Percy Sillitoe* (London, 1975).

9 The individual, Fouad "Flash Fred" Kamil, told his story in *The Diamond Underworld* (London, 1979). It needs to be read with a certain degree of skepticism.

10 For a summary see R.T. Naylor, *Economic Warfare: Sanctions, Embargo Busting, and Their Human Cost* (Boston, 2001), 167–71.

11 See William Reno, *Corruption and State Power in Sierra Leone* (Cambridge, 1995).

12 One of the best works on this topic is by Edward Jay Epstein, *The Diamond Invention* (New York, 1981).

13 For the most thorough investigation, see Janine Roberts, *Glitter and Greed: Inside the Secret World of the Diamond Cartel* (New York, 2003).

14 *Financial Times*, 31 January 2000, 1 July 2000.

15 Roberts, *Glitter and Greed*, 326–34.

16 Nor have they stopped. Global Witness still calls on the public to demand from sales staff if they can reassure them that their stones are "conflict-free" (*The Independent*, 10 February 2006).

17 *Daily Telegraph*, 23 November 2002. The original damage claim was for £12 million.

18 *Washington Post*, 16 October 1999; *Jerusalem Post*, 16 September 1991, 21 September 1999. On Klein's earlier escapades in Colombia and Antigua, see The best account of the affair is in the report of the investigation by Louis Blom-Cooper, *Guns for Antigua* (London: 1990). See also *Daily News* (Virgin Islands), 26 April 1990, 31 August 1990; *Guardian*, 28 April 1990; *New York Times*, 16 June 1990; *Los Angeles Times*, 16 July 1990; *Washington Post*, 18 July 1990; *Middle East International*, 12 October 1990; *Israeli Foreign Affairs*, December 1990.

19 For a thorough dissection of the accusations made by Douglas Farah in the *Washington Post* about al-Qā'idah diamond dealing, see Christian Dietrich and Peter Danssaert, "Antwerp Blamed, Again," *International Peace Information Service*, 16 November 2001.

20 For a sensible view of the "conflict diamond" and terrorist diamond confusion, and the myths created about them, see the testimony of Christian Dietrich to the Commission d'enquête parlementaire "Grands Lacs" of the Sénat de Belgique, 11 January 2002. He comments, "I cannot imagine that Al Qaida agents would be terribly good in dealing in diamonds unless they could take protection fees from somebody."

21 See for example *BBC News*, "Angola Swoops on Diamond Diggers," 10 April 2004.

22 Douglas Farah, *Blood from Stones: The Secret Financial Network of Terror* (New York, 2004).

23 *Financial Times*, 30 June 2004.

24 See www.powow.com/samihossaily. Douglas Farah deserves credit for tenacity. See his "The Use of Gold, Diamonds and Other Commodities in Terrorist Finances," written as a result of his new position as Senior Fellow of the National Strategy Information Center of the University of Pittsburgh. The evidence cited is the usual – unnamed "intelligence sources."

25 See "Tanzanian Government Bans Export of Rough Tanzanite," *Jewellery Business*, August 2005.

26 *Financial Times*, 8 August 2000, 23 May 2001.

27 *Wall Street Journal*, 16 November 2901.

28 Tanzanian Mineral Dealers Association, press release, 21 November 2001.

29 "Gem May Fund Terrorism," ABC News, 14 December 2001. See *Professional Jeweler*, Daily News Archive, 19 December 2001.

30 See the story of how the gem dealer Michael Avram uncovered the real story, recounted by Robert Weldon in "Tanzanite Sleuth," *Professional Jeweler Magazine*, May 2002.

31 *Arizona Daily Star*, 10 February 2002.

32 ABC News, 6 July 2002. An earlier ABC broadcast that effectively merged tanzanite and terrorism, and therefore suggested that buying tanzanite was supporting terrorism, was subject to a blistering attack by Cap Beesley, president of American Gemological Laboratories, the number one laboratory in the world. Beesley quite correctly stated that the program and interviewer "had an agenda that required specific sound bites to support a particular position and create the illusion of completeness." On the other hand, what else is TV "news" all about?

33 And the legend was energetically promoted for its own purposes by Global Witness even after the story had been exposed as bogus (*For a Few Dollars More*, 17–18).

34 Quotations from Douglas Farah in *Washington Post*, 18 February 2002, 3 September 2002.

35 Ibid. See also *Professional Jeweler*, 20 February 2002, 19 June 2002.

36 The illegal gold trade is explained in detail in R.T. Naylor, "The Underworld of Gold," *Wages of Crime*, chapter 5 (Ithaca, 2002, 2004).

37 An excellent overview of the role of the dhow is in Norman Miller, "The Indian Ocean: Traditional Trade on a Smuggler's Sea," *American Universities Field Staff, Africa/Asia*, no. 7, 1980.

38 See Timothy Green, *The World of Diamonds* (London, 1981) for interesting information on the emergence of the Indian diamond-cutting industry and its role in contraband movements.

39 There is a brief, partial overview by Angelina Malhotra, "India's Underground Bankers," *Asia, Inc.*, August 1995. This article incorrectly imputes to the Vietnam War the origins of India's hawāla banking system. In fact it can be traced at least as far back as World War II.

40 Ibid.

41 The accounts by Douglas Farah have the gold being both run to and purchased from Dubai!

42 The one that received the most unwanted attention was ARY Gold, run by a Pakistani émigré, which had previously been in the spotlight because of revelations its boss had allegedly paid a bribe of $5–10 million to the husband of Benazir Bhutto while she was prime minister, to get a two-year legal monopoly on the supply of gold to the Pakistan market (*New York Times*, 8 January 1998).

43 *Associated Press*, 8 July 2002; *Philadelphia Inquiry*, 27 June 2002.

CHAPTER SEVENTEEN

1 Marie Cocco, "U.S. View in Terror Cases: Trust Us," *Newsday*, 3 June 2004. Early in 2006, with outrage over Padilla's treatment growing, the Bush administration suddenly claimed that 4.5 years before they had found "a locker full of applications to join al-Qaeda's war overseas," including one from Padilla, in Afghanistan (*Miami Herald*, 13 January 2006). Apparently Usama had put "help wanted" ads in major newspapers.

2 The notion of madrasas (institutes that teach Islamic sciences) as purported training grounds for suicide bombers etc. is dealt with by Peter Bergen, "The Madrasa Myth," *New York Times*, 14 June 2005.

3 For one of the early hyperbolic accounts of the emerging Islamintern, see Willam Carley and Timothy O'Brien, "Web of Fear: New Kind of Terrorist, Amateur and Ad Hoc, Worries Authorities," *Wall Street Journal*, 17 March 1993. On the case, see *United States versus Ramzi Ahmed Yousef*, Lead No. 98–1041 2nd Cir., 25 August 2000; *United States versus Salameh* 152 F. 3rd 88 2nd Circ., 1998. Yet the FBI labwork implicating the defendants was revealed to be faked, and the case against the man who rented the truck was so full of inconsistencies that it might well have failed – but for two things. The prosecution successfully played on the sentiments of the jury, and the defense tried to rely on contradictions in the prosecution case rather than presenting a proper rebuttal. See John F. Kelly & Phillip Wearne, *Tainting Evidence: Inside the Scandals at the FBI Crime Lab* (New York, 1998), chapter 5.

4 *New York Times*, 6 June 2002. Subsequent number 3s included Mohammed Atef, Ramzi bin al-Shibh, and Abu Zubaida, Haitham al-Yemeni, Abu Faraj

al-Libbi, and Hamza Rabia (*New York Times*, 5 May 2005; *Sunday Times*, 5 August 2005; *Asia Times*, 6 December 2005, etc.).

5 Coll, *Ghost*, 250–1.

6 *Daily Telegraph*, 9 March 2003. There is a sketch of KSM's alleged career in terrorism by Jason Burke in *Observer*, 2 March 2003. Assuming the events portrayed are roughly accurate, what emerges is that KSM ran his own operations and occasionally crossed paths with bin Lāden or Ayman al-Zawahiri but that there was no "merger" of their terror capacities into a corporate whole to justify the management hierarchy notion. On "waterboarding" torture, see "US Hides High Profile Prisoners," *BBC News*, 21 May 2004.

7 On this, see Jane Mayer, "Outsourcing Torture," *New Yorker*, 14 February 2005.

8 Peter Vadja points out with respect to the Bojinka Plot to blow up a dozen US airplanes that it became an al-Qā'idah operation in retrospect not because it was planned by bin Lāden but because the man into whose bank account some money allegedly for the plot had been placed was a brother-in-law of Usama's brother-in-law (Peter Vadja, "The al-Qaidah Myth," McGill University, 2 May 2005).

9 *Middle East International*, 8 August 1997; *United States versus Rahman* 189 F. 3rd 88, 104 (2nd Cir. 1999).

10 Randal, *Osama*, 5.

11 Jamal Halaby, "U.S. Citizen Held in Jordan Freed," *Associated Press*, 23 May 2001.

12 See Judith Miller and Jeff Gerth, "Al-Qaeda-Trade in Honey Is Said to Provide Money and Cover for bin Lāden," *New York Times*, 11 October 2001, and comments by the ever-vigilant Rita Katz in *LA Weekly*, 22 September 2005.

13 At least one prominent Palestinian defendant tried in absentia was a former al-Fatah military commander with no known affiliation with or sympathy for Islamist causes. *Middle East International*, 19 May 2000.

14 *Christian Science Monitor*, 24 October 2001.

15 Godfrey Fisher, *Barbary Legend: War, Trade and Piracy in North Africa 1415–1830* (Oxford, 1957), 10.

16 A thorough account of the conflict is by Alistair Horne, *A Savage War of Peace: Algeria 1954–1962* (London, 1977).

17 *The Economist*, 15 February 1992.

18 *Middle East International*, 8 October 2004; *New York Times*, 21 June 2004.

19 *Financial Times*, 22 February 1994.

20 Probably the best summary of the complexities of the Algerian civil war is Miriam Lowi, "Algeria, 1992–2002: Anatomy of a Civil War," *Understanding*

Civil War: Evidence and Analysis, Paul Collier and Nicholas Sambanis, eds (Washington, 2005). On collaboration between the regime and the insurgents, and of the way Algeria and the US exploit the alleged existence of a North African bin Lāden, see Salima Mellah and Jean-Baptiste Rivoire, "Who Staged the Tourist Kidnappings?" *Le Monde Diplomatique*, February 2005.

21 Allegedly the monks were supposed to be kidnapped; but the faction responsible for the job handed them over to another group, who beheaded them. *Middle East International*, 19 December 2003; Randal, *Osama*, 165–71.

22 *Reuter News Service – Western Europe*, 29 March 1996; BBC *Monitoring Service Middle East*, 3 August 1994; *Le Monde*, 13 October 1994, 15 November 1994; *Sunday Times*, 8 January 1995; *The Economist*, 7 January 1995; BBC *Monitoring Service, Middle East*, 16 December 1994; *The Independent*, 10 November 1994.

23 Randal, *Osama*, 181–2.

24 This was the subject of a reasonably good examination in the *Seattle Times*, 23 June-7 July 2002.

25 United States District Court, Southern District of New York, United States v. Mokhtar Haouari S4 00 Cr. 15, 3 and 5 July 2001.

26 "Man Found Guilty in Millennium Bomb Plot," CNN.com LawCenter, 13 July 2001.

27 *Wall Street Journal*, 16 April 2002.

28 Amar Makhloif, popularly known as Abu Doha, was routinely fingered as a mini-bin Lāden, running a parallel but sometimes cooperative terrorist network based mainly on Algerian exiles. Like bin Lāden and the notorious British cleric Abu Hamza (popularly known as Abu Megaphones) he seems to have been guilty mainly of having a big mouth. See *Chicago Tribune*, 11 March 2003. That gave grist to immigrant-bashing propaganda mills that denounced the British government's lax attitude towards Islamic asylum seekers and decried British mosques as breeding grounds for dangerous radicals (*Observer*, 21 April 2002).

29 On this process, see Olivier Roy, "Britain: Homegrown Terror," *Le Monde Diplomatique*, August 2005.

30 On the twisted career of Abu Qatada, see Daniel McGrory and Richard Ford, "Al-Qaeda Cleric Exposed as an MI5 Double Agent," *The Times* (London), 25 March 2004.

31 *Guardian*, 11 April 2005,13 April 2005.

32 *New York Times*, 14 May 2005.

33 *Globe and Mail*, 15 September 2005.

34 For hagiography, see *Business Week*, 17 June 2002, BBC *New/World/Europe*, Profile: Judge Baltasar Garzon.

35 "Tayseer Alouni" *Foreign Correspondent* – ABC TV, 8 October 2004.

36 *New York Times*, 11 April 2006.

37 An outstanding work on the intricacies of religious politics in Morocco is Malika Zegha, *Les Islamists Morocains: Le défi à la monarchie* (Paris, 2005).

38 *Middle East International*, 9 July 2004. Allegedly, in 2001 there was an early plan for attacks in Morocco that did have something to do with bin Lāden. Their instigator, Mohammed al-Tubaiti, had gone to Afghanistan in 1999 to ask bin Lāden to give him a mission – and was brushed off with a little cash. He was told to come back if and when he had a serious plan. But his "network" was wound up before he could pull anything off. This is consistent with the role bin Lāden might have played not as planner and manager but as a sounding board for ideas created elsewhere and from time to time as a source of a bit of start-up money. The operations are then pulled off by the real planners with no further input from bin Lāden (Jason Burke "Terror's Myriad Faces" *Observer*, 18 May 2003).

39 This, of course, was consistent with the US line, but, representative of the growing schism between the American and European intelligence services, the latter were more inclined to see the elusive Moroccan Islamic Combatant Group less as a "group" than a general sense of ideological commitment shared by a host of completely independent grouplets inside Morocco (*Middle East International*, 30 May 2003, 13 June 2003; *New York Times*, 16 May 2004).

40 *Middle East International*, 9 July 2004.

41 *Middle East International*, 8 August 2003.

42 Zeghal, *Islamists*, 278–81.

43 El Ejido was neither the beginning nor the end of the racist attacks. A general strike by those who lost their homes, their cars, and in some cases their papers identifying them as legal workers, to try to gain compensation and protection against a repetition, failed after their employers threatened to replace them with Eastern Europeans. See *Morocco Times*, 21 February 2005.

44 *Middle East International*, 25 February 2000.

45 *New York Times*, 12 April 2004; *Financial Times*, 5 April 2004.

46 That was the term used by El Mundo. Others were equally unflattering. See: "Spanish Press Slams al Qaeda Verdict," CNN.com, 27 September 2005; "Spain's 9/11 Trial Condemned as a Failure," *London Times*, 27 September 2005; "Spanish Court Jails 18 in al-Qaida Trial," *Al-Jazeera*, 26 September 2005.

47 *Middle East International,* 5 August 2005.

48 *New York Times,* 30 July 2005.

49 Much of the information on this topic is from persons whose identity cannot be disclosed.

50 In the ongoing "Grand Bribery" case, police officers, judges, and lawyers were charged with taking 500,000 Egyptian pounds to issue rulings and overturn previous ones, as well as for forging documents. (*Al Ahram,* 23 February 2006). See also the case involving financial and sexual extortion from an Egyptian businesswoman reported in *Al Ahram,* 21 February 2006.

51 See, for example, *Al Ahram,* 3 March 2006.

52 *Financial Times,* 28 November 2003; *New York Times,* 25 November 2003; *Guardian,* 27 November 2003.

53 *New York Times,* 27 November 2003; *Financial Times,* 28 November 2003; BBC *World News,* 20 December 2003; *Guardian,* 27 November 2003.

54 On the background, see Mehmet Ali Birand, *The General's Coup in Turkey* (London, 1987), and Jacob Landau, *Radical Politics in Modern Turkey* (Leiden, 1974).

55 Properly speaking the translation should be *steppe wolves* but *gray wolves* has become standard. It comes from the legend of a wolf leading the Turks from Central Asia into Anatolia.

56 For a summary and the actions of the most notorious of the Gray Wolf hitmen, see Naylor, *Patriots & Profiteers,* 74–9.

57 On the history of Turkish Hizbullah, see Bülent Aras and Gökhan Bacik, "The Mystery of Turkish Hizbullah," *Middle East Policy,* vol. 9, no. 2, June 2002, 147–60; Asli Aydíntaşbaş, "Murder on the Bosphorus," *Middle East Quarterly,* June 2000, 4; Ely Karmon, "Radical Islamic Political Groups in Turkey," *Middle East Review of International Affairs,* vol. 1, no. 4, December 1997, 4; John T. Nugent, "The Defeat of Turkish Hizbullah as a Model for Counter-Terrorism Strategy," *Middle East Review of International Affairs,* vol. 8, no. 1, 2004, 69–76; *Middle East International,* 19 February 1993, 11 February 2000; "What Is Turkey's Hizbullah?" *Turkey: HRW World Report,* Human Rights Watch, 2000.

58 The official Turkish line was that the bombers were Hizbullah but that their leader was acting on orders from bin Lāden ("Turkey Charges Key Bomb Suspect," BBC *News,* 19 December 2003).

59 See Michael Isikoff and Mark Hosenball, "The World's Most Dangerous Terrorist," *Newsweek,* 23 June 2004, in which almost every subsequently discredited rumor is trotted out. For more sensible accounts, see Jeffrey Gettleman in *New York Times,* 13 July 2004; Thanassis Cambanis in the

Boston Globe, 11 September 2004; Jason Burke in the *Observer*, 27 June 2004; and Pepe Escobar in *Asia Times*, 14 October 2004. See also *al-Jazeera*, 7 September 2004.

60 "Jordanian Court Sentences al-Zarqawi to Death," *Associated Press*, 15 February 2006.

61 This competition was confirmed to German intelligence during interrogation of Shadi Abdallah, supposedly one of al-Zarqawi's top collaborators. Shadi Abdallah in fact moved from bin Lāden to al-Zarqawi because he found bin Lāden's line too indiscriminate, while al-Zarqawi's sole objective was to overthrow the monarchy in Amman and establish an Islamic government there (*Newsweek*, 25 June 2003).

62 There was a chance he did actually go to Baghdad for medical treatment, but it seems the regime was unaware of his presence (Michael Isikoff and Mark Hosenball, "Fabricated Link?" *Newsweek*, 26 October 2005).

63 *Kingston Whig-Standard*, 21 September 2004.

64 *Christian Science Monitor*, 16 October 2003.

65 Patrick Cockburn "US Soldiers Bulldoze Iraqi Farmers' Crops," *The Independent*, 10 November 2003; "Pentagon Should Halt Pillage in Iraq," *Newsday*, 17 August 2004.

66 *Middle East International*, 12 September 2003.

67 Nicolas Pelham, "Siege of Falluja Ignites Wrath of Iraq's Mystical Sufi Masters," *Financial Times*, 21 April 2004.

68 See Jason Burke, "The bin Lāden of Baghdad," *Observer*, 27 June 2004.

69 *New York Times*, 10 February 2004; *Daily Telegraph*, 10 April 2004. Virtually all senior diplomats on the scene wrote it off as a hoax, but Bush administration apologists took it seriously – see Stratfor, *Geopolitical Diary*, 10 February 2004.

70 For example, Abu Azzam. See Michael Isikoff and Mark Hosenball, "The 'Second' Man," *Newsweek*, 28 September 2005.

71 *Associated Press*, 23 October 2005.

72 Pepe Escobar, "Welcome to Civil War," *AsiaTimes*, 16 September 2005; *Sunday Times*, 1 January 2006.

73 For opportunist use of the bin Lāden bogey-man in South East Asia, see Joshua Kurlanktzick, "The Rise & Fall of Imperial Democracies," *Washington Monthly*, January/February 2006.

74 See Zachary Abuza, "Tentacles of Terror: Al Qaeda's Southeast Asian Network," *Contemporary Southeast Asia*, vol. 24, no. 3, December 2002, and "Funding Terrorism in Southeast Asia: The Financial Network of Al Qaeda and Jemaah Islamiyah," *National Bureau of Asian Research*, vol. 14, no. 5, December 2003.

75 *Asia Times,* 25 October 2002.

76 *Tempo Interactive* (Jakarta), 19 September 2002.

77 News of his "escape" was suppressed until the trial in Texas of a US soldier accused of abusing prisoners in Bagram, during which the defense lawyer asked for his testimony (*New York Times,* 3 November 2005). On the theft of equipment from Bagram, see *The Independent,* 13 April 2006, and *New York Times,* 14 April 2006.

78 For a good overview, see Peter Symonds "The Political Origins and Outlook of Jemaah Islamiyah," *World Socialist Website,* 13 November 2003. For a detailed examination of CIA involvement, see Prados, *President's Wars,* chapter 8.

79 *New York Times,* 25 January 2002.

80 *New York Times,* 17 June 2002; Andrew Marshall, "The Threat of Jaffar," *New York Times Magazine,* 10 March 2002.

81 *The Age* (Melbourne), 6 November 2002; *Asia Times,* 25 October 2002.

82 Private communication from onsite diplomats.

83 *New York Times,* 10 March 2002, 23 November 2002.

84 *New York Times,* 3 March 2005.

85 *The Age,* 3 March 2005; *New York Times,* 5 December 2005.

86 "Bali Justice Concerns after Anti-Terrorism Laws Deemed Unconstitutional," ABC Radio, 23 July 2004.

87 *New York Times,* 7 October 2005; *The Independent,* 3 October 2005; *Observer,* 2 October 2005.

88 Actually the identity of the terror-funding Saudi charities (variously identified as Um al-Qura, Al Haramain, and the IIRO) seemed to depend on which issue of the *New York Times* the government spokesperson had last consulted.

89 Noy Thrupkaew, "Follow the (Saudi) Money," *The American Prospect,* 1 August 2004.

90 For an interesting history, see Marites Danguilan Vitan, *Under the Crescent Moon: Rebellion in Mindanao* (Quezon City, 2000).

91 *Financial Times,* 16 December 2001; *New York Times,* 10 and 17 June 2002; John Gershman, "US Takes Antiterrorism War to the Philippines," *Alternet,* 28 January 2002.

92 Geoffrey York, "Former Philippine Rebel Fears Fresh Violence," *Globe and Mail,* 9 November 2003. For an excellent survey of the situation, see Herbert Docena ,"When Uncle Sam Comes Marching In," *Asia Times,* 25 February 2006.

93 John Prados, *President's Secret Wars: CIA and Pentagon Covert Operations since World War II* (New York, 1986), 64.

94 *New York Times*, 27 August 2002; *Asia Times*, 3 April 2004; Kleveman, *New Great Game*, 100–9; "China's Xinjiang Region: An Area of Strategic Interest," *Power and Interest News Report*, 16 September 2004.

95 CNN.com, 15 June 2002.

96 *New York Times*, 3 July 2002. Some claimed that the most likely suspect was Lashkar-i-Jhangvi, a Sunnī underground group with pro-Tāliban sympathies whose only "link" to bin Lāden was the fact that some of its cadres had fought in Afghanistan. In fact the group was sometimes regarded as just a collection of thugs whose sole interest was sectarian killings – it first came to prominence in tit-for-tat attacks on Pakistan's Shiʻa minority.

97 *Pacific News Service*, 15 May 2003; *Middle East International*, 16 May 2003.

98 *Asia Times*, 9 December 2003.

99 *New York Times*, 12 December 2002.

100 See especially *Power and Interest News Report*, 26 August 2004. See the sensible deflation of the hysteria by Stefan Eklof, "Piracy: Real Menace or Red Herring?" *Asia Times*, 4 August 2005. One month after the *MV Superferrry 14* disaster, one of its sister ships (*MV Superferry 12*) collided with another vessel at the cost of sixty lives. No one blamed that on the Abu Sayyaf Group or bin Lāden.

101 *New York Times*, 13 October 2002.

102 "Washington Possibly Examining Militancy Threat in West Africa," *Stratfor*, 14 November 2002.

103 *Middle East International*, 16 April 2004.

104 *New York Times*, 15 November 2005; Paul Garwood, "Jordan Rounds Up 120 in Bombing Investigation," *Associated Press*, 11 November 2005.

105 *Sydney Morning Herald*, 8 December 2002; *Middle-East-Online*, 7 December 2002. Danny Rubenstein, "PA Unveils Israeli Intelligence Scheme," *Haaretz*, 14 September 2005. Later, when Hamas seemed poised to best Fatah in the Palestinian elections, Yasir Arafat's successor, Mahmoud Abbas, tried to play the al-Qāʼidah card against it – claiming that bin Lāden's people were infiltrating the Islamic movement in the Occupied Territories (*Associated Press*, 3 February 2006).

106 Prior to his government position, the minister was a senior official of the Internal Macedonian Revolutionary Organization, which dates back to the early twentieth century, when it made its reputation from assassinating Turkish government officials and extorting money from Muslim businessmen. In its more recent incarnation, it had spawned a new paramilitary organization, the Lions, raised specifically to fight Albanians (*Foreign Report*, 3 June 2004; *New York Times*, 1 and 17 May 2004).

CHAPTER EIGHTEEN

1 See his own account reported in *Globe and Mail*, 26 August 2002.

2 *Washington Post*, 12 June 02; *Southam Newspapers*, 16 August 2002; BBC *World News* , 24 August 2002.

3 For many commentators, al-Marabh had to be guilty – he was an Arab and he was arrested by the Feds. See, for example, "Bush Administration Freed Terror Suspect," *NewsMax.com Wires*, 3 June 2004. This seems to have been largely copied from a *Canadian Press* dispatch ("Terror Suspect Freed") of 2 June 2004.

4 See below, notes 27–31.

5 For Arar's story, see www.maherarar.ca.

6 *Globe and Mail*, 27 November 2003; *Maclean's*, 16 December 2004. As of September 2005, al-Mrei was still in solitary with the "evidence" against him secret.

7 *Washington Post*, 20 March 2003.

8 *Detroit News*, 29 March 2004.

9 "Britney Spears, Trust Our President in Every Decision," CNN, 23 September 2003.

10 *Detroit News*, 29 March 2004.

11 *Los Angeles Times*, 7 March 2004; *Miami Herald*, 29 January 2004. The letter also explained that "Youssef get to telling me the roll he played with the terrorists of Sept. 11, 2001 and how he made ID and documents for them to get around any where in the world." Since no one believed Hmimssa had anything to do with 9/11 or its perpetrators, his prison braggadocio was just further confirmation of what a habitual liar he was.

12 *Associated Press*, 9 January 2005.

13 For a summary, see *Washington Post*, 20 November 2005.

14 *New York Times*, 30 March 2006.

15 *Detroit News*, 27 January 2004.

16 United States District Court, Western District of Pennsylvania, *United States of America v. Ali Alubeidy*, 8 October 2001.

17 "WHO Warns of Bioweapons Risk," BBC News Americas, 25 September 2001.

18 *Seattle Times*, 24 December 2003; *Washington Post*, 12 June 2005.

19 See Michael Niman's account of the press conference and background in *Alternet*, 16 September 2002.

20 This story is told by Mathew Purdy and Lowell Bergmanin in "Unclear Danger," *New York Times*, 12 October 2003. See also the account in Elaine Cassel, *The War on Civil Liberties* (Chicago, 2004), 43–7.

21 Cited in *New York Times*, 12 October 2003.

22 *Globe and Mail*, 22 January 2004.

23 US v. Mohammed Abdullah Warsame, United States District Court, District of Minnesota, "Conspiracy to Provide Material Support to a Designated Foreign Terrorist Organization," 20 January 2004.

24 Affadavit of Detective Terrence McGhee, New York City Police, United States v. Mohammed Abdullah Warsame, United States District Court, Southern District of New York, 21 January 2004.

25 Department of Justice, "Minneapolis Man Charged with Conspiring to Provide Material Support to Al Qaeda." 21 January 2004.

26 United States District Court, District of New Jersey, Crimiinal Complaint, *United States of America v. Hemant Lakhani*, 11 August 2003.

27 United States Department of Justice, "British Arms Dealer, Two Others, Arrested in Attempted Sale of Shoulder-Fired Missile," *Criminal Complaint News Release*, 13 August 2003; "Hemant Lakhani ... British Arms Dealer Receives Maximum Sentence," *The New Criminologist*, 14 September 2005.

28 *India Abroad*, 3 May 2005.

29 *New York Times*, 9 January 2005.

30 United States District Court, District of New Jersey, Criminal Complaint by Special Agent James Tareco; No. 03–7106, 11 August 2003.

31 Petra Bartosiewicz, "Rounding Up Al Qaeda, One Stooge at a Time," *Harper's Magazine*, August 2005.

32 *India Today*, 19 September 2003.

33 "On this, the day after the fourth anniversary of the September 11th terror attacks on America, Hemant Lakhani has received a significant sentence," *New Criminologist*, 14 September 2005.

34 A year later a British citizen of Indian origin also pleaded guilty to laundering money for Lakhani and turned state's evidence (*Hindustan Times*, 16 May 2005).

35 *Money Laundering Alert*, vol. 14, nos 5 and 11, 2003.

36 *Kommersant*, 14 August 2003.

37 "British Arms Dealer, Two Others, Arrested in Attempted Sale of Shoulder-Fired Missiles and Deal for 50 More," *Criminal Complaint News Release*, Newark, NJ, 13 August 2003.

38 *Financial Times*, 14 October 2001; *New York Times*, 11 October 2001; *La Presse*, 20 October 2001; *Money Laundering Alert*, November-December 2001.

39 *New York Times*, 11 October 2001, citing the typically well-founded views of Steven Emerson.

40 *Washington Post,* 11 January 2003. Originally the owner of Al Nur was supposed to be Mohammed Hamdi Sadiq al-Ahdal, but he was then reposing in a Saudi prison, so al-Nashiri seems to have been drafted to take his place, whether by al-Qā'idah or the US Treasury remains unclear.

41 *New York Times,* 4 March 2003.

42 *Christian Science Monitor,* 19 February 2003.

43 *Yemen Times,* 3 and 20 January 2003. Also *Yemen Times* summary from Germany, 13–19 January 2003.

44 See Eric Lichtblau and William Glaberson, "Millions Raised for Qaeda in Brooklyn, U.S. Says," citing Rita Katz, *New York Times,* 4 March 2003.

45 *New York Times,* 4 March 2003.

46 *Washington Post,* 16 November 2004.

47 *Los Angeles Times,* 29 July 2005.

48 *Christian Science Monitor,* 24 December 2004; *Middle East International,* 30 September 2005.

49 For a detailed examination of the government's records, see Center on Law and Security, *Terrorist Trials: A Report Card,* February 2005.

50 *Seattle Times,* 24 December 2003.

51 *New York Times,* 28 September 2003.

52 *Des Moines Register,* 18 July 2004.

53 *Toronto Star,* 8 December 2003.

54 United States of America, Plaintiff v. Sami Omar Al-Hussayen, United States District Court for the District of Idaho, Second Superceding Indictment.

55 *Spokesman-Review* (Boise, Idaho), 1, 17, and 22 July 2004.

56 Geov Parrish, "Long Live the King," WorkingForChange.com, 17 June 2004.

57 *St Petersburg Times,* 4 April 2003. There is a multipart examination of the case on Court TV, 29 October 2005: www.crimelibrary.com/terrorists_spies/ terrorists/dr_robert_goldstein/index.html.

EPILOGUE

1 As in George Bush's recent reverie (*The Independent,* 10 February 2006).

2 By one version, Atta conceived the plan back in 1996 and only brought it to bin Lāden because he lacked resources to do it alone. However, this story came from US interrogation of key suspects who were probably tortured (*Los Angeles Times,* 23 July 2004).

3 *New York Times,* 12 July 2005.

4 See Jeffrey St Clair, *Grand Theft Pentagon: Tales of Corruption and Profiteering in the War on Terror* (Monroe, ME: 2005).

5 "Wars 'useful', Says US Army Chief," *BBC News*, 23 January 2004.

6 *Globe and Mail*, 7 June 2002.

7 (National Commission on Terrorist Attacks Upon the United States, *The 9/11 Commission Report*, authorized ed. (New York, 2004), 186.

8 See R.T. Naylor, "The Insurgent Economy: Black Market Operations of Guerrilla Groups," *Crime, Law & Social Change*, vol. 20, no. 3, 1993, updated in chapter 2 of *Wages of Crime*.

9 Coll, *Ghosts*, 250–1.

10 *Wall Street Journal*, 20 September 2001; *Financial Times*, 24 September 2001.

11 *Washington Post*, 28 August 1998.

12 *New York Times*, 10 January 2003.

13 Thus US federal officials decided early in 2003 to "double the size of the operation" devoted to rooting them out. This followed the discovery that "Terrorist financing links in the United States are more pervasive than they previously thought" (*New York Times*, 10 January 2003).

14 *Al Jazeera*, 17 February 2006.

15 *Money Laundering Alert*, April 2003; *Forward*, 28 February, 2003; *Haaretz*, 18 May 2005; "Al-Arian Likened to Don in Mafia," TBO.com, 8 November 2005; *Tampa Tribune*, 7 December 2005.

16 After the exposure of fabrications around Iraqi WMDs, US media were filled with laments from intelligence officers (usually anonymously) about how they felt betrayed when the government distorted information they had provided to bolster its shabby case. Contrast this to comments from the former assistant chief constable of Scotland who broke ranks to claim that key pieces of evidence implicating Libya in the Lockerbie bombing had been planted by US agents (*The Scotsman*, 29 August 2005).

17 Jacob Hornberger, "The International Terror-and-Drug Cop Is on the Beat," The Future of Freedom Foundation, 14 January 1004. Reproduced in *Alternet*, 16 January 2004. See also *BBC News*, "US Stops 'al-Qaeda drug boats,'" 21 December 2003.

18 Stuart Winter, "Bird Smugglers Bring in 'Plague,'" *Express on Sunday*, 28 August 2005.

19 See, for example, Colonel Dan Smith, "Spying and Lying by the Pentagon," *Counterpunch*, 28 January 2006.

20 This is the central argument of Chalmers Johnson's excellent *The Sorrows of Empire: Militarism, Secrecy and the End of the Republic* (New York, 2004).

21 United Press International, 25 January 2006.

22 The most recent analysis of the power of the lobby is by two Harvard re-
    searchers, John Mearsheimer and Stephen Walt, "The Israel Lobby," sum-
    marized in *London Review of Books*, 23 March 2006. For a contrary view, see
    Noam Chomsky, "The Israel Lobby," *Znet*, 28 March 2006. While Chom-
    sky's countercase has merit, it seems almost obviated by the very fervor with
    which the claims of Mearschiemer and Walt were attacked, including by
    their own university.

23 On the use of this tactic, see Alexander Cockburn and Jeffrey St Clair, eds,
    The Politics of Anti-Semitism (Oakland, CA: 2003).

24 Interestingly, the post-9/11 hate campaign directed against Muslims and
    Arabs by US mass media led to dramatic results. After 9/11, only 14 per-
    cent of Americans admitted to thinking that Islam as a religion incites
    violence against non-Muslims. By early 2006 the proportion was up to
    33 percent with fully 25 percent of Americans willing to state that they were
    personally prejudiced against Muslims. See Juan Cole, "Bigotry Towards
    Muslims and Anti-Arab Racism Grow in the US," See his blog, *Informed Com-
    ment*, 9 March 2006 (www.juancole.com).

Index

Abdullah Azzam Brigade,
  293–4
Abdullah, Mohammed
  Ahmed ibn Sayed, 60
Abraham, Yehuda, 327
Abu Gharib, 301
Abu Sayyaf Group, 179,
  308–9, 312
Afghan Support Commit-
  tee, 176
Afghan-Soviet war, 14
Afghanistan: and Civil War
  (1992–96), 28; coup of
  1978, 19; ethnic divi-
  sions of, 15–16; and fall
  of Soviet Union, 27, 76;
  and hawāla, 159; and UN
  Security Council, 107; US
  response to 9/11, 12
African Gem Resources
  (AfGem), 271–2
Agha, Haji Abdul Manan,
  159
Aideed, Hassan, 135
Aideed, Mohammed Farah,
  128–9, 131, 134–5, 161,
  163

Al Aqsa Islamic Bank, 242
Al Barakaat, 161, 162–6,
  172
Al Haramain Islamic Foun-
  dation, 164, 183–4, 236
Al Jazeera, 288, 292
Al Jihad, 43–5, 67, 89, 92,
  99, 204, 295, 303
Al Khidmat Foundation,
  177
Al Nur Honey Press, 328–9,
  409n40
Al Qadir Traders, 159
Al Rashid Trust, 177–8
Al Sadaqa Foundation, 216
Al Shamal Bank, 171
Al Shifa Honey Press,
  328–9
Al Taqwa Trade, Property
  and Investment Com-
  pany, 172, 233
al-Ali, Suleiman ibn Ali,
  232
al-Aqil, Abd al-Aziz, 183
al-Arian, Sami, 342
al-Aziz ibn Baz, Abd, 38
al-Bakri, Mukhtar, 322

al-Bannā, Hasan, 41
al-Bannā, Sabri. See Abu
  Nidal
al-Bashir, Hassan Ahmed
  Omar, 65
al-Deek, Khalil, 280, 328
al-Fadl, Jamal, 90–2, 95,
  97–8
al-Faruq, Omar, 303–4, 307
al-Fawwaz, Khalid, 235–6
al-Hamzi, Badr, 149
al-Hawsawi, Mustafa
  Ahmed, 235
al-Hussayen, Sami Omar,
  333
al-Ikhwān al-Muslimīn. See
  Muslim Brotherhood
al-Iraqi, Abu Jajer. See Salim
al-Ittihād al-Islāmiyya, 121,
  132–6, 162, 164, 336
al-Khalayleh, Ahmed Fadl,
  297
al-Marabh, Nabil, 315–20
al-Masri, Khaled, 93–4
al-Mouyad, Sheikh Mu-
  hammed Ali Hassan,
  329–31

al-Mrei, Hassan, 317
al-Mujamma al-Islāmī, 207
al-Nashiri, Abd al-Rahim, 329
al-Nasir, Gamel Abd, 41–2, 294, 304
al-Qadi, Yasin, 179–82, 219, 233
al-Qaeda, *See* al-Qā'idah
al-Qā'idah: 3,6; and Albanian insurgents, 313; and bay'a, 91; and Bosnia, 249–250; and counterfeiting, 251–5, 258, 261; and diamonds, 267–9, 272, 397n20; funding, 179, 206–7, 224, 239–40, 376n10; and gold, 273, 275–6; and hawāla, 159, 163; and Independent Task Force on Terrorist Financing, 153–4, 159; origins, 45; and recruitment, 32; and Tāliban, 109–10; and weapons, 111
al-Rahman, Umar Abd, 173, 279–80
al-Rajhi, Suleiman Abd al-Aziz, 230
al-Tawhid wa al-Jihād, 299, 301
al-Turabi, Hassan, 61, 65, 67–8, 86, 199
al-Wahhāb, Muhammad ibn Abd, 38
al-Zarqawi, Abu Musab, 287, 290, 297–9, 301–3, 312, 404n61
al-Zawahiri, Ayman, 45, 67, 118, 301, 303, 323
Albanian National Liberation Army, 313
Albright, Madeleine, 72
Ali, Ilyas, 250–1
Ali, Osman Hassan, 130–1, 135

Alnassi, Mohammed, 328–31
Alouni, Tayseer, 288
Alubeidy, Ali, 320
Alwan, Sahim, 321–2
AMAL Movement, 269
American Gem Trade Association, 272
American International Group (AIG). *See* Maurice Greenberg
Amin, Hafizullah, 19
Ansar al-Islam, 299
Anti-Counterfeiting Consumer Protection Act (1986), 253
Arab Bank of Amman, 200
Arab Liberation Front, 201
Arafat, Yasir, 195–6, 199–205, 208, 214
Arar, Maher, 317
Armageddon Industry, 9
Arnaout, Enaam, 224–6
Ashcroft, John, 52, 150, 207, 221–2, 225, 229, 250, 287, 290, 315, 319–21, 324, 327, 329–31
Atta, Mohammed, 145–6, 288, 337–8, 340, 409n2
Aznar, José, 292
Azzam, Abdullah, 31

Bank of Credit and Commerce International (BCCI), 200, 204
Bank Secrecy Act (1970), 52, 142
Barakat, Assad Ahmed, 256
Barre, Mohammed Sayed, 123–30, 132
Bashir, Abu Bakir, 305, 307
Bedu, 293–5, 297
Begin, Menachem, 186, 189, 192, 202–3, 209, 379n1, 380n17
Beirut Marine barracks suicide bombing (1983), 248

Beit al-Maal, Inc. (BMI), 232–4
Benevolence International Foundation (BIF), 206, 224–6, 237
Bernadotte, Folke, 193
Berri, Nabih, 269
Biheiri, Suleiman, 232–4
Bin Lāden, Usama, 3–8, 28, 75; in Afghanistan, 14, 119, 159; and Al Jihad, 45; and BIF, 225; and embassy bombings, 96–101; and hawāla, 159, 163; and honey trade, 328–9; and international media, 74; and Islamic banks, 171–2; and Islamic charities, 167, 173, 175–6, 206–7, 235; and Islamic radicals, 37; and Jalalabad, 27; and Lackawanna Five, 323; and LRA, 71; and MAK, 32; and Mohammed Abdullah Warsame, 324; and Muwāfaq, 181; origins, 29–30, 39; and Palestine, 34; and RICO, 55; role in 9/11, 13, 105; and Saudi Arabia, 40–1, 89, 105; and Somalia, 120–1, 131–2; and Stinger missiles, 26, 99, 131; and the Sudan, 40, 59, 67, 71, 336; and Sufis, 39; and the Tāliban, 78, 85–6, 118–19; and training camps, 33, 111, 114; and US propaganda, 110
Black Hand, 47–8
Blaize, John, 263–4
Bodansky, Yousef, 92, 98, 258
Boukhari, Salim, 286
Bourgass, Kamal, 287–8

Bozkurtlar (Gray Wolves), 296, 403n55
Bridas Corporation, 81–2
Buffalo Cell. *See* Lackawanna Five
Bush, George H.W.: and Maurice Greenberg, 153; and Somalia, 121–2, 130
Bush, George W., 82, 138; and Al Barakaat, 162, 172; and Axis of Evil, 51; and economic warfare, 139–40, 154, 177, 207; and Hamas, 215–17; and Muawāfaq, 181; and 9/11, 106, 338; and Patriot Act, 327; and Pentagon budget, 5, 337, 344; and Saddam Hussein, 300; and SDGT, 141; and Tāliban, 108; and terrorist listings, 309; and Usama bin Lāden, 103, 377n26
Bush, Laura, 12, 109

Capone, Al, 49
"Carlos," 68, 86, 197–9, 383n42
Carter, Jimmy, 65–6, 197
"Charlotte Hezbollah Cell," 242–9
Cheney, Dick, 251, 394n35
Chertoff, Michael, 225
Chinese Civil War, 309
Christian Solidarity International, 72
Churchill, Winston, 187–8
CIA: Afghan aid, 20; and domestic espionage, 140, 242–7, 322; underground banking, 23, 159
Clinton, Bill, 105; asset freezes, 10, 213, 215–16, 344; and embassy bombings, 86; and IEEPA, 139–40; and Tāliban, 108

Cold War, 5, 7, 11, 50, 128, 343, 345
Committee for the Mass Expulsion of Arabs, 213
Comprehensive Anti-Terrorism and Effective Death Penalty Act, 140
"Conflict diamonds," 262–3, 267, 324, 343
Counterfeiting: product, 251–7, 283, 394n37; of USD, 258–61
Crime War, 7, 46, 50, 343
Currency and Monetary Instruments Report, 142–3
Currency Transaction Report (CTR), 142–3, 245

Dallah Al Baraka Group, 172
Daoud Kahn, Mohammed, 16–18
Dar es Salaam. *See* Embassy bombing (1998)
Darwesh, Kamel, 321–2
De Beers Consolidated, 263–7, 270, 272
Defense of the Honor of the Sinai Communitees, 294
Democratic Front for the Liberation of Palestine, 201
Department of Homeland Security, 151, 230
Dershowitz, Alan, 106, 363n6
Detroit Four, 315–20
Dhafir, Rafil, 228–30, 234
"Dirty bomb," 111, 326
Dome of the Rock. *See* Haram al-Sharif
Dostom, Abdul Rashid, 27–8, 76
Drug trade: Afghanistan, 4, 24, 82–5, 110, 116–18, 249–51, 275; France,

283; Palestine, 203–4; Somalia, 120, 124–6; Sudan, 71
Drug War, 7, 10–11, 51, 143, 148, 225, 250–1, 285, 336, 344–5

East Turkistan Islamic Movement, 309
Economic Warfare: origins, 10, 138–9
Egypt: and Al Jihad, 43; and bin Lāden, 45; and Emergency Law (1981), 294–5; and Gamā'at 43–4; and Muslim Brotherhood, 43–4; and Palestine (1948), 41
Eisenhower, Dwight D., 103
El Ejido riots, 291, 402n43
el-Gindy, Amr Ibrahim, 240–1
el-Hage, Wadih, 99–101, 232, 272
el-Maati, Ahmed, 33–4
Elashi, Ghassan, 221–3
Elfgeeh, Abad, 331
Elgindy, Anthony Abraham. *See* Amr Ibrahim el-Gindy
Embassy bombings (1998), 86, 96, 134, 271
Enron Corporation, 82
Eritrea, 132–3; and Diaspora, 133
Eritrean Liberation Front (ELF), 133
Eritrean People's Liberation Front (EPLF), 133
Eritrean Relief Association, 133
Escobar, Pablo, 11, 339

Fadlalallah, Mohammed Hussein, 247–8
Fakhet, Sarhane Ben Abdelmajid, 292

Fatah, 195–6, 201–2
Fatah Revolutionary Council, 202
Financial Action Task Force, 138
Fleming, Ian, 263–4
Foreign Terrorist Organizations, 140
Franks, Tommy, 113
Freedom of Information Request, 233
Front de libération nationale (FLN), 282–3
Front Islamique du salut (FIS), 282

Gamā'at al-Islāmiyya, 42–5, 69, 204, 256–7, 280, 295, 306
Garang, John, 65–6, 72, 135
Garzón, Balthazar, 288
Gelb, Leslie, 152–3
Global Relief Foundation, 206, 222–4, 226
Gold, 273–6
Goldstein, Baruch, 213
Goldstein, Dr Robert, 333–4
Gore, Al, 108
Green Belt Strategy, 14
Greenberg, Maurice, 153, 175
Groupe salafiste pour prédication et combat, 283
Gulf War (1991), 35, 102, 135, 208
Gurion, David Ben, 190, 193
Gush Emunim, 209

Habash, George, 196
Haddad, Rabih, 223–4
Haddad, Wadi, 196–8
Hadhramout, 39
Haganah, 190–1, 195

Hamas, 5, 92, 154, 184, 207–8, 213, 215–22, 231, 233, 237, 242, 251, 255, 257, 331, 336, 386n5, 387n21, 388n22
Hambali, 306–8
Hamdan, Abd al-Jaber, 223
Hameed, Moinuddeen Ahmed, 327
Hammoud, Mohammed Yousef, 244–9
Haouari, Mokhtar, 285–6
Harakat al-Muqāwama al-Islāmiyya. See Hamas
Haram al-Sharīf: and plots to destroy, 210
Harb, Said, 247
Hassan, Beni, 297
Hassan, Muhammed ibn Abdullah, 126
Hassoun, Adham Amin, 222
Hawāla, 4, 154–60, 273–4, 324, 336, 339
Hawatmeh, Nayif, 201
Hekmatyar, Gulbuddin, 17, 23, 33, 35, 76–8, 116
Help the Needy, 228–9
Herzl, Theodore, 186–7
Hijazi, Raed, 280, 316
Hill, James, 256–7
Hitler, Adolf, 189
Hizb-i-Islami, 17, 76
Hizbullāh, 5, 67, 92, 154, 215, 237, 242–9, 251, 255–7, 268–70, 336
Hmimssa, Youssef, 318–19
Holy Spirit Mobile Force, 70
Hussein, Saddam: and Abu Nidal, 202–4; and Arafat, 204, 208; and bin Lāden, 5, 35, 73, 96, 287, 297–8; and "Carlos," 197, 384n43; and the Sudan, 65; and WMDs, 88, 287

Independent Task Force on Terrorist Financing, 153, 159, 167
India: and hawāla, 156–7
Indo-Pakistan war (1971), 18
Indonesia: and Islam, 304
Inter-Services Intelligence (ISI), 21, 24
International Anti-Counterfeiting Coalition (IACC), 252–3
International Colored Gemstone Association, 272
International Emergency Economic Powers Act (IEEPA), 137, 139, 206, 214–15, 221, 223–4, 228
International Islamic Relief Organization (IIRO), 178, 231–2, 234
International Maritime Board (IMB), 311
International Monetary Fund (IMF), 73, 144, 170, 236, 282
Iran: and counterfeiting, 258–61
Iran-Contra scandal, 26, 77, 180
Iraq: Western crimes in, 6
Irgun Zve-Leumi, 186, 189–90, 192, 196, 211
Isamuddin, Riduan. See Hambali
Islam: and economic philosophy, 168–74; and interpretations, 35–8; pacifism, 6; and radicals, 37
Islamic Action Front, 312
Islamic American Relief Agency (IARA), 235
Islamic Army of Aden, 179
Islamic Association for Palestine, 218–20

Islamic banks, 171
Islamic Brigade, 282, 336
Islamic charities, 31, 84,
89, 167, 173–4, 183,
227–38, 336, 339–40; Af-
ghan refugees, 22; and
Cambodia, 308; and fro-
zen assets, 177; and Gulf
States, 175, 340; and
Jemmah Islamiya, 303;
and legal battles, 218–
26; Mercy International,
232; and Palestine, 216–
18; and SAAR, 230; Sana-
Bell Inc., 232–3; and
Saudia Arabia, 175, 178–
9, 184; and Somalia, 128,
164; and the US, 206–7
Islamic Cultural Institute of
Milan, 173, 328
Islamic Great Eastern
Raider's Front, 295
Islamic Heritage Revival So-
ciety, 176
Islamic Investment Compa-
nies, 172–3
Islamic Jihad (organiza-
tion), 208, 215, 231,
245, 300, 342
Islamic Movement of
Kurdistan, 299
Islamic Movement of
Uzbekistan, 310
Islamic Unity. See al-Ittihād
al-Islāmiyya
Islamic Unity Front. See An-
sar al-Islam
Israel: creation of, 192; and
foreign aid, 194; and
Hamas, 215–17; and Is-
lamists, 207–9; and polit-
ical upheaval, 192–4

Jalalabad, battle for
(1989), 27
Jamait-i-Islami, 17, 24, 76,
116, 177

Jarwan, Ayman, 229
Jemmah Islamiya, 303–8,
336
Jewish Agency, 191–2
Jewish Defense League,
211
Jewish National Fund, 188,
190, 192, 200
Jibril, Ahmed, 201
Jihad, Abu, 203
Jihad al-Bin'ā, 243
Jihādists. See Islamic radi-
cals
Juma'ale, Ahmed Nur Ali,
161, 163
Jund al-Islam. See Ansar al-
Islam

Kahane, Rabbi Mier, 212–14
Kahane Chai, 212–14
Kamel, Fateh, 284
Karzai, Hamid, 116–17
Katz, Rita, 231
Kefauver, Estes, 50–1
Kennedy, Robert F., 51–2
Kerry, John, 56
Kfar Tapuach Fund, 214
KGB, 197–8
Khalfan, Kamal, 268
Khalfan, Mohammed, 268
Khalifah, Mohammed Ja-
mal, 178–9, 234, 279
Khalq, 18–19
Khalq-Parcham coup
(1978), 18
Khan, Ismail, 76–7
Khmer Rouge, 308
Klein, Yair, 268
"know-your-client" (KYC),
142–3, 145
Kony, Joseph, 70–1
Kook, Rabbi Avraham, 209
Kurdish independence
forces, 296–7, 299
Kurdish Workers Party
(PKK), 296–7
Kyoto Accord, 103

Lackawanna Five, 320–3
Lakhani, Hemant, 324–7
Landmark Plot, 279–80
Lashkar-e-Taiba, 177
Laskar Jihad, 306–7
Lebanon: Diaspora, 268;
and Hizbullāh, 242–9;
and wars, 201
Levitt, Matthew, 220, 247
Lewinsky, Monica, 86
Lohamei Herut Isreal. See
Stern Gang
Luxor massacre (1997),
45, 338

Maali, Jesse Issa, 241–3
Mafia, 342–3; and al-
Qā'idah, 47; and Capone
Gang, 49; and Islamic
Terror, 48; and Patriot
Act, 55; and Prohibition,
48–9; and Terror War, 55
Mahdi, Ali, 128, 131
Mahfouz, Khalid ibn,
180–1
Mahjoub, Mohamed Zeki,
99
Maktabah al-Khidmaah
(MAK), 31
Marcos, Ferdinand, 55
Maryam, Abu. See Moham-
med Abdullah Warsame
Marzouq, Mousa Abu, 222,
233
Mas'ud, Ahmed Shah, 17,
24, 76, 78, 83, 109, 278
Millennium Plot, 280–1,
284, 297–8, 316, 328
Mohammed, Ali, 97
Mohammed, Khalid
Sheikh, 256, 278–9, 339,
400n6
Money Laundering Control
Act (1986), 142
Moro, 308–9, 352n12
Moroccan Islamic Combat
Group, 289

Morocco, 289
Moskowitz, Irving, 210
Moussawi, Zacarias, 279, 323
Mubarak, Hosni, 181
Mujahedi Masr (Holy Warriors of Egypt), 294
Mujahideen, 14, 26, 287; and bin Lāden, 31; and hawāla, 159; and Palestine, 200; Saudi Arabia aid to, 20; and Soviet Union, 25; and Tāliban, 78; US aid to, 19–20
Muslim Brotherhood, 41–2, 172, 317; and Saudi Arabia, 230; and Somalia, 134; and the Sudan, 61–2, 67
Muslim charities. See Islamic charities
Mubarak, Husni, 69
Muhamaddiyya, 305
Mussolini, Benito, 188–9
Muwāfaq Foundation, 179–81, 183
MV Superferry 14, 312

Nada, Youssef, 172–3, 231, 233
Nahdalat Ulama, 304
Nairobi. See Embassy bombings (1998)
Najibullah, Mohammed, 25, 27
Nasreddin, Ahmed Idris, 173, 231
National Commercial Bank of Saudi Arabia, 233
National Front for the Liberation of Iraq: and other groups, 300
National Islamic Front (NIF), 61, 67, 71, 199, 275
Nationalist Action Party, 296

Nehru, Jawaharlal, 304
New Kach Movement, 212–14
Nidal, Abu, 194–7, 202–5, 298
Non-Aligned Movement, 304
Noriega, Manuel, 56–7, 111
Northern Alliance (Afghan), 109, 114, 121
Numerically Integrated Profiling System (NIPS), 276

Oakley, Robert, 82
Obada, Abu, 217
Obote, Milton, 70
Öcalan, Abudullah, 81, 297
Office of Foreign Assets Control (OFAC), 139, 145–6, 151, 223
Office of Terrorism and Financial Intelligence, 151
Ogaden, 123, 127, 132
Ojhri Camp, 21
Omar, Mullah Muhammad, 77, 116, 273
Operation Anaconda, 113
Operation Grapes of Wrath, 243
Operation Green Quest, 151
Operation Imminent Horizon, 229

Padilla, José, 222, 277
Pakistan: and Afghan aid, 21; and hawāla, 156–7, 160; and War on Terror, 311
Palestine: Diaspora, 195–6, 200; and the Irgun, 189; and Islamists, 207–8; and political history, 187–9
Palestine Liberation Organization (PLO), 194–6,

199–201, 203, 207, 208, 214–15
Palestine Liberation Tax, 200
Panama, 55–6
Parcham, 18
Partai Nasional Indonesia, 304
Pashtunwali, 78–9
Pataki, George, 229, 320
Patriot Act, 10–11, 52, 137, 140, 143, 145, 153, 214, 287, 322; and banks, 144–6; and IEEPA, 150–1, 223; and "material aid," 149, 251, 314–27; and money laundering, 147, 327; and money seizures, 147–8; and terror money, 152, 160, 165; and Title III, 144
Polisario guerrilla movement, 291
Popular Front for the Liberation of Palestine (PFLP), 92, 196, 198–9, 201, 213, 215
Powell, Colin, 287, 298, 341
Ptech, 182–3

Qadhafi, Mu'ammar, 199
Qadir, Haji Abdul, 83–4
Qāt, 124–6, 129–31, 134, 161, 164, 274, 368n9
Quranic Literacy Institute, 217–20, 233, 241

Rabbani, Burhanuddin, 17, 76, 83, 116, 159
Racketeer Influenced and Corrupt Organizations statute (RICO), 52–5, 89–90, 96, 140, 150, 213–14
Radical Islamic militants in the West, 11, 28, 47, 50, 284, 302, 337

Reagan, Ronald, 26, 197
Red Cross, 129–31
Rehman, Muhammed Habib, 324–7
Reid, Richard, 277, 332
Reno, Janet, 216
Republican Party: aftermath of 9/11, 46; and House of Representatives Task Force on Terrorism and Unconventional Warfare, 92, 258
Ressam, Ahmed, 284–6
Ricin, 287–8
Riyadh and Khobar Towers bombings, 89
Russia. *See* Soviet Union

SAAR Foundation, 230–1
Sadat, Anwar, 42, 294
Salafī, 38, 132, 282
Salah, Mohammed Abdul Hamid Khalil, 217–20, 233, 241
Salim, Mamdouh Mahmud, 97–8
Samudra, Iman, 307
Sanchez, Illich Ramirez. *See* "Carlos"
Saudi Arabia: and Islam, 38; and National Commission for Relief and Charity Work Abroad, 184; and the Tāliban, 85–6; and US influence, 40
Sayyaf, Abdul Rasoul, 33, 278, 305, 309, 378n34
Schoomaker, General Peter, 338
Scientific Socialism, 123
Shamir, Yitzhak, 190, 192, 203, 380n19
Shanab, Ismail Abu, 216
Sharon, Ariel, 207, 213
Sheikh Ez al-Din al-Qassam Brigade, 214–15

Shin Beit, 216, 313
Sierra Leone: and diamonds, 262–3, 265; and weapons, 326
Sillitoe, Sir Percy, 265
Society of In'ash al-Usra, 242
Soeharto, Mohammed, 304–5
Soekarno, Achmed, 304
Somali National Movement, 127–8
Somali Patriotic Movement, 127–8
Somali Salvation Democratic Front, 127, 132–3
Somalia: and Al Barakaat, 162–3; and bin Lāden, 120–1; Diaspora, 120, 128; and drugs, 121; ethnic divisions of, 122; and food supply, 129–31; and forbidden organizations, 134; and hawāla, 161, 163; Muqdisho, 135, 160; political divisions of, 122–4; and qāt, 124–6; and Soviet Union, 123; and Terror War, 121, 160
Soviet Union: in Afghanistan, 16, 19, 25, 27; and oil pipeline, 80–1
Specially Designated Global Terrorists (SDGT), 141
Specially Designated Nationals and Blocked Persons (SDN), 141
Specially Designated Terrorists (SDT), 139
State Supporters of Terrorism (SST), 139
Stern Gang, 189–90, 192–3, 195–6, 210–11
Stinger missile, 25–6, 112, 131, 325
Sudan: and Communist Party, 61; and Demo-

cratic Union Party, 60, 62; and economic reforms, 73; Holy War, 59; and the Lord's Resistance Army (LRA), 70–2; and Muslim radicalism, 59; and religious and ethnic composition, 62–3, 69–70; and Sudan People's Liberation Army (SPLA), 64–72, 93, 135, 204, 361n9
Suez Canal, 187
Suleiman, Mudir Omar, 271
Sultan, Bandar ibn, 237
"Supernote," 258–61
Suspicious Activity Report, 142–4, 245
Syria: and counterfeiting, 258–61

Taba, Egypt (bombing, 2004), 292
Talaeh al- Fatah, 45
Tāliban, 28, 176; and bin Lāden, 86; and China, 310; and drugs, 82, 84–5, 110, 116–18; and gold, 273, 275; and Khalqis, 77; and mujahideen, 78; and rise to power, 76–7; and Saudi Arabia, 85–6; and smuggling, 118–19; and treatment of women, 78–9, 109, 178; and UAE, 85; and US, 107–8, 115–19
Tanzania Mineral Dealers Association (TAMIDA), 271–2
Tanzanite, 270–3
Temple Mount Foundation, 210
Tenet, George, 111
Terror War, 11, 46, 50–1, 53, 89, 121, 128, 136,

138–41, 143–4, 160, 250–1, 307, 310

Terrorist Exclusion List (TEL), 141

Thalib, Jaffar Umar, 306

Tora Bora, 13

Trademark Counterfeiting Act (1984), 253

Trading With the Enemy Act (1917), 139

Triborder Region (South America), 255–6

Turkey: and Hizbullah, 296–7; and NATO, 296

Turkmenistan: and pipelines, 81–2, 116

Umm al-Qura Foundation, 308

Ummah Tameer-e-Nau, 177

Underground banking. See Hawāla, 28, 154–8

UNITA, 262, 266

United Arab Emirates, 85

United Holy Land Foundation for Relief and Development, 206–7, 215, 218–23, 226

United Jewish Appeal (UJA), 190–1

United Nations Development Fund, 243

United Nations Drug Control Program, 84

United Nations Security Counsel: and Resolution 1373, 137

United Somali Congress, 128

United States: and Afghanistan, 83, 112–19; Afghanistan Coup (1978), 19; and Al Barakaat, 164–6; and al-Qadi, 181–2; and bin Lāden and charitable fraud, 227; criminal case, 86, 88; criticisms of War on Terror, 344, 356n29, 410n16; and economic warfare, 141–51, 179–81, 162, 239, 327–8; and Hamas, 214–17; and Hizbullāh, 242–9; and Islamic charities, 174, 176–7, 183; and Isreali aid, 194; and mujahideen, 20; and oil pipelines, 80–1, 87; response to the Sudan, 69; and Saudi Royal Family, 40; and Somalia, 121, 129, 131–2, 135; and Tāliban, 82, 86, 107–8; and Terror War, 137–51, 307; and war on counterfeiting, 252–4

UNOCAL, 82

USS Cole, 108, 178–9, 317

Valachi, Joseph, 53–4, 90, 359n21

Vinnell Corporation, 311

Waheed, Abdurrahman, 305

Wahhābī. See Salafi

Warsame, Mohammed Abdullah, 323

Warsaw Pact, 191

Weapons of Mass Destruction (WMDs), 5, 73, 88, 97, 287, 341

Wechsler, William, 153–4, 175, 218

Weizmann, Chaim, 187

Western Somali Liberation Front, 123

Wolosky, Lee, 153

World Bank, 290, 293–4

World Food Programme, 178

World Muslim League, 230, 233, 316

World Trade Center Attack (1993), 173, 178, 181, 234, 278, 339

World Trade Center Attack (2001): and Patriot Act, 143–4; selection of, 337; and Tāliban, 108; US reaction to, 9, 338

Yassin, Ahmed, 207–8

Yeltsin, Boris, 27

Yousef, Ramzi, 181, 234, 278–9, 339

Youssef, Mohammed Hesham, 222

Ze'evi, Rehavam, 213

Zionism, 186–92, 208–14, 387n15, 387n17

Zubeidah, Abu, 328